Palgrave Studies in Nineteenth-Century Writing and Culture

General Editor: **Joseph Bristow**, Professor of English, UCLA

Editorial Advisory Board: **Hilary Fraser**, Birkbeck College, University of London; **Josephine McDonagh**, Linacre College, University of Oxford; **Yopie Prins**, University of Michigan; **Lindsay Smith**, University of Sussex; **Margaret D. Stetz**, University of Delaware; **Jenny Bourne Taylor**, University of Sussex

Palgrave Studies in Nineteenth-Century Writing and Culture is a new monograph series that aims to represent the most innovative research on literary works that were produced in the English-speaking world from the time of the Napoleonic Wars to the *fin de siècle*. Attentive to the historical continuities between 'Romantic' and 'Victorian', the series will feature studies that help scholarship to reassess the meaning of these terms during a century marked by diverse cultural, literary, and political movements. The main aim of the series is to look at the increasing influence of types of historicism on our understanding of literary forms and genres. It reflects the shift from critical theory to cultural history that has affected not only the period 1800–1900 but also every field within the discipline of English literature. All titles in the series seek to offer fresh critical perspectives and challenging readings of both canonical and non-canonical writings of this era.

Titles include:

Eitan Bar-Yosef and Nadia Valman (*editors*)
'THE JEW' IN LATE-VICTORIAN AND EDWARDIAN CULTURE
Between the East End and East Africa

Laurel Brake and Julie F. Codell (*editors*)
ENCOUNTERS IN THE VICTORIAN PRESS
Editors, Authors, Readers

Colette Colligan
THE TRAFFIC IN OBSCENITY FROM BYRON TO BEARDSLEY
Sexuality and Exoticism in Nineteenth-Century Print Culture

Dennis Denisoff
SEXUAL VISUALITY FROM LITERATURE TO FILM, 1850–1950

Laura E. Franey
VICTORIAN TRAVEL WRITING AND IMPERIAL VIOLENCE

Lawrence Frank
VICTORIAN DETECTIVE FICTION AND THE NATURE OF EVIDENCE
The Scientific Investigations of Poe, Dickens and Doyle

Jarlath Killeen
THE FAITHS OF OSCAR WILDE
Catholicism, Folklore and Ireland

Stephanie Kuduk Weiner
REPUBLICAN POLITICS AND ENGLISH POETRY, 1789–1874

Kirsten MacLeod
FICTIONS OF BRITISH DECADENCE
High Art, Popular Writing and the *Fin de Siècle*

Diana Maltz
BRITISH AESTHETICISM AND THE URBAN WORKING CLASSES, 1870–1900

Catherine Maxwell and Patricia Pulham (*editors*)
VERNON LEE
Decadence, Ethics, Aesthetics

Muireann O'Cinneide
ARISTOCRATIC WOMEN AND THE LITERARY NATION, 1832–1867

David Payne
THE REENCHANTMENT OF NINETEENTH-CENTURY FICTION
Dickens, Thackeray, George Eliot and Serialization

Julia Reid
ROBERT LOUIS STEVENSON, SCIENCE, AND THE *FIN DE SIÈCLE*

Anne Stiles (*editor*)
NEUROLOGY AND LITERATURE, 1860–1920

Caroline Sumpter
THE VICTORIAN PRESS AND THE FAIRY TALE

Ana Parejo Vadillo
WOMEN POETS AND URBAN AESTHETICISM
Passengers of Modernity

Phyllis Weliver
THE MUSICAL CROWD IN ENGLISH FICTION, 1840–1910
Class, Culture and Nation

Palgrave Studies in Nineteenth-Century Writing and Culture
Series Standing Order ISBN 0–333–97700–9 (hardback)
(*outside North America only*)

You can receive future titles in this series as they are published by placing a standing order. Please contact your bookseller or, in case of difficulty, write to us at the address below with your name and address, the title of the series and the ISBN quoted above.

Customer Services Department, Macmillan Distribution Ltd, Houndmills, Basingstoke, Hampshire RG21 6XS, England

'The Jew' in Late-Victorian and Edwardian Culture

Between the East End and East Africa

Edited by

Eitan Bar-Yosef

and

Nadia Valman

First published 2009 by
PALGRAVE MACMILLAN

Palgrave Macmillan in the UK is an imprint of Macmillan Publishers Limited, registered in England, company number 785998, of Houndmills, Basingstoke, Hampshire RG21 6XS.

Palgrave Macmillan in the US is a division of St Martin's Press LLC, 175 Fifth Avenue, New York, NY 10010.

Palgrave Macmillan is the global academic imprint of the above companies and has companies and representatives throughout the world.

Palgrave® and Macmillan® are registered trademarks in the United States, the United Kingdom, Europe and other countries.

ISBN-13: 978–1–4039–9702–9 hardback
ISBN-10: 1–4039–9702–0 hardback

This book is printed on paper suitable for recycling and made from fully managed and sustained forest sources. Logging, pulping and manufacturing processes are expected to conform to the environmental regulations of the country of origin.

A catalogue record for this book is available from the British Library.

Library of Congress Cataloging-in-Publication Data

"The Jew" in late-Victorian and Edwardian culture : between the East End and East Africa / edited by Eitan Bar-Yosef and Nadia Valman.
        p. cm.
    Includes bibliographical references and index.
    ISBN 978–1–4039–9702–9
    1. Jews – England – History – 19th century. 2. Jews – England – History – 20th century. 3. Jews – South Africa – History – 19th century. 4. Jews – South Africa – History – 20th century. 5. Jewish literature – Great Britain – History and criticism. 6. Zionism – Great Britain – History. 7. England – Ethnic relations. I. Bar-Yosef, Eitan. II. Valman, Nadia.

DS135.E5J4155 2009
305.892'404209034—dc22   2008036027

10 9 8 7 6 5 4 3 2 1
18 17 16 15 14 13 12 11 10 09

Printed and bound in Great Britain by
CPI Antony Rowe, Chippenham and Eastbourne

Contents

Acknowledgements

This volume began life as a two-day colloquium entitled 'Between the East End and East Africa: "The Jew" in Edwardian Culture' which convened in July 2003 at the University of Southampton. Organized by the University's AHRB Parkes Institute for the Study of Jewish/non-Jewish Relations, in association with Ben-Gurion University of the Negev, Israel, the colloquium marked the centenary of both the Uganda Proposal and the Report submitted by the Royal Commission on Alien Immigration in August 1903. A second conference – entitled 'Jews, Empire, and Race' – which took place at the same venue in August 2005 (commemorating, this time, the centenary of the 1905 Aliens Act) allowed us to develop further many of the themes explored in this book. We would like to thank the many scholars from many disciplines who participated in these two exciting events; Jo Reilly and Steve Taverner, for their invaluable role in organizing the conferences; and particularly Tony Kushner, Director of the Parkes Institute, for his energetic encouragement. We also gratefully acknowledge the financial assistance of the (then) Arts and Humanities Research Board. Friends and colleagues who offered kind advice and inspiration at various stages of our work include Bryan Cheyette, Abigail Green, David Feldman, Jonathan Schneer, Efraim Sicher, and Adam Sutcliffe. At Palgrave, Paula Kennedy, Joe Bristow, and Steven Hall were enthusiastic supporters of this book. Most of all, thanks to the contributors for their lively and inventive thinking and their good-humoured patience.

Portions of some of these essays have been published previously. The editors and authors would like to thank Wayne State University Press for permission to reprint material from Chapter 7 of Meri-Jane Rochelson, *A Jew in the Public Arena: The Career of Israel Zangwill* (2008); and the Van-Leer Institute and Hakibbutz Hameuchad publishing house, Israel, for permission to reprint material from Eitan Bar-Yosef, 'Lama lo Uganda: ha-mishlahat ha-tzionit le-mizrah Africa, 1905', published (in Hebrew) in *Teoria U-vikoret* 28 (2006): 75–100.

Abbreviations

AJA	Anglo-Jewish Association
BBL	British Brothers' League
BoD	Board of Deputies
BPP	British Parliamentary Papers
CPA	Cape Town Archives
CUL	Cambridge University Library
CZA	Central Zionist Archives
ITO	Jewish Territorial Organization
JC	*Jewish Chronicle*
MLG	Mitchell Library, Glasgow
NA	The National Archives of the United Kingdom
RCAI	Royal Commission on Alien Immigration

Documentation

References to all secondary sources and scholarly works appear in the endnotes of each chapter in shortened form only (author's surname, short title, and page numbers). Full publication details can be found in the volume's Bibliography.

The Bibliography does not include primary material: bibliographical information for all primary sources – including manuscripts, official papers, pamphlets, late-Victorian and Edwardian scholarly accounts, newspaper and periodical reports, published diaries, memoirs, speeches, interviews, travel narratives, works of fiction, films, and so forth – is cited in full in the endnote section of each chapter (a detailed first note, followed by shortened references in subsequent endnotes).

Contributors

Eitan Bar-Yosef is Senior Lecturer at the Department of Foreign Literatures and Linguistics, Ben-Gurion University of the Negev, Israel. Author of *The Holy Land in English Culture, 1799–1917: Palestine and the Question of Orientalism* (Oxford University Press, 2005), he is currently working on a project exploring the role of 'Black Africa' in Zionist culture and literature.

Jasmine Donahaye is Research Associate at the Centre for Research into the English Literature and Language of Wales (CREW), at Swansea University. A regular cultural critic on Wales and Israel/Palestine in *Planet: the Welsh Internationalist*, she is author of two poetry collections, *Misappropriations* (Parthian, 2006) and *Thirst* (Salt, forthcoming), and of chapters and articles on Welsh and Jewish political, cultural, and literary interactions. She is working on a study of Welsh literary constructions of Israel and Palestine, and a critical volume on Welsh Jewish literature.

Nicholas J. Evans is RCUK Fellow/Lecturer in Diaspora Studies at the Wilberforce Institute for the study of Slavery and Emancipation (WISE) and the History Department at the University of Hull. He has previously worked on numerous projects examining migration to, through, and from Britain, 1830–1960, at the universities of Leicester, Hull, Aberdeen, and Cape Town, and is currently editing a series of papers that examine Jewish history, heritage, and culture in Scotland, 1879–2004, as well as writing a monograph on European transmigration via Britain, 1836–1914.

Ben Gidley is a research fellow at the Centre for Urban and Community Research, Goldsmiths College, University of London. An advisory editor of *Engage*, he has researched East London Jewish radicals in the early twentieth century, and is engaged in the formation of the Centre for New Jewish Thought in London. At the Centre for Urban and Community Research he is involved in several research projects on issues of community leadership and community representation in multicultural cities.

David Glover is Senior Lecturer in English at the University of Southampton. His books include *Vampires, Mummies, and Liberals: Bram Stoker and the Politics of Popular Fiction* (Duke University Press, 1996) and *Genders* (Routledge, 2000; co-authored with Cora Kaplan). He is currently working on a cultural history of the 1905 Aliens Act.

Mark Levene is Reader in Comparative History and a member of the Parkes Institute for Jewish/non-Jewish Relations at the University of Southampton.

His recent books include *Surviving Climate Change* (Pluto, 2007; co-edited with David Cromwell), as well as *The Meaning of Genocide* and *The Rise of the West and the Coming of Genocide* (2005), the first two volumes of his *Genocide in the Age of the Nation-State* (I. B. Tauris). He is also co-founder of the Crisis Forum ('The Forum for the Study of Crisis in the 21st Century'), http://www.crisis-forum.org.uk.

Adrienne Munich holds positions in Art, Cultural Studies, English, and Women's Studies at the State University of New York at Stony Brook. Author of works about Victorian culture, modernism, and Amy Lowell, she is co-editor of the journal *Victorian Literature and Culture*. Her current project focuses on changing meanings and cultural implications of the South African diamond discovery.

Simon Rabinovitch is the Alexander Grass Post-Doctoral Associate at the Center for Jewish Studies and the Department of History, University of Florida. He is currently working on a book entitled *Jewish Nationalism and Autonomy in Late Imperial and Revolutionary Russia*. His published and forthcoming articles examine Jewish nationalist thought, folkloristics, and ethnography.

Meri-Jane Rochelson is Professor of English at Florida International University, where she is also affiliated with the programs in Women's Studies, Judaic Studies, Sephardic/Oriental Jewish Studies, and Religious Studies. Her edition of Israel Zangwill's 1892 novel *Children of the Ghetto* was published in 1998 (Wayne State University Press), and she is co-editor of *Transforming Genres: New Approaches to British Fiction of the 1890s* (St. Martin's, 1994). She has published numerous articles on Victorian and Anglo-Jewish literature and culture; her most recent book, *A Jew in the Public Arena: The Career of Israel Zangwill*, was published in 2008 by Wayne State University Press.

Lara Trubowitz is Assistant Professor of English at the University of Iowa. She writes on Anglo-American modernism, twentieth-century British political history, and Jewish cultural studies, and is currently completing a manuscript entitled *Conspiring To Be Civil: The Hidden History of Antisemitism and Modernism*. She is co-editor, with Phyllis Lassner, of *Antisemitism and Philosemitism in the Twentieth and Twenty-First Centuries: Representing Jews, Jewishness, and Modern Culture* (University of Delaware Press, 2008), and co-editor, with Cinzia Sartini Blum, of *Contemporary Italian Women Poets: A Bilingual Anthology* (Italica Press, 2001).

Nadia Valman is Senior Lecturer in Victorian Literature at Queen Mary, University of London. Author of *The Jewess in Nineteenth Century British Literary Culture* (Cambridge University Press, 2007), she has also co-edited *The Image of the Jew in European Liberal Culture, 1789–1914* (Vallentine Mitchell, 2004) with Bryan Cheyette, and *Remembering Cable Street: Fascism and Anti-Fascism in British Society* (Vallentine Mitchell, 2000) and *Philosemitism, Antisemitism and 'the Jews': Perspectives from the Middle Ages to the Twentieth Century* (Ashgate, 2004), both with Tony Kushner.

Introduction

Between the East End and East Africa: Rethinking Images of 'the Jew' in Late-Victorian and Edwardian Culture

Eitan Bar-Yosef and Nadia Valman

On Friday, 17 May 1900, London was awash with some of the wildest celebrations the capital had ever witnessed. For months the public had been following the events in Mafeking, a small British town in the Cape Colony, South Africa, which was besieged by the Boers in October 1899, shortly after their declaration of war on the British Empire. The siege lasted 217 days, and when news reached London that British forces had finally liberated the garrison and the civilians, thousands took to the streets, cheering, dancing, and drinking.[1]

Like their fellow-Londoners, the Jewish immigrants, recently arrived from Eastern Europe to the capital's East End, also celebrated the great victory – even if somewhat belatedly. Indeed, their own Mafeking Night was delayed by 24 hours: 'Although the news ... was already known on Friday evening, East End Jewry did not celebrate the happy event until the conclusion of the Sabbath', noted the leading Anglo-Jewish organ, *The Jewish Chronicle*: 'The Sabbath clothes were not doffed, for was it not a *Yom Tov* [a Jewish religious festival]? Never did Brick Lane and Hanbury Street present such a sight.'[2]

The Second Anglo-Boer War (1899–1902) posed a problem for Jews in Britain. The War broke out as a result of British imperial ambitions in South Africa, exacerbated by the political and economic restrictions placed by the Boer government on foreign residents in the Transvaal, the centre of the flourishing gold mining industry. The fact that many of the foreign mining magnates in South Africa were Jews allowed Liberal and Labour politicians and journalists in Britain to claim that this was in fact a Jewish war, ignited by Jewish capitalists, and fought for Jewish interests.[3] 'For Whom Are We Fighting?' asked the title of a chapter in J. A. Hobson's influential study *The War in South Africa: Its Causes and Effects* (1900). The answer, Hobson believed, was self-evident: the desire to control the Witwatersrand was not

1

limited to those 'international financiers, chiefly German in origin and Jewish in race', who were taking over the gold mines and thus drawing Britain into the war; their less affluent brethren, who were invading South Africa, also partook in this 'Jew-Imperialist design'. Touring Johannesburg, Hobson was dismayed by these newly-arrived immigrants, 'actively occupied in small dealings, a rude and ignorant people, mostly fled from despotic European rule'. Hobson's conclusion was clear: 'not Hamburg, not Vienna, not Frankfort, but Johannesburg is the New Jerusalem'.[4]

British Jews, who supported the war because they felt it was a chance to demonstrate their loyalty to the Queen and the Empire, now had to face the allegation that their support stemmed from Jewish greed, not British patriotism. Mafeking Night offered them a rare chance to participate, unabashedly, in the jingoistic fête. Waving the Union Jack and revelling in the good news ('Mafeking relieved. Mazal Tov, Mazal Tov'), the ecstatic Jews even went as far as suggesting that their own trials and tribulations gave them a better idea of the hardship experienced by the besieged Brits in South Africa: 'They rejoiced at the freedom once more gained by that brave little band far away in South Africa', noted the *Jewish Chronicle*, 'because they themselves knew fully well the misery and wretchedness of being caged up for months and months in a small area, for what after all is the Pale of Settlement of Russia but a large Mafeking with the eager foe watching and waiting outside the gates?'[5]

If Hobson had imagined Johannesburg as Jerusalem, it was only appropriate for Jews to insist that Mafeking resembled the Russian Pale (those territories on the western border region of Imperial Russia in which Jews were allowed permanent residence): although these two geographical projections were meant to serve opposite ideological ends, both employed images of 'Africa', Judaizing quintessential symbols of Britain's imperial ambitions in the 'Dark Continent'. Ironically, just three years later, the fantasy of an African Zion – populated by those 'rude and ignorant people' Hobson saw in Africa – became official British policy, when, in August 1903, Colonial Secretary Joseph Chamberlain offered Theodor Herzl, the President of the Zionist Congress (founded in 1897), a chance to create a Jewish homeland in the Uasin Gishu plateau, part of the British East Africa Protectorate.

The British proposal – the 'Uganda plan', as it came to be known (although the territory in question was actually situated in what is today eastern Kenya) – undoubtedly stemmed from a genuine concern for the persecuted Jews in Eastern Europe, especially after the devastating Kishinev pogroms of April 1903, in which dozens of Jews were murdered, hundreds injured, and numerous houses looted and destroyed.[6] But if the proposal sought to offer a haven for those Jewish immigrants fleeing Eastern Europe, it was also a calculated attempt to divert them from seeking shelter in London. Major William Evans-Gordon, MP for Stepney (part of the East End) and member of the Royal Commission on Alien Immigration which was set up in 1902 to assess the immigration situation and its hostile local response, claimed in his book *The Alien Immigrant* (1903) that 'When visiting the towns of Western Russia within the Jewish pale, I was surprised to find myself in the familiar surroundings of the East End'. This in itself was not remarkable, thought the Major, considering that the Hebrew colony in the East End 'forms a solid and permanently distinct block – a race apart, as it were, in an enduring island of extraneous thought and custom'. 'Many English people living in the neighbourhood have summed up the situation to me in a phrase: "We are living in a foreign country." '[7] It is telling that in August 1903 – the same month Chamberlain made his proposal to the Zionists – the Royal Commission submitted its report, in which it recommended placing stringent restrictions on Jewish immigration to Britain, thus paving the way towards the Aliens Act of 1905, the first such anti-immigration legislation to be passed in peacetime. The Jews, in short, were what Homi K. Bhabha has called 'white but not quite':[8] sufficiently white to settle East Africa for King and Country, but not white enough to settle in the East End.

Johannesburg as the New Jerusalem; the East End as a foreign country; the Russian Pale as the East End; East Africa as the new Zion: different as they are, all these identifications mirror the powerful desires and anxieties associated with the figure of 'the Jew' at the turn of the twentieth century. As Bryan Cheyette has persuasively shown, ambivalent representations of 'the Jew' lie at the heart of modernity;[9] yet the late-Victorian to early Edwardian years stand out in British history as a turbulent period, exceptional for its contradictory imaginings of the Jew and for its projection of these contradictions onto an unprecedentedly broad canvas. Thus Hobson, Evans-Gordon, and not least the residents of Brick Lane on Mafeking Night interpreted the behaviour and experience of actual Jews via the discursive construct of 'the Jew'.[10] More strikingly than ever, 'the Jew' was overdetermined: infinitely wealthy and yet abjectly poor; refusing to assimilate and yet assuming a false English identity; cosmopolitan and tribal; 'alien' and yet almost overly familiar; ideal colonizer and undesirable immigrant; white but not quite. The context of the Empire, we seek to show in this volume, is crucial for an understanding of the new dimensions of late-Victorian and Edwardian semitic discourse. Hobson's description of the 'Jew-Imperialist design' at work in the South African War (or, as H. M. Hyndman termed it, 'an Anglo-Hebraic Empire in Africa'),[11] is, in this sense, just one articulation of a range of readings of the Jewish diaspora as mirroring, mimicking, perverting, or usurping Britain's omnipresence (rightful or otherwise) on the world stage. As the contributions to this volume demonstrate, it is only by examining the vast cultural and geographical grid within which Jews were imagined that we can re-read the ambivalent representation of 'the Jew' in British culture in these tumultuous years.

Transnational, postcolonial, postmodern?

The essays in this volume thus shift between several sites – between the East End and East Africa, between Palestine and the Pale of Settlement, between Britain and the Boer Republics. Chronologically, they focus around the key international events in which Jewish and imperial history intersected, from the onset of Jewish immigration in the 1880s and the rise of political Zionism in the 1890s, to the Boer War (1899–1902), the Royal Commission on Alien Immigration (1902), the Kishinev pogrom (1903), the Uganda plan (1903), and the Aliens Act (1905). It was through this series of events that, their protestations of patriotism notwithstanding, Jews in Britain became enmeshed in a web of links and associations with other Jews worldwide, whether through place of origin, commercial contacts, internationalist political affiliations, or an emerging sense of diaspora consciousness. In particular, we seek through the chronological focus and geographical scope of these essays to consider how the context of Empire produced both a new language and iconography for imagining and making meaning of Jewish difference, as well as new opportunities and pressures for Jews.

By exploring these issues we hope to identify, account for, and eventually address several omissions that have long characterized scholarship on this period. That the historiography of British Jewry has neglected the colonial aspects of its subjects could perhaps be explained by the fact that the discipline of British history as a whole has worked for decades under the assumption that, as Catherine Hall has testified, 'Britain could be understood in itself, without reference to other histories'. It is only recently that historians like Hall have realized that 'in order to understand the specificity of the national formation, we have to look outside it'. Indeed, the entire field known as the 'New Imperial History' has emerged from the premise that 'colony and metropole are terms which can be understood only in relation to each other'.[12]

If British-Jewish historiography has overlooked these colonial connections, even more striking has been the state of affairs in postcolonial studies: although committed to the study of identity, hybridity, and Otherness in the context of colonialism's global legacy, postcolonial critics for a long time ignored the role of 'the Jew' in this context. Alluding to the rise of Zionism in his influential study *Orientalism* (1978), Edward Said famously noted that 'one Semite [namely, the Jew] went the way of Orientalism, the other, the Arab, was forced to go the way of the Oriental'.[13] By associating the Jews categorically with the West and Western knowledge, Said overlooks the long European tradition of imagining the *European* Jew as 'Other'. But, as Ivan Kalmar and Derek Penslar have rightly pointed out, 'if ever there was a people that lives at the borders between cultures and civilizations it is the Jews'.[14]

The Jews' liminality, on the other hand, is all but proverbial in many postmodern theorizations of their relation to western modernity. Zygmunt

Bauman, Julia Kristeva, and Jean-François Lyotard, for example, have all
sought to explain ambivalent responses to Jews in modern Europe as a result
of their capacity to disturb categories of identity, particularly the boundaries of nation.[15] Such thought helps us interpret the contrary currents in
European culture beyond the binary terms of 'antisemitism' and
'philosemitism' that previously dominated the analysis of responses to
Jewish difference. Yet it has, in turn, produced 'the Jew', in Bryan Cheyette's
words, as 'an ethnic allegory for postmodern indeterminacy'. In casting 'the
Jew' as the diasporist par excellence, theorists run the risk of rendering
Jewish experience of homelessness abstracted and aestheticized.[16] This volume, in contrast, aims to re-historicize the figure of the *fin-de-siècle* Jew, by
considering not only the national and racial fantasies that were activated by
the spectacle of Jews crossing the borders of the United Kingdom in the
late-Victorian and Edwardian period, but also the many other social and
political forces to which Jews were subject. The result is to reveal some
unexpected complexities. As Nicholas Evans, for example, shows in his
contribution to this volume, migrating Russian Jews were certainly the
object of vociferous public xenophobia at the turn of the twentieth century;
at the same time, however, as passengers they were essential to the global
market dominance of British shipping companies. Paradoxically, it was the
anti-alien cause – the desire to 'keep Britain British' – that threatened to
undermine a symbol of Britain's mercantile strength by diminishing her
commercial position and hindering the business of ports such as London,
Glasgow, Liverpool, and Southampton. Shaped as much by economic as by
discursive influences, the meaning of Jewish migration could thus reflect
competing forms of contemporary nationalist expression.

Recent attempts to expand the theoretical paradigms of postcolonial
studies have also provided new ways of thinking about the political,
social, and cultural construction of Jewish otherness. For Kalmar and
Penslar, this involves contesting Orientalism's assumed relationship to
imperialism and locating it in a longer cultural-historical framework, 'in
the Christian West's attempts to understand and to manage its relations
with *both* of its monotheistic Others'.[17] Aamir Mufti, by contrast, seeks to
analyse Europe's Jewish Question in the terms of the postcolonial critique of European modernity, 'as an early, and *exemplary*, instance of the
crisis of minority that has accompanied the development of liberal-secular
state and society in numerous contexts around the world'.[18] These
approaches insert the Jews into postcolonial studies as the Other of the
'Christian West' or the 'liberal-secular state'. Yet Mufti's interest in
Jewishness as a minoritarian position of critique, and Kalmar and
Penslar's concern to reposition Jews as 'targets rather than perpetrators
of orientalism', means that both these studies eschew extended consideration of Jews as imperial actors as well as Others.[19] This paradox is
particularly visible in the 1890s, when Jews were appearing in various

roles on the global stage: not only as a troubling, 'primitive', immigrant minority in Britain but also as Empire-builders in South Africa. They were imagined, meanwhile, not only as dirty, disease-ridden, and super-stitious, but also, in a colonial setting – as Adrienne Munich shows in her essay in this volume – as sensual romantic heroes. *The 'Jew' in Late-Victorian and Edwardian Culture*, therefore, aims to explore the Jews' liminal position within the Orientalist tradition, and, moreover, to trace the ways in which this liminality was reflected in the political, social, and cultural aspects of the colonial experience.

Nowhere was this more visible than in the rise of political Zionism in the 1890s. For Theodor Herzl and his contemporaries, the colonial dimensions of the movement were all but obvious, not only because Palestine was to be appropriated, settled, rejuvenated – in a word, colonized – but also because colonialism offered the Jews a chance to identify with or even mimic Western societies, without assimilating into them. As Daniel Boyarin has shrewdly observed, it was precisely by transforming them into colonists that Herzl hoped to convert the physically inferior, effeminate Jews – long imagined in European culture as being black – into virile white men.[20] This is not to say that Zionism was simply a form of Western colonialism; far from it.[21] But neither is it helpful to overlook, as Zionist historiography has done for decades, the obvious colonialist features of the Zionist project – cultural, but sometimes also economic and ideological. As we shall see, while the Uganda plan highlighted these features by imagining a Jewish colony in a typical imperial context ('Darkest Africa'), the Zionist project of settling Palestine has retained many of these aspects. Exploring the links between Zionist culture and the British imperial experience, this volume suggests how the methods of postcolonial criticism may be applied both to the culture of Zionism and to the image of 'the Jew' in the British political imagination.

In the remainder of this introduction, we outline some of the broad political, social, and cultural developments that converged in the late-Victorian and Edwardian period with such discursive force around the figure of 'the Jew'. Firstly, we consider arguments and attitudes concerning the place of Jews in British life, beginning with the public debate about Jewish emancipation in the mid-nineteenth century and encompassing response to alien immigration at the turn of the twentieth. We then focus on several geographical/discursive sites where fears and hopes linking Jews and the imperial nation were projected: shifting from the East End, through the broader national and imperial arena, to the Zionist colonial ethos, each section will seek to highlight the interplay between the historical and the rhetorical, demonstrating how uncertainties about domestic class conflict, international capitalism, and the fate of the Empire were repeatedly expressed – by both Jews and non-Jews – through semitic representations.

Identifying Jews

Judaism had always held a unique place in the British cultural imaginary, whether as a source for republican thought, the object of millennial fervour, or a model for sacred poetry.[22] Jews themselves, however, had been mostly absent from Britain until 1656, and in the 200 years following their readmission remained a tiny religious minority with a low public profile. The issue of the Jews' place in the nation erupted into public discourse with the controversy surrounding the 'Jew Bill', the parliamentary act of 1753 that was to naturalize foreign-born Jews.[23] But it was the nineteenth century that saw the first sustained discussion of the possibility of Jewish participation in the political life of the nation. Such participation had been effectively impossible because entry into Parliament, civic offices, and various professions required the swearing of a Christian oath. From the 1830s onwards, however, with the relaxation of similar restrictions against Catholics and Dissenting Protestants, Jewish emancipation became an object of intense debate by politicians and writers. Crucially, the question of the Jews' status as citizens came into prominence at a time when Britain's religious identity was highly contested; at stake in the arguments about the exclusion of Jews was the Christian character (variously defined) of the nation. In 1858, after many attempts, Lionel de Rothschild was enabled as a professing Jew to take up the seat to which he had first been elected 11 years previously, and in 1866, under the Parliamentary Oaths Act, Jews were finally admitted to both Houses of Parliament.[24]

If the controversy over Jewish emancipation had turned on the significance of the Jews' religious faith, however, the nature of their difference as a minority was far from clear. As part of their campaign to be admitted to the full rights of citizenship, and in accordance with the tenor of religious culture in mid-Victorian Britain, the elite Anglo-Jewish leadership had centralized Jewish representational, religious and welfare institutions and, despite internal differences – their Sephardic (Spanish and Portuguese) or Ashkenazic (Central European) ethnic origins – represented themselves publicly as a unified religious community. Victorian Jews, in other words, were highly acculturated; their devotional practice and communal organization had come to resemble that of the Anglican majority.[25] The granting of emancipation opened up further opportunities for social mobility, and a number of Jews became spectacularly prominent in public life: this was exemplified in the 1860s and 1870s by the success of Jewish financiers and the political career of the Jewish-born Prime Minister, Benjamin Disraeli.[26]

As the last quarter-century began, then, Jews were unprecedentedly visible. At the same time, social and cultural assimilation exacerbated confusion about the scope of Jewish allegiances. Disraeli's political biographer, Frank Harrison Hill, drew attention to such ambiguity in describing the 'Hebrew gentlemen' prominent in the press and Parliament of the period, 'singing the national anthem and patriotic melodies to an amused and excited audience who have shouted and banged their glasses, and have believed in the [Jews'] spontaneity and disinterestedness and genuine British feeling'.[27] The difficulty of ascribing meaning to the changing and inchoate links that may (or may not) have bound together individuals of Jewish origin meant that the spectacle of 'Hebrew' patriotism could not be taken at face value.

The Jews' capacity to espouse 'genuine British feeling' was most vociferously questioned, however, in relation to Disraeli's handling of the 'Eastern Question' crisis of the late 1870s. Attributing the Prime Minister's continued support for Muslim Turkey (despite its atrocities against Bulgarian Christians) to his 'Oriental' sympathies, Disraeli's critics sought to unmask him as a secret Semite, conspiring against England's Christian principles of liberty.[28] The Liberal historian Goldwin Smith demanded, more baldly, in a series of essays in the same period, 'Can Jews Be Patriots?' Smith regarded Judaism as 'a religion of race' that was essentially tribal, and this exclusivity made it incompatible with patriotism. He challenged the Chief Rabbi, Hermann Adler, who had engaged in disputation with him in the pages of the *Nineteenth Century*, to clarify 'what are the relations between country and race in the mind of a strict Jew', and contended that the 'ruling motives of the Jewish community are not exclusively those which actuate a patriotic Englishman, but specially Jewish and plutopolitan'.[29] If liberals had championed the right of Jews to be freed from the restrictions imposed by a Christian state, they were less comfortable with the idea that emancipated Jews might still sustain collective and cosmopolitan ties.

Attempts to define Jews as driven by 'Oriental sympathies' or 'plutopolitan motives' in fact register the difficulty of recognizing and interpreting Jews in the absence of clear markers of religious or cultural distinctiveness. As Deborah Cohen puts it, 'in the late nineteenth century, Jews came increasingly to be identified as a race precisely because they were difficult to differentiate from their fellow citizens'.[30] This difficulty proved an object of fascination for both novelists and investigative journalists, even as their narratives revelled in racial taxonomy.[31] Exploring the literary representation of diamond-seeking and diamond-dealing Jews in South Africa, Adrienne Munich demonstrates in her contribution to this volume how racial indeterminacy played a crucial role in the symbolic economy which identified Jews with diamonds: it was precisely the combination of clearly-marked Jews with Jews of more ambiguous identity that produced the impression that Jews dominated, if not absolutely owned, Kimberley and the great mine at its centre.[32]

Activists attempting to articulate their objections to Jewish immigration into Britain, meanwhile, were driven into logical tangles by the elusive nature of Jewishness. The anti-alienist Arnold White, for example, argued that the

Jews 'reflect, like the chameleon, the texture and the tint of the rock on which they rest', yet this adaptability belied their indelible racial essence.[33] Confusion over whether Jews had a tendency to assimilate or to live separately is also apparent in the evidence presented to the Royal Commission on Alien Immigration. Thus, the same witness (George Brown, resident of Stepney, a photographer's assistant) who complained that the Jews have formed a 'foreign colony in England' – 'determined to deal among themselves, and form a complete colony for themselves, and do as they like' – also criticized the Jewish merchants' tendency to anglicise their names in order to 'pose as English people'. Somewhat baffled, the commissioners found it difficult to 'reconcile the two situations': 'If these people are only served by members of the community', wondered Mr Lyttelton, 'why should they change their name?'[34]

Yet the Commission's own vocabulary – with 'Alien' masquerading as 'Jew' – did little to clarify these issues, especially when collapsing the boundaries between new immigrants and established Anglo-Jews. Here, for example, is part of the evidence given by J. L. Burton, acting editor of the *Shoe and Leather Record*, who described a case in which a Jewish boot manufacturer had fraudulently declared himself bankrupt:

13244. [Evans Gordon] Is he an alien, or an Englishman? –An alien.

13245. Does that appear? –He is an alien.

13246. (*Lord Rothschild*.) You mean to say he is a Jew? –Yes.

13247. That is not an Alien? –He is not a native Englishman.

13248. (*Chairman*.) Does that fact appear? –We do not report it in that way.

....

13263. (*Chairman*.) Do you use the word 'Gentile' there as the opposite of 'alien'? Does it mean native-born? –A man who is native-born.

13264. When you say 'Gentile,' is not that in opposite to the Jew? –Yes.

13265. These are Christians? –I suppose they are.

13266. Then the other side of the account would include English Jews as well as aliens? –Yes.

13267. Do you call a Jew an alien? –Not always.

13268. The Gentiles exclude the Jew. In which category do you put the English Jew who becomes bankrupt? –I would call him an alien if he was in the second generation; if his father came from a foreign country to England I would call him an alien.

13269. Take an English Jew, nothing to do with the foreigners; which category do you put him in, alien or Gentile? –I think he would be in the alien category.[35]

Amid the proliferation of definitions, almost to the point of absurdity, this witness gradually reveals his use of the term 'alien' not as a legal but a racial category.

Race, liberalism, and the question of antisemitism

Victorian scholarly discussion of the Jews' 'racial' character was also deeply implicated in the politics of immigration. Throughout Europe, as Mitchell Hart has argued, 'the racial and anthropological discourse on Jews had its impetus...in the struggles over emancipation, assimilation and national identity that came to be identified as "the Jewish Question"'.[36] Indeed, Jews as well as non-Jews were active in these arguments over self-definition.[37] They appealed to the concept of race, not only in Disraeli's mystical sense of peoplehood but also from within the scientific disciplines of anthropology and medicine, as an apparently measurable and inherited type. While some disputed the stability and permanence of racial traits, others reworked the premises or stereotypes of conventional racial thinking.[38]

One such example is the Australian-born late-Victorian race scientist Joseph Jacobs. Although racial theory in Britain was primarily concerned with imperial subjects and barely touched on Jews,[39] the role of race thinking in promoting ideas of Jewish degeneracy in continental Europe motivated Jacobs to create a Jewish counter-race science designed to prove the racial unity, distinctness, and purity of all Jews. As Simon Rabinovitch shows in his essay in this volume, Jacobs' work must be seen in the context of the politics of Jewish immigration, as an attempt to establish by modern statistical methods that nurture, rather than nature, was responsible for the immigrants' much publicized physical deficiencies. Jacobs' solution to the problems surrounding immigration, moreover, was a quintessentially imperial one, believing that the Anglo-Jewish middle class could and should 'civilize' the primitive East Europeans.[40] The chameleon-like quality of the Jews, for Jacobs, was evidence of their capacity for genuine integration.

The extent to which hostility to Jewish immigrants or Jewish capitalists in the period indicates a significant rise in antisemitic thinking and expression is a subject that has much exercised historians.[41] In general, Britain has been widely regarded as uniquely exempt from the ideological and institutional forms of antisemitism that were emerging in late nineteenth-century Europe – the rise of antisemitic political parties in Germany and Austria, for example, and the framing of Alfred Dreyfus for espionage in France.[42] But, as Colin Holmes argues, the calling into question of Jewish national loyalties at the time of the Eastern Question crisis and the South African War, as well as the popular and organized hostility to Jewish immigration, were situations that highlighted 'what was regarded as the essential incompatibility of certain Jewish and British interests'.[43] In each case, David Feldman also notes, 'the critique was driven by the same oppositions between disinterestedness and corruption, patriotism and the self-seeking influence of the Jews'.[44] In its strongest expressions, Hobson's warnings about a 'Jew-Imperialist design' in global politics shared its rhetoric of malevolent international conspiracy with the *Protocols of the Elders of Zion* (first published in Russian in 1903). Equally, in these terms, Hobson's radical-liberal anti-capitalist thinking converged with that of the influential nationalist and anti-alienist Arnold White: both regarded the Jews as a threat to their respective ideals of the nation.

Yet these dramatic declarations coincided in the period with a strong cultural taboo against antisemitic prejudice. One has only to recall the widespread and ferocious criticism heaped on Richard Burton's *The Jew, the Gypsy and El-Islam* (published posthumously, 1898) for its unproven allegations against Jews (including a revival of the blood libel), described in the mainstream press as 'fiercely, fanatically anti-semitic'.[45] Opponents of immigration restriction readily seized on the charge of antisemitism, to the extent that both government spokesmen and anti-alienist leaders took care to steer clear of the word 'Jew' in discussions of immigration. Nevertheless, counter-forces were also at work: casual discrimination existed across all social classes; hostile stereotypes of Jews as representatives of alien materialism were common both in high literature and popular culture, from *Punch* cartoons to cheap postcards.[46]

This complicated picture of British culture, characterized by no one single tendency but many competing or overlapping voices, is often lost. Claire Hirshfield, for example, in her study of hostility to Jewish capitalists by the organized Left, is unable to reconcile her conclusion that at the turn of the century 'the reductionist logic and tiresome clichés of nineteenth century antisemitism acquired new strength and luster' with her earlier acknowledgement that this rhetoric was in fact limited to the sphere of political debate and made no impact on popular opinion.[47] This tension between the impropriety of antisemitic feeling and its open expression in a number of instances is brought to the fore in Lara Trubowitz's essay in this volume. The contradictions in parliamentary discourse on aliens, she argues, reflected contrary desires both to exclude Jews and to avoid the charge of antisemitism. Such contradictions could be present even within individuals, as the *Jewish Chronicle* noted in its 1889 profile of Arnold White. 'Mr White seems to love and to hate us in a breath', noted the *Chronicle*, 'to at once kiss us and scratch us with proverbial feminine inconsistency'.[48] Seeking to examine the cultural as well as the political dimensions of semitic discourse, the contributions to this volume reflect the complex interplay within British society between philosemitism and antisemitism.

This nuanced approach to the multiple voices at play and interests at stake in *fin-de-siècle* Britain may help to think through further the vexed question of the relationship between 'real' Jews and the hostile cultural stereotypes of the period. Rather than regarding 'the Jew' as entirely a discursive construct, it is important to remember that certain beliefs about Jews – for example, their economic activity – had some basis in fact. Jews were indeed prominent in the exploitation of the South African diamond fields, powerful in international finance, particularly merchant banking, and deeply involved in press ownership. These particular areas of concentration can be explained as one consequence of Jewish history – particularly of the close personal contacts across borders that had proved advantageous in the development of international finance.[49] Nonetheless, as Holmes rightly argues, the actuality of Jewish involvement in high finance or information ownership does not 'clinch the claim that these individual Jews were working in a Jewish interest'.[50]

Certainly, the relationship among economic, class, and ethnic interests that motivated such individuals bears further investigation. But it is the cultural and political appropriation of this semitic representation that concerns us most. Indeed, controversies centring on Jews were frequently figurative articulations of broader themes. For example, the socialist and Liberal critique of Jewish involvement in South African investment took place at a time when the power of finance capital was coming under increasing scrutiny. In Hobson's claim, therefore, that the South African War was contrary to national interests, and in his uneasiness about the resurgent jingoism it inspired, we can see projected, onto Jewish agency, Liberal ambivalence about the role of international capitalism in the modern economy and the pliability of the newly expanded electorate. Equally, behind nationalist objections to the cosmopolitan ties of Jewish financiers and their apparently inscrutable loyalties, lay a consciousness of Britain's declining imperial supremacy in the face of the industrial powers of Germany and America. From this perspective, the visceral, hysterical tone of much writing about the Jews suggests not so much an atavistic hatred of Jews themselves, as profoundly modern fears about money, democracy, and nation in the contemporary world.

East End, West End

The Jewish East End, meanwhile, came to crystallize a different set of domestic concerns, relating in particular to urban deprivation: indeed, Jews became associated as much with extreme poverty as extreme wealth in the last two decades of the century, when the demographic profile of Anglo-Jewry was dramatically changing. In 1828 there were 27,000 Jews in Britain; in 1860 there were 40,000. Before the last third of the nineteenth century, Jews constituted not more than 0.2 per cent of the population; even in London, where most lived, they comprised less than 1 per cent of the capital's total inhabitants.[51] Between 1881 and 1914, however, the Jewish population underwent huge expansion as a result of mass immigration. Although exact figures are impossible to ascertain (given the government's notoriously unreliable methods of data collection), between 120,000 and 150,000 East European Jews settled permanently in Great Britain.[52] As the demography changed, so did the geography of Jewish London: the vast majority of Jews now inhabited the East End.

Jews emigrated from Russia and Poland in response to severe restrictions on their economic life in the 1880s and to pogroms in 1881–82, 1891–92, and 1903–6. Initial public sympathy for the victims of the pogroms during the early 1880s shifted quickly towards hostility, expressed both in sporadic violence in the streets of the East End and in the efforts of upper-class activists to galvanize working-class anti-alienism. In responding to both, the Aliens Act of 1905 was the first legislation to restrict immigration for nearly a century: it gave government inspectors 'power to prevent the landing of undesirable immigrants', unless they could prove they were 'seeking admission…solely to avoid persecution or punishment on religious or political grounds or for an offence of a political character'. An 'undesirable immigrant' was a pauper (who could not show 'that he has in his possession to obtain the means of decently supporting himself and his dependents'), an invalid ('a lunatic or an idiot', or someone whose illness 'appears likely to become a charge upon the rates or otherwise a detriment to the public'), or a criminal ('sentenced in a foreign country with which there is an extradition treaty for a crime').[53] The Act was introduced by the Tory government: the Liberals who came to power in 1906 did not enforce it rigorously; but nor did they repeal it.[54]

Jewish immigrants became the object of such dramatic government intervention not because of their numbers: although the immigrant influx had considerably increased the Jewish population, it remained miniscule in absolute terms (in the 1900s Jewish immigrants constituted one third of Britain's foreign population, which was itself a decidedly unthreatening 1 per cent of the total population). Rather, as Bernard Gainer has argued, 'Immigrant' and 'Jew' became synonymous terms because of the central role attributed to the East End in the British popular imagination and the extraordinary concern for the district's social problems which emerged roughly at the time of the first great wave of immigration.[55]

In the East End itself, popular hostility directed against Jewish immigrants was first and foremost a mechanism that channelled and defused East Enders' anger at their own chronic poverty and insecurity; xenophobia seems to have been a secondary issue. As Tony Kushner points out, alongside traditions of intolerance, relations between Jews and non-Jews were also often marked by co-operation, for example during the strikes of 1889 and 1912.[56] It is telling that violence on the East End streets, such as the stone-throwing and looting in Bethnal Green in 1903, was directly linked to moments of acute strain in the employment or housing market. Jews were accused of lowering the standards of living; in particular, they were associated with the sweating, or small workshop practice of employment, characterized by poor working conditions, long hours, low pay, and seasonal fluctuation, and with the housing shortage that had led to extreme overcrowding. Yet, as Gainer shows in his examination of the myths that surrounded the Jewish immigrant, both problems had beset the East End long before the immigrants' arrival. He ascribes anti-alienism, then, to pervasive popular ignorance not only about the true extent of immigration, but also about the real economic causes of local unemployment, such as trade depressions, mechanisation, and provincial competition.[57]

The problem of urban poverty to which anti-alienism responded was, meanwhile, a question that preoccupied many social reformers and informed their efforts to influence government policy. In this respect, the East End had become a metonym for discontents that were both more widespread and more significant. When William Booth of the Salvation Army sought to denounce the social conditions that led to moral depravity, it was to the East End that he turned: his work, *In Darkest England and the Way Out* (1890), thus echoed both Andrew Mearns' *The Bitter Cry of Outcast London: An Enquiry into the Condition of the Abject Poor* (1883) and Charles Booth's *Life and Labour of the People in London* (1889–1903). The place to which Jews emigrated in the late-nineteenth century was, then, for onlookers as well as residents, already freighted with the most acute of contemporary anxieties.

Nor were Jews especially sympathetic to the plight of the immigrants. Ensconced in the middle class, the established Anglo-Jewish community and its philanthropic wing – the Jewish Board of Guardians – broadly shared anti-alienist assumptions about the deleterious social effects of immigration and put such assumptions briskly into practice. The Board's emigration committee (established in 1879) facilitated the repatriation or assisted emigration of between 30 and 61 per cent of those who arrived in Britain. When it did offer to aid refugees to economic independence, the Board distinguished the 'deserving' from the 'undeserving' poor in the same manner as non-Jewish charitable agencies – to the vocally expressed disgust of the East End Jewish press.[58]

Religion became a battleground between East and West, as the small independent orthodox congregations of the East End energetically resisted the authority of the Chief Rabbi.[59] Politics, too, divided East Enders from their middle-class co-religionists: social democrats and anarchists urged Jewish workers to affiliate themselves with English workers and to resist the forces of masters, capitalists, and religious leaders; East End Zionists were regarded by patriotic West Enders with deep suspicion.[60] At the same time, within the East End itself, ethnic affiliation sometimes provided the means to bridge differences of wealth – as in the case of friendly societies, whose values of mutual aid were shared by masters and workers alike.[61] Little wonder that, observing the domestic lifestyle of East End Jews, Charles Booth's investigators found it persistently difficult to categorize them in terms of class.[62]

Rather than a stable 'community', then, Jews in Britain formed a dynamic collective of interest groups, a population sharing religious origins but otherwise profoundly fissured by differences of class, religious observance, political interest, and ideological commitment.[63] This perspective on Anglo-Jewry as divided and embattled is evident in Ben Gidley's essay in this volume. Gidley traces such divisions in the various responses among Jews to the Kishinev pogroms of 1903, revealing starkly the competing interests at stake in the transnational interpretation and use of Jewish history. Such internal battles provided the Anglo-Jewish author and playwright Israel Zangwill with a rich resource for fiction in his portrait of the diversity of East End life, *Children of the Ghetto* (1892). In both his art and his political work, Zangwill rejected a philosophy of assimilation that merely mimics the dominant ethnicity, advocating instead the possibility of multiple loyalties and identities which complement rather than contradict each other.

It is only appropriate, then, that Zangwill's colourful persona surfaces in many of the essays in this collection: embodying a series of complex affiliations – East End/West End, English/Jewish, Zionist/Territorialist – Zangwill's figure encapsulates the range of tensions and contradictions with which this volume is concerned. David Glover's essay, for example, charts the decisive role that the British political context played in shaping Zangwill's Territorialism (advocating the creation of autonomous or semi-autonomous Jewish territories, not necessarily in Palestine): although many of Zangwill's practical commitments embodied universalistic values and beliefs, 'it was the pressure of events within the British political arena', Glover writes, 'that nearly always propelled him into word and deed'. Indeed, given that Jews contested every aspect of Jewish life among themselves – given that Zangwill himself could personify these contradictory dimensions – it is hardly surprising that Jews were publicly imagined in such contradictory ways.

Jews, the nation, and the Empire

'Distress in London is not the distress of a great city', observed Arnold White, 'it is the distress of a great Empire'.[64] The crisis in the East End attracted so much attention precisely because it reflected, in myriad ways, broader anxieties about Britain's national and imperial position. Even before the massive Jewish migration, the East End/West End divide was often imagined in imperial terms which constructed the Eastern borough as a domestic enclave of otherness: if Booth's *In Darkest England* relied on the vocabulary of African exploration to depict the East End as an urban jungle, teeming with 'heathens', the growing Jewish presence reinforced the inclination to imagine it as an Oriental sphere (already suggested, of course, by the Asian immigrants residing there, not to mention the 'East' in 'East End').[65] As one of the witnesses to the Royal Commission complained, in a typical moment of geographical/cultural projection, Whitechapel and Mile End had become a 'Jerusalem'; another said that it was 'a second Palestine'.[66] Evans-Gordon described the Jewish invasion of the East End in terms that recalled the Israelites' conquest of Canaan in the Old Testament: 'The Christian fares as the Canaanite fared', he wrote in *The Alien Immigrant*: 'He is expropriated. Chapel after Chapel has been closed, many mission halls have been abandoned, and the congregation of the few that remain are dwindling every day'.[67]

Ironically, images like these complicated, perhaps even subverted, the time-honoured tradition of imagining the English as modern-day Israelites, and England itself as a new and better Zion, a Blakean 'green and pleasant land' where Jerusalem is to be built.[68] And not just England: as Linda Colley has argued, the shared Protestant heritage, that bound Britons together by reinforcing the conviction that Britain was God's elect nation, played a crucial role in forging the imperial ethos.[69] Nevertheless, Biblical vocabulary was not always used to cement the nation: different constituencies had often appropriated the image of 'Chosen People' to voice their own ambitions against dominant, hegemonic forces. As Jasmine Donahaye demonstrates in her essay in this volume, the Welsh identification with the trials and tribulations of the Biblical Jews, a practice that could be traced back to the seventeenth century, was a central trope in the emergence of Welsh cultural nationalism in the 1900s. Donahaye shows how the growing visibility of *historical* Jews settling in Wales introduced a semitic discourse which, merging with the nonconformist tradition, stressed the parallels between the two beleaguered nations – sharing, Donahaye argues, 'a "small" sense of nation, language, and distinctive history, which they retain in binary opposition to the politically, linguistically and culturally dominant "other", the English'.

If the analogy between the Jews and the Welsh could challenge the hegemonic myth of Empire from within, the parallels between the Jews and the South African Boers pointed to the forces that threatened Empire from without. The Boers had also reworked Old Testament tropes to create their national myth, and regarded themselves as having re-enacted the Exodus from Egypt in the Great Trek out of the British-controlled Cape Colony earlier in the century. As Nadia Valman shows in her essay, moreover, this analogy attained a new topicality during the South African War, when pro-imperialist propaganda, emphasizing the narrow religiosity and cultural primitiveness of the Boers, suggested inevitable resonances with popular perceptions of East European immigrants.

The array of imperial anxieties triggered by the humiliations of the protracted war in South Africa – the danger of the racial and moral decline of the nation and the prospect of an imminent foreign invasion that would overturn the imperial hierarchy – can also help explain the role of 'the Jew' in *fin-de-siècle* fantasies of reverse colonization, fantasies in which 'savage' forces invade and take over the 'civilized' metropole in a monstrous brutality that mirrors Britain's own imperial practices.[70] M. P. Shiel's *The Lord of the Sea* (1901), Violet Guttenberg's *A Modern Exodus* (1904), and James Blyth's *The Tyranny* (1907) all deal explicitly with the danger posed to the Empire by the migration of Jews into the metropolitan centre. In other cases, the fantasies employ more metaphorical readings: as critics have shown, the representation of Bram Stoker's *Dracula* (1897) – hook-nosed, chameleon-like, bleeding money – relied on antisemitic stereotypes. Reminiscent of Svengali, the malicious Jewish protagonist of George Du Maurier's best-selling *Trilby* (1894), it is Dracula's mesmerizing power that allows him to infiltrate the imperial centre.[71]

These fantasies exposed fears about the deteriorating state of national health, an issue which became increasingly poignant after the military disaster of the War: the Interdepartmental Committee on Physical Deterioration, established in 1904, raised grave doubts about the physical condition of working-class army recruits. The Jews occupied a typically confused place in this discussion. Although medical witnesses failed to come to a unanimous conclusion about whether Jews were particularly prone to trachoma or tuberculosis as alleged, the Royal Commission on Alien Immigration expressed concern about the degeneracy of pauper aliens. As Lara Trubowitz and Nicholas Evans show in this volume, the imagery of disease had penetrated the very language in which immigration was discussed.

More specifically, the press often represented immigrants as an especial threat to the physical condition of the working class.[72] If they were in one sense winning the struggle for existence against indigenous East Enders by being able to subsist on less food, sleep, and space, this lowering of living standards would take its toll on the populace more generally. The implications for the imperial future were not difficult to fathom. In *The People of the Abyss* (1903), the American author Jack London spelt out the consequences of adding to a stock already degenerate: 'Brutalized, degraded and dull, the Ghetto folk will be unable to render efficient service to England in the world struggle for industrial supremacy which economists declare has already begun.'[73] It is in this light that Daniel Pick regards the 1905 Aliens Act not 'as a mere anomaly, nor, exclusively, as part of some timeless, centuries-old phenomenon of anti-semitism, but in relation to that wider contemporary attempt to construct a racial-imperial identity'.[74]

It was the language of Empire, then, that gave opposition to Jewish immigration its most persuasive rhetorical coherence. While East End anti-alienism failed to take off as an organized movement in the 1890s, it gained rapid ground in 1901 in the wake of the South African War. By 1902 the anti-alienist British Brothers' League (BBL) claimed 12,000 members in east London. Its public meetings were characterized by a bombastic display of imperial patriotism that united elite leadership with popular membership. While the Conservative Party grew unhappy with its association with the BBL, the strength of feeling expressed by the League provided the incentive for the Royal Commission and eventually the Aliens Act: as David Feldman argues, 'the immigration question negotiated the space between the experience of the East End electorate and imperial politics'.[75]

The triangulation of Empire and metropolis through the 'Jew' was not limited to native Britons. In her work on Olive Christian Malvery, a Punjabi photojournalist who settled in Edwardian London, Judith Walkowitz has shown how Malvery's creation of her public persona as a favoured 'daughter of the Empire' – identifying with and defending the interests of London's Cockney working women – was given greater force by her journalistic presentation of East End Jews as irredeemably alien. Malvery was thus able to construct an 'us' that included both British and imperial subjects, only with reference to the 'foreign' European Jew. Demonstrating the richness of inter-articulating 'racial' representations through the lens of Empire, Walkowitz shows how Malvery's work complicates a simple relationship between colonizer and colonized by employing the 'Jew' as the ultimate Other.[76]

All these examples, from the orientalisation of the East End to fantasies of degeneration and otherness, suggest the meanings of 'the Jew' in the discursive aspects of imperial culture. But Jews were also active players in Britain's imperial expansion throughout the nineteenth century and beyond. The Jewish involvement took many forms: Jews functioned, for example, as agents of Britain's 'informal' imperialism in territories which were not under direct British control, like areas of the Ottoman empire. This was true of British Jews (such as the philanthropist Moses Montefiore, who travelled time and again to the Middle East), but also of indigenous Jews who lived in these 'contact zones': as merchants, translators, or mediators, they employed their linguistic skills and vast commercial ethno-religious networks to advance British financial, strategic, and cultural interests in these areas. In return, they often enjoyed the protection of the British consulate.[77]

More directly, Jewish capital played an increasingly significant role in the making of the British Empire. When, in 1875, Disraeli – himself a quintessential empire-builder – purchased 44 per cent of the Suez Canal Company shares without the consent of Parliament, it was to Lionel de Rothschild that he turned for a short-term loan of £4 million. Following the discovery of gold and diamonds in South Africa in the 1870s and 80s, Jewish 'Randlords' like Alfred Beit, Lionel Phillips, and Barney Barnato (born Barnett Isaacs) became key players in South African financial and political life. In 1895, Cecil Rhodes staged an unauthorized British attack on the Boer republics (the abortive 'Jameson Raid') in an attempt to overthrow Paul Kruger's Boer government: both Beit and Phillips helped plan and finance the failed venture. Phillips was among those arrested by the Transvaal authorities for his part in organizing the raid and was condemned to death (he was eventually pardoned and fined £25,000); Beit, like Rhodes, was found guilty by the House of Commons inquiry. This association between Jews, capital, and imperial intervention would be distilled, as we have seen, by the Anglo-Boer War. Yet even seemingly domestic affairs like the two Edwardian scandals which implicated senior Jewish politicians and businessmen had crucial imperial connections: the Marconi scandal (1912) centred on a contract to construct an Empire-wide chain of wireless stations; the Indian Silver scandal (1913) involved the supply of silver for the British government of India.[78]

As David Feldman has noted, 'the capacity of empire to provide opportunities for some Jews to pursue profit for themselves and their firms is beyond dispute'.[79]

But Empire was about more than just profit: for middle and lower-class Jews, imperial culture offered a way of exhibiting their patriotism and loyalty, while the Empire itself 'provided a field of activity in which Jews were able to justify their emancipation'.[80] This imperial energy, as Feldman has noted, was manifested in numerous spheres and contexts: the Chief Rabbi was the religious head of the United Hebrew Congregations not only of Britain, but of the British Empire as a whole; the *Jewish Chronicle* included regular columns dedicated to 'Colonial and Foreign News' and 'Jottings from South Africa'; numerous Jews were involved in fighting for and administrating the Empire;[81] and even those who remained in Britain could take to the streets and celebrate illustrious imperial moments, like the relief of Mafeking.

Most significantly, perhaps, Jews settled across the Empire, in Canada, Australia, South Africa, and elsewhere. In some cases, British Jews – like many other Britons – emigrated overseas in search of better living conditions and opportunities. In other cases, the move was forced: the Empire offered the leaders of British Jewry a way of coping with the escalating pressures of immigration. A significant minority of the East European Jews who were assisted by the emigration committee set up by the Jewish Board of Guardians was sent to colonial destinations like Australia and South Africa.[82] Similarly, as Aubrey Newman has shown, the Poor Jews' Temporary Shelter, an East End charity established in 1885, worked closely with shipping companies in order to facilitate the movement of transmigrants from Lithuania – via the Port of London – to South Africa.[83]

A survey of the Jewish imperial experience is beyond our scope here: we should note, however, that the liminal nature of the imperial frontier and the relationship between white settlers and indigenous populations highlighted and sometimes complicated the ambivalence of 'the Jew'. 'The Jews, as a category, transgress the two major discourses on which Australian population policy has been constructed: race and nation', wrote Jon Stratton in his contribution to a significant volume edited by Sander L. Gilman and Milton Shain, dedicated to the question of Jewries at the Frontier, 'It is no wonder that general discussions of Australia's migrant-population history and policy have ignored the Jews'.[84]

Colonial Zion

The Jewish involvement in Empire acquired a new dimension with the rise of political Zionism, a movement committed to 'the creation of a home for the Jewish people in Palestine to be secured by public law':[85] this was the programme adopted by the First Zionist Congress which convened in Basle in 1897 under the leadership of Theodor Herzl, a Viennese journalist and playwright who had published, a year earlier, an influential treatise entitled *Der Judenstaat* (*The Jewish State* or *The Jews' State*).

An assimilated Jew, devising his Zionist programme independently, Herzl was not aware of his predecessors in Central and Eastern Europe, figures like Moses Hess (author of *Rome and Jerusalem*, 1862) or Leo Pinsker (*Auto-Emancipation: An Appeal to His People by a Russian Jew*, 1882) who had already envisioned the founding of an autonomous Jewish political entity. Ironically, some of these Jewish thinkers were influenced by the Protestant eschatological tradition which first surfaced in Britain in the seventeenth century and re-emerged in the nineteenth. Convinced that the restoration of the Jews to the land of their fathers was a crucial stage in the series of events which would culminate in Christ's Second Coming, Evangelical premillenarians conceived various plans for the restitution of a Jewish polity in the Holy Land, plans which often conflated millenarian and imperial interests.[86] As Abigail Green has recently argued, the eschatological logic was often fused with humanitarian concern for oppressed Jews (especially in Muslim lands) and the wish to spread the values of Victorian civilization through an 'imperialism of human rights': along with anti-slavery, British support for the Jewish cause played an important role in legitimising Empire.[87] In 1840, Lord Shaftesbury, the eminent Evangelical reformer, convinced Foreign Secretary Palmerston (his step-father-in-law) to encourage the Jewish colonization of Palestine as a policy that would benefit the Empire.[88] The plan was never realized, but, as Gideon Shimoni has argued, it was the threat of premillenarian projects like these – threat, because the Jews were expected not only to migrate, but to convert as well – that spurred the Jews themselves into action.[89]

Equally influential was George Eliot's proto-Zionist novel, *Daniel Deronda* (1876), published at the height of the Eastern Question excitement. Written as a reaction against the conventional Evangelical plot (rather than converting to Christianity, the 'gentile' Deronda discovers himself a Jew), the novel was received enthusiastically in Jewish circles, playing a key role in spreading Zionist aspirations among Jewish readers.[90] For Eliot, Deronda's quest at the very end of the novel ('The idea that I am possessed with is that of restoring a political existence to my people, making them a nation again, giving them a national centre') is idealistic, more visionary than practical: as Gillian Beer has reminded us, 'his success in his Zionist endeavour would have seemed far less certain for the first readers (and the author) than it may do now'.[91]

Yet by the 1880s, Zionist visions were beginning to be realized. In 1882, motivated by the violence in Russia, groups of East European Jewish settlers began establishing small agricultural communities in Palestine. At the same time, however, with numerous difficulties facing the settlers – not least the Ottoman suspicion of massive Jewish immigration, combined with the local

Palestinians' resistance – it was clear that sanctuary for Jewish refugees must be found elsewhere. In 1891, for example, the French-Jewish philanthropist Baron Maurice de Hirsch established the Colonial-Jewish Association (JCA) which aimed to facilitate the mass migration of Jews from Eastern Europe by settling them in agricultural colonies, especially in Argentina. Arnold White, on the other hand, proposed that Jews should be settled in Turkish Armenia, 'rich in soil, benign in climate, half populated and inhabited in part by a semitic race which [would] get no harm from contact with the Jews'.[92] These various solutions, dubbed 'Territorialist' (as opposed to the 'Zionist' emphasis on Zion alone) continued to stir Jewish public opinion well into the twentieth century.

Meanwhile, influenced by the increasingly antisemitic mood on the Continent (Herzl was the *Neue Freie Presse*'s Paris correspondent in 1894, when the Dreyfus Affair broke out), Herzl succeeded in consolidating the sporadic Zionist fractions into a unified force. Predominantly an East European movement, Zionism was much less successful in Britain. Herzl was quick in mobilizing the assistance of Israel Zangwill, but although East End Jews tended to support Zionist ideas – Herzl addressed several cheering East End rallies in 1897–1899 – respectable West End Jews, always more intent on assimilation, were slow in warming up to the Zionist idea.[93]

Yet despite the limited support for Zionism among Anglo-Jewry, Britain was significant for Herzl because he saw the British Empire as the ideal patron of the Zionist cause. Struggling, in vain, to gain a franchise from the Ottomans for the colonization of Palestine, and frustrated by his inability to gain German diplomatic support, Herzl turned to Britain: her liberal tradition, the relative lack of antisemitism, and even the Evangelical interest in the restoration of the Jews to Palestine – all these contributed to Herzl's admiration;[94] but it was Britain's imperial power, and particularly her presence in the Middle East, that appealed to Herzl most. London thus gradually became a centre for Zionist activity. The Jewish Colonial Bank (or Trust), the financial instrument of the Zionist Organization, was registered in London in 1898. In 1900, Herzl decided to hold the Zionist congress in London, the imperial metropolis, where the vibrant newspaper scene guaranteed mass coverage. In July 1902 Herzl appeared before the Royal Commission on Alien Immigration: quoting passages from *The Jewish State* ('The unfortunate Jews are now carrying the seeds of anti-Semitism into England'),[95] his testimony suggested that it was in Britain's interest that the Jews should attain their own national home.

A few weeks later, desperate to secure a territory for Jewish colonization – at least as a temporary measure – Herzl began to negotiate with British officials in an attempt to obtain El-Arish, in the Sinai Peninsula (under British control since the 1882 annexation of Egypt). But Lord Cromer, the British council-general in Egypt, opposed the plan, and the Zionists were forced to seek a different territory. Herzl desired Cyprus – like El Arish, adjacent to the

Holy Land – but the British, in April 1903, offered 'Uganda', that is, the Uasin Gishu plateau in British East Africa.

With the Uganda Affair, political Zionism and the British Empire found, for the first time – though certainly not the last – a shared interest: for Zionists, this signalled the possibility of creating an autonomous Jewish state, recognized and sponsored by the world's most powerful Empire; for the British, this was a chance to increase the 'white' population in East Africa (where an expensive train line had just been built) and, at the same time, to divert Jewish immigration from Britain itself. The goal, as Chamberlain candidly explained in an East End rally in December 1904, was 'to find some county in this world of ours, if possible under the aegis of the British flag', where these 'poor exiles from their native land, who do not leave it out of caprice, or with any desire to injure us, could dwell in safety, following their own religion and their own aspirations, and where they could find subsistence without in any way interfering with the subsistence of others'.[96]

Typically, these issues were swiftly picked up by Israel Zangwill. As Meri-Jane Rochelson demonstrates in her essay in this volume, adopting the racialist language of imperialism in his praise of the British gift of East Africa, Zangwill could, in nearly the same breath, remind Jewish listeners that the threat of British (and American) immigration restrictions added to the need for Jewish settlement in Africa. Zangwill's Zionism and Territorialism, Rochelson argues, were both idiosyncratic and emblematic, combining a desire to meet pragmatic resettlement goals with a larger need to define Jewishness as race, religion, and nationality for a Europe inclined to dismiss it as all three.

The fact that the Uganda plan was eventually aborted has allowed Zionist historiography to approach the entire affair as a marginal, even eccentric episode.[97] Nevertheless, as Mark Levene notes in his essay in this volume, the vision of an 'African Zion', far from being an anomaly, was in fact rooted in the ideological and cultural origins of Herzl's Zionism. Employing some of the tools of 'speculative' or 'counterfactual' history, Levene argues that although *The Jewish State* does not mention Africa by name, it is profoundly influenced by the European colonial impetus, and particularly the late nineteenth-century 'Scramble for Africa'.

Levene's argument thus helps explain why the Uganda Affair has been relegated from Zionist historiography. Insisting that Zionism should be understood in the context of the nineteenth-century European rise of nationalism, Zionist scholars have customarily rejected or considerably qualified claims about the affinity between Zionism and colonialism, claims that have become more audible since the 1980s with the work of young historians and sociologists, stimulated by the publication of Edward Said's *Orientalism* (1978) and *The Question of Palestine* (1979).[98] Seeking to repudiate these arguments, Zionist historians have pointed out that, unlike typical

European settlement colonialism, Zionism lacked a unified metropolitan centre which had initiated the colonial venture in the first place; that, rather than exploit the local labour force in Palestine in order to produce a considerable revenue for metropolitan investors, Zionism encouraged the work of Jewish labourers and actually invested in Palestine more than it had ever earned; and, finally, that Zionism was in effect an *anti*colonial movement which sought to liberate the Jews from their historic position as an oppressed, persecuted – in a word, colonized – people.[99]

While these observations certainly suggest that a straightforward analogy between Zionism and colonialism would be simplistic and ultimately unrewarding, conventional Zionist accounts all but ignore the discursive, cultural, and even practical affinities between Zionism and settler colonialism. European Zionists were shaped by the imperial ethos of the *fin de siècle*: hence they sought to create and employ various colonial practices (a Colonial Bank, scientific surveys, the establishment of settler plantation colonies); embraced the civilizing mission of bringing progress to a backward territory (a desert that must be made to bloom); adopted Orientalist tropes in their attitudes towards the native population (the Palestinians as noble savages, romantic yet primitive); and, as we have seen, recognized the range of shared interests, strategic as well as cultural, between the Zionist movement and the British Empire. 'You are far ahead of us in all technical industries, just as the great politicians of your country were the first to see the necessity for extending your Colonial possessions', Herzl declared in a speech to the annual conference of the Zionist Federation in London in 1899: 'This is the reason why the flag of Greater Britain waves over every sea, and, to my mind, this is why the Zionist idea, which is a colonizing plan, should be easily and quickly grasped in England.'[100] As Daniel Boyarin has argued, it was by mimicking the colonial European settler – by transforming the Jews into 'white' colonists – that Herzl's Zionism attempted to answer, once and for all, the 'Jewish Question'.

What the Uganda affair contributes to this heated debate is an opportunity to explore these colonial tropes from a perspective that transcends and yet highlights the conventional Palestinocentric view. Void of the historical, religious, and romantic dimensions of the Jewish colonization of Palestine, the vision of an 'African Zion' – though short-lived – laid bare the colonialist logic (or mimicry) of the Zionist 'anticolonial' project. Drawing on the narratives produced by and about the Zionist commission sent in 1904 to survey the designated East African territory, Eitan Bar-Yosef's essay in this volume explores how the Zionist travel narratives appropriated the conventions of the exotic African adventure. While supporters of the plan attempted to project the sacred image of 'The Promised Land' onto East Africa, ultimately it was the symbolic aura of 'Africa' – the colonialist, racist, and cultural dimensions of the 'African fantasy' – that fed into the Zionist project in the Promised Land.

Balfour and beyond

The prospect of a Jewish state in Africa was not to be fulfilled, but the bond between Zionism and the British Empire would intensify, leading eventually to the Balfour Declaration of November 1917, in which the British Government committed itself to the 'establishment in Palestine of a national home for the Jewish people'.[101] Henceforth, the allegation that Zionism was indeed an agent of western imperialism (first British, then American) would continue to haunt the Zionist movement. The establishment of the state of Israel in 1948, following 30 years of British rule in Palestine, allowed Zionists to see their national project as a *post*colonial venture (similar to other emerging nation-states in Asia and in Africa); the 1967 war, however, brought about a new phase: controlling and exploiting a vast population of Palestinians, Israel now underwent 'a rapid evolution into a colonial state'.[102] The massive building of Jewish settlements in the occupied territories escalated the oppression: by the end of the 1990s, the combination of militarised colonial outposts, road blockades, and highways solely for Jews would add undeniable force to accusations, both in Israel and abroad, about the parallels between Zionism and Apartheid rule.[103]

The analogy between Jerusalem and Pretoria (that is, before South Africa's 1994 transformation into the 'Rainbow Nation') brings us back to the series of geographical projections with which we began this introduction: the East End as a foreign country; the Russian Pale as Mafeking; Johannesburg as the New Jerusalem. While we hardly wish to collapse historical differences, it is nevertheless telling that more than a century after the turbulent events depicted in this volume, 'the Jew' (though sometimes only 'the Zionist' or 'the Israeli') continues to evoke contradictory images, raising, yet again, disconcerting questions about the possibility of distinguishing stereotypes from reality, and highlighting the forces and conditions which render these representations so ambiguous.

It is significant, furthermore, that these contradictory attitudes towards Zionism and Israel relate not only to the historical uncertainty surrounding 'the Jew', but also to the memory and legacy of British colonialism itself, which in many ways remain unresolved. For many British commentators today, the critique of Israel seems to offer a convenient way of exorcising their own colonial guilt without having to address Britain's own direct contribution to the Middle Eastern muddle.[104] To dwell on these questions would be to go beyond the limited theme of this book. Nevertheless, like those Mafeking celebrations in the East End – delayed by 24 hours, yet equally exultant – the essays in this volume should also be projected ahead, allowing us to ponder how late-Victorian and Edwardian representations of 'the Jew' will continue to resonate long after the 1900s had passed.

Notes

1. Krebs, *Gender, Race and the Writing of Empire*, ch. 1.
2. 'Mafeking Day in the East End', *JC*, 25 May 1900, 11. In the original piece, the phrase 'Yom Tov' appears in Hebrew.
3. Holmes, *Anti-Semitism*, 66–70, 81–83; Hirshfield, 'The Anglo-Boer War'.
4. J. A. Hobson, *The War In South Africa, Its Causes and Effects* (1900; New York: Howard Fertig, 1969), 189, 226.
5. 'Mafeking Day in the East End', *JC*, 25 May 1900, 11.
6. On the international political and cultural impact of the Kishinev pogrom, see Penkower, 'The Kishinev Pogrom'.
7. W. Evans-Gordon, *The Alien Immigrant* (London: William Heinemann, 1903), 10, 7–8, 9.
8. Bhabha, *The Location of Culture*, 89.
9. Cheyette, *Constructions of 'the Jew'*.
10. For theoretical discussions of the distinction between 'the *abstract Jew*, the Jew as a concept located in a different discourse from the practical knowledge of "empirical" Jews', see Bauman, 'Allosemitism' and Bauman, *Modernity and Ambivalence*, ch. 2.
11. H. M. Hyndman, 'The Parting of the Ways', *Justice*, 16 May 1896, 4.
12. Hall, *Civilising Subjects*, 9, 12.
13. Said, *Orientalism*, 307.
14. Kalmar and Penslar, *Orientalism and the Jews*, xx.
15. Bauman, 'Allosemitism'; Kristeva, *Powers of Horror*, 4, 185; Lyotard, *Heidegger and 'the Jews'*.
16. Cheyette, '"Ineffable and Usable"', 296, 311.
17. Kalmar and Penslar, *Orientalism and the Jews*, xiv, our emphasis. See also Omer-Sherman, *The Cultural and Historical Stabilities*.
18. Mufti, *Enlightenment in the Colony*, 7, original emphasis.
19. Kalmar and Penslar, *Orientalism and the Jews*, xv.
20. Boyarin, *Unheroic Conduct*, 271–312. On the Jew as black see Gilman, *Jewish Self-Hatred*, 6–12; Gilman, *The Jew's Body*, 171–200.
21. Penslar, 'Zionism, Colonialism, Postcolonialism'.
22. Salbstein, *The Emancipation*, 33–36.
23. For more on the 'Jew Bill' see Singer, 'Great Britain'; Endelman, *The Jews of Georgian England*, 24–64; Felsenstein, *Anti-Semitic Stereotypes*, 187–214; Shapiro, *Shakespeare and the Jews*, 195–224.
24. On the debates about Jewish emancipation see Salbstein, *The Emancipation* and Feldman, *Englishmen and Jews*, 21–47.
25. Feldman, *Englishmen and Jews*, 48–71.
26. Feldman, *Englishmen and Jews*, 78–82.
27. Frank Harrison Hill, 'The Political Adventures of Lord Beaconsfield', part I, *Fortnightly Review* (August 1878), quoted in Feldman, *Englishmen and Jews*, 115.
28. Feldman, *Englishmen and Jews*, 94–120; Ragussis, *Figures of Conversion*, 174–233. See also the essays in Endelman and Kushner, *Disraeli's Jewishness*.
29. Goldwin Smith, 'Can Jews be Patriots?', *Nineteenth Century*, 3 (January-June 1878), 887, 875.
30. Cohen, 'Who Was Who?', 461.
31. On Jews and race in literary discourse see Cheyette, *Constructions of 'the Jew'*; Freedman, *The Temple of Culture*; Ragussis, *Figures of Conversion*; Malchow, *Gothic Images*, 148–165; Valman, *The Jewess*, 173–205.

32. For another reading of the relationship between Jews, diamonds, and British imperial ambitions see Kaufman, 'King Solomon's Mines?'.
33. Arnold White, review of Dreamers of the Ghetto by Israel Zangwill, Academy and Literature, 53 (1898), 342, quoted in Cohen, 'Who Was Who', 478.
34. British Parliamentary Papers (BPP) 1903, IX, Royal Commission on Alien Immigration (RCAI), Minutes of Evidence, Vol. I, qq. 2,452–455.
35. RCAI, Vol. I, qq. 13,244–248, 13,263–269.
36. Hart, 'Picturing Jews', 160. See also Patai and Patai, The Myth, ch. 1.
37. Efron, Defenders of the Race; Hart, Social Science; Hart, 'Jews, Race and Capitalism'.
38. Endelman, 'Anglo-Jewish Scientists', 52.
39. Efron, Defenders of the Race, 33–57.
40. Efron, Defenders of the Race, 78.
41. On the South African War see Hirshfield, 'The Anglo-Boer War'; on Hobson see Holmes, 'J. A. Hobson'; Mitchell, 'Hobson Revisited'; on the BBL see Holmes, Anti-Semitism, 94–97.
42. See, for example, Endelman, 'English Jewish History'; Endelman, 'The Englishness'; Feldman, 'Was Modernity Good for the Jews?'.
43. Holmes, Anti-Semitism, 13.
44. Feldman, Englishmen and Jews, 266.
45. Holmes, Anti-Semitism, 49–62.
46. Holmes, Anti-Semitism, 104–114; Cowen and Cowen, Victorian Jews.
47. Hirshfield, 'The British Left', 110, 107.
48. JC, 1 April 1889, 19, quoted in Garrard, The English and Immigration, 65.
49. Holmes, Anti-Semitism, 66–86.
50. Holmes, Anti-Semitism, 81.
51. Salbstein, The Emancipation, 37–38.
52. Gainer, The Alien Invasion, 1–14; Endelman, The Jews of Britain, 128–129.
53. 'Aliens Act, 1905', <http://www.movinghere.org.uk/deliveryfiles/pro/Aliens_Act_1905/0/3.pdf>.
54. For a detailed account of the passage and administration of the Act, see Pellew, 'The Home Office'.
55. Gainer, Alien Invasion, 3.
56. Kushner, 'Jew', 40
57. Gainer, Alien Invasion, 16–23.
58. Feldman, Englishmen and Jews, 299–306, 320–322.
59. Feldman, Englishmen and Jews, 312–328.
60. Feldman, Englishmen and Jews, 332, 344–345.
61. Feldman, Englishmen and Jews, 312–319.
62. Englander, 'Booth's Jews', 565.
63. For accounts that highlight some of these fissures see Feldman, Englishmen and Jews; Fishman, East End Jewish Radicals; White, Rothschild Buildings; Black, The Social Politics.
64. Arnold White, Problems of a Great City (1886), 226, quoted in Gainer, Alien Invasion, 74–75.
65. According to the OED, the first modern usage of 'East End' (as the 'Eastern part of London') is in 1846. See also Fishman, East End 1888; Lindeborg, 'The "Asiatic"'.
66. Quoted in Holmes, Anti-Semitism, 17; see also Steyn, The Jew, 59–78.
67. Evans-Gordon, The Alien Immigrant, 12.

68. Bar-Yosef, *The Holy Land*, ch. 1.
69. Colley, *Britons*, ch. 1.
70. Brantlinger, *Rule of Darkness*, 234–236. See also Arata, 'The Occidental Tourist'.
71. Davison, *Anti-Semitism*, 120–157; Pick, *Svengali's Web*.
72. Holmes, *Anti-Semitism*, 37–39; Feldman, *Englishmen and Jews*, 275.
73. Jack London, *The People of the Abyss* (1903; New York: Lawrence Hill, 1995), 231.
74. Pick, *Faces of Degeneration*, 215.
75. Feldman, *Englishmen and Jews*, 279.
76. Walkowitz, 'The Indian Woman'.
77. Green, 'The British Empire'.
78. Endleman, *The Jews of Britain*, 153–155.
79. Feldman, 'Jews and the British Empire', 72.
80. Feldman, 'Jews and the British Empire', 77.
81. Feldman, 'Jews and the British Empire', 71.
82. Lipman, *A Century of Social Service*, 97–100.
83. Newman, 'The Poor Jews' Temporary Shelter'.
84. Stratton, 'The Color of Jews', 311.
85. Vital, *Origins*, 368.
86. Sokolow, *History of Zionism*; Bentwich and Shaftesbury, 'Forerunners of Zionism'; Pragai, *Faith and Fulfilment*; Bar-Yosef, *The Holy Land*, ch. 4; Valman, *The Jewess*, ch. 3.
87. Green, 'The British Empire'.
88. Frankel, *Damascus Affair*, 302–310; Friedman, *The Question of Palestine*, xi–xxvii.
89. Shimoni, *The Zionist Ideology*, 61–64.
90. Werses, 'The Jewish Reception'.
91. George Eliot, *Daniel Deronda*, ed. Graham Handley, World's Classics (1876; Oxford: Oxford University Press, 1988), 688; Beer, *George Eliot*, 227.
92. Holmes, *Anti-Semitism*, 26.
93. Cohen, *English Zionists*.
94. Beller, 'Herzl's Anglophilia'.
95. *RCAI*, Vol. I, q. 6,244.
96. *Alien Immigration*, Trade and the Empire series, no. 67 (Birmingham: Imperial Tariff Committee, [1904]), 2–3.
97. Cf. Friedman, 'Herzl'.
98. Kimmerling, *Zionism and Territory*; Shafir, *Land*; Pappé, 'Zionism'.
99. Bareli, 'Forgetting Europe'; Shimoni, 'Postcolonial Theory'.
100. *The Messenger of Zion*, July 1899, 14.
101. See, among numerous other studies, Fromkin, *A Peace*, 297.
102. Penslar, 'Zionism, Colonialism, Postcolonialism', 97.
103. See, for example, Chris McGreal, 'Worlds Apart', *Guardian*, 6 February 2006, <http://www.guardian.co.uk/israel/Story/0,,1703245,00.html>.
104. Bar-Yosef, 'I'm Just a Pen'.

1

Jews and Jewels: A Symbolic Economy on the South African Diamond Fields

Adrienne Munich

The 1867 discovery of diamonds by Europeans in South Africa accelerated the imperialist 'scramble for Africa'.[1] A global stampede headed for the diamond fields, including large numbers of Jews from everywhere in the Diaspora.[2] Immediately, if not sooner, the diverse population of Jews seemed to forge a closed fraternity, a guild that not only dealt in diamonds, but – in a metaphoric cluster that is the subject of this essay – was itself identified with diamonds.[3] The diamond fields, furthermore, provided an opportunity to represent a frequently unholy partnership between Jew and African, adding to the sinister symbolism of racial representations and the meanings of African diamonds. Jews and Africans, whatever the many differences carefully delineated among and between them by nineteenth-century ethnographers, cast crudely raced shadows on the purest of gems. This symbolic economy served the evangelical project in bringing capitalism to Africa, converting Africans to miners and Protestants.[4] Jews, I will suggest, were cast as an engine of commerce, but also as a problem, both exotic and admired.

Inspired by the promise of a glittering plot in an exotic locale, novelists necessarily confronted a symbolic economy that identified Jews with diamonds. Could the diamonds of Kimberley bear meaning independent of the terrible mine and diamond-dealing Jews, which was their pedigree? Could novels set there portray the Jewish presence independently of the luxurious product they seemed to enable? The Jewish/diamond nexus governs the plot and the problems in three South African diamond fields novels where the source of diamonds is also the setting of the novel. This unique place in the midst of desolate karoo, with its Jews and diamonds so coupled, presents special difficulties in signifying a diamond as pure, valuable beyond cost, an amulet sacred to the highest reaches of Western (Christian) society, an emblem of what nineteenth-century Western culture has deemed love without boundary. This essay considers the manner in which three novels confront the problem of the Jew in the jewel.

Kimberley: diamond city of the Big Hole

By the time Louis Cohen embarked from London, in 1872, 'on the good ship, *European*' for the South African diamond fields – equipped with minimal mining gear, modest cash, and a 17-year-old's thirst for adventure – what he called the 'Diamond City of the Plains' teemed with people of differing tribes, including a reassuring abundance of his own.[5] As in the Biblical Cities of the Plains, the all-too recognizable Hebrews are marked by Cohen as beings of questionable character:

> A few, a very few, appeared well bred, but most of them postured like pilfering tinkers who had got their best clothes out of pawn. They were, as a rule, smoking large cigars. On driving up the Main Street, I had noticed the self-same species of gentlemen standing in front of their framed canvas habitations, and when I read on the signs displayed outside these tented offices that Abraham, Isaac, and Jacob had recovered from their long celestial sleep, and gone in for earthly diamond buying, 'at the very highest prices for the European market,' I felt a real glow of hope as I inwardly ejaculated, 'Thank the Lord I'm with my own people – and it's not Jerusalem!' But they certainly looked as if they had come from the Sublime East – of London. (18)

Cohen's mordant vision of patriarchal resurrection in a land of riches offering hope for the Jews also recognized that the Jews once again were delivered into a land already chock full of other claimants: 'Upon each mound I saw I climbed and accosted the workers. They were of all nations, Englishmen, Irishmen, Scotchmen, Africanders [*sic*], Germans, Boers, &c.' (24). Despite the racial diversity on display, he discovers that the claims are mostly held by 'this breed of miners, Anglo-Saxon to the core...big, brawny, fine-made fellows' (26). Cohen not only links diamonds to Jews without claims, but, in a symbolic economy that continues in the writings I examine here, he associates jewel and Jew with shady dealing, with unkept promises, with wickedness, even with death. The diamond fields recall Sodom and Gomorrah.

In striking contrast to the European invasion of the New World, and its evocation of the New Jerusalem and the Garden of Eden, Cohen portrays the racially diverse pilgrims to Africa as descendants of the sinful Cities of the Plains; if Jews are the Chosen People of the Diamond, this symbolic association condemns as much as it honours. Cohen's wit disguises his unconscious condemnation of Jewish diamond dealing; after all, he joins with his own people to seek his fortune. But his gaze is not

parochial: scanning the human panorama, he marvels at 'such a cosmopolitan and heterogeneous population' (13). His racial survey, a tendency
of diamond fields writing, categorizes humanity with the fine precision of
nineteenth-century ethnographic texts – not only kinds of Jews, but kinds
of Africans, Celts, and others. In his novel, *Mixed Humanity* (1892),
J. R. Couper reproduces such conventional racial taxonomies and describes
the diamond fields as a human potpourri, including nation-identified yet
essentialized Jews:

> Malays and Capeboys…Men of all nations, colours, and complexions
> thronged the thoroughfares – Indians, Arabs, Kaffirs of all tribes,
> Europeans, from the swarthy Italian to the fair, blue-eyed Scandinavian;
> and those of the Hebrew race seemed very numerous… [T]he majority of
> the dealers were Jews, who, though from all parts of the world, retained
> the characteristics of their own race, resembling in a marked manner the
> inhabitants of the different countries they hailed from.[6]

Cohen's evocation of a Biblical Jew, resurrected on the diamond fields,
notes that the dirty poor Jews, with their shabby reclaimed raiment, clearly
emerge from a specific geographic origin: London's East End. To Cohen's
localizing of a certain kind of Jew, Couper adds another characteristic – some
Jews' ability to resemble non-Jewish compatriots. This chameleon nature
enables Jews to tilt their identities to 'the different countries they hailed
from', thereby muting their racial distinctiveness and, perhaps, diffusing it.[7]
The proliferation and diversity of Jews in Kimberley, whether clearly marked
or of more ambiguous identity – all engaged in activities associated with the
diamond business – produces an impression that Jews dominate, if not
absolutely own the town with the great mine at its centre.[8]

By its very excess, the Kimberley diamond mine instituted the symbolic
terms for imagining South African diamonds. The mine inspired superlative
description; 'awe' strikes all observers in fiction and memoir alike when
confronted with the massive digging. Known familiarly as 'the Big Hole',
the largest hand-dug excavation in the world, the mine had a surface area of
42 acres and a depth of 2,625 ft. By 1914, 22.5 million tons of earth had
been excavated, yielding 2.7 tons of diamonds. The place was dangerous,
insanitary, chaotic. Eventually, because of the steepness of the diggings,
walls would cave in, burying African worker and his employer alike: 'Every
day nearly there are two or three niggers killed', explains a character in
Mixed Humanity (20). The production site, littered with dead Africans, might
seem to dim the diamond's glitter: morally, the landscape of the Big Hole
offered a special vision of hell; psychologically, the pit could be conceived as
a particular kind of horror at the feminine, a place where men enter, never
to emerge.[9] It is telling that the one illustration featured in Anthony
Trollope's two-volume work on South Africa (1878) showed a map of the

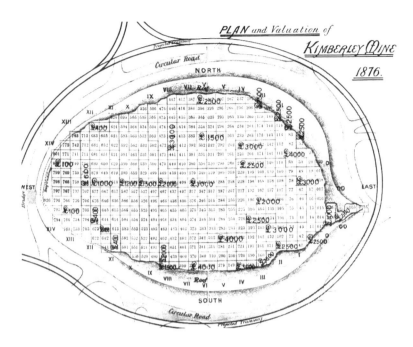

Figure 1.1 'Plan and Valuation of Kimberley Mine, 1876'
Source: From Anthony Trollope, *South Africa*, 2 vols. (London: Chapman & Hall, 1878), vol. II, between 178–79.

Kimberley Mine, an image that could be viewed as encompassing both of the above meanings (Figure 1.1).[10]

In *Mixed Humanity*, the awesome Big Hole – with almost naked African workers at the bottom of the pit, digging and shovelling – inspires metaphors of insects:

> A great yawning chasm it appeared to Senior, as he gazed upon it some-what awestruck…. Kaffirs, like swarms of ants, were to be seen working at the bottom of the mine, under the supervision of white overseers, whose duty it was to see that the precious gems were not stolen. Senior thought of the Kaffir whom he had seen carried along on the stretcher, and the many lives lost in trying to unearth these stones held in so much value simply for ornaments; then, thinking of those of whom he had heard so much, the illicit diamond buyers, more generally known as the I.D.B., he wondered how many of them had forfeited the best years of their lives by being tempted to buy stolen diamonds from the Kaffir workmen. (20–21)

Viewing the same chasm, Trollope cannot decide which insect the workers at the Big Hole most resemble – ants or flies – but his description of their actions might more accurately be likened to bats or demons: 'They come as flies come up a wall, only capering as flies never caper, – and shouting as they come. In endless strings, as ants follow each other, they move, passing along ways which seem to offer no hold to a human foot' (175). The depiction of African miners as sub-human connects them to a literal underworld, criminal and dangerous. These workers secrete diamonds on (or in) their bodies, selling them to the IDBs. Couper describes the part of the Africans in the illicit trade: 'Senior had now become well experienced in the tricks of the wily African. Every dodge had been tried on him in the concealing of stolen diamonds ... All parts of the body they used for this purpose – ears, nose, stomach, hair – and they even made cuts in their legs to hide the precious stones' (45).

Receivers of the African's looted stones were identified in memoirs, newspapers, and novels as Jews, the typical IDBs.[11] Couper describes IDB Faganstine: 'His face was long and thin, his eyes bloodshot, his head was nearly bald. He had side-whiskers and moustache, dark in colour. He was rather well dressed, had on a long-tail coat and spotless white waistcoat, which, being low cut, allowed a broad expanse of white shirt to be seen. The cast of his features was decidedly Hebraic' (25). With his formal attire in the most unlikely setting for it, Faganstine anticipates Bram Stoker's Dracula, while his name echoes Charles Dickens's Fagin.

In fact, the Kimberley air could not have sustained Faganstine's pristine attire for more than two minutes. According to Trollope's novelist eyes, between the dust and the flies, one's lungs – not to say one's shirt – would carry a permanent layer of grime and specks,

> of dust so thick that the sufferer fears to remove it lest the raising of it may aggravate the evil, and of flies so numerous that one hardly dares to slaughter them by the ordinary means ... [A] gust of wind would bring the dust in a cloud hiding everything, a cloud so thick that it would seem that the solid surface of the earth had risen diluted into the air. (190–191)

Because keeping any clothing white would be miraculous, the whiteness at the centre of Faganstine's body appears unnatural, even sinister. This is not the whiteness of purity, but the whiteness of stolen diamonds. Faganstine's spotless white body and his dirty trade reproduces the duality of Jew/jewel, providing a linkage in dirty dealing between Africans whose only interest in diamonds is their exchange value and those Jews for whom the diamond represents a livelihood in a valuable and lightweight commodity. Flies (or African miners) and dust (or Jewish dealers) taint the diamond.

At the very lip – or mouth – of the awesome mine, diamonds cannot appear independently of dangerous, degraded conditions of production, and commercial motives of buying and selling. All gemstones begin their history mired in impurity, in the mucky probing of the ground and crass bargaining with Jews in dusty tents. The vicissitudes of diamonds in novels chart their meanings – as the ultimate jewel of romance, as the ultimate commodity, as the ultimate material sign of the Jew.[12] Combining these three functions of diamonds, the jewel/Jew stands at the centre of contested meanings in South African Diamond Field writings. Can such writing exalt the diamond, maintain its glitter? Can the diamond's 'Jewishness' be disappeared?

South African domestic novels and diamond-loving heroines

Although the variety of kinds of Jews and kinds of Africans assembled together in various ways at the diamond fields provides the exotic interest and the drama of the South African diamond novel, the plot centring on the heroine categorizes the three novels discussed in this essay as a type of the domestic novel. The domestic novel, regarded as a female genre, merges here with the adventure novel, the quintessential novel of mas-culinity. This hybrid form was adapted to the imperialist setting by encompassing bourgeois domesticity as a normal aspect of imperialist escapades. Beauteous heroines frequently assume names reminiscent of bodice rippers – Dainty Laure in Louise Vesalius Sheldon's *An I.D.B. in South Africa* (1888) or Loraine Loree Temple in Cynthia Stockley's *Pink Gods and Blue Demons* (1920) – where both heroines succumb to the seductions of sexy, racialized Lotharios, irresistible Jews. Their counterpart in *Mixed Humanity*, May Leslie, is a seductive and diamond-dealing Jewess; her radical difference from the Christian leading ladies provides a way of understanding the functions of both Jews and heroines in colo-nial domestic novels. In different ways, then, these three novels address the spectacle of Jews on the diamond fields, each identifying the Jew with the jewel.

Mixed Humanity, Couper's mixed genre novel – *bildungsroman*, domestic novel, adventure tale, and detective story – follows the loves and losses of Jack Senior, a fine Irish lad, boxer, and mine worker, while an important sub-plot follows May Leslie, mistress of IDB Ikey Mosetenstine.[13] Couper's fascinating novel presents a complex rendering of Jews by creating a range of stereotyped Jewish characters who nonetheless spill out of their typical behaviour in surprising ways. *Mixed Humanity* even features a Jew, Joseph Leonard, as the hero's best friend, whose father had been an honest but failed diamond dealer, and who is stereotyped, albeit rather mildly, as advanced in maturity for his age. He earns his keep as a civil servant, teaches Senior's lover to play the piano, and offers firm, though narrow, ethical advice to his friend.

The rest of Couper's Jewish characters deal in diamonds, and all the Jewish diamond dealers are IDBs. The most wealthy and successful is Ikey Mosetenstine, whose endearing quality is his having earned the undying loyalty of a brilliant and talented Basuto, who acts as his agent and trains newly-arrived miners to steal and sell to him. But, wealth aside, the most complex Jewish figure, combining stereotypes of Jewish women and men, is Ikey's mistress, May Leslie. Whereas Mosetenstine represents the stereotypical materialistic corpulent Jew – with a luxurious home, loyal Basuto gem-runners, and an unmistakable Yiddish accent ('Zometimes I tink I go, and zometimes I tink I stay') – May possesses characteristics both of the beautiful Christian heroines, familiar from other diamond field novels *and* the (male) Jewish heroes. Her greed and her conscious manipulation of her beauty as a theatrical display provide a dark mirror to the other domestic heroines' purity. While the novels in general play on the symbolic linkage between the pure white European woman and the white purity of the diamond, Couper's text associates the diamond with the sultry, capitalist Jewess.

Indeed, her awareness of her sexuality, her acting on her sexual desire, and her full identification with precious jewels ally May Leslie with the dangerous male diamond/Jew. A temptress, she is a greedy diamond dealer. In addition, like a fantasy of the beautiful Jewess (Marlowe's Abigail, for example, or Shakespeare's Jessica) she would yield all her treasure to a Christian man – in this case Searight, a ne'er do well, whose only apparent charms are his forthright Christian good looks and a taste for brutality.

Although May is not labelled as a Jew, her looks, her activities, and her use of Yiddish phrases ('mozel' for 'luck') identify her ethnicity. From ages 15 to 19 she enjoyed a short successful career as an actress, recalling spectacular nineteenth-century Jewish actresses, Rachel and Sarah Bernhardt. Couper's delineation includes intelligence, beauty, sexuality, and emotionality – all familiar from the stereotypical Jew:

> May Leslie, now nineteen years of age, was of medium height, of slender and exceedingly graceful build. ... Her complexion was of a dark olive tint, yet delicate and transparent. She had large bright eyes, the blue of which contrasted strangely with the darkness of her hair, eyebrows, and complexion; her teeth also perfect in shape, shone with a dazzling whiteness against the dark skin. The lines and expression of her face bespoke a curious mixture of passion and shrewd intelligence, of pathos and strength of character; and the somewhat thick rosy lips of her small pouting mouth gave her a faint suggestion of sensuality. (70)

Hoarding jewellery as portable, personal, and private riches places May in the literary tradition of Jewish merchants, well-known from early modern drama – characters such as Barabas from *The Jew of Malta* and Shylock from

The Merchant of Venice – recapitulated famously in Charles Dickens's Fagin. *Mixed Humanity* reveals May as these characters' legitimate descendant:

> From her childhood she had shown a strange fondness for jewellery, though curiously she wore but little. She was always buying some ornament, which, together with her numerous presents, she hoarded up, and like a miser brought forth in secret, to look at and feel with her light fingers. ...
> Leading the way into her room, she went to...an empty box ... and lifting the cover exposed a small safe.... [S]he unlocked the safe and produced gem after gem, jewel after jewel, ring after ring, ladies' tiny watches, tiaras, pendants, charms, lockets, gentlemen's pins, childish baubles she had stored up almost from her infancy. ...She gazed fondly at her treasures, the hoarding of which had been the greatest pleasure of her life. ...Then May Leslie put an arm round his [Searight's] neck, and clasping his hand, and drawing his face down until it reached hers, cheek against cheek, she whispered softly: 'They are all yours, darling, and I am yours, yours for ever.' (70, 76)

Without the diamond connection, May's literary prototypes appear in such pornography as 'The Beautiful Jewess in the Boudoir'.[14] The combination of the corrupted sexuality of the female porn star with economic savvy – and the sexual connection between May's jewel box and the Kimberley mine – produce a creature born and bred in the colonial racial imagination.

Different from the Jewish May, innocent and Protestant Loraine Loree, the heroine in *Pink Gods and Blue Demons* never yearned for diamonds, apparently content with her diligent Scots husband's gift of an add-a-pearl necklace. When she encounters the jewel, the diamond mine, and the Jew, she enters into the diamond/Jewish symbolic economy, falling into erotic knowledge and sophistication. That is, in symbolic terms, she *becomes* a Jew, and thus the plot must rescue her from commodity culture:

> [I]t was only since she came to Kimberley that the romance [of diamonds] had taken hold of her imagination. It was seeing 'the biggest hole in the world' that started it. She had gone by herself and gazed long into the vast excavation delved by the hands of men in search for those strange little cadres of imprisoned light...
> She wondered what became of diamonds. They seemed indestructible, yet where were all the millions of them that had been taken from this one great hole alone – that, down there, out of the light, were still being dug and groped and sweated for? And it was all for women! That gave her a thrill she had never felt before.[15]

Loree invokes the well-established symbolism surrounding gemstones. Diamond has been divorced from the market economy and linked to durable love rather than durable goods. Yet such a divorce must remain incomplete in the teeming presence of the Big Hole; Loree's correct exclamation about the miners wearing out their lives should have been, 'And it was all for money!' This crucial substitution of lust for greed eroticizes the diamond. In the novel, both sins – lust and greed – are deeded to the Jew, tainting the gems associated with him, but with an enticing blue light. Loree's meditation depends on diamonds' economic value, while it momentarily suspends them from actual economic exchange. A love diamond signifies the immense worth placed on the beloved, yet its allure includes its envelope of danger, darkness, and, here, the Jew's amorous genius.

The heroine's romance fantasy recasts the dangerous scene of production as a chivalric tale, conflating (mostly black) miners' miserable deaths with the love tokens of white knights and whiter ladies. Lorraine Loree's racial profile – she is a 'Jersey Lily with French blood' – references Lily Langtry, mistress of Bertie, Prince of Wales, and suggests Loree's potential. Her husband's erotic torpidity matches his occupation: Donald Temple (his name suggests the commercialisation of religion in a colonial setting) sells cold-storage plants and what the author calls 'corpses', that is beef and mutton. As a consequence, Loree's passionate register remains unmeasured until she sees the Big Hole and meets Hazeltine Quelch, owner of a diamond mine, a character who resembles May Leslie – sensual, passionate, fiscally sharp, and irresistible. In him, the affinity between Jews and diamonds appears somatic, even genetic. The impossibility of divorcing the gem from the mine, along with the diamond/ Jew equation, produces this character. At the very end, slow-witted (part of her attraction as a mannequin) Loree grasps Quelch's open secret: 'This strange Eastern man with his gentle un-English eyes while she stood considering him – how un-English he was to have tears running down his cheeks like that; that he *must* be a Jew (as she had often supposed) to be so emotional, so unreserved, so piercingly sapient – the truth came to her like an arrow' (187).

Quelch differs from Cohen's dark East End Jews with cigars, crassly masculine and certainly not gentlemen. This un-English gentleman Jew shows himself not only joining the Captains of Industry, but also having the capacity for single-minded passion, great displays of generosity, and womanly manifestations of grief. The author liberates this character from any national origins and casts him as an Orientalized and feminized exotic, one who nonetheless educates his son at an exclusive English public school. And although he owns a diamond mine, he is not portrayed as buying and selling for profit. Rather, he lavishes diamonds on women as seductive gifts. In addition, like May, but more saturated within the symbolic Jew/jewel economy, Quelch gives himself when he gives diamonds. May craves diamonds, deals in diamonds; Quelch is a diamond.

At the novel's outset, Loree languishes alone in a comfortable hotel, formerly a club where Kimberley mining princes used to retreat when tired of domesticity, a place imbued with the aura of illicit sex and diamonds. Into this suggestive setting, Quelch enters and casts his un-English eyes upon our heroine:

> Immediately Loree experienced the same odd prickling in her blood as the rays of the diamond seemed to cause her. Only she no longer felt that she was missing something or that life was passing her by … He was a dark, gracefully-built man with thick dark hair brushed back smoothly on his well-shaped head. Everything was right about him, from his hair to his shoes. He was the kind of man who could not make any mistake about dress, and gave distinction to anything he wore. His name was Quelch, and Loree was aware that he was a power in the hotel and in Kimberley. (12–13)

Quelch sends roses to her room. As she 'stuck' his rose in the 'V of her gown, her hands trembled a little and her veins thrilled again as if in answer to some magnetic current which, whether it came from a magic stone or from a man's eyes, made her feel curiously alive and daring … His voice held a melancholy cadence; the dark beauty of his face suggested the East where women are addressed with a caressing softness' (15–17). With his jewel voice Quelch romances her with stories of stones, 'the Orloff, the Taj-e-mah, the Star of Africa … It was wonderful to hear Quelch speak of them. It seemed to Loree that his words were like the gems themselves sparkling and rippling and tumbling in cascades' (21). Very soon the gem-inflected voice magically materializes in the shape of real diamonds in Loree's room – one magnificent rose-pink diamond, which she wears between her breasts – 'hiding under her heart a little pink god smiled and sparkled' – and a 'chain of diamonds, two blue diamonds on each side of the clasp, and one of these diamonds has three dots or defects in it that, held in a certain light give the impression of a tiny death's head grinning at you' (109). Kimberley diamonds, with their association of corpses, emerge in the Diamond City of the Plains. The diamond gift from the Jew passes on as contamination, a warning of the wages of sin.

Pink Gods differentiates this enticing Jew from his more crass brethren while assigning them all intimate, though differing, relationships to diamonds. Whereas diamonds associated with Quelch glitter in an exotic light cast by the harem, other Jewish diamonds mark the wearer's vulgar conspicuous consumption. These mercantile Jews share with Quelch possessive, enveloping passions, unnamable sorrows, and glorious diamonds, but their lives and their diamonds result from greed rather than lust. Mrs Solano (a plump and still beautiful high-spirited Jewess) with her husband Mikey (who dies a madman) had been IDBs until Mrs Solano inadvertently choked their infant son to death when he sucked down his tiny throat a huge golden illicit diamond hidden in his sugar bag. Because she has killed her baby in the course of dirty dealing, the widow Solano wears the glittering diamond on her forehead as a mark of her transgression. And although Loree seems to join the Jewish crowd by enhancing her Paris frock with the glorious death's head diamond chain, Quelch keeps her name out of the society pages to protect her reputation. Only Jews are listed in print as mannequins for ostentatious diamond displays: 'Mrs. Ikey Mosenthal's famous tiara; Mrs. Solly Moses' wreath of Jagersfontein roses. Miss Rebecca Isaac's magnificent necklace and pendant of water white stones. Lady von Gugenheim's priceless plaque of black diamonds' (123–124).

Its Jewish provenance doubles the illicit significance of Loree's dazzling necklace. The necklace turns out to belong technically to Mrs Solano, who sold it but was never paid. Thus, the diamonds come to Loree indirectly from an IDB jewel-box through her illicit Jewish lover, who voids Mrs Solano's claim by paying her buyer's debt. Nonetheless, the term 'blue demon' warns that this glorious jewel cannot be separated from its pecuniary history. After the connection between her necklace and the mercenary Solano is revealed, there is nothing for Loree but to escape her illicit connection with Jews, pink gods and blue demons. With the help of Irish Mrs Cork, who had been in a liaison with Quelch, she disguises herself as a boy, escaping the Jew's silken clutches to her cold-storage meat salesman and bourgeois respectability, where she will wear her pearl necklace in progress. This deadened domesticity constitutes a satisfactory ending, with Mrs Cork having the last moral caution: '[S]he produced a little parcel of sparkling stones wrapped in a silk handkerchief and laid it on the table. A foolish girl returns you these,' she said ... She left you tonight to join her husband. ... Forget her, and let her forget you' (188). Thus, the plot empha-sizes giving up the Jew and his jewels in favour of a Protestant ethic, which preaches simplicity over show and sanctifies industriousness, chastity, and discreet modest wealth, while disapproving of stimulation, display, and pleasure.[16]

Romancing the African jewel

Presenting a seemingly different version of the Jew/jewel economy, American-born Louise Vesalius Sheldon's *An I.D.B. in South Africa* (1888) offers two appealing un-English characters, who illustrate the same dilemma. This novel adds significant African characters, doubling the diamond stigma (and its concomitant attraction), while placing the Jew in intimate relation to an exotic African. The title announces its illicit theme and its economic motive; and although the main IDB in this novel is not Jewish but Scottish, he nev-ertheless appears in the context of illicit dealers who are Jewish: the first character caught with an IDB, Count Telphus, is likely to be a thoroughly assimilated Jew, who commits suicide when he is apprehended. Jews in the novel identify with him, while observing his lack of élan in the illicit jewel trade: ' "Father Abraham," exclaimed a sympathizing Israelite, "how could he be so careless with such a blazer".'[17] Herr Schwatka, the character we first encounter with Count Telphus, represents a trace-of-the Jew and shares characteristics with Hazeltine Quelch, a careless, passionate, sapient seducer.

Every character in the book lives out and through a racial identity. The plot centres on Dainty Laure – the daughter of a Zulu princess and an English soldier – who does not know that her husband Donald, an 'impulsive Scotchman from the cold North', is an IDB.[18] Dainty's domestic decor mirrors her African/English blood: 'Her home seemed a part of herself – a bright light creature, glorifying the materialities about her with a certain radiance' (32). The 'certain radiance' pairs the heroine with diamonds and their common African origins. Her cottage is itself a displaced European structure imposed on a colonial landscape dominated by the Big Hole:

> Within rifle-shot of the 'ninth wonder of the world', the great Kimberley Mine, stood a pretty one-story cottage nestling among a mass of creepers... The walls were artistically hung with shields, assagais, spears, and knob-kerries and in either corner stood a large elephant's tusk, mounted on a pedestal of ebony.
>
> A small horned head of the beautiful Hesse-bok hung over a door – India matting over which was strewn karosses of rarest fur, a piano stood in one corner, while costly furniture, rich lace and satin hangings were arranged with an artistic sense befitting the mistress of it all. (12)

The blood in the heroine's veins instantiates what Robert Young describes as 'colonial desire', the colonizer's desire for the colonized Other and the persistent interest in English fiction in the precarious ethnicity of English identity. 'Englishness', Young observes, 'has always been riven by its own alterity... It is striking that many novelists... write almost obsessively about the uncertain crossing and invasion of identities... So much so, indeed, that we could go so far as to claim it as *the* dominant motif of much English fiction.'[19] Dainty Laure genetically embodies the conflict Young describes: this concern with the 'uncertain crossing' of English racial identity comes explicitly to the fore in South African diamond novels, where every character's racial composition, meticulously described, seems to tell readers about a natural English essence, yet many have buried connections to non-English identity. In *An I.D.B.*, the love affair between Dainty and Schwatka – between the secret African and the hidden Jew – forms one romance plot that reflects on other, 'purely' European couples in the novel. Dainty's parents produced a creature desirable (in Young's terms) by a white Briton, but, as the plot reveals, her dangerous magnetism must be ultimately contained: by being attracted to each other, Dainty and Schwatka, uniquely glamorous and involved with each other in their daring romance, avert the danger of a continuing dilution of the 'races of Britain'.

Dainty embodies 'the crossing and invasion of identities' while always bearing the sign of the racialized other: 'Bracelets of dewdrop diamonds encircled her wrists, and with the rubies and diamonds at throat and ear completed a toilet which might have vied with that of some semi-barbaric Eastern princess. Such was the woman in whose veins ran the blood of European and African races' (14–15). Her racial profile conjures post-colonial accounts of Orientalism, as if Dainty's mixed blood has produced a Semite, the 'semi-barbaric Eastern princess' resembling Lady von Gugenheim with her 'priceless plaque of black diamonds', or, indeed, Quelch, the Eastern prince.[20] The author diagnoses racial mixing as fascinatingly pathological:

> But the union of European with African produces, in their descendants, beings endowed with strange and inconsistent natures. These two bloods mingle but will not blend; more prominently are these idiosyncrasies developed where the Zulu parentage can be traced, and naturally so, for the Zulus are the most intelligent of the African tribes. Now they are all love, tenderness and devotion, ready to make any sacrifice for those on whom their affections are placed; again revengeful, jealous, and vindictive. (3)

Dainty's unconscious sexuality and dormant savagery mark the inevitability of her racial heritage: 'On a divan, the upholstering of which was hidden by a karosse of leopard skins, reclined Dainty Laure,... Occasional motion of a fan of three ostrich feathers, lids slowly unveiled those dark languorous eyes, which seemed like hidden founts of love. Should occasion come, she could smile with her eyes, while her mouth looked cruel' (13–14). Zulu characteristics of sexuality and languor combined with ruthlessness resemble the Jewish Quelch, and also May Leslie's inherent sensuality.

At the same time, Dainty, like Loree, has preserved a Victorian virginity:

> She was, as yet, unconscious of the powers that lay dormant in her; under her child-like exterior was a soul of which even her husband knew nothing... [T]he strange truth of which she herself was entirely oblivious, that the great pulsating power of Love had not yet inspired her... [B]orn of an English soldier and the daughter of a savage warrior, there slumbered in her soul a possibility of passion that needed only to be aroused to burst into flame. (32–33)

The talent to kindle passion's flames lies in a sexy yet impervious Jew: fearless and careless of the soupçon of sadism revealed by the Zulu cruelty of Dainty's mouth, the enigmatic Herr Schwatka, seductive and assimilated, fulfills this role. Like Quelch, Schwatka has casually seduced women with his innate, compelling sexuality. Also like Quelch, he does not resemble ethnographic descriptions of the Semite. Not sallow, swarthy, greasy, or greedy, he is 'a fair-haired Austrian of distinguished appearance and engaging manners, cool-headed, strong-willed, materialist whose spirit of determination dominated most of those with whom he came in contact' (34). Schwatka is the kind of Jew of Couper's perception, who adopts the physical characteristics of the nation he inhabits but retains the Jew's materialistic essence. Bryan Cheyette reminds us that such figures represent the double nature of the Jew whose ability to blend in threatens traditional delineations of race.[21] Here Jew and African, both sexy and irresistible, pose threats to the fixed categories of European national identities. This unspoken otherness quickens their two alien hearts: Schwatka quietly knows that Dainty passes for white; they recognize the Other in each other.

Dainty discovers that her husband will be sent to jail for illicit diamond buying, but with the cooperation of her trusty Bushman servant Bela, 'who in his fantastic proportions resembled a heathen idol in bronze' (29), she hides the diamond in his eye-socket, behind the adoring servant's glass eye. Here, sensationally, the ancient African icon incorporates the illicit diamond, like a jewel inserted in an Indian god's forehead. Bela, akin to a strange god, like the pink diamond of Stockley's novel, serves as the ageless, almost supernatural spirit, a guardian angel to Dainty, his qualities uniquely qualified to save her. Sheldon carefully delineates his race:

> Bela was a 'Bosjesman' or Bushman, with features of the Negro type, and short, crispy black hair. He was about four feet in height, being one of the race of pygmies, nearly extinct. They are the oldest race known in Africa .... [T]heir traditions tell of a mighty nation who dwelt in caves and holes in the ground, who were great elephant hunters, and who used poisoned arrows in warfare. (82)

Native loyalty and hereditary cunning enable Bela to slip into neutral territory and return the diamond to the fleeing Dainty, her husband, and Herr Schwatka. Escaping from the law to England, Dainty discovers that Donald maintains a faithful Scottish wife. Donald regretfully signs over the diamond to Dainty; she falls into Schwatka's arms; they disappear with their illicit jewel, perhaps to America, home of hopelessly muddled races, bearing the sign of the Jew in the jewel, into the eternity of 'the end'. The melodramatic finale of *An I.D.B. in South Africa*, with the Jew/Austrian, the Zulu/Scot, and the illicit diamond sailing off together, can be understood within the symbolic economy traced in this essay. The Scot bigamist IDB escapes ultimate judgment, like Loree, returning to his racially pure spouse, his cold Northern country's frigid conjugality, without any glitter to warm it. In keeping with that economy, impurity is exported to a shore where mixed breeds can enjoy the sensual pleasures endemic to their kind and live off their stolen goods.

* * *

The taint of death and the illicit clings to intensely desirable and envied diamonds. Some of the Jews in the South African diamond novels stand for this aspect of the diamond – yearned for, a sign of romance and uncountable wealth, extravagantly admired, but associated with what must be given up to maintain middle-class respectability, the Protestant ethic, and white racial purity. The immense value and the extravagant meanings of diamonds issue from their transformation from dusty, dull stones to faceted gems and then to ornaments endowed with pedigrees, stories, promises. To achieve these meanings, the jewel stands apart from its origins in the classical Marxist sense that the fetish of the commodity appears independent of its production. Or they gleam like Walter Benjamin's *phantasmagoria*, where the reified object exists as a sign of unconscious desire, magically free of its conditions of production, a thing in itself, swathed in myth. Yet because of the setting at the Kimberley mine, the magic trick turns transparent, the myth too anchored to its diamondiferous soil. So ubiquitous on the diamond fields, so intimately connected with every aspect of its production as a commodity, the Jewish characters are fused to the jewel. The novels resolve their ambivalence about the Jew by forcing British Protestant characters to renounce the jewel, however reluctantly. While the jewels retain their lustre – it is true, not so dazzlingly when worn by Mrs Ikey Mosenthal – the Jew, so deeply associated with them, clings to their meanings. South African diamond novels leave the jewels to the Jews. And the Jew, like the diamond, a white hole of representation, still glitters and gleams, but somewhere else, as an object of perilous allure.

Notes

Deepest thanks to Susan Gubar's generosity, not only for suggesting the title but for giving me courage to write about Jews. And thanks to Timothy Johns for leading me to the Comaroffs.

1. As Schreuder notes (*The Scramble for Africa*, 27): 'Looked at in a long-term perspective...diamonds may even be said to have begun the uneven 'modernisation' of Southern Africa.' This, as John Comaroff and Jean Comaroff argue (*Of Revelation and Revolution*, 5), means 'civilizing' by giving the natives a sense of entering time, of entering history.
2. Kanfer, *The Last Empire*, 52.
3. The connections between Jews and gems extend back at least to King Solomon, so that the symbolic economy at the diamond fields is prepared for in myth and history.
4. Focusing on Protestant missionaries to Africa, Comaroff and Comaroff (*Of Revelation and Revolution*, 8–90) describe connections between religious and

economic effects and values: 'The impact of Protestant evangelists as harbingers of industrial capitalism lay in the fact that their civilizing mission was simultaneously symbolic and practical, theological and temporal. The goods and techniques they brought with them to Africa presupposed the messages and meanings they proclaimed in the pulpit, and vice versa. Both were vehicles of a moral economy that celebrated the global spirit of commerce, the commodity, and the imperial marketplace.'

5. Louis Cohen, *Reminiscences of Kimberley* (1911; facs. rpt. Kimberley: Historical Society of Kimberley, 1990), 12, 17. Subsequent page numbers will be cited parenthetically in the text.

6. J. R. Couper, *Mixed Humanity: A Story of Camp Life in South Africa* (Cape Colony, South Africa: J. C. Juta, 1892), 20. Subsequent page numbers will be cited parenthetically in the text.

7. Bryan Cheyette (*Constructions of 'the Jew'*, 12) observes about the Jew in English representation: ' "The Jew," like all "doubles," is inherently ambivalent and can represent both the "best" and the "worst" of selves. Unlike marginalized "colonial subjects" who were, for the most part, confined racially to the "colonies" in the late nineteenth century, Jews were, simultaneously, at the centre of European metropolitan society and, at the same time, banished from its privileged sphere by a semitic discourse.' The Jews are at the centre of diamond discourse, spectacular at the diamond fields and in South African diamond novels. Most Jewish characters in these novels do not escape stereotyping, but rather call forth a range of stereotypes. The only Jewish character I have encountered in South African diamond novels who is not a stereotype is Joseph Leonard (Jack Senior's friend in *Mixed Humanity*), and he, interestingly, has nothing directly to do with the diamond business.

8. The 'Jewish' attribution of the town is also apparent in common references to Johannesburg, often shortened to 'Jo'burg' – that is, 'Jewburg'.

9. Jill Matus, in a private conversation, told me that South Africans used the resonance of the sexual meaning to taunt a girl or women of easy virtue by dubbing her 'Kimberley'.

10. Anthony Trollope, *South Africa*, 2 vols. (1878; London: Dawsons of Pall Mall, 1968), vol. 2, between 178–179. Subsequent page numbers will be cited parenthetically in the text.

11. Barney Barnato – East End Jew, briefly a partner with Louis Cohen, and eventually a partner with Cecil Rhodes in De Beers, final owner of the Kimberley Mine – was suspected of IDB. Cohen accuses Barnato of nefarious practices, but it is not clear if these charges are simply sensationalized for the purposes of Cohen's memoir. James Leasor (*Rhodes and Barnato*) describes the situation of Barnato's partner and nephew, Isaac (afterwards, Jack) Joel, who was accused of IDB. Joel, however, skipped bail, and the case was never tried. Barnato's reputation was not spotless, but no one openly accused him of shifty dealings.

12. See Freedman, *The Temple of Culture*, on the 1870s Jew as figure of a simultaneous disgust and pleasure in capitalism.

13. I do not know if Couper is inspired by George Eliot's plotting in *Daniel Deronda* (1876), but it is striking how the two plots in his novel mirror hers. Instead of Eliot's Jewish hero, Couper's Jewish main character is a woman, and the limited, athletic, Christian Gwendolen is replaced by Jack Senior, a boxer.

14. 'The Beautiful Jewess in the Boudoir', *Venus Schoolmistress: A Victorian Collection* (New York: Grove Press, 1984).

15. Cynthia Stockley, *Pink Gods and Blue Demons* (London: Cassell, 1920), 8. Subsequent page numbers will be cited parenthetically in the text.
16. For a provocative speculation on this Calvinist ethic and its ties to materialism see Weber, *The Protestant Ethic*. Weber links the Protestant ethic to a branch of independent, Evangelical Protestantism, Chapel rather than Church. In this regard, Stockley giving her Scottish hero the name of Temple is symbolically suggestive of the enterprising, upwardly mobile, yet emotionally frigid and stingy capitalist.
17. Louise Vesalius Sheldon, *An I.D.B. in South Africa* (London: Trübner, 1889), 8. Subsequent page numbers will be cited parenthetically in the text.
18. It is significant that both Donald Laure and Pat Temple are Scottish and are cold and materialistic. The materialism of the Scot as a stereotype extends to his being an IDB, joining the Jewish IDBs in Veselius Sheldon's racial grid; Stockley associates her Scot with dead meat.
19. Young, *Colonial Desire*, xii, 3.
20. For the association between Oriental Jews and Africa earlier in Victorian literature see Benjamin Disraeli's *Coningsby* (1844) which asserts: 'From time immemorial they [Hebrew Arabs] had sojourned in Africa' (*Coningsby, or The New Generation* (London: J. M. Dent, 1959), 174).
21. See Cheyette ('Introduction: Unanswered Questions', 4): 'This particular "Jew" is, above all, a sign of confusion or indeterminacy.'

2
Little Jew Boys Made Good: Immigration, the South African War, and Anglo-Jewish Fiction

Nadia Valman

Public debate about and among Jews in Britain at the end of the nineteenth century focused on two seemingly unrelated, even contradictory, phenomena – the influx of poor, ghetto-minded immigrants to the metropolitan centres, particularly the East End of London, and the rise of the Jewish plutocracy. Yet it was in these two developments that the hopes and fears invested in Jews during the second half of the nineteenth century converged, giving new urgency to the longstanding question of their capacity for improvement, integration, and national feeling. Jewish patriotism – always under scrutiny during wartime – was an object of especially charged discussion in this period, because the South African war of 1899–1902 directly implicated Jews.

Southern Africa had given Jews – impoverished immigrants as well as those with established business and banking connections – opportunities for spectacular success, first in the diamond fields of Kimberley (the Cape Colony) in the 1880s and, later, in the gold mining industry of the Boer-governed Transvaal. By the 1890s these newcomers, economically significant but politically restricted and heavily taxed by the Boer government, had common cause with British imperialists aspiring to annex more of South Africa; indeed, several Jews were involved in the failed coup attempted in the Jameson Raid of 1895. As pressure mounted on the British government to intervene on behalf of the unenfranchized *Uitlanders* (foreign residents), the anti-war movement charged that a conspiracy between imperialists and Jewish capitalists was deliberately destabilizing the Boer Republics and leading Britain astray into military conflict. In the critique of the war as well as in the fervently nationalist climate of wartime, then, Jewish questions were paramount.

These questions, I will argue, were formative for Anglo-Jewish writing at the *fin de siècle*. In this chapter, I explore the competing meanings attached to the Jewish entrepreneur in public discourse at the time of the South

African War, the political assumptions they encoded and the different rhetorical forms in which they were articulated. I identify first of all the two dominant tropes that shaped the interpretation of Jews in this period: the story of the immigrant's rise from poverty to prosperity and the terrifying image of the vampiric capitalist. Influentially expressed by the social investigator Beatrice Potter and the anti-imperialist theorist J. A. Hobson, these tropes articulated not just literal anxieties about the Jews' place in the nation but also much broader concerns about changing relationships among labour, capital, and Empire at the end of the century. For Anglo-Jewish novelists, meanwhile, the spectacle of Jewish success was an equally compelling subject. In examining, in the latter part of the chapter, the writing of Samuel Gordon, Benjamin Farjeon, Julia Frankau, and Israel Zangwill, I trace the replication and rewriting of prevailing metaphors and narratives of Jews. Rather than simply contesting stereotypes, however, Jewish writers actively participated in the political fantasies provoked by the ambiguous figure of the Jewish entrepreneur.

The politics and poetics of Jewish success

Discussion of Jewish enterprise predated the South African War. It was a keynote, in fact, of much analysis of Jewish immigrant life in the East End of London, which had by the late Victorian period become the object of widespread interest. Parliamentary inquiries, investigative journalists, philanthropists, and anti-alienists sought to document the complex social, political, and domestic organization of the Eastern European Jews and to discuss the significance of their cultural distinctiveness in a liberal nation.[1] Public discussion of the East End, however, frequently stretched beyond this local context to suggest a framework for interpreting the psychology and behaviour of Jews on the world stage in the 1890s.

One of the most celebrated accounts of East End Jewish life was produced by Beatrice Potter in 1888–9 in her role as investigator for Charles Booth's *Life and Labour of the People in London*. Drawing on a combination of quantitative and qualitative data, Potter's essays aimed to describe the trade practices, religious and secular institutions, and psychic life of Jewish immigrants in order 'to estimate...their character and capacity as members of our social and industrial state'.[2] Discussing 'the reasons of the Jews' success' and of their resentment by their Gentile neighbours, Potter's analysis of the Jews' rapid rise out of the gutter was rigorously environmentalist (187). She considered Jews to be advantaged in commerce by their cultural and religious traditions, including intellectual training, moral and physical discipline, and familial cohesion – and also by their historic experience of persecution, which had 'weeded out the inapt and incompetent' and honed the Jewish intellect into 'an instrument for grasping by mental agility the good things withheld from them by the brute force of the Christian peoples' (188).

The result of this heritage is illustrated by the vivid narrative at the centre of Potter's essay that tells the story of Jewish immigrants fleeing persecution in Eastern Europe and arriving in London. Potter describes the men's 'look of stubborn patience; in their eyes an indescribable expression of hunted, suffering animals, lit up now and again by tenderness for the young wife or little child' (183). The scene stages the warm expressions of family feeling between the new arrivals and relatives already established in London, then narrows its focus to the tableau of one young immigrant boy, whose ambitions are aroused at the sight of the newly-acquired wealth he sees displayed by the father who arrived before him. The story of the archetypal immigrant follows: often exploited, he quickly acquires marketable skills and, by undercutting the wages of others, immediately begins to master his destiny. Soon he is himself a small-scale employer, and is 'in a fair way to become a tiny capitalist – a maker of profit as well as an earner of wage' (185). In entering into the competitive market, 'he has become a law-abiding and self-respecting citizen of our great metropolis, and feels himself the equal of a Montefiore or a Rothschild' (186).

Potter's observation of contemporary Jewish life is rapidly subordinated to her narrative teleology. In a similar way Booth himself evokes, in the final volume of *Life and Labour*, 'the picture of a little Jew boy in a very poor street, playing pitch and toss all by himself, studying the laws of chance in this humble fashion' – giving his empirical account of gambling amongst the various elements of East End society a suggestive narrative dimension that invites the reader to imagine the Jew boy's destiny.[3] But both Potter and Booth seem unsure what their own response should be to such tales of dogged individualism. While Potter's essay ends by pointing to the social deterioration wrought upon local working-class life by unregulated, unorganized labour, the Jewish *Bildungsroman* that it sketches also represents a compelling example of immigrant self-betterment that benefits both individual and national community.

Belying, as David Feldman has noted, the plurality of opportunities, interests, and conflicts that intersected in the crucible of East End labour,[4] this potent image of the Jewish worker – disciplined, determined, aided by familial and fraternal contacts, unencumbered by wider ties of class or nation, and above all driven by racial instinct towards capitalism – was extremely influential. In the course of the following decade, moreover, it slipped easily into a more sinister register. As the crisis in South Africa loomed, in particular, the same nexus of beliefs was mobilized to explain the threat posed by Jews not only to labour conditions in the East End of London but to the national interest as a whole.

The Jewish background of many of the financiers prominent in the South African economy was, Claire Hirshfield argues, used opportunistically by opponents of the Boer war to attempt to discredit the Conservative government and to inflame public opinion.[5] Yet however flawed their argument was in fact, its rhetorical coherence successfully relied on a number of commonplace assumptions about Jews which had by the turn of the century passed into the realm of uncontested truth. The Jews' insular devotion to family and philanthropic generosity towards co-religionists noted by Potter, and frequently reiterated by others, was now writ large onto the globe as a secret racial brotherhood. The Jewish 'instinct' for capitalism rather than wage-earning also took on gigantic proportions. For socialists, who had vehemently defended rights of asylum for poor immigrants, an ambivalence about how Jews made money was now given free rein. In his leaders for *Justice,* the organ of the Social Democratic Federation, for example, party leader H. M. Hyndman accused the 'loan-mongering fraternity' – 'begotten in Judaea and "made in Germany"' – of seeking 'the extension of modern capitalist slavery though the dark continent' via 'a great project for the constitution of an Anglo-Hebraic Empire in Africa, stretching from Egypt to Cape Colony and from Beira to Sierra Leone'.[6] The mysteries of the Jewish diaspora – individuals internationally dispersed yet viscerally linked – suggested a particular and sinister affinity with imperialism.

The economic theorist and anti-imperialist J. A. Hobson, perhaps the most significant critic of 'Jewish capitalism' in the late 1890s, had earlier drawn heavily on Potter's essays in his *Problems of Poverty* (1891). Here he replicated Potter's claims about the deleterious effect of Jewish immigration on the East End economy through the driving down of wages and the proliferation of small workshops. The Jew, physically resilient and ruthlessly amoral, he argued, was 'the "fittest" person to survive in trade competition' and possessed a 'natural aptitude' for becoming an employer.[7] In his writing on the Transvaal conflict, published initially in the *Manchester Guardian* and later as *The War in South Africa* (1900), these ideas were extended in an account of the South African economy as dominated by Jews, who, '[b]y superior ability, enterprise, and organisation,...out-competing the slower-witted Briton, have attained a practical supremacy'.[8] The racial conflict of the East End had been exported to South Africa.

What interests me here is the character of Hobson's rhetoric. In the figurative language that he uses in writing about Jews, Hobson moves from an analysis of economic forces to an invocation of terror. In *Problems of Poverty*, Hobson added a hyperbolic overtone to Potter's sober, statistically-based observations about Jewish labour practices: he claimed, for example, that German, Polish, and Russian Jews were 'coming over in large battalions to steal all the employment of the English working man, by underselling him in the labour market'.[9] The suggestion here, of a deliberate, strategic, and militarily organized collective conspiracy was to find echoes in Hobson's writing on the South African War. In 'Capitalism and Imperialism in South Africa', an article published in the *Contemporary Review* in 1900, Hobson's argument links the interests of capital and Britain's pursuit of war but his language at moments dives unexpectedly into dramatic metaphor. The Jews in the Transvaal, he declares, 'went there for money, and those who came early and made most have commonly withdrawn their persons, leaving their economic fangs in the carcase [*sic*] of their prey'.[10] Imperialism is merely a pretext for capitalists, who 'have certain economic advantages to gain by assuming this pseudo-patriotic cloak'.[11] They rely, in the last resort, 'upon one powerful secret ally which ever lurks in the recesses of the national character ... that race-lust of dominance'.[12] Hobson here associates Jews with vampirism, manipulation, and masquerade, suggesting also that they possess the power to call up latent atavistic forces in the population as a whole. He evokes both the vulnerability of the electorate and the all-powerful grasp in which it could be held by the Jews.

It is important to note that this gothic imagery was not confined to the Left but was equally evident in the popular anti-alienism whipped up by nationalists in the East End at the turn of the century. In his statement to the Royal Commission on Alien Immigration, James Johnson, Chairman of the British Brothers' League, ascribed declining standards of living in East London to aliens who 'live on us like parasites, sucking out our heart's-blood, because we wish to live and will as far as possible, a little bit decent ... We ask are they not persecuting us? Have they not come from persecution to persecute? Are they not revenging themselves on us ... They openly tell us they are going to have this country.'[13] While the League attempted to rally the 'decent' community under attack, Johnson went on to warn the Commissioners of the dangers of ignoring working-class feeling about immigration. In this respect, Johnson, like Hobson, was raising the spectre of popular power through an image of Jewish terror.

Potter's and Hobson's (and the BBL's) thinking, then, overlapped in surprising ways: both shared a view of the Jew as having a propensity for commerce and lacking the public spiritedness to regulate it. But the different modes in which they articulated this vision are telling. Potter's linear, literary narrative expresses her belief that the social behaviour of the Jews could be analysed within a rational framework and understood. For Hobson, especially in *The Psychology of Jingoism* (1901), where he developed his account of the conflict in South Africa, wartime patriotism revealed that under industrial capitalism the British public was reverting increasingly to savage, irrational instincts.[14] In his language of violence and excess, Hobson evokes the incomprehensible, ungovernable nature of the forces undermining the rational ordering of democratic society, the very same forces that James Johnson tried to use to press the government into anti-alien measures. In the following sections of this chapter, I want to demonstrate how both of these immensely powerful tropes – Potter's immigrant *Bildungsroman* and Hobson's gothic nightmare, and the competing visions of modern Britain from which they stemmed – shaped Anglo-Jewish writing too.

Moralizing South African wealth: Samuel Gordon, Benjamin Farjeon, and the immigrant *Bildungsroman*

Victorian Anglo-Jewish fiction, produced in the context of the campaign for Jewish emancipation and thus characterized by an apologetic tendency, was predominantly concerned with explaining the congruities of Judaism with Christianity, often safely distanced through an historical setting.[15] By the late nineteenth century, however, the question of doctrinal difference had disappeared from literary representation, replaced with an emphasis on the secular life of contemporary Jews, in particular the dilemmas of assimilation and social mobility. As the terms of public discussion of the Jews shifted to encompass their capacity to identify with shared national cultural values rather than religious faith, Anglo-Jewish fiction began to display a concern with the ethics of Jewish family and community life, frequently examined through the story of the rise of a Jewish immigrant or East End-born male. In this section, I examine the reappearance of Beatrice Potter's Whitechapel *Bildungsroman* in stories by the little-known German-born, Cambridge-educated novelist Samuel Gordon, who wrote for a predominantly Jewish readership, and the prolific and popular writer Benjamin Farjeon. Considering these turn-of-the-century novels alongside Potter's ethnographic writing, I will argue, we can see more clearly the liberal ideology that shaped their perceptions of the Jewish immigrant entrepreneur.

The acquisition of wealth is the central subject of both Gordon's *Sons of the Covenant: a Tale of London Jewry* (1900) and Farjeon's *The Pride of Race* (1901), and South Africa is its source. The fortune of the hero in these two East End-to-West End tales begins with successful speculation in South Africa. Farjeon's protagonist, the multi-millionaire Moses Mendoza, starts his career as a financier with a gift of diamond shares from a compatriot: 'A Jewish lad, born in the East End of London, Whitechapel way, who had gone out to South Africa in the steerage, and landed there with fourpence in his pocket, came home first-class, and set up his carriage. Another followed suit; and another. The air pulsed with golden rumours. The wonders of Aladdin's cave were eclipsed'.[16] Eschewing the glitter of South African minerals, Gordon has his capitalist hero, Leuw Lipcott, invest in property close to the mines, perceived perhaps as a less dubious form of profitmaking. Both novels, however, plot the movement of Jewish capital, acquired via South Africa, back to England and to the common good. Lipcott funds an improvement scheme for the Jews of the East End, with the aim of combating their insularity and fostering instead their social spirit. Mendoza's vast wealth enables him, in a 'magnificent and unprecedented act of patriotism' to donate a battleship to the nation. He also finances the political career of his son Raphael, a man whose freedom from the corruptions of the privileged classes enables him to see more lucidly the necessity for increased public spending on defence, and thus to serve more loyally 'a nation's honour, a nation's safety'.[17]

The repeated insistence in these two novels on the altruism and unerring – even heightened – patriotism of the South African capitalist registers the impact on Anglo-Jewish writers of the increasingly vocal critique of Jewish financial power as conspiratorial and treacherous. Published in this climate, Gordon's and Farjeon's novels have been seen as an anxious reinvigoration of the apologetic tradition of Anglo-Jewish literature.[18] Indeed, while the story of the moral career of the Jewish immigrant evidently owes much to Beatrice Potter, Potter herself was heavily influenced in her research by the Anglo-Jewish elite, whose upwardly mobile self-mythology she duly replicated in 'The Jewish Community'.[19] Thus Potter and her co-investigators, David Englander has argued, 'presented [the Jews'] alleged preoccupation with social advancement as the secular expression of sacred precepts'. At the same time, however, Booth's researchers held similar values themselves, sharing with their editor the assumption that the desire for self-employment and social self-betterment were universal, natural, and admirable.[20] If *Life and Labour* suggested the ascent of the little Jew boy through enterprise to the role of 'law-abiding and self-respecting citizen of our great metropolis', Gordon and Farjeon stress even more emphatically his route via South African speculation to devoted service to the nation.

These literary paeans to the virtues of Jewish capitalism, moreover, should be read within the wider context of late-Victorian liberal thought, in which the Jews, and in particular working-class Jews, had come to embody anew the Smilesian ideals of industry, thrift, and sobriety. For Samuel Smiles, prophet of mid-Victorian self-improvement, the competition that arose from virtuous labour was both natural and moral, while the habit of saving was essential to the wellbeing both of society and of the individuals who composed it.[21] The Jewish immigrant, John A. Garrard argues, took on for many Liberals a symbolic role, 'the symbol of [this] slowly crumbling but still nostalgically satisfying Victorian economic and social morality'.[22] Anglo-Jewish fables of the rise from poverty to prosperity of an East End Jew, supported by communal philanthropy and advancing through a combination of enterprise and self-denial to the position of responsible and respectable citizenship, enthusiastically endorse this particular, liberal brand of late-Victorian philosemitism. The young Leuw Lipcott, in Gordon's novel, is a transparent mouthpiece for Smilesian 'Self-Help': aspiring to become his own boss he declares that 'freedom means self-respect, and self-respect means strength, and strength means victory'.[23] In another of Farjeon's novels, the protagonist, a virtuous Jewish businessman, declares that the Jew is 'industrious and enterprising, he excites emulation and stimulates the commercial activity of his neighbour, by which the wealth of the general community is increased'.[24] Extending Gordon's message to a wide popular readership, Farjeon was not so much pleading a special case for the

Jews as utilizing the figure of the Jewish immigrant to illustrate the benefits of work, responsible charity, and measured consumption that were the focus of all his writing.[25] These novels, then, seen in a broad perspective, provide a fictional counterpart to the efforts among Liberals at the end of the century to reassert the values of free trade, religious tolerance, and individualism in the face of increasingly radical challenge.

Sons of the Covenant, indeed, is so thoroughly imbued with Smilesian philosophy that even its romantic subplot is expressed as a tale of 'the economy of [the] heart' (476). Lipcott's success in the harshly competitive environment of the East End is ensured by his continence in finance and feeling – but the true value of such steely self-control is not initially recognized by the object of his affections, the wealthy Dulcie Duveen. When Lipcott fears the failure of his suit he finds himself employing the familiar financial lingo:

> All these years he had heaped and hoarded his love, refusing to expend a single grain of it, because he had hoped one day to bestow it where any man might have been proud to bestow it. And now, what was he going to do with it, with the dead weight, the refuse, unmarketable stock, to which it had turned and which was pressing him to earth? ... Probably it required only a little wise manipulation to convert what at first appeared to him an irredeemable loss into a considerable profit. (476–477).

However, it is not Lipcott's 'manipulation' of his emotional stock that succeeds in the end, but his patience in a volatile market. Ultimately, saving rather than squandering – and resisting the temptation to speculation – proves the route to prosperity in love as well as in money. In Gordon's *Sons of the Covenant*, then, affective relations are governed by the same rules as capitalism. Indeed, these principles are reflected everywhere in the world of the novel, including, according to another character, in the racial evolution of the Jews. The absence of 'real master minds' amongst them, he claims, is due not, as Jews like to think, to the lingering effects of Gentile hostility, but 'something more radical, more fundamental. It is an astonishing manifestation of the wise economy wherewith the race of the Covenant husbands its vitality. Instead of exhausting its resources in the production of genius, it prefers to consummate itself more frugally in brilliant mediocrity.' Providing against physical 'degeneracy' through cerebral 'over-exertion', the Jews as a racial body unconsciously practise the same values of thrift and sobriety that are the hallmarks of the individual success story of Leuw Lipcott (463). Crucially, the symbolic hero of this success story is not a powerful 'genius' who could threaten social or economic stability but a modest 'mediocrity' who will sustain it. Gordon's novel thus adapts Beatrice Potter's immigrant *Bildungsroman* to explain the benefits to society more generally of the proverbial individualism of 'the Jew'.

Just as the liberal idealization of the Jew was not the only response to immigration at the turn of the century, however, the cheerful optimism of Farjeon and Gordon was not the only current in Anglo-Jewish literature. In turning now to fictional narratives by Julia Frankau and Israel Zangwill, I seek to explore two more complicated contemporary responses to the question of Jewish patriotism and economic activity. Necessarily framing this question at the turn of the century, moreover, is the South African context. Although Britain was in fact engaged in bitter and controversial warfare in the Transvaal at the time Farjeon's and Gordon's novels were published, South Africa figures for them only in its pre-war incarnation as a source of sudden and great wealth – a plot device that enables the narrative to unfold as a demonstration of the 'wise economy' of the Jews while avoiding entirely the more troubling implications of the war. But Jews were widely perceived at the time of the conflict as unrestrained in their pursuit of profit and oblivious to the interests of the nation. In their writing, Frankau and Zangwill address more directly the role of Jews in the war itself, as, respectively, financiers and fighters.

Between civilization and barbarism: Boers and Jews in Julia Frankau's *Pigs in Clover* (1903)

In the rhetoric of socialist opposition to the South African War, the Boers were frequently idealized as a simple, pious, agrarian people, valiantly holding out against the encroachment of modern capitalism.[26] For imperialists, however, the conflict in South Africa was cast as a battle between the civilization of the Empire and the barbarism of the Boers. In one of his letters to the *Daily Graphic* in 1891, Lord Randolph Churchill notoriously described the Boer farmers as 'ignorant', 'uncultivated', 'hopelessly unprogressive', uninterested in developing their land beyond basic farming or their minds beyond Bible-reading.[27] The focus on the religious orthodoxy, lack of hygiene, and primitiveness of the Boers became commonplace in public debate about the war, and was revived in the controversy over the British use of concentration camps, when 'barbarism' became a hotly contested term between liberal pro-Boers and the pro-government press.[28]

These images recur in *Pigs in Clover*, published in 1903 after the end of the war by the Anglo-Jewish novelist Julia Frankau. Set during the 1890s as the conflict brewed, Frankau's novel firmly insists on the pro-imperialist view of Boer culture. Her message is carried by the heroine, herself a novelist – an expatriate Englishwoman living in Cape Colony, who writes a book about the oppression of Africans under the rule of the Boers, which galvanizes British readers into moral fervour:

> The rough egotism of the Boers was vivid in the book, their brutalities, their cunning also; one saw their strength, but one turned sick at their

hypocrisy. One realised through Joan de Groot's pages the superficial religion that taught the Boers neither virtue nor charity; their Biblical learning that yet left them a prey to every superstition, while the lessons of cleanliness in the Old Testament were as little regarded as the lessons of mercy in the New. It was a nation that passed before the reader's eye, a winding pageantry of ignorance, strong and menacing, a danger to civilisation.[29]

In Frankau's novel, however, these terms also provide an alternative framework for imagining the Jewish immigrant in England. The novel's Trollopian plot concerns the relationship between a declining aristocratic family – the politician Stephen Hayward, his sister Constantia, and his daughter Aline – and two East End Jewish businessmen prospering through Transvaal gold, the altruistic Karl Althaus and his adopted brother, the mendacious Louis. In *Pigs in Clover*, Jewish capitalists are divided between those who seek to serve the Empire and those who present, like the Boers, a 'danger to civilisation'.

Julia Frankau's portraits of villainous Jews in her earlier novel *Dr Phillips: A Maida Vale Idyll* (1887) and in *Pigs in Clover* have been read as expressions of 'Jewish self-hatred', or an 'internalised...racial discourse about Jews'.[30] Analysing her private and public statements, Todd Endelman has concluded that Frankau was a radical assimilationist whose writing on Jewish themes was driven by 'a strong desire to escape identification with the common run of Jews by distancing herself from them'.[31] In *Dr Phillips* she drew brazenly on the rhetoric of contemporary antisemitism, which represented the Jewish male as sexually exploitative and racially repellent, and the outrage the novel caused may have motivated the more complicated representations of Jews in *Pigs in Clover*.[32] In this fiercely patriotic novel Frankau includes regular references to the errors of prejudice against Jews, and takes special care to dissociate Jewish capitalists from the charge of conspiracy in South Africa (81).[33] Furthermore, as Bryan Cheyette has argued, *Pigs in Clover* can be seen alongside Farjeon and Gordon as a version of the Anglo-Jewish apologetic novel, in which 'elements of the "Jewish plutocracy" [are identified] with the good of the nation as a whole'.[34]

Here, Frankau tells once again the story of the little Jew boy made good. Rand millionaire Karl Althaus is born into poverty, and rises into prominence because 'he was untiringly industrious, orientally generous, and he had graduated in sharpness in the streets of Whitechapel' (118). As a youth he was helped by Jews, but only, as he explains, 'because I was one of themselves' (105). Supporting his old, frail mother, and his adopted baby brother Louis, Karl 'worked and starved, and stole perchance, but never begged, resolution and strength growing in him the while and an indomitable greed. All around he saw what he wanted...all around he saw money, and the things that money could buy' (116). Continuing this ethnographic tradition,

Frankau places great emphasis on Karl's exemplary family feeling, but also on his conflicted attitude towards religion. He explains that 'Judaism is to me what England is to you, part of myself, the best part', but also regards Judaism as lacking in spirituality, 'a thing of forms and foods', and 'in all his moments of restlessness and rare depression, he longed for Christianity and its early lessons' (105, 106, 107).

Karl's story takes a new turn, however, when he meets the imperialist novelist Joan de Groot in Cape Town. She teaches him 'that there were things in life more worth having than money or works of art...his place in the Empire, his stake as an Englishman' (81). In South Africa, Karl's paternal instincts and warm generosity extend beyond his own family: 'He was learning love for his country, now that out there it seemed weak, despised, despicable' (195). But it is Judaism, above all, that stimulates Karl's imperialist enthusiasm – or rather, Judaism's inadequacies. Filling the void left by an unspiritual religion, it is literally the conversion he has longed for, a new, mystical 'luminosity in the soul of the big South African millionaire' (82). Frankau's narrative of the Jewish capitalist, then, unlike Gordon's liberal *Bildungsroman*, does not see patriotic virtue merely in the feat of self-betterment. Indeed, Karl's materialistic immigrant mentality is rendered virtuous only through his attachment to the cause of the British Empire – an attachment which emerges, contrary to the leftwing stereotype, not as a means of furthering his personal or tribal interests, but as a route to transcending them. Previously uninterested in politics, he becomes enlisted in the battle for 'civilization'.

The cause, however, is undermined by his brother. Louis, the son of a prostitute and a parasitic Polish-Jewish immigrant, is the 'descendant of that wheedling, ringleted son of a weak race that is no longer a nation' (142). In Karl's brother the attributes ascribed to immigrant Jews are given a different set of meanings. Heartless and unattached, the moustache-twirling Louis is an arch-manipulator whose compulsive wheeling and dealing in South Africa is made the reason for the Jameson Raid's failure. Powered by a crude vengeful desire to possess the property of the Hayward family and the body of its young heiress, because 'it would be something of a personal triumph to force the stronghold of exclusiveness' (247), Louis' primitive drives threaten to wreck social and political order. If much of the energies of the novel are devoted to eulogizing Karl's conversion to the good cause, far more of its imaginative charge erupts in the depiction of Louis' villainy. And although Frankau seeks to counter the Liberal/left stereotype of the conspiratorial capitalist in the figure of Karl, the gothic elements in contemporary anti-capitalist discourse also resonate in her text, in a lurid romantic melodrama revolving around Louis.

Images of parasitism and mysterious power were not only the prerogative of political ideologues like Hobson and Johnson. Gothic terror was also, by the end of the century, perhaps the most favoured literary mode for representing Jewish males. The villainous and power-hungry Jew appeared in Oscar Wilde's *The Picture of Dorian Gray* (1891), George Du Maurier's *Trilby* (1894), and Marie Corelli's *The Sorrows of Satan* (1895), in each case posing a special threat to, and attraction for, British women.[35] Bram Stoker's *Dracula* (1897), in particular, has been seen as figuratively encoding anxieties about Jewish immigration.[36] Like these novels, *Pigs in Clover* similarly interarticulates political and sexual danger. While Karl is chivalrous towards women and loyal to the Empire, Louis is both 'lecherous' and 'treacherous'; Louis' cosmopolitan rather than national loyalties are reflected in his 'sympathetic, adaptive faculty…, one of the secrets of his successes with women' (128, 306). Even the 'strong and self-reliant and powerful' Joan de Groot falls victim to Louis' irresistible force when he tries to get his hands on a Boer farm which she is to inherit and which he believes lies over a valuable mining reef (131). The mysterious sado-masochism of sexual desire in the novel thus becomes a metaphor for the racial threat posed by the Jewish immigrant.[37]

In the figurative language describing the love affair between Jew and Englishwoman, Frankau puts a different moral cast on South African wealth from Farjeon and Gordon. Louis 'held her by indissoluble bonds through the magic of the flesh, the chain that eats into a woman's heart and holds a man's conscience lightly in its weakest link. The chain was gold as yet, brilliant and uncorroded, set with rare jewels; hung about her grandly, and the glamour of it was in her eyes.' (151).[38] Although Joan valiantly resists Louis' attempts to take possession of the South African lands, the corruption of 'gold' and diamonds has nonetheless entered her soul. It is through sexually degrading her that Louis gains power over Joan; the ardour that had expressed itself in her patriotism is absorbed by her enslavement to him: 'Louis had coaxed and wheedled, sacked and undermined, left [her modesty] fallen and ruined before his exactions and encroachments, made her utterly defenceless before him' (382). In this metaphor, Louis' sexual conquest of Joan constitutes a sustained attack on the heart of the Empire. As a brutal slavemaster, he is implicitly linked with the cruel and 'dangerous' rule of the Boers in Africa. Focused around the imperial trope of endangered white womanhood, then, Frankau's novel aligns Jews on the one hand with enlightened support for the imperial cause and on the other with Boer barbarism.

The dualism that shapes *Pigs in Clover*, Bryan Cheyette has argued, is an expression of a particularly Anglo-Jewish anxiety to 'differentiate between the moral and immoral aspects of "Jewish finance"'.[39] Frankau's novel, however, is also structured by an unresolvable tension between rationalistic defences of the Jews – 'one of their community cannot misbehave without earning opprobrium for their whole body' (296) – and a violent gothic language of abjection and racial degeneration more typical of contemporary antisemitic discourse. During the South African mining boom of 1895, for example, London society is seen to be invaded by

> men with unpronounceable names, with impenetrable accents, masquerading now as Germans, now as Dutchmen, yellow men with bitten nails, and Mongol cheek-bones, men with whisky concessions, rich and fat with the dregs and refuse from the black man's drunken orgies, men with bald heads, black eyes, vulture noses, men, aye, and women too, whom no country owned, and no race claimed, the slime, the scum of nations... women who had been of the Cape Town pavement, but were now dwelling on the inside of the doors of Piccadilly, instead of loitering before them. (189)

If the social and sexual licence that characterizes colonial adventurer society is overtaking the metropolitan centre, however, Frankau's narrator lays the blame for this change as much on the aristocratic 'gold-seekers' of London as on the Jewish 'gold-bringers' of South Africa (189). Indeed, the target of the novel's critique is more broadly an English decadence that is revealed, rather than impelled by the Jews. In this respect, the novel can be read not so much as an articulation of a specifically Anglo-Jewish ambivalence, but as part of what Patrick Brantlinger has identified as the sub-genre of Imperial Gothic, which 'expresses anxieties about the ease with which civilization can revert to barbarism or savagery and thus about the weakening of Britain's imperial hegemony. The atavistic descents into the primitive experienced by fictional characters seem often to be allegories of the larger regressive movement of civilization, British progress turned into backsliding'.[40]

This allegory is most apparent in the novel's strikingly apocalyptic conclusion, the suicide of Joan de Groot. Despite an atoning marriage to the altruistic Karl, Joan believes that her seduction by Louis has marked her beyond redemption. Karl's chaste chivalry is feeble in the face of Louis' erotic power. For in arousing her sexual passion, the novel suggests, Louis has Judaized Joan – has provoked in her a reversion to primitive sexual instinct: 'The panther in Louis, the mere beast she saw too. *And the beast within her leapt to it!*' (393, original emphasis). Joan kills herself acknowledging that 'the enemy was within, not without; it was herself she had to fight, not Louis' (391). The Jew here is merely a catalyst to the descent of the vulnerable British heroine into barbarism. By the end of the novel, similarly, the aristocratic Hayward family, financially bankrupt and emotionally impoverished, has succumbed to the temptations of speculation and sex provided by the Althauses.

Thus, although the novel looks proleptically towards military victory over the Boers in the later 1890s, its plot presents the battle for 'civilization' as deeper, more ongoing, and less certain of success. In the gothic images of racial invasion which engulf the English heroine at the novel's conclusion, in fact, Frankau's novel moves beyond discussions of Jewish capitalism that dominated the years of the South African War. Instead, it articulates the fears of national degeneration that intensified in the postwar period, and that found one form of expression in increasing demands for the restriction of alien immigration.

The Boer War and the Jewish soldier:
Israel Zangwill's 'Anglicization' (1907)

Such concern with the impact of Jewish immigration was shared, rather than challenged, by the established Anglo-Jewish community. For middle-class Anglo-Jews, the charge that the war in South Africa was a Jews' war, coinciding with the growth of anti-alienism in the East End, meant that their loyalties too were under intense scrutiny. For this reason, Richard Mendelsohn has argued, Anglo-Jewry 'seized upon the distant imperial war as an opportunity to demonstrate the depth of its patriotism and of its integration into English society, to give the lie to those who, witnessing the influx of exotic Eastern European Jews into Britain, saw the Jew as alien and as such essentially unpatriotic and unassimilable'.[41] The Anglo-Jewish rabbinate enthusiastically promoted the cause of the war in the pulpit, the wealthy elite and Jewish-owned firms contributed substantially to supporting the volunteer units, congregants organized fundraising concerts.[42] In his short story 'Anglicization', Israel Zangwill satirized with bitter irony the gestures of national belonging that the South African war elicited from Jews. Faithfully documenting the 'war-sermons', militaristic Chanukah services, and *Jewish Chronicle* listings of patriotic donations, Zangwill's story was published in 1907, a year after such gestures had received a chilling reply in the Aliens Act.

In 'Anglicization', Zangwill presents a complex portrait of Jews at a critical moment of social change, differentiating through a shifting narratorial point of view three distinct perspectives on the war: that of a prosperous garment trader of immigrant origins, his Polish wife, and his assimilated son. The story begins with the migration to London from a provincial seaport town of Solomon Cohn, a successful, pompous businessman and town councillor who 'had distinguished himself by his Anglican mispronunciation of Hebrew and his insistence on a minister who spoke English and looked like a Christian clergyman'.[43] Cohn, the narrator insists, was not 'anxious to deny his Jewishness ... he was merely anxious not to obtrude it' (49). Unable to jettison his religious pedantry but anxious for respectability, Cohn thinks he can control the terms of his integration into British public life and refuses to face its contradictions. He believes that he has left the ghetto behind him, yet in London discovers that he is way behind in the ascent to anglicisation. In a small town his figure possessed 'the rotundity that the ratepayer demands'; in the city he finds himself 'an abdomen without authority' (50, 55). Whereas Cohn's piety and prosperity formerly guaranteed his public status in the gentile world, in the *fin-de-siècle* metropolis these no longer suffice. The course of the immigrant *Bildungsroman*, in Zangwill's hands, runs less smoothly.

It is in response to this new context, Zangwill suggests, that Cohn becomes an enthusiastic jingoist. In London, his opinions become formed by his newspaper and by the popular feeling he picks up from his workers, and he joins in the patriotic fervour echoing resoundingly in the synagogues and pages of the Jewish press at the time of the South African War. His business, too, flourishes with the insatiable demand for khaki. Withholding judgement, the narrator participates in the excitement, with only the slightest hint of ironic dissonance, as '[t]he brightly-dressed worshippers, lingeringly exchanging eulogiums on the "Rule Britannia" sermon, made an Oriental splotch of colour on the wintry pavement' (58). As the Jewish commercial classes loudly display their loyalty to the Empire, they seem unaware of their own marked cultural difference and its perils. When his son declares his desire to enlist, however, the unresolved tensions in Cohn's identity erupt. At the sight of Simon in uniform, '[w]ild hereditary tremors ran through him, born of the Russian persecution, and he had a vague nightmarish sense of the *Chappers*, the Jewish man-gatherers who collected the tribute of young Jews for the Little Father' – tremors that cannot be wholly quashed by his new found patriotism (60).

The ambivalence that Cohn acts out without fully understanding is not, however, shared by his son. Simon looks 'every inch an Anglo-Saxon', feels himself to be a descendant of Nelson and Wellington, and discovers that with the call-up 'some new passion that surprised even himself leapt to his breast – the first call upon an idealism, choked, rather than fed by, a misunderstood Judaism' (62). Patriotism, for Zangwill as for Frankau, holds a particular attraction for the secularized – and therefore presumptively spiritually impoverished – Jew. Yet Simon is ultimately forced to recognize the relationships of power that are masked by the rhetoric of national identity. After the war, he falls in love with the sister of a comrade whose life he saved on the battlefield. But in the xenophobic postwar climate, her father has joined the League of Londoners for the suppression of immigration, and she herself considers that 'it is only natural – isn't it? – that after shedding our blood and treasure for the Empire we should not be in a mood to see our country overrun by dirty aliens' (82). Simon, who initially mocks the irrationalism of this thinking, is finally devastated when his sweetheart refuses him because he is a Jew. 'Our country', which expanded to embrace Simon in wartime, has now contracted to exclude him.

The third perspective presented by the story is that of Simon's mother Hannah. Imported from Poland to marry Solomon Cohn and always self-conscious of 'the danger of slipping back unconsciously to the banned Yiddish', Hannah's precarious sense of belonging in England is at last stabilized when she sees her son marching shoulder to shoulder with the British army (51). Zangwill sets the scene of her revelation in St Paul's Cathedral at a service for new recruits prior to their sailing for South Africa. Initially apprehensive about the prospect of attending a church service, Hannah is amazed by the similarity of the liturgy to that of the synagogue: 'Surely there had been some monstrous mistake in conceiving the two creeds as at daggers drawn, and though she only pretended to kneel with the others, she felt her knees sinking in surrender to the larger life around her' (66). The free indirect discourse used by Zangwill here brings the reader closer to Hannah's inner thoughts than to those of the other principal characters – and closer to the immense appeal of being embraced by the 'hurrahing hordes that fused themselves with the procession and became part of its marching' (66). Above all, Zangwill invests Hannah alone with the capability of moving beyond the parochialism of Anglo-Judaism towards a kind of ecumenical universalism. Like Karl Althaus in Frankau's novel, Hannah finds redemption in the inclusive promise of imperialism.

In light of the way that the story unfolds, however, this scene appears in retrospect laced with irony. It illustrates not the transcendence of Hannah's limited horizons but the illusion of national belonging to which she succumbs in response to the pageantry of patriotism. Zangwill's text, unlike the others considered in this chapter, is profoundly sceptical about the nation's capacity to include Jews – undoubtedly because it was written following the exclusionary gestures of the Aliens Act. Indeed, if Solomon Cohn embodies the myth of the immigrant entrepreneur who rises, in Beatrice Potter's words, to 'become a law-abiding and self-respecting citizen of our great metropolis', that myth is decisively debunked in the story of his son Simon, whose opportunities, one generation later, are determined by race, not willpower.

Yet Zangwill's tale is concerned not only with the resurgence of British intolerance, but also with the confusions and contradictions over identity experienced by anglicised Jews themselves. While Solomon Cohn, for example, sagely advises that intermarriage is the only solution that will enable Boers and British to live together harmoniously in a future South Africa, he is unwilling to apply the same lesson to Jews and Christians in England. Conversely, when Simon indignantly refuses the attentions of a Jewish matchmaker, his mother is anxious at the thought of his abandoning the faith, and yet, at the same time, also feels 'vaguely exalted by it, as by the organ in St. Paul's ... Ah! How this new young generation was snapping asunder the ancient coils! how the new and diviner sap ran in its veins!' (74). As much as Zangwill is interested, in this story, in exposing the hypocrisy of British nationalism, he is equally concerned to catch the subtle interplay of desire and disavowal that characterizes Jews' relationship to Britishness.

This ambivalence is articulated most strikingly of all in Hannah's response to Simon's letters from the front, proudly read out loud by the father who had so steadfastly opposed his enlisting. Simon repeats the conventional imperialist view of the Boer as

> [a] canting hypocrite, a psalm-singer and devil-dodger, he has no civilization worth the name, and his customs are filthy. Since the great trek he has acquired, from long intercourse with his Kaffir slaves, many of the native's savage traits. In short, a born liar, credulous, and barbarous, crassly ignorant and inconceivably stubborn ... Is it to be wondered at that the Boer farmer, hidden in the vast undulations of the endless veldt, with his wife, his children and his slaves, should lose all sense of proportion, ignorant of the outside world ...? (68)

Yet these words are heard by Hannah 'with a stab of insight that he was reading a description of himself – nay, of herself, of her whole race, hidden in the world, awaiting some vague future of glory that never came' (689). Zangwill's position is at its most elusive with this analogy. Here, in the mind of the character most identified with the narratorial voice, is a critique of Jews as archaic and primitive, buried in the 'endless veldt' of the ghetto mindset – an insight revealed by the discourse of the South African War and the Jews' unthinking response to it. If the conflict in South Africa is a war against barbarism, Zangwill proposes, this implicates Jews as much as Boers.

While Frankau's portrayal of Jewish vice was motivated by her radical assimilationism, for Zangwill, in contrast, a belief in Jewish universalism permeated his writing (and personal life – exemplified, for example in his own practice of intermarriage).[44] Hannah's 'stab of insight', then, may well suggest the author's own view of anglicised Jewry as, like the 'Boer', narrowly religious, ignorant, and unmodern, stubbornly rejecting the inclusive promise of 'the outside world'. And yet, the story's final, poignant tableau is a fierce embrace between the disappointed Simon and his mother, both forcibly, rather than voluntarily, excluded from this promise, 'their love the one thing saved from Anglicization' (86). In these last words, Zangwill returns to the period's most cherished image of the Jewish family, now revisited with bitter irony. Beatrice Potter's supportive, inward-looking Jewish family unit reappears here, its insularity a bulwark against Gentile cruelty. Indeed, by the end of the story, the progressive values of 'civilization' are no longer synonymous with 'anglicisation'.

Conclusion

Anglo-Jewish novelists, Bryan Cheyette argues, negotiated the contrary demands of universalism and particularism 'by taking prevalent Jewish representations – such as the Jewish financier or ... the Jewish alien – which are then re-written in terms which make them "acceptable" to the majority values of English culture'.[45] But Gordon, Farjeon, Frankau, and Zangwill were not only responding defensively to current stereotypes of Jews. Rather, as I have shown by reading them within the context of *fin-de-siècle* political discourse, the figure of the alien entrepreneur had become a cipher, for both Jewish and non-Jewish writers, for ways to imagine the national future.

Gordon's and Farjeon's narratives seek to insert the enterprising Jew boy into the mid-Victorian philosophy of liberal individualism and bourgeois respectability as adumbrated by Beatrice Potter. For Frankau, the instinct for profit that motivated Jews was less benign, but it could be harnessed and transcended by the idealism of Empire. Although in this respect Frankau shared with Gordon the view that Jews could participate in the progress of civilization, this faith is ultimately overwhelmed in her novel by a contrary, terror-ridden vision. The imagery of national degeneration, resonating with the gothic rhetoric of both the political right and left, is in Frankau's novel exemplified by the economic and social ascendance of the Jews.

The scepticism towards modernity expressed in different ways by Hobson and by Frankau is cast in a particularly complex and poignant way by Zangwill. In the triangulation of perspectives that structures his text, Zangwill strikingly eschews the schematically binary opposition of good Jew/bad Jew that characterizes semitic representation in the period. His characters are not only little Jew boys seeking respectability or political power, but others too, differentiated by age, gender, birthplace, memory. Zangwill's Anglo-Jews are all internally divided and conflicted – certainly the consequence of a legacy of persecution and its continuing echoes in the present, but just as much an effect, also, of their own unresolved confusion about exactly how much they want of 'modernity' and 'anglicisation'. In posing this question, Zangwill moves the reader's focus away from the hackneyed debate about the Jews' capacity for civilization and towards a much more demanding question about the nature of contemporary 'civilization' itself.

Notes

1. See Englander, *A Documentary History*.
2. [Beatrice Potter], 'The Jewish Community', in Charles Booth (ed.), *Life and Labour of the People in London, III, Blocks of Buildings, Schools, and Immigration* (London: Macmillan, 1892), 178. Subsequent page numbers will be cited parenthetically in the text. On Webb's research for these essays see O'Day, 'Before the Webbs', 226–240.
3. Charles Booth, *Life and Labour of the People in London, XVII, Final volume: Notes on Social Influences and Conclusion* (London: Macmillan, 1902), 57. This image comes from section 3, 'Betting', in Part II, 'Habits of the People'.
4. Feldman, *Englishmen and Jews*, 185–257.
5. Hirshfield, 'The British Left', 95.
6. H. M. Hyndman, 'Imperialist Judaism in Africa', *Justice*, 25 April 1896, 4; Hyndman, 'The Parting of the Ways', *Justice*, 16 May 1896, 4.
7. J. A. Hobson, *Problems of Poverty* (London: 1891), 98, 60, quoted in Holmes, 'J. A. Hobson', 130–131.
8. Hobson, *The War in South Africa: Its Causes and Effects* (London: James Nisbet, 1900), 189.

9. Hobson, *Problems of Poverty*, 58, quoted in Holmes, 'J. A. Hobson', 129.
10. J. A. Hobson, 'Capitalism and Imperialism in South Africa', *Contemporary Review*, 77 (1900), 4–5.
11. Hobson, 'Capitalism', 15.
12. Hobson, 'Capitalism', 16.
13. James Johnson, *RCAI*, 1903, vol. II, 286–288, quoted in Garrard, *The English and Immigration*, 64.
14. Mitchell, 'Hobson Revisited', 407. For an account of Hobson's view of the Jews in the context of his developing economic thought, see Holmes, 'J. A. Hobson', 144–150.
15. See Cheyette, 'From Apology to Revolt'; Valman, 'Semitism and Criticism'.
16. B. L. Farjeon, *The Pride of Race. In Five Panels* (London: Hutchinson, 1901), 38, 307.
17. Farjeon, *The Pride of Race*, 71.
18. Cheyette, 'From Apology to Revolt', 256–260. On Farjeon see Persell, 'Capitalism'.
19. Englander, 'Booth's Jews', 560–561.
20. Englander, 'Booth's Jews', 557.
21. Garrard, *The English and Immigration*, 94.
22. Garrard, *The English and Immigration*, 96.
23. Samuel Gordon, *Sons of the Covenant: a Tale of London Jewry* (Philadelphia: The Jewish Publication Society of America, 1900), 107. Subsequent page numbers will be cited parenthetically in the text.
24. Benjamin Farjeon, *Aaron the Jew* (1894), quoted in Persell, 'Capitalism', 206. These ideas are repeated verbatim by Liberal parliamentary politicians in the Aliens debate. In 1898, for example, Lord Grey described Jews as 'the people possessing the best enterprise and endowed with the best brain power. These men, when they arrive, may come destitute, but the evidence goes to show that, after a few years' stay…when they become assimilated to our English life, they form an industrious portion of the community, contribute to the taxation of the country and become a source of wealth'. Quoted in Garrard, *The English and Immigration*, 98.
25. Persell, 'Dickensian Disciple'.
26. Hirshfield, 'The British Left', 103–104.
27. Lord Randolph Churchill, *Men, Mines and Animals in South Africa* (1892), quoted in van Wyk Smith, 'The Boers', 429.
28. Krebs, *Gender, Race and the Writing of Empire*, 49–51.
29. Julia Frankau [Frank Danby, pseud.], *Pigs in Clover,* 3rd edn (Philadelphia: J. B. Lippincott, 1903), 100. Subsequent page numbers will be cited parenthetically in the text.
30. Cheyette, 'The Other Self', 104; Endelman, 'The Frankaus', 127–135; Galchinsky, ' "Permanently Blacked"'.
31. Endelman, 'The Frankaus', 131.
32. On the criticism that *Dr Phillips* provoked see Endelman, 'The Frankaus', 132. On Frankau's use of antisemitic discourse in this novel see Galchinsky, ' "Permanently Blacked"' and Valman, *The Jewess*, 193–200.
33. On Frankau's self-identification as a patriot, see Malcolm C. Salaman, 'Obituary: Death of "Frank Danby". A Personal Tribute', *Jewish Chronicle*, 24 March 1915, 22.
34. Cheyette, 'The Other Self', 105.
35. Davison, *Anti-Semitism*, 133–134.

36. For analyses of *Dracula* in these terms, see Malchow, *Gothic Images*, 148–166; Halberstam, 'Technologies'; and Davison, *Anti-Semitism*, ch. 5.
37. For an extended discussion, see Valman, *The Jewess*, 193–203.
38. For more on Jews and jewels, see Chapter 1 in this volume.
39. Cheyette, 'The Other Self', 105.
40. Brantlinger, *Rule of Darkness*, 228.
41. Mendelsohn, 'The Jewish Soldier', 12.
42. Mendelsohn, 'The Jewish Soldier', 12–13.
43. Israel Zangwill, 'Anglicization', in *Ghetto Comedies* (1906; London: Globe, 1925), 49. Subsequent page numbers will be cited parenthetically in the text.
44. For an extended discussion, see Rochelson, ' "*They That Walk in Darkness*" '.
45. Cheyette, 'The Other Self', 111.

3
Acting like an Alien: 'Civil' Antisemitism, the Rhetoricized Jew, and Early Twentieth-Century British Immigration Law

Lara Trubowitz

> No one will be much or little except in someone else's mind.
>
> Djuna Barnes, *Nightwood*

It has been more than 20 years since the historian Colin Holmes, in his influential work on twentieth-century British antisemitism, stated that 'at no point between 1876 and 1914 did any [governing party in Britain] introduce discriminatory legislation specifically against Jews'.[1] His claim has since become a truism of contemporary scholarship on Anglo-Jewish relations. This essay reconsiders Holmes's assertion in light of what I call 'civil antisemitism', a highly nuanced form of anti-Jewish rhetoric operating within the British Parliament during the first part of the twentieth century. Civil antisemitism, like the fanatical anti-Jewish ideologies espoused by radical right-wing groups such as the Britons, draws a clear demarcation between Jews and non-Jews, decries Jews' degenerate properties, and promotes a belief in the threat of Jewish influence; it relies, however, on more rhetorically complex techniques to convey its attitudes and theories. It has received limited critical attention from scholars of British antisemitism, precisely because it rarely appears to be as militant, or as dangerous, as the hate mongering we associate with demagogues like Arnold White and Oswald Mosley.[2] Indeed, because civil antisemitism distills fanatical antisemitic rhetoric into an 'acceptable' medium for differentiating Jews both from British citizens and from other immigrants, it has frequently been mistaken for philosemitism, not only by politicians and journalists of the period, but also by contemporary literary scholars and historians.

In this essay, I focus on debates surrounding the passage of anti-immigration legislation in 1904 and 1905, laws that were known collectively as the 'Aliens Acts'. I describe the techniques by which civil antisemitism is constituted within the debates, and show how British parliamentarians cultivate such techniques in order to avoid charges of antisemitism, targeting Jewish immigrants but, ironically, often without mentioning Jews at all.[3] The complexity of these techniques, and hence of the Acts themselves, points not only to a woefully neglected strain of British antisemitism, but also to the critical impact of antisemitic thought on public policy debates in Britain at large, debates that, contrary to Holmes's claim, ultimately give rise to a 'rational' and distinctly anti-Jewish immigration platform sponsored by the British government. In the process, a powerful but indirect rhetoric about Jewishness is established, one that will continue to influence public debate long after the 1904 and 1905 Acts cease to be a centrepiece of discussions either about Jews or about Anglo-Jewish relations.

The Aliens Acts: a brief history

On 24 April 1902, Britain's Royal Commission on Immigration began heated deliberations over immigration trends, an issue that many parliamentarians considered especially pressing, given the large influx of Eastern Europeans who had begun arriving in Britain in the early 1880s.[4] Commission sessions were held until 21 May 1903. In August of that year, the Commission offered its recommendations for instituting new and comprehensive restrictions on immigration. The report was widely praised by members of Balfour's Conservative government, and would become an important catalyst in the Conservative party's fight for the passage of the Aliens Act, an anti-immigration bill first introduced into parliament in 1904. The administrative and legal powers ceded to the government by the bill were extensive: it enabled the government to deny entry to any alien who was without visible means of support, had been sentenced to three or more months of imprisonment in a foreign country, or was 'of notoriously bad character'. In addition to these strict landing regulations, the bill gave officials the authority to monitor, detain, and deport any immigrant deemed by the Home Office capable of sedition; it also bestowed upon local government boards permission to designate as off-limits to immigrants those areas where overcrowding could be attributed to a prior increase in the alien population.

Not enough votes were gathered for the 1904 bill to pass, but within one year, in July 1905, a revised bill was approved by both the House of Commons and the House of Lords;[5] on 10 August 1905, it was presented for Royal Assent. The 1905 bill, which Jill Pellew describes as 'the first modern act to regulate immigration into Britain',[6] remained in effect until 1914, when a modified act, the 'Aliens Restriction Bill', was passed under the threat of war. In the discourse surrounding the 'Aliens Restriction Bill' – indeed, in the very appellative of the bill itself – we get a clearer articulation of the primary goal of the earlier 1904 and 1905 Aliens Acts: to control what lawmakers present as the unrestricted movement of 'undesirable aliens' within and through Britain, a movement, as I will show, that is defined, by Conservative and Liberal parliamentarians alike, as primarily and essentially Jewish.

Scholarly analyses of both the 1904 and 1905 Acts typically proffer two seemingly paradoxical views of the legislation: on the one hand, a belief espoused initially by leaders of the Jewish community, and later by historians of the legislation, that Jews are the primary target of the laws;[7] on the other hand, the notion, most recently articulated by Pellew, that the imprecise wording of the laws, and of the surrounding debates, make the Acts' intended target ambiguous at best. Indeed, as John Garrard notes, the laws and debates over the Acts' ratification often appear not to be explicitly about Jews at all.[8] Rather than see this contradiction as the product of diverging textual and historical interpretations, I will argue not only that both suppositions are true, but, more importantly, that together they demonstrate the highly insidious methods by which antisemitism operates amidst debates over the passage of the laws, and within early twentieth-century British politics more generally. In the following pages, I will analyse the rhetorical devices behind such methods, focusing on speeches that Major William Evans-Gordon delivered before the House of Commons on 2 May 1905 during debates over immigration restrictions. Evans-Gordon was, at the time, MP for Stepney and had been a major architect of the 1904 bill.

Among the most common and striking of these devices are apophasis and metalepsis. Apophasis is a bifurcated statement, in which a speaker makes a claim by pointedly refuting the significance of the very assertion he or she wishes to emphasize. For instance, Harry Lawson, MP for Mile End and one of the government's most ardent proponents of immigration legislation, employs a simple apophasis when he says, addressing his fellow parliamentarians on the need for immigration restrictions, 'I do not think it is necessary to point out that...Jews suffer from an invasion of people of their own faith.'[9] Evans-Gordon produces a more complex version of apophasis when he states, in a speech before the House of Commons, that 'immigration is by no means wholly Jewish', but then declares that '[t]he Jewish emigrants do form a very large part of the whole', and proceeds to focus solely on Jewish immigration trends (2 May 1905; 735).[10]

In metalepsis, one figure in an extended series of figures is substituted for another, effectively occluding a central term of the figural series as a whole. We see metalepsis at work when Evans-Gordon, during the same 1905 speech, laments the 'process of transformation and wholesale substitution of foreign for English population going on daily under [one's] eyes' (717). Moments later, he equates the word 'foreign' with the term 'alien', which refers, he explains, not to the Italian, French, and German immigrants arriving in Switzerland, who 'are in no way aliens except in a purely technical sense' (718), but rather to those who are 'eating up the native population' and causing the 'churches' of the natives to be 'continually left like islands in the midst of an alien sea' (717). In this instance, 'foreign' is a metonymy for 'alien', and 'alien' is a metonymy for what Evans-Gordon will elsewhere call 'a race apart', a race that threatens the existence of churches, the latter being a metonymy for the Gentile, hence British, population as a whole.[11] 'Jew' is of course the crucial term left out. Over the course of these debates, the rhetorical interchangeability of Jews, immigrants, and aliens becomes a crucial component of the agenda of parliamentarians, who wish to restrict Jewish immigration without having to name Jews as their target.[12]

In short, the fact that the figure of the Jew in parliamentary debates is often only indirectly readable is no mere coincidence, but rather a powerful rhetorical effect. Conservative parliamentarians such as Evans-Gordon and Lawson actively cultivate this effect, transforming what might have been perceived as a distinctly antisemitic political platform into a viable and 'reasonable' immigration policy. It is precisely this transformation that makes possible the passage of the 1905 bill, and would later enable critics to claim that antisemitism did 'not make any significant headway into conventional politics'.[13]

Evans-Gordon and the 'alien' immigrant

Let us examine more closely the rhetorical mechanisms at work in Evans-Gordon's speech of 2 May 1905. In the speech, Evans-Gordon turns what appears to be a very general assessment about the nature of immigration into a commentary on the essential quality of Jews, transforming migration into the characteristic that defines Jewish difference as such. He begins as follows:

> I would remind the House that year by year some 1,500,000 human beings of every age, sex, and religion, the healthy and hopeful, the diseased and hopeless, good, bad, and indifferent, are on the move from the South and East of Europe pressing toward the West. (707)

These opening remarks can be characterized as quantitative, designed primarily to communicate the extensiveness of contemporary immigration movements. And yet, it is not through the numbers that Evans-Gordon underscores the enormity of the movement; rather, the movement is 'great' because of its commonplace or prosaic nature, that is, precisely because it involves 'human beings of every age, sex, and religion'. Having established the quantitative parameters of immigration, Evans-Gordon then shifts to a specific description of Jewish immigration. As we have already seen, the description starts with a repudiation:

> This immigration is not by any means wholly Jewish. The Jewish emigrants do form a very large part of the whole, and in their case, it may be said to take the form of a national migration. There are 5,500,000 Jews in the Russian Empire, but we cannot consider all these people to be possible

emigrants, though a large number of them must be considered in that light, unless affairs in Eastern Europe undergo a profound modification. As things are, it is the poorest and the least fit of these people who move, and it is the residuum of these again who come to, or are left in this country. Having realized the magnitude of this movement, the problem for us is what steps should we take. (707–708)

Evans-Gordon's premise appears to be that a description of Jewish immigration will give us a sense of the quality of immigration overall – in other words, that Jews are merely an example of immigration, but not exemplary. However, this premise itself assumes the acceptance of two axioms: that Jews immigrate, and that Jewish immigration as such has distinct and recognizable characteristics or qualities. Evans-Gordon affixes to Jewish movement this quality of *is*-ness when he describes such movement as a 'national migration', bestowing upon Jews the status of a nation, and specifically, a nation that moves. To describe the Jews as a nation unto themselves was, at the time, a platitude. And yet, it is precisely the conventionality of the statement that frees Evans-Gordon from any need to explain his claim. His argument can be unravelled as follows: if, as Evans-Gordon suggests, the Jews are distinct from other nations, one can only assume that they are also distinct from Russia and, hence, already immigrants, even before their impending 'national migration' to Britain. Such logic, of course, presupposes the occurrence of a prior migration, say, into Russia, which in turn reinforces the correlation between Jew and immigrant. Evans-Gordon reads this migration of Jews into Russia synecdochally, as representative of the Jews' future migrations, and therefore his predication of the Jews' imminent migration into Britain is, more accurately, the anticipation of the *recurrence* of Jewish migration. Such a recurrence can be presumed only if Jewish immigration is understood to be itself essentially permanent, always occurring and recurring.

Indeed, for Evans-Gordon, permanent impermanence is the *is* of Jewishness, the quality that separates Jews from others. This is a view he iterates in his 1903 book, *The Alien Immigrant*, depicting Jewish residents of the East End as 'descendents of Pharaoh's brickmakers', as if to remind his readers that, historically, Jews have always migrated, at least since their Exodus from Egypt, and thus do not come from Russia at all.[14] When he describes Jews as immigrants in his speech before the House of Commons, he is, in effect, reasserting this stereotypical idea of the Jew as the essential wanderer, slipping between the terms immigrant and wanderer without ever having to elucidate the slippage as such.

This slippage between the qualities of immigrants and stereotyped Jews is no idiosyncratic artifact of Evans-Gordon's jingoism. That categories of identity be presented as definitive is demanded by a central criterion of legal discourse itself: the clear demarcation of the object of the law, which, in the case of the Jew, means translating impermanence into a characteristic permanent enough to warrant legal attention. And yet, the slippage alone is not enough to legitimise immigration restrictions. Evans-Gordon must also present Jewish movement as a force noxious to British society. In some cases, this noxiousness is expressed thematically, while in other cases the structure or force of the rhetoric itself performs the task. We can see the latter in Evans-Gordon's contention that the immigrant is the root cause of migratory movements, a claim that emerges as part of a complex and powerful sub-narrative about the relative strength of immigrants in relation to the political forces confronting them.

In essence, for Evans-Gordon, it is not primarily external forces that create immigrants, but rather immigrants themselves who cause immigration:

> The expulsive forces which cause this great movement are in the main mis-government and oppression. But other forces are at work. The enormous number of these people who have gone before make a drawing force to the people who are left behind, and this great travelling mass of humanity has produced among the shipping companies, and people connected with railways and other transport, a fierce competition. Every single person who can be induced to travel is another ticket sold. All these forces add naturally to the number of people who are on the move. (707)

His description of 'these people', or Jewish immigrants, as both a 'drawing force' and a 'travelling mass of humanity [that] has produced among the shipping companies … a fierce competition' emphasizes the efficacy of the Jews themselves. Moreover, it has the rhetorical effect of diminishing, by comparison, Evans-Gordon's own allusions to such external agents as 'oppression', 'mis-government,' and 'the affairs in Eastern Europe', categories he invokes with little attention to detail. Indeed, the more detailed nature of the portrayals of the immigrants makes their power at least commensurate with the forces afflicting them: the descriptions establish the immigrants' strength as proof of their increasing numbers, and the immigrants' increasing numbers as proof of their strength.

The Acts and public testimony

Evans-Gordon generally expresses two of the most prevalent philosophical suppositions about Jews that circulate, and are fused, amidst debates on the passage of the Acts. On the one hand, Jewishness is presented as an ontological or essential condition – one either is or is not Jewish – while on the other hand, Jewishness is represented as a form of contagion, which presupposes the belief that contact with the Jew can, in effect, make non-Jews into Jews. Although seemingly paradoxical, together the two suppositions supply British lawmakers in 1904 and 1905 with a key rationale for anti-immigration legislation. The first supposition gives officials a set of charac-teristics they can define as inherently non-British, enabling them to sub-ject any entity with these characteristics to immigration regulations. The second supposition gives an urgency to the passage of the laws: lawmakers need to protect Britain from the danger of a plague-like influx of Jews whose very presence threatens to turn '[s]treets and districts [that were] formerly entirely English...entirely foreign in character'.[15] It isn't simply that the Jew carries diseases; it is that Jewishness itself is the disease, and it is spreading.

But this latter supposition, given its inflammatory nature, could not be accepted as straightforward content in such polite public discourse as parlia-mentary debate. Therefore, the MPs often turn to the public to make their claims for them, not because the public's claims offer greater insight into any real referent, but rather because of several useful rhetorical effects of this type of assertion by proxy. Indeed, what we uncover in the use of public statements about Jews by parliamentarians is evidence of a 'rhetoricized' Jew, a constructed figure absolutely necessary to the legal narrative being played out, but also necessarily concealed as part of the cultural drama unfolding within British public life more generally.

It is common in debates to find the MPs incorporating public assertions directly into their speeches. For instance, in the 1905 debate cited earlier, statements are included from English and German municipal officers, British Customs officials, heads of Jewish committees, Jewish writers such as Israel Zangwill, and social historians such as Charles Booth. The most frequently cited source of these statements is the Royal Commission on Alien Immigration.[16] For 13 months beginning in January 1902, the Commission, under the direction of Lord James of Hareford, heard testimony from shopkeepers, borough councillors, doctors, port inspectors, and a vari-ety of residents of the East End – a district that was rapidly being settled by more and more Jews – on the state of immigration in Britain.[17] Lawmakers use these statements both to illustrate the impact of aliens on the British population and, more importantly, to indicate their own deference, not to individual agendas and ideologies, but to what they present as an objective assessment of a widespread cultural problem.

Indeed, of paramount importance to the MPs is the perception that what public statements articulate are not individual or idiosyncratic views about the Jewish immigrant but rather precisely what is 'true' about Jews. Thus, MPs frequently downplay the individuality of public speakers in order to commu-nicate the strictly factual quality of the assertions they cited. We see this, for instance, in Harry Lawson's speech before the Commons in 1905:

The case in regard to immigration in this country is summed up by the words used by German officials at the ports of the embarkation: 'Utterly destitute and friendless who can just afford a ticket to Grimsby go to England.' .... The truth is that we get the floating scum – those who would go anywhere .... (2 May; 737–738)

The anonymity of the speakers in such statements is important. The 'German officials' are presented as nothing more than conduits for facts that exist prior to the officers' utterance, hence the single statement – 'utterly destitute' – placed into the mouths of the plural 'officials'. This does not mean that the Germans are extraneous, for some conduit or figure is required to assert a 'truth' that Lawson cannot express on his own. At the same time, the officials are a synecdoche for a larger public whose 'sighting' of the immigrant carries greater weight than Lawson's alone. The implication is that when Lawson describes immigrants as 'floating scum' he is merely characterizing events whose occurrence the public has previously described and verified. Here Shoshana Felman's assessment of testimony applies: 'the witness's speech', she says, 'is one which ... transcends the witness who is but its medium'. Yet MPs also approached public testimony positivistically, 'not as a mode of statement of, but rather as a mode of access to ... truth'.[18]

Indeed, the integration of accounts of public sentiment into official speeches can be likened to the use, in the United States, of a victim impact statement in the penalty stage of a capital trial: in such instances, the victim provides evidence, not of the occurrence of a crime, but rather of the impact of that crime on another. That the victim has suffered, has experienced the impact, is assumed to be an irrefutable fact and, as such, cannot be challenged; the victim's perception of the crime becomes the truth of the crime. In the immigration debates, witness statements carry weight precisely because perception is treated and presented as incontestable and incontrovertible, a direct access to fact: specifically, the detrimental effect of Jews, and of other immigrants, on the sustainability of British communities and British identity.[19] It is precisely this understanding of the function of public statement that undergirds the following claim by Evans-Gordon, as he repudiates a colleague's insistence that the growth of Britain's immigrant population is much smaller than proponents of restrictions would argue. Evans-Gordon, of course, here refers not to Jews themselves, but rather to London's East End:

There is not a clergyman or responsible resident in the East End of London who does not see this process of transformation and wholesale substitution of foreign for English population going on daily under his eyes .... Not all the Blue-books or statistics in the world can controvert these incontrovertible facts. (2 May 1905, 716–717)

In this way, the public is charged with the task of describing, as Evans-Gordon on his own cannot, the Jews' noxious effect on Britain.

Evans-Gordon again establishes the power of the public by citing Inspector Malveney and an unnamed Commissioner of the Metropolitan Police:

> We have the evidence of Chief Inspector Malveney, of the H Division, that in six years 107 whole streets in Stepney went out of English occupation into foreign occupation; and there is the statement of the Chief Commissioner of the Metropolitan Police, who said in his last Annual Report that the alien colony in the East End continued to increase rapidly, and the area which it occupies is extending accordingly. (716–717)

Moments later, he reinforces his earlier description of the Jews as a 'travelling mass of humanity', and a 'national migration' with comments made by the Bishop of Stepney in 1902. In the following passage, it must again be kept in mind that the 'East End' was commonly considered an increasingly Jewish area; hence the assertion that what 'immigrants' threaten are 'churches':

> The East End of London was being swamped by aliens who were coming in like an army of locusts eating up the native population or turning them out. Their churches were being continually left like islands in the midst of an alien sea. (717)

The Bishop's description makes Britain, and the British, a miniscule or defenseless entity – prey to the immigrants who are, in the Bishop's mind, a devouring mass of (Biblical) insects as well as treacherous waters, swarming over or drowning, as the case may be, the British Christian.

Descriptions such as these by the Bishop of Stepney suggest that Jews are not just a momentarily dangerous immigrant but, indeed, the corporeal embodiment of a form of movement whose nature and effect are in general monstrous: so great is the force of the movement that it *both* swallows *and* submerges the native population. Elsewhere, the migration of Jews is described in terms of infectiousness, as a contagion so communicable that MPs such as Lawson worry it will irreversibly transform Britain, causing Britain's 'backward march to physical deterioration' (740).

Contagiousness proliferates

During this period, expressions of hysteria over Jewish contagion run the gamut, from diatribes against the Jews as carriers of disease to the presumption that the Jews themselves are a disease. That the Jews' susceptibility to disease is a key theme within debates over the Acts is now commonly noted by critics.[20] But more crucial are the ways in which the idea of Jewish difference, as itself transferable to others, as migratory or movable, is rhetorically enacted and authenticated. In the following few pages, I will suggest some of the ways in which thematic claims about Jews importing disease are transformed into rhetorical arguments. Indeed, it is the proliferation of the rhetoric itself, quite aside from the supposed proliferation of Jewish aliens, that comprises one of the central mechanisms of civil antisemitism.

In testimony before the Royal Commission frequently quoted by historians, Dr F. A. C. Tyrrell reports that Jews are 'peculiarly prone to trachoma', a highly virulent disease of the eyes, explaining further that trachoma is 'largely a disease of race' (29 May 1902).[21] Evans-Gordon, in his statements of 2 May 1905 before the House of Commons, makes similar claims about the immigrant's proclivity to diseases, even though he is more cautious than Tyrrell about directly naming Jews as any disease's primary source.

> [S]mallpox and scarlet fever have unquestionably been introduced by aliens within the past few months, and ... trachoma, a contagious disease, which is the third principle cause of total loss of sight, and favus, a disgusting and contagious disease of the skin, have been, and are being, introduced by these aliens on a large scale. (711)

Having established, through metaleptical association, that Jews (aliens with trachoma) are carriers of disease, Evans-Gordon can now suggest that Jews are themselves 'verminous' in their ability not only to carry but to proliferate disease: 'We found some of them suffering from loathsome and unmentionable diseases, the importation of which into this country might and does lead to very serious results, and we found most of them verminous' (722). The subtle shift from his first assertion (the Jews carry disease) into the latter (the Jews actively proliferate the disease) is attributable to the metalepses in Evans-Gordon's language, metalepses which set the stage for the structural transformation of Jewishness itself into a *principle* of contagion.

Indeed, the spreading of the Jew is accompanied and perpetuated by an overflowing of the very figures that supposedly describe Jewishness, making the rhetoric itself into the very Jewishness it depicts – infectious and overflowing. Thus, in a precursor to Evans-Gordon's rhetoric, an anonymous author – writing in the *Pall Mall Gazette* in 1901 after an outbreak of smallpox – can describe Jewish immigrants variously as a disease attaching itself to the arm of Britain, a scourge of Biblical proportions, infectious filth, *and* foreign sewage. Jews are, according to the author,

> loathsome wretches who came grunting and itching to our shores .... [T]he small-pox now creeping through London, this agony now throbbing and scorching in my arm is caused (make no mistake about it) by the scum washed to our shores in the dirty waters flowing from foreign drainpipes.[22]

To the extent that the Jew is thought to be spreading, rhetoric about the Jew is out of control as well. Yet, this excessiveness does not lead to accusations of the rhetoric as false; instead, the rhetoric's seeming failure gives further proof of its very accuracy, and in turn, of the need for legislation. To illustrate the crucial and oddly productive role of the contagious rhetoric of the Jew – productive, precisely because the more it loses control over its subject matter, the more it reinforces the dangerous nature of the subject it describes – I return to comments recorded by the Royal Commission, the body charged by Parliament to collect public evidence of the impact of immigration on Britain.

A 1903 report from the Commission includes the following statement by East End resident William Rose, a local carpenter. '[The Jews are] like the waves of the sea', Rose says, 'they simply keep spreading, but they do not retreat like the waves of the sea do' (302).[23] It is not in Rose's metaphor that the power of his statement lies. Rather, the potency of his remarks is most striking in that moment when the metaphor fails – that is, when the incongruity between Jews and the sea becomes greater than the similarity, precisely because the Jews do not 'retreat like the waves'. This 'failure' is, in effect, the metaphor's success, for it dramatizes the Jew's transcendence of the very terms of the analogy and, in doing so, provides evidence for the notion that Jews keep spreading, indeed, can't be 'fixed'. Thus, a cyclical logic is established: the more the Jew's wandering nature is substantiated by a proliferating series of metaphors, and metaphoric 'failures', the more urgent is the need for descriptions that will demarcate or 'fix' the Jew. As the need expands, so the figurative complexity of the descriptions increases, proof that Jews slide through (or out of) conventional descriptions and categories.[24] And so the wandering nature of the Jews is again established and reinforced. In this way, Rose's rhetoric demonstrates not only its own distinction from any 'real Jew' but, ironically, the disappearance of the Jew *into* a rhetoric that takes the Jew's place, that is, the becoming Jewish of the rhetoric itself. In fact, Rose's speech exemplifies the paradox at the heart of immigration law: that discourses of immigration inevitably become the very thing they seek to describe, until the concrete figure of the Jew itself is no longer needed to support anti-immigrationist claims. Jewishness is detached from the Jew, indeed ceases to be distinctly Jewish, as it metamorphosises into exactly that which discourses of contagion proclaim: a transferable trait, and moreover, one infecting everything around it – a trait that need not be *of the Jew* to be 'essentially' Jewish.

Indeed, in comments such as Rose's, the failure of the analogical structure of the claim is precisely what constitutes the 'truth' of the figure of the Jew. The figure is created by the inadequacy of a conceptual mode of thought, and yet that very inadequacy comes to signify a seemingly coherent truth about Jews. In the process, all actual agents of a potentially antisemitic immigration platform are removed, with the exception of the rhetoricized

'Jew' himself, who now effectively operates as the implicit cause of immigration, of the legislation against it, and even of the excessive rhetoric invoked to support the laws that will soon restrict such decisively 'Jewish' movements.

Once the proliferation of rhetoric about Jews succeeds in establishing 'truths' about, or the reality of, Jewish traits and Jewish movement, MPs can proceed with relative impunity to make all sorts of claims about 'the Jew', investing the process of anti-immigration legislation with an empirical inevitability under which any specific political agenda is effectively submerged. Earlier, I cited Evans-Gordon's assertion that Jews themselves are the root cause of immigration. In the following speech before the Commons, Harry Lawson will further argue that Jews are the chief instigators of anti-immigration legislation. Here the mobility and mutability of the figure of the Jew is both productive and counterintuitive, permitting Lawson to transform a distinctly antisemitic law or rhetoric into an effectively philosemitic one, an extreme, but not unprecedented illustration of civil antisemitism. To support his arguments, Lawson reminds his colleagues that he himself is half-Jewish and, as such, could never vote for a law based on 'that damnable heritage from the Middle ages – the spirit of Jew hating and Jew baiting' (734). 'Happily', he declares, 'there has been no antisemitic feeling in this country'. Lawson's logic is as follows: a Jew cannot support antisemitism; if he, as a Jew, would vote for the law, then the law itself cannot be antisemitic. Rhetorically, his own Jewishness becomes both a metonymy for Britain's innocence, and the mechanism of his advocation against the very group from which he himself is descended.

Later, Lawson will explain to his colleagues that Jews themselves are among those who want restrictions placed on Jewish immigration. Using the apophasis I cited earlier in the essay, he states: 'I do not think it is necessary to point out that...Jews suffer from an invasion of people of their own faith whom they do not want to see here and who are an unnecessary burden' (735).[25] Indeed, Jewish desire for anti-immigration laws becomes the proof Lawson requires to depict support for immigration legislation as both manifestly unproblematic and philosemitic in nature: 'There is no question that those who have the longest heads and those who have most at heart the interest of the English Jews are not opposed to this Bill, and in fact are anxious to see this stain removed from the fair fame of those for whom they care so much' (735). If Lawson had earlier been a metonymy for the English, he now metaleptically becomes a stand-in for Jews in general, the Jewish spokesman for Jews who want to prohibit other Jews from landing in Britain. Indeed, the more the English Lawson enumerates his reasons for supporting legislation, the more the half-Jew Lawson transmogrifies into the Jew he cites, another Jew who wants Jews kept away from Britain. And so the half-Jew synecdochally becomes the whole Jew, calling for restrictions on Jewish immigration, and asking the Englishman to help out. Lawson's 'transformation', enacted on the rhetorical level of his speech, supports the thematic idea that Jewishness 'spreads' and 'takes over', simultaneously eliminating 'English' volition while expressing a fundamental 'truth' about the condition of immigration. Rhetorically, we can read his speech as both support for, and a symptom of, the hysteria over Jewish contagion. Politically, Lawson's advocacy of a Jewish position, his temporary inhabiting of Jewishness as a whole, ironically helps to legitimise desire for the Jew's exclusion. Thus, at one and the same time, the Jew vociferously spreads and proliferates, and politely requests to be contained – the paradoxical double figuration required by lawmakers, who fear both the Jew and charges of antisemitism.

Conclusion

The fervor that undergirds this type of rhetorical proliferation of 'the Jew' within immigration discourse demands that we recognize a crucial continuity between the highly veiled 'civil' antisemitism of anti-immigra- tionist parliamentarians such as Evans-Gordon and the more obviously rabid anti-Jewish demagoguery of later right-wing militants and organiza- tions such as Mosley and his British Union of Fascists. While the latter's invectives against Jews may be more familiar to scholars of antisemitism, Evans-Gordon's and the other parliamentarians' anti-alien agitations were perhaps just as dangerous, precisely because they appeared to be politically legitimate. This legitimacy was no mere by-product of anti-immigrationist arguments, but rather the necessary foundation of such argument, which could be politically and publicly persuasive only by appearing decisively unfanatical. Indeed, critical neglect of the techniques of civil antisemitism has led to an impasse in British studies: the failure to see, first, the integral role of antisemitism in centrist political and literary debates over English national identity and, second, how the prevalence of civil antisemitism in Britain left the British government and public unprepared to confront the growing malice toward Jews both in 1930s Germany and in Britain itself.

Notes

1. Holmes, *Anti-Semitism*, 89.
2. White, author of *The Modern Jew* (1899), was an ardent restrictionist and, in 1902, testified in favor of anti-immigration legislation before the Royal Commission on Alien Immigration (*RCAI*). For transcripts of his testimony, see *RCAI*, Minutes of Evidence, Vol. II (28 April 1902), 15–28. Mosley was founder of the British Union of Fascists.
3. Holmes, in his work on the British Brothers League, describes the reluctance of politicians, in particular leaders of the Tory Party, to be perceived as antisemitic or to be associated with groups that seemed to tolerate or promote antisemitic attitudes. 'Towards the end of 1902', he explains, 'anti-alien Tory MPs were

apparently warned [by Tory leaders] about their involvement with the British Brothers League' (*Anti-Semitism*, 92). Indeed, he tells us, '[t]he Tory Party...was quick to reprimand those MPs whose activity seemed to draw them towards sources [linked with antisemitism]' (26–27). The party's changing approach to antisemitism can be attributed, in part, to the fact that overt expressions of antisemitism were, during this period, increasingly considered unseemly for politicians, indeed, an affront to notions of British civility. Changing perceptions of the Jews' economic and social status also prompted politicians to avoid anti-Jewish sentiments. By 1904, parliamentarians had already begun to regard Jews as a potentially influential constituency, one that neither they, nor their political parties, could afford to offend.

4. For a synopsis of the anti-immigration movements and policies that immediately preceded the 1904 legislation, see Pellew, 'The Home Office'.

5. The 1904 bill was opposed by a majority of members of parliament, particularly those in the Liberal party, who argued, on the one hand, that the bill threatened a long-standing tradition of political asylum in Britain and, on the other hand, that the terms of the bill were too vague to be efficiently legislated. In the 1905 Act, which was drafted in response to criticism of the 1904 law, safeguards were established to protect immigrants seeking political or religious asylum, references to the moral character of immigrants were clarified, and the clause on the creation of prohibited areas for immigrants was eliminated.

6. Pellew, 'The Home Office', 369.

7. See, for instance, David Feldman's work on British politics and the formation of Anglo-Jewish communities in *Englishmen and Jews*.

8. Garrard, *The English and Immigration*, 57. See also Holmes, *Anti-Semitism*, 101 and 106.

9. 'Aliens Bill', *The Parliamentary Debates (Authorised Edition)*, Fourth Series, CXLV (London: Wyman & Sons, 1905), 2 May 1905, col. 735. All subsequent references to the parliamentary debates, unless otherwise noted, are from the Commons, and will be cited parenthetically in the text and in the endnotes by date and/or column number.

10. For additional details on Evans-Gordon's role in the shaping of the Aliens bills see M. J. Landa, *The Alien Problem and Its Remedy* (London: P. S. King & Son, 1911), 29–30, 175. According to Landa, Evans-Gordon, unlike White, 'was no doctrinaire politician, or demagogue appealing [to the public] with melodramatic phrases' (26); rather, he used 'the gift of clever argument' to convince parliament of the detrimental effects of the 'concentration of aliens' on native-born Englishmen and women (29).

11. William Evans-Gordon, *The Alien Immigrant* (London: William Heinemann, 1903), 7.

12. This slippage is noted by Holmes in his discussion of the anti-alien tirades of Robert Sherard. According to Holmes, 'Sherard did not spell out that his references [to aliens] were to Jews – although, in fact they were and his readers would have recognized them as such' (*Anti-Semitism*, 38).

13. Field, 'Anti-Semitism', 26.

14. Evans-Gordon, *The Alien Immigrant*, 11.

15. Evans-Gordon, *RCAI*, Vol. II, Minutes of Evidence, 2 May 1905, col. 716.

16. Evans-Gordon was a member of the Commission, as were Lord Rothschild, the Hon. Alfred Lyttelton, Sir Henry Norman, William Vallance, and Sir Kenelm Digby, Under-Secretary for the Home Department.

17. The 'East End' was one of many metonymies used by MPs in the course of the parliamentary debates to invoke Jews; others included areas of embarkation such as Russia, or more generally, Eastern Europe, and professions such as 'tailoring, cabinet-making and shoemaking' (2 May 1905, col. 730).
18. Felman, 'Education and Crisis', 3, 16.
19. We can explain the function of public testimony in the debates more fully as follows: the public provides evidence of an *experience* of events that is received and reiterated by parliamentarians as if it were simply testimony of the events themselves, and, more importantly, indication of the general impact of immigration within the public arena. Evans-Gordon emphasizes the importance of public testimony when he suggests to his fellow parliamentarians, during debates over the 1905 Act, that public accounts of immigrant activity generally offer a more accurate assessment of the problem of immigration than the numerical figures presented by institutions such as the Jewish Board of Guardians. Drawing attention to inconsistencies in the figures offered to the Royal Commission, he says that 'the case [for restrictions] does not rest upon these figures at all. It rests upon other evidence. Such evidence as our own senses; those of us who are familiar with the facts have senses, and they should not be despised' (716).
20. See for instance Holmes, *Anti-Semitism*, 37–40, 42; and Landa (*The Alien Problem*), who, by 1911, was already commenting on this tendency.
21. In associating trachoma with race, and with the Jewish 'race' in particular, Tyrrell disregards fully the contention, offered by other medical researchers of the period, that trachoma was in fact not an inherited, or distinctly 'racial' condition, but rather was spread by poor living conditions, especially overcrowding in urban areas. For Tyrrell's testimony see *RCAI*, Vol. II, Minutes of Evidence (29 May 1902), 127–129.
22. Quoted in *JC*, 6 December 1910, 8. The article originally appeared in the *Pall Mall Gazette* on 29 November 1901.
23. *RCAI*, Vol. II, Minutes of Evidence (31 July 1902).
24. Here we might call on Bakhtin's notion of grotesque realism to characterize the way in which Jews are constituted within rhetorical practice as that which exceeds the parameters or terms of the rhetoric itself (*Rabelais and His World*). In other words, what we have in that moment when the metaphor fails to contain the figure is the creation of a grotesque realism by linguistic means, even though no precise image of grotesqueness is ever evoked.
25. This sentiment is later echoed by Evans-Gordon, who describes the Jewish Board of Guardians' various attempts to discourage 'undesirable' Jews from immigrating to Britain.

4
Commerce, State, and Anti-Alienism: Balancing Britain's Interests in the Late-Victorian Period

Nicholas J. Evans

At the end of the nineteenth century, Britain governed one-quarter of the globe; her merchant and naval fleets ruled the waves. Yet despite being the most powerful industrial nation on earth, Britain panicked in the last decades of the Victorian era, as inward migration from Eastern Europe began to dominate its political and manufacturing heartlands. With foreign culture and commerce increasingly infiltrating the East End of London, the Leylands area of Leeds, and the Gorbals district of Glasgow, the more Conservative newspapers and their anti-alien spokesmen began to question Britain's policy of unrestricted asylum.[1] By 1902 there was sufficient political support to bring about a parliamentary review of immigration in the form of a Royal Commission on Alien Immigration.[2] Yet the proposals by the Conservative party to restrict alien immigration in the 1900s threatened Britain's liberal policies of asylum and free trade which had brought about much of Britain's economic strength.

This chapter demonstrates that commerce was as crucial to late-Victorian culture as anti-alienism: it is impossible to understand how the restrictions on immigration were gradually introduced in the late nineteenth century without recognizing the balancing act that stood behind them. The first section considers the crucial economic aspects of the passenger shipping business and the fears that the British merchant marine, already reeling from the effects of intense foreign competition, would be unduly hindered by the impact of draconian passenger shipping legislation. The role played by these commercial considerations in the making of the Aliens Act suggests that the vocal opposition of right-wing MPs was neutered in order to preserve Britain's liberal trading interests. The chapter then moves on to examine the evidence presented to the Royal Commission by maritime and medical authorities, and reproduced by the media. Although these findings were not typical of the experience of the majority of migrants, they were instrumental in reinforcing contemporary associations between disease and race, leading to longer-term medical racialization at the Edwardian quayside. Placing Britain's response to alien immigration in the wider context of self-governing dominion states within the British Empire, the final section of this chapter will ask why some states introduced restricted immigration while others retained more liberal policies. The imperial relationship – Britain as an imperial power, not just as a domestic entity – adds another dimension to the interplay between these three elements – state, commerce, and anti-alienism. While British politicians sought to impose restrictions on alien migration into Britain, transmigration to the dominions was seen as an indispensable by-product of free trade in which British participation was to be encouraged.

The growth of passenger shipping and the emergence of anti-alienism

Most Europeans arrived in Britain via the Humber ports. Travelling third class as transmigrants, they were expected to leave Britain within 14 days of arrival. They chose to migrate to the United States, Canada, or South Africa via Britain because they deemed it cheaper, quicker, or safer than to journey on those direct emigrant services provided by Britain's competitors based in Hamburg, Bremen, Rotterdam, Antwerp, Copenhagen, and Le Havre. Hull was their main point of entry, Liverpool the main port of departure. The overland journey between these two ports was catered for by the provision of third-class trains called 'emigrant specials'. Others came via the Thames, arriving on immigrant tickets, hoping to purchase a ticket for the next stage of their journey upon arrival in London. It was this latter flow of aliens that came under the greatest scrutiny in the Parliamentary debates of the 1900s.

The question of restricting immigration was nothing new at the time of the Royal Commission. During times of political crises – like the French Revolution and the Napoleonic Wars – Britain had revised the Aliens Act that had first been introduced in 1793 to protect the country from the perceived political dangers of revolutionary Europe.[3] Following the passing of the 1836 Aliens Act, the movement of people was to be monitored at all of the major points of entry, with quarterly returns sent by passenger ports to the Home Office (and, after 1873, to the Board of Trade). These figures enabled the government to quantify the scale and character of the alien influx.[4] Yet the Act had ceased to be an effective indicator of alien movement by the late 1850s. When large-scale immigration emerged in the late Victorian period, officials' failure to quantify the problem caused popular concern. The 1888 Select Committee on the Immigration and Emigration of Foreigners concluded that more reliable data needed to be collated on the various movements into, through, or from Britain.[5] After May 1890, the results were presented annually to Parliament.[6] Nevertheless, even this data showed regional variation in the accuracy of the information returned. As a report by the Board of Trade to the House of Commons noted in April 1892, 'with so vast a passenger movement as that to and from the United Kingdom it would probably be impossible to obtain a minutely complete return'.[7] While government statisticians could generate volumes of data on diverse topics ranging from railway accidents to the scale of guano imports, maintaining an accurate account of alien arrivals into Britain was seemingly beyond the capabilities of late-Victorian bureaucracy. To those concerned with the appearance of concentrated pockets of foreigners in Britain's major urban areas, this was a danger associated with Britain's liberal asylum policy.

Such weaknesses were of particular significance in London, where many of those arriving were classed as 'immigrants', even though they were actually transmigrants. This mislabelling fuelled tension, since it led to the perception that immigration was far higher than it was in reality. As one Edwardian noted, unrestricted asylum, particularly as the influx was dominated by Jews, would enable Jewish influence to dominate British commerce as it had already done in Italy. In the frontispiece of his copy of W.H. Wilkins's *The Alien Immigrant* (1892), this anonymous individual noted that the long-term effect would be the emergence of 'Cosmopolitan Jewry' whose 'great object is the *Business & financial control* of the World'.[8] Politicians like William Evans-Gordon (Conservative MP for the Stepney Division of Tower Hamlets, and member of the Royal Commission) and Harry Samuel (Conservative MP for the Limehouse Division of Tower Hamlets) were quick to cash in on these anxieties: maximizing the ambiguity of official passenger statistics, they highlighted the increased presence of the foreign-born population in key areas of London and Britain's industrial heartlands. Such anti-alienists pointed out that it was necessary to restrict immigration to ensure that British workers would not have their wages reduced by aliens under-pricing their services. If only the influence of the foreign menace could be minimized, they argued, Britain would remain firmly British.

Nevertheless, there were other issues to consider – issues that were equally critical for Britain's political interests and imperial standing. After all, the idea of restricting alien entry and thus reducing passenger traffic posed a serious threat to British commerce, challenging the liberal policy of free trade which had benefited British maritime expansion since the repeal of the Navigation Laws in 1851. Britain's ship-owners had emerged during the nineteenth century as the largest providers of passenger shipping. Though the market was highly competitive, companies like Cunard, White Star, Union-Castle, Allan, Anchor, and Guion helped to turn the British mercantile marine into the most powerful merchant fleet on earth. As the *Fortnightly Review* noted in 1903, Britain and her Empire had 8,532 steamships registered under their flag, Germany 1,365, the United States 1,094, France 630, and Russia 544.[9] Yet while Britain's share of the inter-continental market had grown, her dominance of the intra-European trade had weakened, as European nations invested heavily to develop their shipping interests. By 1900, the short-sea routes to Britain were largely in the hands of German, Dutch, Danish, Belgian, and French lines. Though Britain shared the Baltic routes with Germany and Denmark, and continued to dominate the Scandinavian routes, expanding foreign fleets controlled the main North Sea routes upon which immigrants were conveyed to Britain.[10]

In other words, any restriction on the shipment of aliens to Britain from the Baltic (and from Europe in general) threatened to lessen Britain's involvement in intra-continental passenger shipping even further. It would have done so by reducing the revenue generated through transporting immigrants (or by impairing the quick turn around of migrant-carrying vessels), and, even more crucially, by threatening the supply of transmigrants who, after arriving in Britain – often on the same boats as immigrants – sailed from Britain elsewhere. These transmigrants were needed to fill third class steerage berths on ocean liners leaving Liverpool, Glasgow, London, or Southampton. Indeed, to retain the commercial advantage, Britain's steamship operators were building ever-larger vessels. New crafts launched during the Edwardian era – such as *Aquitania*, *Olympic*, or *Mauretania* – cost huge sums of money to build, maintain, and operate. Too large to transport British emigrants only, their future success relied on the constant supply of European transmigrants, needed to fill the third class compartments.[11]

The significance of these huge ocean liners was not merely commercial. It is enough to read Kipling's poem, 'The Secret of the Machines', to realize that vessels like Cunard's *Mauretania*, launched in 1906, were seen as mighty symbols of British imperial power.[12] Since 1840, Britain had held the coveted Blue Riband, the award given for the fastest transatlantic crossing. But in 1897 the situation changed when Germany successfully challenged Britain's supremacy with Norddeutscher Lloyd's *Kaiser Wilhelm der Grosse*, which emerged as the fastest vessel afloat. German companies, namely the Norddeutscher Lloyd and the Hamburg-America Lines, subsequently won for the ensuing nine years.[13]

Paradoxically, then, it was precisely the anti-alien cause – keeping Britain British – that threatened to undermine a symbol of Britain's mercantile strength by reducing her commercial position and hindering the business of ports such as London, Glasgow, Liverpool, and Southampton (from which transmigrants left Britain). As maritime historian Francis Hyde has noted, 'The fear of the foreigner had been transferred from the purely political into that of an economic environment. In the field of shipping, foreign competition was at first a convenient scapegoat [for Britain's narrowing commercial lead over Europe]; but it later became an effective basis for pressure to be exerted on the Government to obtain reductions in the irksome passenger regulations.'[14] With the emergence of anti-alien sentiment, as the Royal Commission was scrutinizing the business of migration and as Conservative

MPs looked certain to limit Britain's domination of transatlantic passenger shipping by restricting *all* aliens who arrived in Britain – no wonder that those engaged in the 'legitimate' business of transmigration leapt to its defence. Men like Charles Henry Wilson (Liberal MP for West Hull) and Christopher Furness (Liberal MP for Hartlepool), who had accrued substantial wealth through their shipping concerns, championed free trade – wishing, of course, to maintain their own lucrative businesses.

Interestingly, not all shipping moguls rejected the anti-alien cause. For example, Charles Wilson's nephew, Arthur Stanley Wilson (the Conservative MP for the East Riding of Yorkshire), voted against Furness and Charles Wilson in many of the debates on the Aliens Bill. It seems that for him, party loyalty was more important than the income he derived through this aspect of his family's business.[15] Similarly, although he was a member of a prominent Anglo-Jewish family, Harry Samuel – who joined Evans-Gordon's campaign – preferred 'English' sentiments to sympathy with his co-religionists.

Medical evidence and the Royal Commission on alien immigration

The anti-alien Conservatives captured their opponents' seats by emphasizing the alien menace, the 'foreignness' infiltrating Britain's inner cities. The alien was depicted as dirty, inferior, a threat to British workers;[16] but the most alarming feature was the notion of the alien as a carrier of pestilence. Indeed, for Evans-Gordon, the medical evidence presented to the Royal Commission was as crucial as evidence about East End working and living conditions.

As we have seen, the immigrant market had, by the end of the nineteenth century, become dominated by foreign companies.[17] Nevertheless, despite fears expressed about the medical dangers associated with the conveyance of migrants on these foreign-owned vessels, the majority of immigrants arrived in a relatively good standard of ships. Foreign fleets were controlled in terms of sanitation, ship design, and passenger comfort by comparable merchant legislation as British-registered vessels; standards varied, but on the whole, the merchant fleets of Holland, Belgium, France, Germany, Norway, and Sweden did not pose the medical threat of infiltrating the British capital with disease on a similar scale to that which had brought the Hanseatic port of Hamburg to near disaster in 1892.[18]

There was, however, one noticeable exception – those passengers carried under the Danish flag from Russia to Britain. Vessels of Det Forenede Dampskib Selskab (DFDS) had transported emigrants between the Baltic port of Libau and the British capital since 1893, enabling Denmark to retain a share of the 'Jewish market' by conveying emigrants from the Pale of Settlement direct to Hull or to London without calling in at a Danish port *en route*. When the Kiel Canal was opened in 1895, the number of vessels destined for Britain via this Baltic route increased, as the journey was reduced from five to six days to three to four days. The passengers were transported in the 'tween decks of ships not designed for this purpose. Since the Danish-owned vessels did not enter Danish ports, the medical dangers associated with the trade never created concern within Denmark, the country under whose maritime laws the DFDS was regulated. Under a loophole in international law, flouting the standards with which British-registered vessels had to comply on a regular basis, the Danish vessels left passengers exposed to the evils associated with ocean travel in the early nineteenth century.[19]

Not surprisingly, it would be the vessels of the DFDS that would be selected by Evans-Gordon for closer scrutiny by the Royal Commission. Like his careful use of members of the British Brothers' League to answer questions on life in London's East End, Evans-Gordon provided the Royal Commission with exceptional, atypical evidence to gain maximum exposure. Here, for example, is the evidence presented to the Royal Commission by the Port of London's Medical Officer of Health, Dr. H. Williams:

On the 21st May [1902] the ss. 'Hengest,' of Aarhus, from Libau, arrived at Gravesend with 171 Russian immigrants. The vessel left Libau on the 17th May. The immigrants were carried in the after main 'tween decks in a space with a total capacity of 7,172.9 cubic feet, giving 50.16 cubic feet per head only. The total floor space measured 393.3 square feet, an area of 2.3 square feet only per head being available. The quarters occupied by the immigrants were in a filthy condition, the floors being strewn with all kinds of refuse, and offensive liquid from the horses carried on the same deck had leaked through into these quarters. No attempt had been made at cleansing this space since the vessel had left Libau. Two temporary closets were provided, and both were used indiscriminately by the sexes. The only ventilation provided was by means of the bunker hatchways, and by two 12-inch ventilators, one of which was without a cowl, and closed.[20]

Medical Officers in Hull had regularly complained about aliens being shipped in horrific standards; indeed, it was in Hull in 1882, and not in London, that the issue of diseased alien arrivals had first caused political concern.[21] Yet in the lengthy published minutes from the Royal Commission, the obsession with matters affecting Thames-based arrivals implied that the problem centred on London, the Imperial metropolis.

Evidence from DFDS vessels was also employed by Evans-Gordon in his best-selling book *The Alien Immigrant*, which described, in alarmist terms, what was allegedly a typical journey of Jews from departure in a Baltic port to arrival in Britain. Although his description of the DFDS was contradicted by Albert Kinross in the *Pall Mall Gazette*, both writers perpetuated the perceived links between Jewish passengers and the conditions from which disease would emanate.[22]

In fact, the problems associated with diseased aliens arriving in Britain had been monitored since the passing of the 1872 and 1875 General Health Acts, long before the beginning of mass Jewish immigration.[23] Moreover, the conditions on board were as applicable to Slavs, Finns, Lithuanians, Rumanians, and Hungarians arriving in Britain as they were to Jewish immigrants.[24] No single vessel was known to have conveyed only Jewish immigrants, but, since the majority of their human cargo was increasingly of the Jewish faith, Jews were seen as the main carriers of disease.[25]

Attempts to curtail immigration through using such medical evidence at the time of the Royal Commission did, however, serve some useful purpose.[26] After the findings on the poor state of Danish vessels were heard and subsequently published, the Danish government intervened and brought about much-needed improvements – most probably because the company was a source of national pride. Although the problems associated with the trade – overcrowding, the lack of adequate sanitary arrangements, and the carriage of horses in the same part of the vessels as passengers – were reduced, such conditions might have been eradicated far sooner had British government officials simply contacted their Danish counterparts with sufficient medical evidence.

The lack of intervention in the trade during the late 1890s surely raises questions about whether or not Presidents of the Board of Trade – who were preoccupied with profit derived from transmigrants conveyed to Britain – placed the interests of British trade ahead of those of the Home Office. Why did British diplomats not adequately intervene when the problem first surfaced? What was the reason for Britain not seeking to reduce the risks associated with maritime trade? Why was Britain unable to prohibit the arrival of high-risk vessels? The answer might lie in the difficulties of communication between government departments and the numerous layers of bureaucracy. But it is also arguable that action was only taken once the issue of the conditions in which passengers travelled to Britain had become a *commercial* threat. As George Harwood (MP for Bolton) noted during the reading of the Aliens Bill:

> Within the last few months he had seen advertisements at railway stations in Russia and Germany warning emigrants that it would be very much better not to go through England, but to go direct by German lines, because they would have less trouble. Unless the conditions to which we subjected them were civilised the trade would be driven away. It was perfectly absurd for the Government to try to ride two horses. They were pretending to do something, but they would not pay the money to do it properly.[27]

When the findings of the Royal Commission were published in 1903, it seemed to British ship-owners – and those engaged in the support industries of victualling, shipbuilding, and railways – that Britain's commercial interests would be challenged not by the advancement of the American or Imperial German merchant fleets, but by anti-alien sentiment in the East End of London.

Yet despite such vocal consternation, measures designed to protect trade and not domestic interests took precedence in the three months prior to the passing of the Aliens Act. Powers to restrict, or at least police, passenger shipping were watered down by MPs keen to defend free trade. Charles Wilson, Christopher Furness, and Austin Taylor (MP for Bootle) each raised questions in the House designed to draw attention to the damaging effects of the anti-alien cause.[28] Despite Evans-Gordon's scare tactics, when the Aliens Act was finally passed in August 1905, it had been mitigated sufficiently for even the opposing Liberals to endorse it. While the Act forced companies involved in the trade to purchase Bonds ensuring the alien remain genuinely in transit, and restricted the trade to a limited number of ports, the business was not unduly hampered. On the passing of the final amendment affecting transmigration, in May 1905, Charles Wilson asserted that 'the Home Secretary is not likely to hurt our legitimate transmigrant trade'.[29] How true: having finally achieved what three Parliaments had failed to enact, Britain's first piece of alien legislation for sixty-nine years had been watered down sufficiently for Britain's commercial interests to triumph over domestic Conservative policy.

The Aliens Act and increased racial scrutiny

From a shipping perspective, the Aliens Act was not seen as a source of concern. Memoranda had to be re-sent to various shipping lines and their port-side agents during 1906 to remind them that they had to register and comply with the terms introduced under the Act. However, with the status of an immigrant ship varying according to which Home Secretary was in power, the main effect of the Act was the accumulation of more reliable data at Britain's registered ports of entry. Finally beginning to record the true picture of alien migration – demonstrating that the majority of aliens were actually transmigrants – the new statistical returns made under the Aliens Act also showed the declining importance of London in transatlantic passenger shipping.

But the Act had another, more disturbing, effect: the growing awareness of Jewish identity in the eyes of medical and commercial agents. Anti-Jewish and anti-alien racial sentiments were exacerbated, propelled by the Royal Commission to the forefront of contemporary opinion. The application of the regulations laid out in the 1906 Merchant Shipping Act – which required the documentation of aliens passing through Britain's ports – revealed an increasing level of racial scrutiny in some ports (though not in all). For example, at the Scottish port of Glasgow, the so-called 'second city of

Empire', alien transmigrants and non-transmigrants (alien emigrants who had been residing in Britain) were now labelled in both ethnic *and* national terms, rather than just the latter. Such classification was not the result of the inconsistent application of government policy by government employees, but rather the work of clerks of those companies that shipped aliens across the Atlantic. The agents taking bookings tended more and more to label Scottish-born and English-born Jewish emigrants who had immigrant parents as alien Jews or Hebrews.

This racial tagging was relatively new, a by-product of increased racial awareness which was also found in the Annual Reports of the Operations of the Sanitary Department for Glasgow.[30] Although large numbers of Russians (mainly Jews and Finns) had passed through the port of Glasgow as early as the 1840s, they were never then labelled as Jews or Hebrews.[31] The Chief Sanitary Inspector referred to such migrants as 'persons coming from Russian ports'.[32] But this changed after 1899: diseases such as typhus, trachoma, and cholera arriving with immigrants via the port of London would be linked with Jews leaving Scottish ports. Those isolated, as the following entry demonstrates, were identified by race and not just nationality: 'The fumigation by the Shipping Companies of emigrants' baggage from the Continent has again been resorted to, but only in the case of luggage from foreign ports where Russian Jews embarked.'[33] These tendencies were reinforced after 1906 and became more widespread throughout other British ports.

Such racial labelling was also imposed by commercial agencies.[34] Jewish passengers would be the only group identified by race rather than nationality.[35] Although the Allan Line would be the first company to record racial status, they were followed a year later by their Clydeside competitor, the Anchor Line.[36] In 1906 such labelling allows us to identify that Jewish emigrants represented 16 per cent (370 out of 2,274 passengers) of the Allan Line's third-class transmigrant contingent, while for the Anchor Line Jews represented 24 per cent (2,937 out of 12,336 passengers) of their transmigrant customers.[37] Though the number of Jews migrating through Scotland had declined to 678 by 1908, they still formed 22 per cent of the continental transmigrant business undertaken by both companies.[38]

By 1909 the racial labelling had apparently ceased to be of importance to the Glasgow Sanitary Department, as the trade in Russian transmigrants had declined significantly.[39] Yet on the Board of Trade's passenger lists, such ethnic labelling continued.[40] What had begun as an occasional reference to 'Hebrew', 'Jewish' or 'Jew' in the years preceding the Aliens Act developed between 1908 and 1914 into a constant feature of the ethnicity recorded of aliens leaving Scotland's premier ports (Glasgow and Greenock).[41] In 1910, 288 transmigrants and 199 non-transmigrant aliens were identified in the passenger lists as being Jewish (see Table 4.1):[42] the lists, more detailed in this year than for other years, described 14 types of Jews or Hebrews – often prefixed with their nationality.

Table 4.1 Jewish Emigrants appearing in the passenger lists of ships leaving Glasgow and Greenock in 1910 for non-European destinations

Label	Non-Transmigrant	Transmigrant
Russian Jew	138	222
Russian Hebrew	15	24
Austrian Jew	1	23
Austrian Hebrew	0	6
British Jew	1	0
British Jew (born in Scotland)	10	0
Russian Jew (born in Scotland)	12	0
Russian Jew (born in England)	7	0
Russian Hebrew (born in Scotland)	5	0
Russian Hebrew (born in England)	0	0
Polish Jew	1	0
Hungarian Hebrew	0	9
Hebrew	0	2
German Jew	0	2
Total	190	288

Source: Digital photographs of original passenger lists held at The National Archives, BT/27/646–649.
These images have been sampled by the author as part of a project to examine out-migration from Scotland between 1890 and 1960 at the AHRC Centre for Irish and Scottish Studies, University of Aberdeen.

Such ethnic labelling, supplied by the commercial agents of the Anchor and Allan Lines, was not a requirement of the Board of Trade. Glasgow's shipping companies participated in this form of racialized demography because of the increased awareness of the financial costs associated with shipping passengers back to the European port of embarkation (at the shipping company's expense) if the immigrants were rejected by the U.S. Immigration Service as medically unfit. As medical historian Kenneth Collins has demonstrated, the port of Glasgow was the main source of those rejected due to trachoma.[43] Yet it can also be argued that for the Edwardian shipping companies, the label 'Jew' in general was equated with commercial hazard because of the perceived greater risks of disease.

Ethnic labelling was not the only way of identifying such hazardous passengers. In a printed advertisement dated 1910, the Canadian Pacific Railway stated 'NO FOREIGNERS EXCEPT SCANDINAVIANS CARRIED THIRD CLASS FROM LIVERPOOL'.[44] Scandinavian emigrants – always regarded in Parliamentary debates and the Royal Commission as being of a healthier, 'more acceptable class' – were to be conveyed without difficulty. Yet Jews, and Russian Jews in particular, were not to be carried on at least Canadian ships. While advertisements for the Canadian Pacific's ocean liners may have been openly racist, few companies promoted their Jewish credentials.[45]

It is possible that this evidence from medical and other official records at Glasgow represents a personal or localized response to the alien immigrants. After all, while sectarianism was the by-product of the mass Irish immigration into Liverpool and Glasgow during the earlier part of the nineteenth century, Jewry in Scotland as a whole did not seem to experience antisemitic prejudice at first hand.[46] What is certain, however, is that attitudes varied throughout cognate parts of Britain – as they did throughout Britain's Empire.

The alien menace and Britain's Empire

Concerns about the alien problem were not limited to Britain. In the United States, Germany, France, and many parts of the British Empire the problem of race had caused widespread alarm. During the 1880s prejudice over coloured immigrants, particularly Chinese, led the United States to pass the Chinese Exclusion Act (1882). It was followed by similar acts in Canada, Victoria, South Australia, Tasmania, and New Zealand.[47] In the late 1890s this anti-alienism was increasingly directed towards East Europeans of non-Teutonic origin.

In the British Empire, responses to the 'non-colour' race question varied. Australia passed the Immigration Restriction Act in 1901, and New Zealand passed a revised Aliens Act in 1908. Both have been seen as colonial racism against the non-whites via policies designed to retain such colonial outposts as 'British'.[48] In Canada, the 1906 and 1910 Immigration Acts were intended to prevent the immigration of political, moral, physical, or criminally undesirable aliens – bringing the country in line with the 1891 U.S. Immigration Act. In South Africa, home to a large number of Litvak Jewish migrants, the authorities responded in a similar manner to Britain, seeking to limit Jewish immigration, particularly during the political crisis of the Boer War. By contrasting the South African response to Jewish migration with Canadian attitudes, the final section of this chapter will consider the interplay between liberal trading policies and conservative immigration policies in the imperial context.

Between 1880 and 1900, the Jewish population in South Africa grew from 4,000 to approximately 10,000.[49] While the immigrant Jewish community was scattered throughout the Cape and Natal provinces, concentrated pockets of Jewish settlement emerged in Johannesburg, where they began to present a visible ethnic enclave. In Cape Town, South Africa's major point of entry for immigrants, the community intermingled successfully with other aliens in the District 6 region; but the continued influx of Jews throughout the late 1890s began to cause alarm within some sectors of Cape society, especially after the Jewish population had reached a critical mass in excess of 10,000. During the Boer War, the complexities of racial tensions within the war-torn colony meant that resentment against the foreign-born population – especially the Jewish community, but also Indians – became more vocal and virulent than in any other part of the British Empire.

The restriction of Jewish immigration was seen both as a political and economic defensive measure. The Prime Minister of the Cape Colony, Sir Gordon Sprigg, sought to achieve this through a number of measures: in September 1901 he asked London for martial law to be extended to South Africa's ports of entry, and – once this was approved, not without 'difference of opinion'[50] – he requested further powers to restrict dangerous races, namely, Jews and Indians. The British authorities, however, were not thrilled. In response to this request, the Colonial Secretary, Joseph Chamberlain, wrote to the High Commissioner, Alfred Milner:

> You should inform your Ministers that it does not appear to be possible to differentiate against nationality or colour under the permit regulations but that their views have been communicated to the India Office who have been requested to acquaint the Government of India that it is desirable that due circumspection should be exercised in furnishing permits to Indians about whose means to maintaining themselves any doubt may exist as presence in Cape Colony in existing circumstances is deprecated by the authorities there. His Majesty's Consul, Riga, has been communicated with in a similar sense with regard to Polish Jews in view of your telegram of 6th December, No.1.[51]

On the other hand, when the British Foreign Secretary, the Marquess of Lansdowne, advocated the temporary cessation of *all* migration to the Cape in 1902, this was not deemed necessary by the Cape authorities: 'The Cape Government evidently wish that no difficulty should be placed in the way of the immigration to the Colony of a certain class. Viz: – British working men, clerks and shepherds. For whom there is great demand'.[52]

Such views on the need for British immigrants, who were seen as loyal to the British crown, stood in stark contrast to those concerning Polish Jews – the so-called Peruvians. When Europeans, particularly Jewish immigrants, continued to arrive in Cape Town after the introduction of a visa requirement (and possession of £100) in 1902, Chamberlain was asked to intervene. His actions showed that Britain wielded little control over officials representing the State in Europe, and particularly in Russia. Despite the apparent need for documentation and possession of funds to prevent them becoming a fiscal burden, migrants were rarely checked by British consular representatives before embarkation. Too many were still arriving: when the *Goth* landed in Cape Town with 32 impoverished Jews onboard, the Cape authorities heavily criticized the British administration.[53] Although martial law came to an end in September 1902, the British authorities had shown an inability to control the issuance of permits or flow of aliens from British ports, and similar disregard for the Cape authority's desire to control her own ports during the Boer War. While British politicians sought to restrict immigrants from entering Britain, transmigration to South Africa was seen as a by-product of free trade in which British participation was to be encouraged.

The Cape Colony was not the only part of the Empire whose complaints over domestic immigration matters were ignored by Britain during the period. Britain, as the Imperial nation, showed similar disregard for the interests of other dominions - perhaps a reason why many sought to legislate on the topic of immigration as soon as they had reached sufficient maturity to be granted self-governing status and thus control their own immigrant policy. Overall it would be Britain's liberal attitude to the conservatism expressed in parts of the Empire that continued to cause the greatest resentment. Indeed, far from being confined to Colonial Parliamentarians or to political correspondence, hostile attitudes to foreigners arriving *en masse* became increasingly visible in newspapers and popular publications. As Marjory Harper noted,

> Basil Stewart's pamphlet, published in 1909 and entitled *No English Need Apply: Or, Canada, as a Field for the Emigrant*... pulled no punches in his vilification of the immigration authorities for 'frightening away the better and well-conducted classes of Englishmen and women, and attracting only the hewer of wood and drawer of water of other nations', thereby causing Canada to lose 'that cultured and refining influence of which she stands much in need'. 'Russian and Galician Jews, Greeks, Germans, Dutch, Poles, Hungarians, Italians... Syrians and Turks... are not the kind of material from which the British Empire has been made, nor of which it should be built in the future'.[54]

Canada, however, did not show the degree of anti-Jewish sentiment expressed in South Africa, perhaps because the small Jewish community was dispersed throughout the country. As the *Jewish Yearbook* showed in 1896, the country's 3,711 Jews were spread out accordingly: Quebec (2,703), Ontario (2,501), Manitoba (743), British Columbia (277), North West Territories (85), New Brunswick (73), Nova Scotia (31) and Prince Edward Island (just 1).[55] This confirmed what the Canadian Prime Minister had originally conceived when he had authorized immigration officials to allocate land for Jewish agricultural settlers: a 'sprinkling of Jews in the Northwest would be good' for they would 'at once go in for peddling and politicking, and be of much use in the new country as cheap jacks and chapmen'.[56]

Canada's positive response towards Jewish immigrants could be traced back to 1882, when the Canadian High Commissioner Alexander Galt attended a London Mansion House meeting to discuss the plight of Russian Jews under the Tsarist regime and how the settlement of refugees in Manitoba could assist those who had fled state-sponsored persecution. Recognizing the benefits that Canada could gain from being a haven to the oppressed, he decided – unlike his South African counterparts – to accept a number of the migrants. Consequently, many of those arriving in Canada after 1882 did so under schemes organized by the London Mansion House Committee or Baron de Hirsch's schemes which provided for the needs of aliens before and after they had arrived in their place of settlement.[57]

Instead of the Jewish alien being perceived as a menace, as Valerie Knowles has noted, it was the influx of Europeans Slavs (particularly Hungarians) from eastern and central Europe which had a profound impact upon the Canadian labour markets and which consequently became the cause of popular resentment. It was something about which the Canadian Trades and Labour Congress grew increasingly alarmed, echoing concerns similar to those expressed by British Trade Unions about the Jewish influx into Britain: 'As far as the congress was concerned, only rigorous enforcement of the [Alien Labour Act] would prevent Canada from being inundated with "ignorant, unfortunate... non-English speaking aliens," who do irreparable damage to the community.'[58] Canada, in short, showed wider concern for protectionism based upon ethnicity, than upon antisemitism.

Conclusion

Although the Aliens Act did not decrease the number of alien migrants travelling to Britain, it ultimately defined the numbers, nationality, and destination of those arriving at and departing British ports each year. What the medical evidence – presented to the Royal Commission, and reproduced in contemporary newspapers and journals – failed to highlight was that far more aliens arrived through ports outside London than ever arrived via the Thames. However it was precisely by drawing attention to politically-concentrated zones, such as the East End of London, that anti-alienists were able to challenge Britain's national policy of free trade.

Nevertheless, the intervention of MPs with vested interests in passenger shipping protected the transmigrant trade as the immigrant trade became increasingly restricted by Edwardian legislation. Charles Wilson described the trade as being that of Scandinavians and Russians, without reference to religion or ethnicity; he protected the market by championing trade rather than race. To be sure, unlike William Evans-Gordon, Wilson benefited greatly from the alien market; but his rhetorical stance on immigration is as important to the understanding of attitudes towards aliens as the more noted impact of Evans-Gordon. Indeed, even when anti-alienism was at its height, Britain would always place her commercial well-being at the forefront of government policy.

Attitudes towards immigration in the late-Victorian period were characterized, in other words, by a political balancing act: both sides of the political divide failed to control the issue of aliens confidently. On the one hand, the Liberals delayed Conservatism within the Empire, yet could not stop it once countries such as New Zealand and Australia had gained self-government. On the other hand, the Conservatives' policy on immigration (demonstrated at the time of the Royal Commission) was watered down due to the business interests of Liberal MPs. The Conservative administration introduced a piece of legislation that would be immediately enforced by a new Liberal Government in 1906. Once in power, the Liberals oscillated over what was deemed an immigrant ship; at times they appeared more conservative than their political opponents, and even considered, in 1910, the introduction of a London version of an Ellis Island.[59] For lawmakers on both sides of the political fence, balancing Britain's interests – commercial, domestic and foreign – was thus a difficult prospect, anticipating a century of similar difficulties.

Notes

Research for this chapter was undertaken as part of a Caird Research Fellowship at the National Maritime Museum (2000–02) and during a Research Assistantship at the AHRC Centre for Irish & Scottish Studies based at the University of Aberdeen (2003–05). Financial assistance was provided by the University of Hull, the Institute of Migration in Finland, and the Kaplan Centre at the University of Cape Town. I would like to thank Professor Aubrey Newman, Debbie Beavis, Dr Angela McCarthy, and Dr Sheila Boll for their assistance with this chapter.

1. Winston Churchill, MP, stated during the debates on the Aliens Bill that it was only in these districts 'that the alien question had produced a problem of a grave and complex character'. *The Parliamentary Debates (Authorised Edition)*, Fourth Series, CVLVII (London: Wyman & Sons, 1905), 858.
2. British Parliamentary Papers (BPP), *Royal Commission on Alien Immigration (RCAI)* (London: HMSO, 1903), Vols I–V.
3. The original Bill was revised in 1814, 1815, 1816, 1826, and 1836.
4. BPP, Board of Trade (Alien Immigration), *Reports on the Volume and Effects of Recent Immigration from Eastern Europe into the United Kingdom* (London: HMSO, 1894), 2.
5. The conclusions of this Committee were later summarized in the Board of Trade's *Reports on the Volume*, 2. The report of the 1888 Committee, by Sir William Thackeray Marriott, was published in 1889; see *Select Committee on Emigration and Immigration (Foreigners)* XI.419. The findings of this investigation caused the re-enforcement of the 1836 Act in 1890. See *RCAI*, Minutes of Evidence, Vol. II, M.28 (London: HMSO, 1903).
6. The operation of the previous Aliens Act was altered slightly by Orders issued by the Board of Trade in 1890 and 1894. See Nicholas J. Evans, 'Indirect Passage'.
7. *Copy of the Statistical Tables Relating to Emigration and Immigration from and into the United Kingdom in the year 1891, and the Report to the Board of Trade Thereon by Henry G. Calcraft* (London: HMSO, 1892), 12.

8. Part of 12 pages of anonymous comments written in 1910 and contained within the inside cover of a copy of W. H. Wilkins, *The Alien Invasion* (London: Methuen, 1892), later deposited in the University of Aberdeen's library. The same commentator also disliked the influence of the Catholic Church.

9. J. L. Bashford, 'The German Mercantile Marine', *Fortnightly Review*, 73 (1903), 288.

10. *Report of the Departmental Committee on the Establishment of a Receiving-House for Alien Immigrants at the Port of London: Volume I, Report and Appendix* (1911, X.87), 103; Nicholas J. Evans, 'Aliens *en Route*'.

11. During the debates on restricting alien immigration, Christopher Furness (MP for Hartlepool and a ship-owner) noted that the government had awarded the Cunard Steamship Company £2,000,000 as a subsidy for maintaining the large emigration trade between Britain and the United States See *Parliamentary Debates*, CVLVII, 870.

12. Rudyard Kipling, 'The Secret of the Machines (Modern Machinery)', in *Rudyard Kipling's Verse, Inclusive Edition, 1885–1918* (London: Hodder & Stoughton, 1921), 766–767. The verse was first published in 1911, five years after the launch of *Mauretania* and a year after she had won the Blue Riband.

13. Lee, *The Blue Riband*, 231–235.

14. Hyde, *Cunard*, 95.

15. It is telling that Charles Henry Wilson and his brother Arthur considered their sons ill equipped to manage the family firm when they retired. Instead, they appointed a Managing Director (Oswald Sanderson) over the company from 1902.

16. Cf. Joseph O'Brien, 'Some Types of Russian Aliens, Drawn from the Life in the East End of London', *English Illustrated Magazine*, 33 (1905), 585.

17. An opinion confirmed by Newcastle MP, George Renwick, during the Committee meetings discussing the Aliens Bill. See *Parliamentary Debates*, CVLVII, 346.

18. Richard J. Evans, *Death in Hamburg*.

19. Coleman, *Passage to America*, 100–118.

20. *RCAI*, Minutes of Evidence, Volume II, M.6, 176.

21. The issue was raised in the House of Commons, but the subsequent report that was published by Parliament placed Britain's commercial interests ahead of the needs of the alien passengers. *Reports by the Board of Trade and Local Government Board relating to the Transit of Scandinavian Emigrants through Port of Hull* (1882), LXII.87

22. A. Kinross, 'At Sea with the Alien Immigrant', *Pall Mall Gazette*, 16 (1898), 19–26.

23. These Acts had established Port Sanitary Authorities at each of the main ports in England and Wales with each authority employing suitably qualified Port Medical Officers of Health to police Britain's ports.

24. *Parliamentary Debates*, CVLVI, 1230.

25. For coverage of the Hamburg cholera see 'The Cholera', *The Times*, 31 August 1892, 3; 'The Shadow of the Great Death', *The Times*, 17 September 1892, 8.

26. *RCAI*, Minutes of Evidence, Volume II, M.6, 970–977, 156.

27. *Parliamentary Debates*, CVLVII, 436.

28. The DFDS was in the process of signing a pooling agreement with the Wilson Line at the time of the Royal Commission. A few years afterwards, the company noted the increasing importance that passenger revenues from the Russia-to-London route generated in its financial reports. It is worth noting that the income

derived from passengers on the 'Russian trades' represented only 1 per cent of the company's earnings (in 1909) and 2 per cent (in 1910) on the 'homeward' voyages. Passenger Money Outward (between London and the Baltic) grew from £1,436 (in 1909) to £2,162 (in 1910). Passenger Money Inward (between the Baltic ports and London) grew from £1,707 (in 1909) to £3,019 (in 1910) due to the increased use of the Wilson Line to convey transmigrants destined for South Africa via the ships of the Union Castle Shipping Company. Of greater importance to the company was the ability to negotiate a pooling agreement with DFDS for freight - a deal negotiated because the Wilson Line challenged DFDS's dominant role in conveying migrants to Britain. University of Hull Archives and Special Collections, Ellerman Wilson Line Archives, DEW (2)/3/99.

29. Reference contained within a letter sent from the Wilson Line's Managing Director (Oswald Sanderson) to Charles Henry Wilson, 26 May 1905, in response to a telegram sent by Wilson to Sanderson on 25 May 1905. University of Hull Archives and Special Collections, Ellerman Wilson Line Archives, DEW 4/10.

30. Data from these sanitary reports has been discussed by Collins, 'Scottish Transmigration', 49–52; and Collins, *Second City Jewry*.

31. Passengers embarking from the Scottish ports of Glasgow and Greenock were not recorded until 1908 (The National Archives, BT 27/560) and continued until 1914 (based on research for the author's AHRB project based at the University of Aberdeen.)

32. Mitchell Library, Glasgow (MLG), E1/34/2, Peter Fyfe, *Twenty-Eighth Annual Report on the Operations of the Sanitary Department of the City of Glasgow for the year ending 31*st *December 1897* (Glasgow: Robert Anderson, 1897), 5.

33. MLG, E1/34/4, Peter Fyfe, *Thirtieth Annual Report ... 1899*, 14.

34. MLG, D-TC/23, Peter Fyfe, *Thirty-Third Annual Report ... 1902*, 12.

35. The continental passengers travelling via the Allan Line were described as 'Scandinavians, Icelanders, Finlanders and Continentals (Russians, Austrians, Hungarians, Poles, & c., principally of the Jewish persuasion)'. Fyfe, *Thirty-Third Annual Report*, 12.

36. MLG, D-TC/23, Peter Fyfe, *Thirty-Fourth Annual Report ... 1903*, 10.

37. MLG, C2/1/7, Peter Fyfe, *Thirty-Seventh Annual Report ... 1906*, 13. Those by the Allan Line were described as 'Continentals (Russians, Austrians, Hungarians, Poles, & c., principally Jews)'.

38. MLG, C2/1/9, Peter Fyfe, *Thirty-Ninth Annual Report ... 1908*, 13.

39. MLG, C2/1/9, Peter Fyfe, *Fortieth Annual Report ... 1909*, 16.

40. Based upon detailed analysis of the outward-bound passenger manifests created by the Board of Trade for the port of Glasgow in 1910. The National Archives, BT/27/645–649. This project was part of the Diaspora Programme based at the AHRC Centre for Irish and Scottish Studies, University of Aberdeen. (See http://www.abdn.ac.uk/emigration.)

41. Such labelling did not take place in any regular manner at Britain's other important passenger ports (Bristol, Liverpool, London or Southampton).

42. References to the ethnic origin of the aliens were always described by the Anchor Line and rarely by the Allan Line. Most of the Jews were destined for New York. The Jewish transmigrants often arrived in Scotland via the services of the Gibson Line to Leith. Other nationalities described included Japanese, Austrian, Croatian, Bulgarian, Finnish, Spanish, Polish, Hungarian Slovak, Galician and Russian Pole.

43. Collins, *Be Well!*, 97–114.

44. National Maritime Museum (Greenwich), Ephemera Collection, P 29, Advertisement for the Canadian Pacific Railway dated 21 February 1910.

45. For example, most Edwardian companies offered Kosher services to potential passengers. Unfortunately, advertisements for Kosher food have not survived in the extensive ephemera collections of the National Maritime Museum in Greenwich nor the archives of the Allan Shipping Company held at the University of Glasgow. The only example known to promote such Kosher facilities are advertisements, dating from 1887, held in the private collections of David Jacobs.

46. Kenefick, 'Jewish and Catholic', 216–217.

47. Wilkins, *The Alien Invasion*, 36–146.

48. Docker and Fischer, *Race, Colour, and Identity*, 24.

49. Kaplan and Robertson, *Founders and Followers*, 22.

50. Cape Town Archives (CPA), PMO 81, Letter from the Prime Minister's Office, 24 September 1901.

51. CPA, PMO 83, Telegram from the Secretary of State to the Governor, 30 January 1902.

52. CPA, PMO 84, Letter from the Prime Minister's Office, 6 June 1902.

53. CPA, PMO 858, Letter from Major Sir Henry H. Settle to the High Commissioner of South Africa, Johannesburg, 4 July 1902.

54. Harper, 'Settling in Saskatchewan', 97–98.

55. *The Jewish Yearbook* (London: Greenberg & Co., 1896), 28–30.

56. Irving Abella, *A Coat of Many Colours: Two Centuries of Jewish Life in Canada* (1990), quoted in Kelly and Trebilcock, *The Making of the Mosaic*, 75.

57. Knowles, *Strangers*, 55.

58. Knowles, *Strangers*, 78.

59. BPP, *Report of the Departmental Committee on the Establishment of a Receiving-House for Alien Immigrants at the Port of London: Volume I, Report and Appendix* (1911, X.87), 103.

5

The Ghosts of Kishinev in the East End: Responses to a Pogrom in the Jewish London of 1903

Ben Gidley

The story of the Kishinev massacre has become familiar within Jewish collective memory. It was coming up to the Russian Orthodox Easter in 1903. In the Russian empire, the Easter weekend was traditionally a focus of blood libels, combining the representation of the Jews as the murderers of Christ with images of sacrifices and other bloody rituals associated, in the antisemitic imagination, with the Jewish festival of Passover. A violently antisemitic campaign had been circulating in the regional newspaper in Bessarabia, where the town of Kishinev lay, including an inflammatory article by the local police chief.[1] On the eve of the Easter weekend, the body of a Christian child was found and a Christian young woman patient committed suicide in a Jewish hospital, giving rise to a blood libel story. There followed, over 19–20 April, a weekend of violence: according to official statistics, 49 Jews lost their lives and more than 500 were injured, some of them seriously; 700 houses were plundered and destroyed and 600 businesses and shops were looted. About 2,000 families were left homeless. One feature of the pogrom (the violent anti-Jewish riot) seemed to be an official collusion, with the police involved, a garrison of 5,000 soldiers taking no action to quell the violence, and local theological seminary students playing a leading role.

Kishinev was neither the first nor the worst pogrom of the era. As David Roskies has written, 'The timing of the violence remained unchanged from generations past'; the 'springtime of ritual murder' blossomed regularly in those decades. Kishinev 1903, however, marked a new level of violence: 'In all the pogroms of 1881–1883, fewer Jews were killed than in Kishinev' that fatal Passover, pointing towards the even higher death tolls to come, as in 1905–06 and 1919.[2] And thus Kishinev has taken on an iconic status in Jewish history and memory.

What this chapter will explore is how its echoes were heard in Jewish London, and what these reverberations meant for the Jewish community there. We will look at five different responses: the official responses of the Anglo-Jewish leadership; spontaneous responses by migrant associations (*landsmanshaftn*) in London's East End; the attempts made by Zionist leaders at channelling these spontaneous responses; the responses of East London radicals; and, finally, the very different response made by the Anglo-Jewish writer, intellectual, and ideologue Israel Zangwill.

First, however, I will briefly introduce the historical context in which these reactions emerged and locate my account in relation to the dominant historiographies of Anglo-Jewry.

East End and West End: London's internal Orient

The modern period of Jewish presence in London begins with resettlement in the seventeenth century. The first resettlers were Sephardic Jews (that is, expelled from Spain and Portugal) who came to England via the Netherlands. This population was supplemented by other Western European Jews, such as Ashkenazim from the Rhineland. By the last quarter of the nineteenth century, a large proportion of British Jews had to a great extent assimilated into English public life, though continuing, crucially, to follow Jewish religious law. This assimilated community was dominated by a handful of wealthy Sephardic and Ashkenazic families (like the Rothschilds, Montefiores, and Montagus) who were known as 'the Cousinhood'.[3] Through the nineteenth century, wealthier Jews began to shift westward to places like Bayswater and the West End.[4] Signalling the upward social mobility of the established families, this westward shift indicated a new-found confidence, coinciding with the slow process of Emancipation – the attainment of full citizenship – in which members of the Cousinhood, like Nathan Rothschild, played a major part. Political emancipation and the westward move, as well the formation of new communal institutions like the United Synagogue and the Board of Deputies in the West End at the same period, were the foundations of the Anglo-Jewish community.

This Anglo-Jewish community was not monolithic. It included both Ashkenazic and Sephardic congregations and a growing number of Reform ones; there was a degree of political pluralism, with a growing number sympathetic to Zionist politics; and although its institutional heart was in the West End, its members were not confined to that locale. What united Anglo-Jewry in this post-Emancipation moment, though, was a self-conception as 'English citizens of the Jewish faith': in other words, they identified themselves not as an ethnic or cultural collectivity, but as a *community of faith*. Mark Levene and others have described this conception of citizenship as 'the Jewish liberal compromise', which

> upheld the view that the English Jew should have the same status in society as a Congregationalist or Quaker. One's Jewishness was henceforth not a collective interest...but purely a matter of individual religious choice.... [T]his view argued that being Jewish in no way cut across one's

identification with the British nation, nor could it be deemed to cut across one's loyalty to or ability to serve the British state.[5]

In addition to these assimilationist aspects of Anglo-Jewish liberalism, I want to stress a further dimension of the Anglo-Jewish liberal compromise: that at its heart is the notion of *community* or *the communal*. Within sociological accounts, assimilation is often seen as the breaking down of communal authority.[6] Certainly, the assimilationist logic, in which Jewish difference is dissolved at the level of the individual, has a tense relationship with the logic of the communal. However, under the logic of the communal, Jewish difference is re-inscribed at the level of 'the community', in order to serve as the basis for the political legitimacy of the communal leadership, despite the adherence of the latter to the politics of assimilation.

The two logics were combined in the concept of a 'community of faith' and of Jews as 'co-religionists' rather than members of a common ethnicity.[7] As writers like Brian Alleyne, Clive Harris, and Uma Narayan suggest, the logic of the communal reinforces the notion of the unalterable difference *between* and sameness *within* 'communities'. Its logic cannot always accommodate the notion that differences within may be of greater significance than differences between; in particular, the notion of 'community' can obscure the complex social networks or webs of social relations, and conjunctures of the local and global, which make up diasporic peoples.[8]

From the late nineteenth century, a new group of Jews began arriving: Yiddish-speaking Eastern Europeans, mainly from the small communities (*shtetlekh*) and towns of the Jewish 'Pale of Settlement' in the Western parts of the Russian empire. In the wake of the 1881 assassination of Tsar Alexander II by a terrorist group, waves of pogroms swept across Russia. That year, a quarter of a million Jews left the Pale; this marks the start of mass Jewish migration from Eastern Europe to the West. It also, therefore, marks the start of the expansion of the Jewish ghetto in East London. From this time, the Jewish population in Britain rose from around 50,000 to nearly 200,000 (the majority in London, but with sizeable communities in Leeds, Manchester, Glasgow and elsewhere). These immigrants, often arriving at the docks of the East End, settled in precisely the areas that the wealthier Jews were beginning to vacate. It was in this period that the phrase 'the East End' entered the English language,[9] swiftly passing into Yiddish.

The docks remind us that the London in which the Yiddish migrants arrived was an imperial city. Indeed, Imperialism came to provide observers with an epistemological framework through which to understand London; colonial imagery (the jungle, the Dark Continent) was employed to think about, to make visible, the denizens of the capital. Specifically, Oriental otherness was mapped on to London's East End; in Judith Walkowitz's apt phrase, Empire and East End 'imaginatively doubled' for each other.[10] T. H. Huxley, for example, wrote that 'the Polynesian savage in his most primitive condition [was] not so savage, so unclean, so irreclaimable as the tenant of a tenement in an East London slum'.[11] No wonder that the East London street children were dubbed 'street-Arabs'.[12]

The presence of aliens in general – Jews, but also the multiracial (primarily Malay, Chinese, Yemeni, and Somali) maritime proletariat – served to further render the East End as an alien terrain. In this sense, the East End became what Mary Louise Pratt has called the 'contact zone', 'the space of colonial encounters, the space in which peoples geographically and historically separated come into contact with each other and establish ongoing relations, usually involving conditions of coercion, radical inequality, and intractable conflict'.[13] The riverine East End 'represented an insertion of [the] colonial other into the very heart of empire, a tangible intrusion of far-flung territories that were normally inaccessible to the eyes of Londoners'.[14] It was '"an internal Orient" to be discovered and tamed'.[15]

If the East End represented London's internal Orient, the Oriental Jew who dwelt there became 'the inner demon in the assimilationist soul'.[16] As Geoffrey Alderman has observed, the post-Emancipation generations

> felt that they were on trial, that they had to prove, and continue to prove, that they were worthy of the rights and freedoms Anglo-Christian society had extended to them, and they must somehow conform to what they felt were Gentile expectations of acceptable Jewish behaviour…. In the cultural sphere, this preoccupation – almost obsession – had a stultifying dehumanizing influence.[17]

The arrival in large numbers of Jews from the East threatened native Anglo-Jewry's sense of itself as 'English citizens of Jewish faith'. As William J. Fishman writes, 'the socially eminent … feared social retrogression through being identified with such unpalatable co-religionists.' Consequently, they made every effort to re-make their arriving co-religionists into English citizens as swiftly as possible.[18] The Anglo-Jewish leaders consistently sought to make the ghetto dissolve itself into English society at large and throw off its old-fashioned, particularistic, and peculiar rituals, its debased jargon, and, above all, its radical politics. To this end, the Cousinhood pursued a variety of strategies: coercion, bribery, charity, repatriation, missionary work to civilize the foreign Jews, anti-emigration propaganda in Russian papers, and even support for anti-immigration and pro-deportation policies.[19]

The assimilation project assumed an equation between citizenship and (Western) civilization; 'anglicisation' (cultural conformity) was the measure and precondition of the right to citizenship. Englishness was conflated with the universal, while Jewishness was seen as particularism or peculiarity. The Russian Jews' problem, opined the *Jewish Chronicle* in the midst of the bloody pogroms of 1881, was 'their exclusive attitude'.[20] Two decades later, on the eve of the Kishinev pogrom, Anglo-Jewish leader Lucien Wolf could still proclaim in *The Graphic* that

While the wealthier Jews of the North, West, and South of London are but little distinguishable from the Gentiles with whom they consort, the large body in the East End form a compact and characteristic community. The predominance of the Hebrew type is very noticeable, and the alien character of the population is accentuated by the peculiarities of the large foreign element...

Still they need many of the graces of civilisation, and the necessity of anglicising them has been readily acknowledged by their richer co-religionists... special services are held in the Great Synagogue with a view to impressing upon them from the pulpit an enlightened conception of their duty as English citizens. They prove a very ductile material to work upon.[21]

Yet, as the range of responses to Kishinev indicates, not all the denizens of the East End were prepared to pay the price of assimilation.

Before assessing these responses, we must recognize that the 'liberal Jewish compromise' continued to shape the Anglo-Jewish establishment's conception of its history. As Raphael Samuel noted in 1980, 'Jewish history in Britain in so far as it exists, is heavily institutional in bias, and entirely celebratory in tone, recording the progress of the "community" in terms of political status and professional and commercial success.'[22] The dominant model within Anglo-Jewish historiography up until that point – epitomized by the historians associated with the Anglo-Jewish institution, the Jewish Historical Society of England, founded in 1893 – had taken the nation-state framework for granted, seeing Jewish immigration to England as a one-way once-and-for-all prelude to assimilation or integration into the nation-state and largely celebrated this assimilation.[23] It is telling that in the work of these historians, Anglo-Jewish responses to Kishinev are absent.

From the 1970s, following the pioneering work of William Fishman, a handful of historians, including Jerry White, Bill Williams, Geoffrey Alderman, and David Cesarani, have tried to narrate the story of Jewish immigration in a different way: in terms of the everyday struggles of the people of the ghetto, focusing on *differences within* the Jewish community (particularly class differences), as well as highlighting the mechanisms of exclusion which the Jewish immigrants faced within the wider society.[24] These historians have shown that the path to citizenship was uneven and that belonging in England was always problematic.

Nevertheless, even this body of work has, on the whole, continued to accept the framework of the nation-state as the appropriate unit of narrating history and to see Jewish migration as a unilinear flow of 'immigrants' to a 'host' country (albeit regarding this host as much less hospitable than in the earlier Anglo-Jewish historiography). Often, too, these historians have not recognized the importance of Britain's imperial context. In contrast, I would like to stress the *spaces and places of belonging* through which the East Enders navigated: the local, the national, the imperial, the diasporic, and the international. In what follows I will show how these different spaces were evoked in complex ways in the responses to Kishinev.

Echoes of Kishinev in the West End: assumptions of unanimity

Considering the emblematic role Kishinev has subsequently taken, the reaction in London was in fact relatively slow in starting. The first reports of Kishinev in the British press came nearly two weeks later. The Society of Friends of Russian Freedom was one of the first organizations to cry out at the events, in the first week of May.[25] The same week, the two main (West End-based) bodies of Anglo-Jewish communal leadership, the Anglo-Jewish Association (AJA) and Board of Deputies (BoD), both met; the AJA discussed Kishinev but could not decide on a course of action, while the Board made no mention of it at all.[26]

The first official statement from Anglo-Jewry came only on 18 May, a fortnight later, when the BoD and AJA sent a joint letter to the *Times*. The letter, in classic assimilationist style, does its best to show the Jewish community not making too much of a fuss:

> Sir – On behalf of the Jewish communities of Great Britain we crave the hospitality of your columns for a formal protest against the horrors perpetrated on our co-religionists of Kischineff. ... Until two days ago we cherished the hope that an appeal to public opinion outside Russia would not be necessary, but on the fifth [of May – i.e. thirteen days previously], we received from St Petersburg the full text of [the Russian government's official statement on the pogrom] and we feel that [as the document is inaccurate and expresses indifference] we should be neglecting our duty were we to remain silent any longer.[27]

The letter epitomizes the style of the Anglo-Jewish communal leadership in the English public sphere: a tone of almost craven respectfulness, subjection and self-effacement ('we *crave* the *hospitality* of your columns'), combined with an insistence on the sole right to represent and speak for the Jews of England.

A subtext beneath Anglo-Jewish quiescence (sometimes hinted at in meetings of the BoD and AJA during the period) was the on-going debate within the wider British public sphere on immigration restriction. The Royal Commission on Alien Immigration was still convening, and the Anglo-Jewish leadership felt that too much attention on Eastern European Jews – and any perception of transnational Jewish loyalty taking precedence over loyalty to England – would strengthen the anti-alien position.

But beyond this, the statement points towards the key elements in the West End Anglo-Jewish worldview. First, it emphasizes an assimilationist form of universalism which was unable to articulate a sense of Jewishness beyond Judaism. Their identification with the victims – and this was the phrase they use in the letter – was as 'co-religionists', a term that suggests that their solidarity with the Jews of Russia was purely religious, that there were no ethnic or cultural ties. Second, it emphasizes the logic of the communal, which was always premised on *unanimity*, on the repression or disavowal of internal differences. This assumption of unanimity was precisely the basis for the authority of communal institutions, such as the United Synagogue, the AJA, and BoD. When the latter two bodies wrote to *The Times* that they were making their complaint 'On behalf of the Jewish communities of Great Britain' and out of a clear 'duty', they were articulating, in other words, their right and responsibility to represent the Jewish community with a single voice.

East End responses: spontaneity, representation, legitimacy, and mediation

We can contrast this slow, quiet, official communal reaction to the spontaneous response of East End immigrants. Joseph Finn, for example, a trade union leader, wrote to the *Jewish Chronicle* urging action, while smaller friendly societies in the East End, like the Plotsker Relief and Sick Benefit Society and the Hebrew New Year Benefit and Divisional Society, were among the first to pledge money.[28] These were *landsmanshaftn*, mutual aid organizations created by *landslayt*, migrants from the same areas of the Pale. They were swift to respond because, for them, Kishinev had a concrete reality it lacked for the Anglo-Jewish leadership. The *landsmanshaftn*, as spaces of trans-national or diasporic identification, sharply diverged from the liberal forms of political belonging practised by the West End-based leadership. For the communal institutions, the victims of the pogrom were simply 'co-religionists'; but many East Enders, linked to the pogrom victims by a dense web of affective ties, responded in ways that simultaneously recognized both differences within (such as class antagonisms) and samenesses across Jewishness, leading them to articulate forms of belonging which could operate both below and across the nation-state.

While West End leaders feared such autonomous East End action, some recognized that their role in representing the whole community, and indeed the legitimacy of their communal authority, rested on their ability to voice the concerns of the immigrants. A group of communal leaders, including many Zionists such as Moses Gaster and Joseph Cowen, formed a Kischineff Atrocities Relief Committee to raise awareness of the victims. Their first meeting, the same night as the AJA/BoD letter appeared in *The Times*, was held in East London and attracted a large East End crowd, but, crucially, remained under the patronage of West Enders, who took the chair and committee seats. The meeting was mainly conducted in English, although a request for funds was made in Yiddish by the chair.

Several speakers from the floor drew attention to the contrasting responses of the East End and the West End. This was explicitly rejected from the platform though, by Anglo-Jewish leader Herman Gollancz: 'He had heard, he remarked, of the strong line of demarcation between the East and the West, which had been so frequently referred to that evening. He thought they were acting contrary to the spirit of [their aims] in making any such distinction.'[29] Denying the differences within Anglo-Jewry articulated by the immigrants, the speakers on the platform reaffirmed the unanimity of the community.

The main action resolved upon in the meeting was to form a delegation, composed largely of West Enders, to 'wait upon various representative Jewish bodies respecting the Kischineff outrages'[30] – in other words, to lobby, not the British public at large, but the Jewish communal leadership, and thus to maintain the East End in a subordinate position in relation to the communal leadership. We can see these sorts of events as attempts at *mediation*: the East Enders were not to represent themselves in the official public sphere, but to be represented by their betters.

The delegation's attempts at influencing the West End oligarchs, however, had limited success. The AJA, and particularly Lucien Wolf, continued to oppose holding a public meeting, with Moses Gaster (the spiritual leader of the Sephardic community) acting as a lone voice of dissent. By mid-June, Gaster had succeeded in converting a number of AJA members, but the BoD refused to participate and the AJA didn't have the courage to take independent action.[31]

The communal was a space where the differences within – the internal antagonisms within the community – were suppressed. In this light, the Kishinev pogrom can be seen as a moment of crisis for communal authority, a moment in which the legitimacy of Anglo-Jewish leadership was challenged by the East End immigrants, while the West End-based leadership sought to re-impose their communal authority through a politics of mediation and representation.

The East End radicals: proletarian internationalism

The visibility of alien radicals, in particular, alarmed the Anglo-Jewish leadership. Communal leader Samuel Montagu, at a meeting of the BoD, opposed a public meeting on the grounds that 'Unfortunately, [the Jewish community was] cursed with Nihilists in this country and some of them would undoubtedly attend any meeting that might be held and utter seditious cries. Such a meeting would probably undo all the good that had hitherto been done.'[32] Figures like Montagu wanted the Jewish community to appear to the English public and the British state as homogenous – as subscribing to one set of values, English values.

Despite the Kischineff Atrocities Relief Committee's attempt at containment and mediation, these 'nihilists' did indeed organize. Jewish trades unions called a protest meeting, raising money toward the relief fund which the tailors' union's (non-Jewish) president, Social Democrat Herbert Burrows, sent on to the *Jewish Chronicle*.[33] A couple of days later, the Social Democrats held a protest meeting in Mile End. Interestingly, there were almost no Jewish speakers. Chaired by a member of the International Peace and Arbitration Association, the meeting included speeches and letters of support from labour and trades union leaders. Felix Volkhovsky, a veteran non-Jewish Russian revolutionary, spoke in English and Russian. G. Beck, the non-Jewish Russian leader of the East End Social Democrats, was the only speaker in Yiddish. The only Jewish speaker was I. Ellstein, a trade unionist who spoke in English. But it seems that the audience, in contrast to the platform, was overwhelmingly Jewish; one of the speakers, Harry Quelch, a Social Democrat, drew attention to this fact in very ambivalent terms. He

> regretted that the meeting was not composed more largely of Englishmen. He would much rather see an overwhelming meeting of the latter to protest against the outrages committed against a common humanity, particularly because the victims were a race having no recognized nationality or country and rightly belonged to those countries where they dwelt.[34]

This meeting, then, expresses the tension between Kishinev's call to Jewish identity and a proletarian universalism that spoke in terms of 'a common humanity'. The organizers, as 'internationalists', explicitly disavowed the particular Jewish dimension of the protest, but the East End masses who attended were motivated by more complex loyalties and identifications.

Yiddish trade unions and radical groups set up an International Kischineff Massacres Protest Committee to organize a public protest. The new Committee decided their task was not fund-raising but political work: 'steer clear of philanthropy and leave it to others. [Confine ourselves] to the work of organizing an effective protest', as one participant said.[35]

The Committee organized a mass meeting at Hyde Park in mid-June. A procession began on the Mile End Waste, led by the banners of the Jewish trades unions and the anarchist Workers' Friend group. Although many Jewish leaders were present (Israel Zangwill, Harry Lewis of Toynbee Hall, and Zionists Herbert Bentwich and Joseph Cowen), almost all of the speakers, as at the Mile End meeting, were non-Jews. Speakers included English Social Democrats and Russian revolutionaries (speaking in both English and Russian). A text written by the anarchist leader Prince Kropotkin, who was too ill to attend, was read out. Many of the speakers alluded to the composition of the crowd: Volkhovsky, a Russian speaker, said 'the faces before him reminded him of his country', implying a Russian audience; Kropotkin spoke of addressing 'the Jewish workers'; Hunter Watts, an English socialist, 'paid a tribute to the services rendered by the Jewish workers to the cause of

Social Democracy'. Another, Houghton Fisher, said: 'You remember your Kischineff.... We remember our Featherstone and our Peterloo'; his use of 'you' implies a Russian Jewish rather than English audience. But many of these allusions are not just to a Jewish crowd but to a *proletarian* Jewish crowd: Kropotkin and Hunter Watts referred to 'the Jewish workers', while Houghton Fisher's reference is to Peterloo, a pivotal moment in English labour history. Herman Cohen, the only Jewish speaker, 'wished that there were more Hebrews there from more parts of London than one', implying that the East End had come while the West End stayed away.[36] The speeches from the platform, then, again exemplify the tensions between the call to particularist Jewish identification in the response to the trauma of Kishinev and universalising trans-ethnic solidarities, such as the world-citizenship of the working class.

The radical tone of the Hyde Park meeting distressed West End Anglo-Jewry. Joseph Prag reported to the AJA that 'it was a calamity that the meet-ing...was presided over by a member of the Social Democratic Federation [and] attended by Socialists and Anarchists to plead on behalf of the Jews'. He spoke of 'people who preyed upon the feelings of their Russian and Polish brethren', like Prince Kropotkin 'who condemned Jewish capitalists as well as the Russian Government'.[37] As exemplified by Prag's comments, Anglo-Jewish assimilationism was also unable to respect the internal differences (such as those between Jewish workers and Jewish capitalists) that striated Jewish communities in both London and the Pale. The Social Democrats, on the other hand, were tied to particular versions of internationalism which denied the specificities, the samenesses, which bound East End Jews to Jews '*inderheym*' – 'back home' in the Pale. For these radicals, internationalism was an abstract, absolute and categorical imperative, and it required the transcending of any non-'international' (i.e. culturally specific) forms of belonging or identification. In practice, this meant orientation (even assimilation) to the local 'national' proletariat. It entailed the disavowal of Jewish particularist belonging, and an identification with the proletariat as a universal identity which dissolves and supersedes all other identities or particularities.[38]

I now want to turn, finally, to an attempt to articulate both the differences within and samenesses across Jewishness, which stretched the categories of belonging found in liberal assimilationism and socialist internationalism.

Israel Zangwill: between brotherhood and citizenship

In mid May, there was a Zionist meeting at Shoreditch Town Hall in East London. Israel Zangwill, who had not yet broken with the Zionist move-ment, was the main speaker, and his presence attracted a large audience from the East End. He spoke at great length and on many topics, including the aliens issue, Zionism, and Kishinev. Describing the pogrom in lurid terms, Zangwill concluded with

> the dragging out of men's entrails and stuffing their stomachs with feathers, after the fashion of the Apache Indians. As for the Jack-the-Ripper atrocities committed on Jewesses I dare not describe them. No, while the bulk of the world's Jews live in Russia, they actually live in the Middle Ages. Even literally, Russia counts time by the Old Calendar, and this bloody Easter Sunday fell upon the same day and the same souls as in the Dark Ages. It is because the rest of Europe also tends to slide back into the Dark Ages, that we more fortunate English Jews watch with such experienced anxiety the ALIEN ENQUIRY COMMISSION... such of us as are English-born and English-bred believe freedom to be England's grandest tradition. We are so often more English than the English in a ridiculous manner; let us for once be more English than the English in a noble manner, and save England from being false to herself. Secondly, as Jews we remember the teaching of Moses 'Thou shalt not oppress a stranger; for ye know the heart of a stranger, seeing ye were strangers in the land of Egypt.' It has been painful to see how new-comers who could scarcely talk English have turned against newer-comers. I was myself invited to join a Committee of Dukes, Earls and M.Ps, for the Reform of Immigration. I replied that MY OWN FATHER WAS AN ALIEN IMMIGRANT and I dared not shut out others. And thirdly, we Zionists object to anything that lowers the status of our people and restricts its freedom of domicile. Desirous as we are of establishing our people in a home, we cannot give up the right of individual Jews to live where they please, just as individuals of other nationalities would be free to settle among us.[39]

After briefly describing the history of 'the English Jews, I beg pardon, the Jewish Englishmen' and their medieval banishment, he continued: 'I believe England – the mother of liberty and free parliaments – is incapable of sinking so low again... I believe the heart of England is sound, and she will not turn away the outcast and the refugee without helping to find him a home.' However, he added, they had a similar conviction in France, but the Dreyfus affair disproved it.[40]

Zangwill's description of Kishinev is extremely interesting. First, while the Anglo-Jewish leadership refrained from making the connection between Kishinev and the Aliens Commission, Zangwill made the link explicit, framing his discussion of the latter in terms of the former. Second, he employs intriguing metaphors: Apache Indians, Jack the Ripper, and the Dark Ages. With the Apaches, he uses racist images of Native Americans to express the savagery of the Russians. With Jack the Ripper, he evokes an image more frequently deployed to racialise and criminalize the Jews and the East End.[41] Turning to the Dark Ages, he associates Russia with a primitive past, implicitly juxtaposed against Western modernity. These sorts of appeals – to a liberal conception of progress located in the West, while darkness and pastness are located in the East and the colonies – are familiar rhetorical devices used by Anglo-Jewry to command English sympathy for the victims of Russian terror, as is the appeal to English traditions of liberty and tolerance.[42] But Zangwill's use of this has a less familiar twist: he projects orientalising, primitivist images away from Jews and towards Christian Europeans.

Indeed, he explicitly subverts the linear, teleological chronology usually associated with this language: he writes that England, like Dreyfus-era France, can easily return, 'slide back', into the Dark Ages. Further, by shifting so quickly from Kishinev to the Aliens inquiry, he seems to equate the two, subverting the notion of England's superiority over the East.[43]

Zangwill also puts specifically Jewish traditions of empathy for the refugee on an equal footing with (much younger) English traditions of liberty and hospitality. When Zangwill evokes specifically Jewish traditions of concern for the refugee – 'for ye know the heart of a stranger, seeing ye were strangers in the land of Egypt' – he is relying on Exodus 23 and the Passover story; since Passover coincides with Russian Orthodox Easter, these are the words Jews all over the world were repeating at the time of the Kishinev pogrom. Zangwill's iteration of this phrase indicates his sensitivity to the cultural and ritual practices of Jews (although he himself was secular, and married to a non-Jew). For him, Judaism and Yiddish folk practices were a resource for building a new politics of hospitality to the refugee.

His comments on Englishness and assimilation are also interesting – especially given that the highly assimilated Zangwill was responsive to the cultural world of the East End: he came from a Whitechapel Russian/Polish immigrant family, was schooled at the assimilationist Jews' Free School in Spitalfields, and entered English and Anglo-Jewish high society through his literary success. In the speech quoted above, Zangwill scorns the assimilationist attempt to be 'more English than the English in a ridiculous manner', attacks the disavowal of a refugee background by anglicised Jews, and mocks the pretension of English Jews to be 'Jewish Englishmen'. Rejecting a philosophy of assimilation that mimics the manners and habits of the dominant ethnicity,[44] Zangwill asserts the possibility of multiple loyalties and multiple identities: he is English *and* Jewish *and* Zionist, and these complement rather than contradict each other.[45] Following from this is a demand for a form of pluralism: every individual should have freedom of domicile; any Jewish home will not be a pure Jewish space, but people of other nationalities shall settle amongst them without assimilating, just as people of other nationalities should have the right to settle amongst the English. This belief begins to uncouple citizenship from nationality, and thus point to an alternative way of thinking about citizenship.

Set against the backdrop of the Kishinev pogrom, Zangwill's play *The Melting Pot* (conceived in 1905, first performed in 1908, and published in

1909[46]) explores these tensions further: evoking 'the ghosts of Kishinev' and their call to ethnic identity, it also suggests their transcendence in a new, plural citizenship signified by the melting pot of the title. The play's main character, David Quixano, and his mother have made a home in America after fleeing the massacre, in which his father and brother were slaughtered. He falls in love with Vera Ravendal, whose father, a Russian baron, was present at and responsible for the massacre. This history of tragedy is one of the obstacles the couple must overcome. In a speech in the final scene, David says to her: 'cling to me till all these ghosts [of Kishinev] are exorcized, cling to me till our love triumphs over death'.[47] The 'ghosts' of Kishinev, David's slaughtered father and brother, represent the call to Jewish kinship and identification arising out of the trauma of violence. Zangwill's play recognizes the power of this call, but gestures towards its transcendence (or exorcizing) in a sort of cosmopolitan democracy.[48]

In Zangwill's melting pot, then, citizenship becomes a project which celebrates differences, rather then seeking to dissolve them through the undignified mimicry of the dominant ethnicity, which we saw him scorning in his 1903 Kishinev speech. His image is of 'melting up', a process in which the best of every culture will be preserved in a higher unity.[49] Kishinev called Zangwill to a sense of Jewish identity seen in terms of kinship, but also inspired him to grope towards a form of poly-ethnic citizenship (the melting pot) that transcended blood ties.

Where other responses presented the East Enders with an either/or choice – the Jewish nation *or* the English nation, class *or* ethnicity – Zangwill stressed multiple identity, multiple loyalty, multiple belonging. Against the logic of the communal, Zangwill was able to imagine both the specificities of Jewish life, which bound East End Jews to the ghosts of Kishinev, and the differences between Jews.

Notes

Thanks to Victor Seidler, Michael Keith, Paul Gilroy, Max Silverman, Eitan Bar-Yosef, Nadia Valman, and Monica Moreno for comments on earlier versions of this chapter.

1. *JC*, 8 May 1903, 2. On other responses to Kishinev see Roskies, *Literature of Destruction*, 150–188.
2. Roskies, *Against the Apocalypse*, 62, 82.
3. Cf. Bermant, *The Cousinhood*.
4. Bloch, *Earlham Grove Shul*, 2; Newman, *Migration and Settlement*; Newman and Massil, *Patterns of Migration*. This movement can be seen as part of a wider phenomenon, traced back to the sixteenth century, of those attaining respectability by moving westwards. See Ackroyd, *London*, 676–677.
5. Levene, *War, Jews, and the New Europe*, 4. On the 'Jewish liberal compromise' see Kadish, *Bolsheviks*, 55–60, 132; Hyman, *Jews in Britain*, 11. The phrase was coined by Bayme, 'Jewish Leadership', 34.
6. Cf. Bauman, *Modernity and Ambivalence*, 104–111.
7. Cf. Finestein, *Jewish Society*, 39.

8. In addition, it can obscure the fact that 'ethnic identity' itself is contingent and relational, continuously undergoing processes of translation, creolization, syncretization, and hybridization: culture as 'invariably promiscuous and chronically impure'. Gilroy, *Between Camps*, 129.

9. Ackroyd, *London*, 675.

10. Walkowitz, *City of Dreadful Delight*, 35. See also Marriott, 'In Darkest England'.

11. Quoted in Steyn, *The Jew*, 83.

12. Ackroyd, *London*, 679.

13. Pratt, *Imperial Eyes*, 6–7.

14. Looker, 'Exhibiting Imperial London', 14.

15. Back, *New Ethnicities*, 18.

16. Bauman, 'Exit Visas', 57–58.

17. Alderman, *Modern British Jewry*, 138–139; Finestein, *Jewish Society*; Todd Endelman, 'Communal Solidarity'.

18. Fishman, *East End Jewish Radicals*, 65.

19. Fishman, *East End Jewish Radicals*, 64–68, 90; Kadish, *Bolsheviks*, chs. 2–3.

20. *JC*, 10 June 1881, quoted in Fishman, *East End Jewish Radicals*, 66.

21. Quoted in Cowen and Cowen, *Victorian Jews*, 93–95.

22. Quoted in White, *Rothschild Buildings*, x.

23. See, among many others, Roth, *A History of the Jews*; Lipman, *A Social History of the Jews*. More recently, Rubinstein (*A History of the Jews*, 172) has sought to revive this school, arguing that there has been a 'unique symbiosis of Britain and Jewry' and minimizing both the story of antisemitism in Britain and that of class domination within Anglo-Jewry.

24. Cf. Fishman, *East End 1888*; Alderman, *Modern British Jewry*; White, *Rothschild Buildings*; Bill Williams, *The Making of Manchester Jewry*. Closely related are Holmes, *Anti-Semitism*; Kushner, *The Persistence of Prejudice*. Following Cesarani, *The Making of Modern Anglo-Jewry*, there have been efforts to revise the 1970s view with a more complex understanding of the intersection of class with ethnicity, gender, nationality, and acculturation. See, for example, Feldman, *Englishmen and Jews*. Amongst the post-1970s writers, Kishinev is mentioned in passing in some texts, but with no sustained discussion.

25. It held its annual meeting at Clifford's Inn; Nikolai Tchaikovsky, a veteran Narodnik, spoke about the pogrom. *JC*, 8 May 1903, 12. The Society was not a Jewish organization, although some Jews were involved.

26. *JC*, 8 May 1903, 12.

27. *JC*, 22 May 1903, 14.

28. *JC*, 15 May 1903, 18.

29. *JC*, 22 May 1903, 9.

30. *JC*, 22 May 1903, 10.

31. *JC*, 19 June 1903, 11; 16 June 1903, 13. Gaster, from Romania, was a Yiddish-speaking anthropologist specializing in Eastern European (Jewish and non-Jewish) folk traditions. For a longer discussion, see Chapter 6 in this volume.

32. *JC*, 29 May 1903, 14.

33. *JC*, 5 June 1903, 17.

34. *JC*, 26 June 1903, 10.

35. *JC*, 5 June 1903, 28.

36. *JC*, 26 June 1903, 11.

37. *JC*, 26 June 1903, 11.

38. See Gidley, 'Citizenship and Belonging', ch. 9; Wistrich, *Revolutionary Jews*; Traverso, *The Marxists*. This disavowal, I believe, was the reason for the lack of Jewish speakers at the Social Democrats' protests.
39. *JC*, 22 May 1903, 20.
40. *JC*, 22 May 1903, 20–21.
41. See Steyn, *The Jew*, 15; Gilman, *The Jew's Body*, 127; Walkowitz, *City of Dreadful Delight*, 191–228.
42. See Feldman's discussion of the 1881 pogroms (*Englishmen and Jews*, ch. 4), or the Foreign Jews Protection Committee's use of this rhetoric (Gidley, 'Citizenship and Belonging', ch. 9).
43. Arguably, Zangwill's notion of 'sliding back' resonates with ideas of degeneration current in Edwardian England, but it is unusual to see anti-alien prejudice, rather than aliens, associated with degeneration.
44. He made the same point in an 1893 speech, 'The Maccabeans': 'The "mimicry" by which insects assimilate in hue to the environment has made backboneless Jews indistinguishable from "the heathen." ' Israel Zangwill, *Speeches, Articles and Letters*, ed. Maurice Simon (London: Soncino Press, 1937), 44. Zangwill called Disraeli a 'Ghetto parvenu' and declared those who hid their Jewishness guilty of 'Marranoism': formerly 'sailing under false religious colours', now 'sailing under false racial colours [which is] still more vulgar and degrading'. Quoted in Leftwich, *Israel Zangwill*, 162.
45. Elsewhere he wrote that 'The human heart is large enough to hold many loyalties'. Quoted in Leftwich, *Israel Zangwill*, 147.
46. Also performed in a Yiddish version in 1912. For the English text of the play, and Zangwill's wartime 'Afterword', see Israel Zangwill, *The Melting Pot* (London: William Heinemann, 1914).
47. Zangwill, *The Melting Pot*, 197.
48. Sollors, *Beyond Ethnicity*, analyses the play in terms of 'consent' (the melting pot, love, citizenship) triumphing over 'descent' (the old world, death, kinship, blood). The motif of kinship (blood and brotherhood) used here by Zangwill was persistently employed to call for aid for Jewish sufferers. One example is the widely circulated appeal made by the group of Jewish intellectuals in Russia of which historian Simon Dubnov was part: 'Brothers – the blood of our Kishinever brothers cries out to us: rise up from the dust, cease pleading for mercy, stretch out your hand no more to your enemy! You must help yourself, by your own hand!' (Quoted in Simon Dubnov, *Dos Bukh fun Mayn Lebn* [*The Book of My Life*] (Buenos Aires: Congress for Jewish Culture, 1961), 378. My translation). The word 'brother' appears seven times in this short text, from the first word to the penultimate one. Bialik, one of the co-writers of this text with Dubnov, wrote his epic poem 'The City of Slaughter' in response to the pogrom. See full text in Roskies, *The Literature of Destruction*, 162–167. See also Mintz and Roskies, *Kishinev in the Twentieth Century*.
49. The play is often represented as an assimilationist call for differences to be melted *down* in a homogeneous Americanness, a reading that is not sustainable from the text itself.

6

Jews, Englishmen, and Folklorists: The Scholarship of Joseph Jacobs and Moses Gaster

Simon Rabinovitch

Between 1870 and 1910, English interest in folk literature and customs expanded dramatically, and became increasingly organized, scholarly, and influenced by emerging anthropological theories. Building on the foundations created by earlier British collectors and enthusiasts, a small group of private scholars founded the Folk-Lore Society in 1878 (the first of its kind anywhere), which attempted to apply more rigorous and scholarly methods to the study of folklore, and to create what one founder, George Laurence Gomme, called a 'science of folklore'.[1] The new science was based on the application of biological and anthropological evolutionary theories to the study of folklore, and in particular, E. B. Tylor's doctrine of survivals, which claimed it possible to identify, in the cultures of non-primitive societies, customary survivals from earlier stages of cultural development. Members of the Folk-Lore Society debated amongst themselves whether folklore should be considered a branch of anthropology or independent of it, but they all viewed folklore through the lens of evolutionary theories.

English folklore studies during this period were pursued mainly by Victorian gentlemen of varied professions who in their spare time devoted themselves to advancing their humanistic interests.[2] Even considering that most were primarily concerned with British customs and traditions, the nationalist undertones prevalent in anthropology and folkloristics as practiced on the Continent at the time were comparatively muted in England. That two Jewish newcomers to the country, Joseph Jacobs (1854–1916) and Moses Gaster (1856–1939), could gain acceptance in English society through contributions in this field is evidence that being a Victorian gentleman was not limited to Englishmen only. At a time of increasing resistance to East European immigration to England, the manner in which Jacobs and Gaster's very different approaches to folklore and anthropology also illustrate how elite Jews sought to reveal to the general population what Jacobs called, in the title of one of his books, *Jewish*

Contributions to Civilization. By analysing the late-Victorian and Edwardian folkloristic and anthropological scholarship of Joseph Jacobs and Moses Gaster, this chapter examines how two integrated and prosperous London Jews viewed their new immigrant brethren, their English colleagues, and their own roles in the world of English culture and scholarship. The scholarly work of each reflects two very different approaches to how one could (or should) strive to be both Jewish and English, demonstrating the uses and limitations of folklore and anthropology for gaining acceptance in English society.

Joseph Jacobs: an English folklorist in late-Victorian England

Joseph Jacobs moved from Australia to England in order to attend St John's College, in Cambridge, as one of the first Jews to enter that university after the Statute Law Revision Act of 1863. Despite having been a highly regarded student, Jacobs was not offered a fellowship after receiving his Bachelor of Arts. It is impossible to know whether this was due to existing parlour antisemitism at Cambridge;[3] but as a result of Jacobs's failure to find a full-time appointment at a university, he was forced to diversify his literary interests and take on numerous editorial, journalistic, and literary posts to support himself.[4]

After gaining his Bachelor of Arts from Cambridge, but before becoming a widely published folklorist, Jacobs spent several years engaged in studying, anthropologically, the physical characteristics of the Jews in England. Large-scale Jewish emigration from Eastern Europe began in 1881, and with it came a debate over the value of such immigrants to England, with increasing attention paid to the subject in the English press. While anti-Jewish sentiment certainly existed in England, especially among opponents of Jewish immigration, political antisemitism on the Continent during the same period was much more explicit and increasingly based on supposedly scientific grounds.[5] In an effort to combat racial antisemitism and refute scientifically the claims of those who argued that the Jews were biologically inferior to other Europeans, Jacobs became an amateur anthropologist, and in his spare time undertook several studies of comparative anthropometry, using the Jews in England as his subject.[6]

Possibly in order to pre-empt racial science from being employed by anti-Jewish and anti-immigrant forces in England, Jacobs created a Jewish race science which aimed to prove that the new Jewish arrivals who lived in London's East End, while deficient in some ways, would adapt and eventually become as English as the members of the longer-standing Jewish community in the West End.[7] One method of doing so was proving that both sets of Jews belonged to the same race, and in Jacobs's article for the *Journal of the Anthropological Institute of Great Britain and Ireland*, entitled 'On the Racial

Characteristics of Modern Jews', he articulated his view that the Jews are a unified yet separate and even pure racial type. Jacobs was even willing to accept that certain physical deficiencies were apparent in contemporary Jewry, but these deficiencies were in Jacobs's opinion social, not racial, in their causes, and therefore rectifiable.[8] Jacobs explained differences between the Jews and the general population as resulting from both European imposed isolation and Judaic practices, both of which had positive and negative consequences on Jewish physical development. Jacobs tested many of his hypotheses in his study 'On the Comparative Anthropometry of English Jews' by collecting anthropometric measurements for Englishmen, as well as two classes of Jews he bluntly described as 'the better nurtured inhabitants of the West End and descendants for the most part of Jews who have been long settled in this country' and 'the less fortunately situated Jewish dwellers at the East End, the parents of whom in many cases were born abroad'.[9] Jacobs's study and carefully-crafted charts concluded that English Jews compared unfavourably in almost all anthropological measurements (for example, height, arm-span, and keenness of sight) with his English subjects. Nevertheless, when one isolates the statistics for the West End Jews – who, according to Jacobs, 'were probably of very nearly the same class' as his English subjects – 'the inferiority vanishes almost entirely'.[10] As the West End Jews, according to Jacobs, were unquestionably of the same race as the East End Jews, then logically, any racial deficiencies prevalent among Jews at the time were the result of nurture, not nature.[11]

   In attempting to demonstrate Jewish racial parity with the European population, Jacobs even published his own 'Distribution of Jewish Ability' – based on Francis Galton's equivalent for Englishmen – in which he compiled a list of prominent people of Jewish descent in order to prove that Jews had produced at least as many geniuses per million as other European races.[12] Jacobs's 'Distribution of Jewish Ability', as well as his cultural and racial anthropology, focused on refuting the increasingly popular notion that Jews themselves, as opposed to just their religion, were inherently deficient and therefore incapable of integration into European society. But as part of his participation in the anthropological discussion, Jacobs conceded, or even emphasized, two important points: that the Jews are a pure race unconnected to European stock,[13] and that contemporary Jewry did possess some deleterious qualities. These two points were not unconnected, as Jacobs could argue that the Jewish race had the capability of becoming as great as European races, if not greater, while simultaneously pushing Jews – in particular 'East End' (read East European) Jews – to reform themselves.[14] Jacobs thereby employed the theories of the anthropologist E. B. Tylor (integrating them with those of Darwin and Galton) to explain what he perceived to be the evident disparity between Western and Eastern European Jews in their cultural and physical evolution.[15] Tylor frequently spoke of human cultural development in terms of 'mental evolution', and Jacobs applied a similar logic in arguing that the maintenance of supposedly primitive cultural traditions by East European Jews continued to stunt their evolution both culturally and physically.

As an editor and major contributor to the *Jewish Chronicle* and an important figure in the Mansion House Fund established to aid Jewish victims of Russian persecution, Jacobs toiled tirelessly on behalf of East European Jewry, both reporting on the situation in the tsarist empire and helping in the resettlement of new immigrants.[16] Jacobs, however, did not attempt to cloak his disdain for the many elements of East European Jewish culture he considered harmful – marriage practices being a favourite target. In his belief in the backwardness of much of traditional East European Jewish culture, Jacobs reflected typical Central and West European Jewish attitudes toward the *Ostjuden*; but Jacobs was especially emphatic in his desire to Westernise these Jews. As John Efron has observed, for Jacobs, the Jews of England were the ideal model for modern Jewry to follow, and therefore the customs of Anglo-Jewry should become the standard by which East European Jewry should model itself.[17] Efron even suggests that Jacobs wanted English Jewry to perform a similar 'civilizing mission' among other Jews, as England had undertaken among its Empire's subjects. The paradox of Jacobs (and Jewish race science in general) was that a discipline that emerged in reaction to the increasing antisemitism in anthropology and medicine still separated the scientist (in this case a West End Jew) from his subject (East End Jewry) and maintained the existence of ideal types.[18]

Despite the recognition he received through his publications in the *Journal of the Anthropological Institute of Great Britain and Ireland*, racial anthropology was Jacobs's secondary interest to a related discipline, folkloristics, through which he derived employment by writing widely circulated publications.[19] As Tylor's doctrine of survivals made European folklore the main source for data supporting his evolutionary theory of uniform cultural development, the creation of the English Folk-Lore Society provided an arena for Tylorian scholars such as Jacobs to focus their intellectual energies.[20] Between 1888 and 1895, Jacobs committed himself to the collection and publication of British and other folklore. Within that period, Jacobs collected, edited, and published half a dozen volumes of English and Celtic folklore, as well as other folklore from Europe and India, in addition to being one of the founding members of the English Folk-Lore Society, the sole editor of the official publication of the Folk-Lore Society, *Folk-Lore*, as well as a major contributor until he resigned in 1893 because of other commitments.[21]

By the time of his resignation from *Folk-Lore*, Jacobs had riled many members of the Folk-Lore Society, in particular by not accepting the prevailing folkloristic concept of popular creativity. While the field of folkloristics in England was not as inclined to nationalist romanticism as its equivalent German discipline (*Volkskunde*), the belief that folklore was born and changed according to the spirit of the folk was still a bedrock principle of the discipline. Stemming from 'antiquarian studies', British folkloristics may have developed independently from the Continent, but this idea of folk creativity – embodied in the work of the enormously influential Jacob Grimm – was nearly universally accepted among both Continental and British folklorists.[22] In a paper read to the Folk-Lore Society, and subsequently published in *Folk-Lore* under the title 'The Folk', Jacobs argued rather heretically that the individuality of artistry in folklore stems from the 'folk' about as much as popular novels arise spontaneously from their subscribers.[23] Jacobs stated, 'when we come to realise what we mean by saying a custom, tale, a myth arose from the Folk, I fear we must come to the conclusion that the said Folk is a fraud, a delusion, a myth'.[24] And later, more emphatically: 'The folk is simply a name for our ignorance: we do not know to whom a proverb, a tale, a custom, a myth owes its origin, so we say it originated among the Folk.'[25]

Jacobs's theoretical approach arose in part as a defence against members of the Folk-Lore Society who accused him of having compromised the integrity of British folklore in his attempts to improve its readability and make it available to a wider audience. In response, Jacobs argued that he could not recognize any 'hard and fast distinction' between the creation of oral folklore by the 'folk' and written literature.[26] To the extent that the folk did exist, according to Jacobs, any individual (such as himself) who participated in any process of collecting or passing on folklore was a member of said folk. As Jacobs stated, 'Books are but so many telephones preserving the lore of the Folk, or more often burying it and embalming it. For, after all, *we* are the Folk as well as the rustic, though their lore may be other than ours, as ours will be different from that of those that follow us.'[27]

There were broader implications to Jacobs's call for his inclusion in the folk, and against collective folk creativity, than simply defending his own publications. In doing so Jacobs simultaneously negated any exclusionary definitions of 'the folk' and challenged any cultural distinctions between himself, a Jew, and European civilization in general. Hence he later claimed that national literature was exactly that, literature, and did not simply emanate from the popular spirit. In this context, Jacobs may have felt justified in participating culturally in British society, as without popular creativity, British folklore could not be considered the exclusive purview of those who traced their origins from there.

The debate over popular creativity came to the fore particularly during the controversy over the origins of the tale of Cinderella which engulfed the Society in 1893 and 1894. Jacobs, as a lone diffusionist, challenged the self-defined 'anthropological' folklorists over their claim to the British origins of the Cinderella tale. In contrast to those who believed in popular or folk creativity, adherents of diffusion and borrowing theory argued that each folktale stemmed from an individual artistic act which was then modified, re-interpreted, and transmitted over many generations and often across thousands of miles.[28] Diffusionists such as Jacobs tended to examine folk-tales for their literary and artistic rather than anthropological merits.[29] While English folkloristics had far fewer nationalist undertones than any equivalent on the Continent, the Cinderella controversy pushed the limits of neutrality in English folklore scholarship. In this rather complicated controversy, the most prominent folklorists in the society, even those who had long embraced diffusion and borrowing theory, clarified or modified their theoretical convictions to support Alfred Nutt's contention that despite some evidence of Indian origin and numerous similar Cinderella plots, the Cinderella tale originated in the British Isles, and evolved to embrace various ancient traditions of the folk. Despite being essentially a Tylorian argument in agreement with the doctrine of survivals, Jacobs's belief that individual folk-tales were created in a single act by individuals and then diffused did not sit well with Nutt and even diffusionist folklorists when the subject at hand was seemingly quintessential British folklore. Nutt accused Jacobs of ignoring the applications of evolutionary theories in the study of folklore, and of inconsistency between his Darwinist views in racial anthropology and lack thereof in cultural anthropology. In response to Jacobs's article 'Cinderella in Britain',[30] Nutt asked in *Folk-Lore*,

> What is the utmost claim of the anthropologist? That a number of tales originate in a social and intellectual stage out of which our *own* race has emerged, and in which *other* races have remained. ... I cannot understand why Mr. Jacobs who accepts that evidence, who is, in sociology, an evolutionist, should hesitate to accept evolution in folk-literature, should range himself on the side of the revelationist and 'degradationist', if I may coin an ugly word for an irrational thing. Has man struggled upwards from savagery? If so, then most assuredly his tales have struggled upwards with him.[31]

As used here by Nutt, race seems intended to take on the cultural meaning of the term, as Nutt surely would not include Jacobs's race among the 'other' races which remained in a savage state. Thus, although underlying Jacobs's initial argument against popular creativity may have been his desire to be included, or at least not excluded, from the English folk, it is ironically in the attempted refutation of this argument that an English scholar comes closest to confirming Jacobs's inclusion in the English cultural race. From the perspective of an Englishman such as Nutt, however, Jacobs's argument was not only illogical, but suggested a disconnection between folk-literature or lore, and national history. According to Nutt, folk-literature 'aims at depicting man in the sum total of his activities and emotions'; and he added, 'Literature then cannot disassociate itself from the past of the race: for artist, what has been, is'.[32]

In countering Nutt's claims of inconsistency, Jacobs argued that the very essence of his position was both evolutionary and anthropological (in the spirit of Tylor and Andrew Lang); qualitatively good folklore survives, and bad folklore does not. In his paper 'The Problem of Diffusion: Rejoinder' Jacobs argued with some success that a given folk-tale, if good, is both borrowed and improved upon, and the improved version often becomes the dominant version everywhere, even supplanting the original in its place of origin (Jacobs suggested the hegemony of Grimm's fairy-tales to be the example par-excellence). As folk-tale variants constantly multiply and disappear, Jacobs suggested that folklorists should concentrate on studying the history of the diffusion of specific tales, and refrain from seeing individual tales as reflecting the collective history of any single culture.[33]

Brian Maidment suggests that Jacobs's ardent defence of positions he alone held within the Folk-Lore Society led many of his contemporaries to consider him eccentric.[34] Furthermore, his success in making the non-literary folk heritage of Britain accessible as middle-class literature for children and parents who had lost touch with their oral heritage may not have endeared him to his contemporaries, whose standards and aims, in Maidment's terms, 'were perhaps more pretentious and less attainable'.[35] Yet, in stark contrast to his work on British folklore, Jacobs showed no interest in improving the accessibility of Jewish folklore for the children of West End Jews like himself. Despite his extensive research in British and European folklore, and Jewish physical anthropology, Jacobs denied the existence of an expressly Jewish folklore. In his 1888 lecture to the Jews' College Literary Society entitled 'Jewish Diffusion of Folk-Tales', as well as later articles in the *Jewish Encyclopedia* (published in New York in 1903), Jacobs argued that although Jews were historically responsible for transmitting folk-tales from east to west, Jews never developed their own folklore due to what he considered the intrinsically irrational nature of folklore, and the fundamentally rational nature of Judaism.[36] In the *Jewish Encyclopedia*'s entry for 'Folk-tale', Jacobs wrote that 'there is little evidence of Jews having had folk-tales of their own',[37] and in the entry for 'Folk-lore' he declared, 'in essence there is no Jewish folk-lore; yet practically ... there have been survivals of Jewish folklore in all stages of its development'.[38]

Jacobs conceded that some folkloristic elements exist in both the Bible and the Talmud, but he also claimed that Jewish folkloristic creativity ended with the dispersion, and that persisting Jewish customs which were folk-loric in basis were primarily borrowed from non-Jewish cultures.[39] Jacobs explained in 'Jewish Diffusion of Folk-Tales' that the 'bizarre elements of folk and fairy tales' which are survivals of 'savage and idolatrous practices and beliefs involving the grossest and crassest superstitions' were the very same practices that, according to Jacobs, 'were stamped out for ever by the majestic utterances of the prophets, and died away utterly after exile'.[40] Jacobs concluded from this line of reasoning that post-exilic Judaism provided infertile ground for the creation of folkloric literature, as 'Folk-tales could not, therefore, flourish in an atmosphere denuded of nearly all the superstitious material out of which they are formed'.[41]

Much of Jewish folklore did naturally originate from the peoples among whom the Jews lived. Nonetheless, Jacobs was particularly concerned to emphasize that in his opinion, rational Judaism is intrinsically at odds with folklore, a fundamentally irrational art. In the process of painting the Jews as more European than Europeans, Jacobs participated in a recasting of Jewish history and culture common to many trying to modernize the religion at the time. The thousands of Jews who moved to England and North America from Eastern Europe brought their superstitions with them. For Jews like Jacobs, desperately trying to combat negative stereotypes of Jews and Judaism, the fact that traditions persisted among East European Jews which were nothing less than folkloric in basis undermined their arguments against the supposed 'backwardness' of Jews. Arguing against the existence of Jewish folklore may have been doubly intended to persuade Jews to forsake such backwardness and to convince non-Jews of the misguided nature of their stereotypes of Jewish culture.

Jacobs's anthropological and folkloristic beliefs, although perhaps not as inconsistent with one another as Nutt argues, do reflect his personal agenda and conflicted Anglo-Jewish identity. On the one hand, Jacobs argued through racial anthropology that the Jews were indeed a race apart from the rest of Europe, and due to environmental factors were in some ways even physically deficient. On the other hand, Jacobs's desire for cultural inclusion in England is evident in his work for the English Folk-lore Society and also in his attempt to portray Judaism as inherently at odds with irrational folklore. Thus Jacobs's folkloristic writings reflect his desire to bring about his anthropological hypothesis: if the Jews were to do away with superstition, participate in and embrace English culture – if the Jews, in short, were to become model West End Englishmen as he had – then their physical deficiencies would disappear, and their genius become known to the world. In 1896 Jacobs stated, 'As we hold to the past as Jews, we can look forward to the future as Englishmen, now that we have been admitted on the closest terms into the great nation with whose future history that of the habitable globe is inextricably bound up.'[42] Yet, despite his belief in the shining future of English Jewry, despite the fact that Jacobs considered Anglo-Jewry the ideal type for global Jewry to model itself, and despite being an accomplished literary and anthropological scholar, he was unable to find steady employment in England. In 1900 he moved to New York.

Moses Gaster: a Jewish folklorist in Edwardian England

Moses Gaster was a Jew and a folklorist in England whose career overlapped with that of Jacobs and continued long after. At first glance, the two men had much in common. They were both Jewish members of the English

Folk-Lore Society, and were each involved from the earliest stages in the creation of folklore as a scholarly discipline in England.[43] Both had rather diverse academic interests, and were vocal advocates on behalf of East European Jewry. Both were also immigrants: Gaster had been forced to leave Romania, while Jacobs came voluntarily from Australia. Lastly, Gaster and Jacobs were fellow members of the elite London Jewish intellectual dining club, the Maccabaeans.[44]

Gaster and Jacobs socialized in the same circle of the London Jewish elite, as well as with the same English folklorists, but in many ways they are a study in contrasts. Moses Gaster was not only a scholar, but also a leader of some stature among Anglo-Jewry. A controversial *Haham* (akin to Chief Rabbi) of the Sephardic community, a militant Zionist influenced by Peretz Smolenskin and Leon Pinsker, and an early Hebrew revivalist, Gaster was born in 1856 into an elite Jewish family in Bucharest that was sympathetic to Western liberal thought. From his early adulthood he used his family connections to lobby on behalf of his countrymen, and was even involved in the negotiations for the emancipation of Romanian Jewry during the Congress of Berlin in 1878. In the years following the Congress, Gaster became a leading Romanian Jewish intellectual fighting antisemitism, and gradually came to be considered by the Romanian government as an agitator. At the age of 29, in 1885, Gaster was expelled from Romania supposedly for providing details to the West of Romanian antisemitic abuses, and he subsequently immigrated to England in 1886.[45]

After being expelled from Romania, Gaster increasingly shifted his political focus to Zionism, but he always continued to identify with Romanian culture. As Victor Eskenasy has observed, although Gaster's adult life in Romania was marked by his progressive transformation into a proto-Zionist militant, remarkably, 'the political disillusionment which hastened his Judaic militancy did not hamper his recognition as a scholarly authority on the Romanian scene'.[46] Nor did Gaster ever completely sever his own cultural affinity with Romania. Long after becoming an important British scholar, Gaster continued to publish in the *Anuar* (*Anuaral pentry israeliti – Annual for the Israelites*), the *maskilic* journal of Romanian Jewry, indicating that he continued to feel culturally connected to the Jewish community of his native country.[47]

Gaster published a large number of folkloric studies in Romanian, German, English, and Hebrew over the course of a long career.[48] Beginning with his doctoral dissertation at Leipzig University on the historical phonetics of the Romanian language, Gaster eventually became Europe's pre-eminent authority on Romanian folklore. Almost immediately upon his arrival in England, he was invited to give the Ilchester lectures in Greco-Slavonic literature at Oxford, in which he lectured on the relationship between Greco-Slavonic literature and the folklore of Europe during the middle ages. Gaster understood the significance of this appointment. As he later stated in his memoirs (with typically little humility), 'I was the first Jew who had ever been elected to that post [Ilchester lecturer at Oxford] and it made a great impression on the Jews, although they understood very little of what it meant. There were not at that time in Oxford more than eight or ten Jewish students.'[49]

Gaster, unlike Jacobs, believed that Jewish folklore was a real and extant phenomenon. In fact, one of the last endeavours of his life was to translate into English the *Ma'aseh Book*, a Yiddish compilation of Jewish tales and legends which Jacobs had earlier unequivocally suggested did not qualify as evidence of a Jewish folkloristic heritage. Even before this book, Gaster had published many studies of Jewish and Samaritan legends and tales relating to magic, as well as anthologies of rabbinic folk legends. He saw no contradiction between supposedly irrational folk-belief and rational Judaism, and even criticized other folklorists for systematically neglecting the religious elements apparent in all folklore. As Gaster stated in an article published in 1896, 'The element of religious belief, and I take this expression in the widest sense, is one of the most important features in the history of the origin and spread of fairy tales.'[50] The differences between Jacobs and Gaster on Jewish folklore reflect their disparate origins. Gaster may have been a western-influenced modernizing rabbi, but having grown up in Eastern Europe, he was comfortable with the superstitious elements of both Jewish religion and culture, whereas Jacobs, in contrast, felt compelled to portray Jews as more civilized than even Europeans, in order to push East European Jewry toward West European culture.

Like Jacobs, Gaster valued folklore more for its literary than anthropological merits. But what in particular distinguished Gaster's approach to the study of folklore was his emphasis on the art form's universal human quality. In his presidential address to the English Folk-Lore Society in 1908, Gaster explained that he felt personally involved in the world of fairy tales, charmed by its unbroken spell since his days in nursery. As a romantic he lamented that modern rationalism had lost something beautifully imaginative which existed in the past ('An enchanted world, a weird world, but none the less as real and true as the world in which we are moving now'[51]). The very beauty of tales, according to Gaster, is that they do not aim to address any narrow religious questions, but rather provide an escape from reality, and exist only as stories in which the conventional rules of the earth do not apply. Thus, their appeal is universal, and not only are all people inclined to create these tales, but once created, folk-tales are universally understood. As Gaster explained, 'The secret of the fairy-tales is that they are thoroughly human, no difference of faith or race, or station of life is recognized. They draw man to man, thereby weaving a spell over our mind.'[52]

For Gaster, folklore represented the summation of lost innocence in the modern period. Fairy tales and other folklore harkened back to a time when distinctions were not made between humans on the basis of faith or religion.

As a Jew whose interest in folklore began with both Jewish tales and a love for the bird and beast stories of his native Romania, he was well equipped to speak of the universal appeal of folklore. In fact, Gaster proudly attributed his appreciation and wide breadth of folkloric knowledge to his place of upbringing, stating, 'Born and bred in the East, I had greater facilities of coming in contact with the most varied elements of the populace than those given by the artificial and highly secluded form of education in the civilized world of the West.'[53] In suggesting his eastern upbringing as superior to the 'artificial and highly secluded' western education experienced by the members of the Folk-Lore Society, Gaster expressed the extent to which he prized his East European, or at least Romanian, origins.[54] Although Gaster was *Haham* of the small but long established and highly acculturated London Sephardic community (as opposed to the Ashkenazic community), his pride in his East European origins explain why he did not share Jacobs's interest in civilizing eastern Jews.

Gaster's affectionate descriptions of the fantasy world of tales, and the equilibrium established in them between all inhabitants of the earth, human and non-human, are likely a reflection of his own struggles at the time for the Zionist cause as well as for the improvement of living conditions for the Jews in Romania and tsarist Russia. Hence Gaster points out in his 1908 presidential address that the central theme in most tales is an imbalance in the natural order, stating that the 'final act in the little romance is always, justice done to the wronged'.[55] Although the metaphor was not necessarily intended, it is worth pointing out that Gaster's presidency of the English Folk-Lore Society also coincided with the most intense period of Zionist activism in his life. In addition to serving as vice-president of several Zionist congresses, helping to establish Jewish colonies in Palestine, and lobbying the British government, he was president of the English Zionist Federation in 1907.[56] Whether or not he was intentionally alluding to Zionism, his speeches to the Folk-Lore Society seem to express his Zionist idealism. Lamenting the lack of creativity, unity, and justice in the world, and proclaiming the need to find people with the necessary creativity and will to make changes, Gaster argued in these speeches that the utopian elements found universally in folk-tales reflect human yearning for the creation (or re-creation) of a better and more just world. Folklore, in other words, could doubly serve as inspiration for the achievement of those goals:

> As such an ideal state cannot be found in the real world, the poetic imagination of mankind, – the divine gift placed in the cradle of man at his birth, – has created this imaginary world of unity, beauty, and justice, and has transplanted thither all the ideal hopes and aspirations of man. For what have been the ideals which have inspired man from the

beginning and which animate him still in his noblest pursuits? Are they not the desire to realise some of the pictures of the fairy-tales? to create a world that is better, happier, and more glorious; where the differences between man and man have disappeared; where illness and troubles, fleeting shadows like the clouds, are dissipated by a warm and radiant sun; where justice reigns instead of wrong and oppression, and where virtue is rewarded. We may call such a picture a vision or an [sic] Utopia, for we look more to the difficulties which prevent its realisation.[57]

Although Gaster did not explicitly refer to the situation of the Jews in this speech, having been forced from his native country and currently engaged in a utopian experiment – Zionism – he seems at least implicitly to be relating his own personal experiences. The message Gaster drew from folklore – the need for creativity, high ideals, and belief in the seemingly impossible in addressing the problems of the day – complemented his Zionist idealism, as did his claim that a philosophy that aspires to create a world that is 'better, happier, and more glorious' is only considered utopian because 'we look more for the difficulties that prevent its realisation'.

Gaster was a Zionist and Jewish nationalist, but his underlying cosmopolitan humanism is evident in his folkloric work. He was a Zionist because he had seen first-hand the effects of antisemitism in Eastern Europe, and Zionist ideology appealed to his strong sense of justice and desire to correct the vulnerable position in which the Jews found themselves at the time. As a Zionist, Gaster would have also been aware of the extent to which a cultural foundation is necessary for national identification. There were other Jews during just this period who, also largely because of political disillusionment, came to the same realization: Yiddishists such as I. L. Peretz and Semyon Ansky, and Hebrew revivalists such as H. N. Bialik and M. J. Berdiczewski all collected or reformulated Jewish folklore as part of a national awakening in Eastern Europe.

In his presidential address to the Folk-Lore Society of the following year (1909), Gaster shifted from arguing about the universal virtues of folk-tales to focusing on the need for the study of folklore. Gaster claimed in this address that we must study all elements of folklore as they are the 'poetical flowers' containing 'that ancient knowledge which has permeated the world, and the fragrance of which is keeping the human soul fresh whenever it is wafted upon it'.[58] These are words which rabbis, even modern ones, tend to reserve for the Talmud, but Gaster was convinced by the ability of folklore to further human understanding. As he reflected upon the short history of folkloristics, 'The further students penetrated into the realm of the "Folk," *i.e.* that knowledge which is the property of the "Folk," the greater grew the similarity between one nation and another.'[59] Thus, according to Gaster, the significance of folkloristics is as 'a bridge between anthropology and psychology, mere man and mere soul, showing unity in spite of difference'.[60]

Unlike Jacobs, Gaster was not concerned with questions relating to Jewish racial distinction. He accepted national differences, but believed that folklore's universalism demonstrates the common qualities shared by nations, what he called 'unity in spite of difference'. Where Jacobs believed the folk to be a 'fraud', Gaster believed that we collectively belong to a greater folk, as demonstrated by folklore's ability to reveal the shared characteristics and unity of all nations. Gaster, unlike Jacobs, would have considered the idea that Jews had no folklore ridiculous, not least because he was a Jewish folklorist, but more importantly, because he believed no nation exists without its own folklore.

Conclusion

The experiences of Jacobs and Gaster suggest a considerable degree of openness in late-Victorian and Edwardian England to Jewish participation in both English cultural production and scholarly discussion. The study of folklore in England, as elsewhere, grew out of a desire to trace national consciousness back historically, but the discipline as it developed – and perhaps also, by implication, English nationalism at the time – was sufficiently inclusive that Jewish individuals such as Gaster and Jacobs could be prominent members of its scholarly society and participate in developing folkloristics as a field of study in England. Each used this forum as a means to minimize national distinctions: in the case of Jacobs, by arguing against the existence of the folk (in which he faced considerable opposition); and in the case of Gaster, by emphasizing the universal qualities of folklore.

Jacobs believed in the exceptional status of modern English Jewry and he attributed its success to a number of historical circumstances stemming from the early decline of feudalism and the rise of commercialism in England, and the religious toleration which was, according to Jacobs, *sine qua non* for the British imperial project. Most importantly, however, Jacobs believed that the gradual process of emancipation in England ensured its permanence: 'The Jews had time to prove themselves worthy for admission into the national fold before the gates were unbarred. They took part in all sides of the national life so far as they were permitted.'[61] As Jacobs fully accepted the premise that Jews had needed first to prove themselves worthy of emancipation, he personally attempted to continue to prove Jewish worth both by taking part in 'the national life', and also in working to demonstrate that the latest wave of Jewish immigrants to England would over time become English in a similar manner.

Gaster, like Jacobs, considered England to be a particularly unrestrictive society, both academically and socially. As he later reflected upon his first impressions of the country, 'There was altogether a different spirit of liberty in England, a different atmosphere in every way, a cordiality and understanding for the demands of human civilisation and human progress.'[62]

Nonetheless, neither individual was ultimately fully successful in achieving their desired aspirations in England. Although Gaster held a few temporary lecturing positions and fellowships, like Jacobs, he was never granted a permanent post at an English university, despite being considered a pre-eminent thinker in his day.[63] In fact, though both men received accolades later in their lives, such recognition was not from English institutions. After moving to the United States in 1900 to become an editor of the *Jewish Encyclopedia*, Jacobs became a lecturer at the Jewish Theological Seminary of America and was even granted an honorary doctorate from the University of Pennsylvania, something he failed to achieve in England. Gaster was awarded numerous honours from his native country (from which he had been expelled); he was made an honorary member of the Romanian Academy, was a Holder of the Romanian Order of Merit, 2nd and 1st classes, and was a Grand Officer of the Order of the Romanian Crown.

While Jacobs held West End Anglo-Jewry to be the model for East End and indeed all of East European Jewry to emulate, Gaster remained very much in touch with his East European roots, and was unthreatened by its culture. And yet, the unexpected irony in this comparison relates to how Gaster, a Zionist Romanian rabbi, was (relatively speaking) more accepted among his English colleagues in the field of English folklore studies than Jacobs, the Cambridge-educated Australian who published several tomes of English and Celtic folklore. Part of the reason for his greater acceptance lay in the fact that Gaster came to England already with a PhD, his studies were more scholarly, and his opinions less at odds (at least in their expression) with the majority of English folklorists. Perhaps because of these factors, as well as his East European upbringing and his Zionist philosophy, Gaster was confident enough to be not only an English folklorist who was Jewish, like Jacobs, but also an English folklorist of the Jews.

Notes

1. G. L. Gomme, 'Folk-Lore Terminology', *The Folk-Lore Journal*, 2.11 (1884), 348. See also Dorson, 'Folklore Studies', 308. The term 'folklore' was first used in 1846 by the antiquarian William John Thoms.
2. See Dorson, 'The Great Team'.
3. Although it would be reasonable to so speculate, Jacobs never concluded as such, even stating in the introduction to his 1896 collection of essays, *Jewish Ideals and Other Essays*, 'Here in England we are almost absolutely free from any taint of anti-Semitism.' Joseph Jacobs, *Jewish Ideals and Other Essays* (London: David Nutt, 1896), xvi. Nevertheless, one essay in this collection ('Mordecai: a Protest against the Critics', 61–83), an ardent defence of George Eliot's *Daniel Deronda*, may suggest that Jacobs at times felt otherwise.
4. See Maidment, 'The Literary Career'.
5. British anthropology (unlike its German counterpart) generally took a rather limited and not characteristically negative interest in Jews, reflecting the comparatively benign English perception of the Jews. One notable exception was

Robert Knox, who in the mid-nineteenth century imported much of the biological racism of the Continent to England. Efron, *Defenders of the Race*, 33–57.

6. Anthropometry is the practice of measuring the dimensions of human bodies for the purpose of comparative physical anthropology.

7. For an overview of Jacobs and Jewish race science see Efron, *Defenders of the Race*, 58–90; Hart, *Social Science*, 177–179.

8. Jacobs asked, 'What are the qualities, if any, that we are to regard as *racially* characteristic of Jews?' His answer: 'Much vague declamation has been spoken and written on this subject. All the moral, social, and intellectual qualities of Jews have been spoken as being theirs by right of birth in its physical sense. Jews differ from others in all these points, it is true.' Joseph Jacobs, 'On the Racial Characteristics of Modern Jews', *The Journal of the Anthropological Institute of Great Britain and Ireland*, 15 (1886), 25.

9. Joseph Jacobs and Isidore Spielman, 'On the Comparative Anthropometry of English Jews', *The Journal of the Anthropological Institute of Great Britain and Ireland*, 19 (1890), 77. This study, as well as other relevant material from *The Journal of the Anthropological Institute of Great Britain and Ireland*, in addition to Jacobs's 'Studies in Jewish Statistics' (originally published in the *Jewish Chronicle*), were reprinted jointly in Joseph Jacobs, *Studies in Jewish Statistics: Social, Vital and Anthropometric* (London: David Nutt, 1891).

10. Jacobs and Spielman, 'On the Comparative Anthropometry', 80.

11. The pioneering anthropologist Franz Boas, a German Jew, was at the time working along similar lines. In 1900 Boas conducted a study among the immigrants to New York demonstrating that skull shape can change due to environment.

12. Francis Galton, a cousin of Charles Darwin, was also an early mentor of Jacobs at Cambridge. See Joseph Jacobs, 'The Comparative Distribution of Jewish Ability', *The Journal of the Anthropological Institute of Great Britain and Ireland*, 15 (1886), 351–379.

13. Jacobs's *Studies in Biblical Archaeology* (London: David Nutt, 1894) aimed to prove specifically the supposed purity of the Jewish race.

14. Jacobs, as Mitchell Hart states (*Social Science*, 178), 'provides an excellent example of the way in which racial notions could be employed for liberal (i.e., integrationist) purposes'.

15. Tylor claimed that he had developed his argument independently from the theories of Darwin and Spencer. Stocking, *Victorian Anthropology*, 163.

16. Jacobs later claimed he had written most of the paper's editorials in the important year of 1881. Cesarani, *The Jewish Chronicle*, 68. Jacobs was also editor of the periodical *Darkest Russia*. For more on the Mansion House Fund and the Mansion House Committee (the Russo-Jewish Committee after 1882) see Black, *The Social Politics*, 254–267.

17. Efron, *Defenders of the Race*, 78.

18. Efron, *Defenders of the Race*, 78.

19. Very few individuals in England could at this time derive their employment primarily from anthropology. As George Stocking states (*Victorian Anthropology*, 267), 'until nearly 1900, there were probably no more than a dozen men whose professional life was given over solely to anthropological activity, and with the qualified exception of Tylor none of them was regularly involved as an anthropologist in training men who would later devote their own professional lives to anthropology'. Jacobs also wrote extensively as a literary critic, journalist, and historian.

20. Stocking, *Victorian Anthropology*, 163, 262.
21. Within that period, Jacobs collected, edited, and published folklore collections including: *The Earliest English Version of the Fables of Bidpai*; a collection of *Indian Fairy Tales*; two collections of *Aesop's Fables*; *English Fairy Tales*; *Celtic Fairy Tales*; *More English Fairy Tales*; *More Celtic Fairy Tales*; *The Most Delectable History of Reynard the Fox*; and *Barlaam and Josaphat: English Lives of Buddha*.
22. Dorson, 'Folklore Studies', 310. See also Dorson., *The British Folklorists*.
23. Joseph Jacobs, 'The Folk', *Folk-Lore*, 4.2 (1893), 235.
24. Jacobs, 'The Folk', 234.
25. Jacobs, 'The Folk', 236.
26. Jacobs, 'The Folk', 237.
27. Jacobs, 'The Folk', 237, my emphasis. The idea that folklore is not merely a relic of the past, but is continually reshaped and created as a result of communication and performance (identical to Jacobs's argument) is now an accepted anthropological principle.
28. Borrowing theory, developed by the German scholar Theodor Benfey in the 1850s, purported that European folklore was sourced in ancient India and passed westward over many years.
29. In reference to his opponents, Jacobs stated, 'These gentlemen, as I have put it previously, are fortune-hunters, who seek to get as much anthropological wealth out of the folk-tale as they can; I and a few others love her for herself alone. And out of this love springs my protest against their use as *copora vilia* for the anthropologist, and generally I protest against the practice of regarding folk-lore as solely so much material for anthropology, so much contribution to the study of institutions and their evolution. ... I claim to be an anthropologist also. But my anthropology includes likewise the study of the evolution of man's artistic nature.' Joseph Jacobs, 'The Problem of Diffusion: Rejoinders', *Folk-Lore*, 5.2 (1894), 145.
30. Joseph Jacobs, 'Cinderella in Britain', *Folk-Lore*, 4.3 (1893), 269–284.
31. Alfred Nutt, 'Some Recent Utterances of Mr. Newell and Mr. Jacobs. A Criticism', *Folk-Lore*, 4.4 (1893), 442, my emphasis. It is worth noting that in the long run, Jacobs's theories had greater posterity than those of Nutt and the other evolutionists of the Folk-Lore Society. As Richard Dorson states ('Folklore Studies', 306), 'When anthropology rejected the theory of unilinear cultural evolution in favour of cultural pluralism, the scaffolding of English folklore research collapsed.'
32. Nutt, 'Some Recent Utterances', 447.
33. Jacobs, 'The Problem of Diffusion', 129–146. For more on this controversy see Dorson, *The British Folklorists*, 306–310.
34. Maidment, 'Joseph Jacobs', 189.
35. Maidment, 'Joseph Jacobs', 196.
36. Joseph Jacobs, 'Jewish Diffusion of Folk-Tales', *Jewish Ideals*, 138.
37. Joseph Jacobs, 'Folk-tales', *The Jewish Encyclopedia* (New York: Funk & Wagnalls, 1903), 5:428. Jacobs justified his negation of the existence of post-exilic Jewish folk-tales based on the very narrow parameters by which he defined the term. Although Jews did compose some tales and borrowed others throughout the European ghettos, according to Jacobs, these are not by definition folk-tales, 'since nothing fairylike or supernormal occurs in them' (428).
38. Joseph Jacobs, 'Folk-lore', *The Jewish Encyclopedia*, 5:423.
39. Jacobs stated, 'Spread among all the peoples of the earth, the Jews appear to have borrowed customs from each of them, and when found among them to-day it is

most difficult to determine: first, whether the custom is at all Jewish; and, secondly, if non-Jewish, whether it belongs to the country where the particular folk-lore item is found or has been brought thither from some other country.' Jacobs, 'Folk-lore', 5:424.

40. Jacobs, 'Jewish Diffusion', 138.
41. Jacobs, 'Jewish Diffusion', 138.
42. Joseph Jacobs, 'The Typical Character of Anglo-Jewish History', *Jewish Historical Society of England: Transactions*, 3 (1896–98), 143. This is the published version of an address by Jacobs to the Jewish Historical Society of England on 14 November 1897.
43. Gaster evidently had considerable respect for Jacobs as a folklorist: 'Jacobs was very clever, very industrious, very keen in his judgement, very quick in his perception of facts and an extremely hard worker; he had to make a livelihood....He was a very good man.' Bertha Gaster (ed), *Moses Gaster: Memoirs* (London: 1990), 71–72.
44. The Maccabaeans (whose membership also included such notables as Israel Zangwill, Israel Abrahams, Lucien Wolf, Oswald John Simon, Arthur Davis, Herbert Bentwich, Solomon J. Solomon, and Solomon Schechter), officially formed in November 1891 from a group of intellectuals previously known as 'The Wanderers'. The *Jewish Chronicle* devoted a large amount of space to covering the group's events and publishing verbatim its members' speeches and debates. Cesarani, *The Jewish Chronicle*, 90.
45. What Gaster completed of his memoirs were edited, collated and printed privately by Bertha Gaster under the title, *Moses Gaster: Memoirs* (London: 1990). A more widely circulating publication, Victor Eskenasy (ed.), *Memorii (fragmente) Correspondată/Moses Gaster* (1998) is primarily in Romanian, but includes a short English summary of Gaster's memoirs and letters as well as a small amount of Gaster's English correspondence. Also see Bar-Avi, *Dr Moses Gaster*.
46. Eskenazy, 'Gaster', 172.
47. Stanciu, 'A Promoter of the Haskala'.
48. For a complete list of Moses Gaster's publications see Schindler, *Gaster Centenary Publication*, 23–40.
49. *Moses Gaster: Memoirs*, 71. Gaster wrote the Ilchester lectures in German, and paid Joseph Jacobs to help him translate them into English. Gaster's failure to thank Jacobs in the introduction to the published edition, according to Gaster, led to resentment on the part of Jacobs. *Moses Gaster: Memoirs*, 76–77.
50. Moses Gaster, 'Fairy Tales from Inedited Hebrew MSS. of the Ninth and Twelfth Centuries', *Folk-Lore*, 7.3 (1896), 220.
51. Moses Gaster, 'Presidential Address', *Folk-Lore*, 19.1 (1908), 12.
52. Gaster, 'Presidential Address' (1908), 30.
53. Gaster, 'Fairy Tales', 218.
54. Gaster was rather defensive about western Jewish perceptions of Romanian Jewry and argued that the Romanian Jewish experience was historically exceptional within Eastern Europe. As Gaster stated in his memoirs, 'People in the west thought the Jews of Roumania to be half educated and an eastern lot. They did not know that the Jews there had received an education much superior to, or at least on a level with the Jews in the West, and they were in many ways far superior as far as their character was concerned.' *Moses Gaster: Memoirs*, 60.
55. Gaster, 'Presidential Address' (1908), 23.
56. For a detailed account of Gaster's Zionist activities see, Black, 'A Typological Study'.

57. Gaster, 'Presidential Address' (1908), 28.
58. Moses Gaster, 'Presidential Address', *Folk-Lore*, 20.1 (1909), 15.
59. Gaster, 'Presidential Address' (1909), 18.
60. Gaster, 'Presidential Address' (1909), 18.
61. Jacobs, 'Typical Character', 139.
62. *Moses Gaster: Memoirs*, 66.
63. Part of the problem related to the difficulties faced by folklore studies in England in gaining academic recognition at the most important English universities, Oxford, Cambridge, and the University of London. When English social anthropology became established at these universities, the field had little interest in folklore. Dorson, 'Folklore Studies', 305. Still, Gaster was well-qualified for other academic posts as he held a PhD, was widely recognized as a gifted linguist, and served as a member, councillor, and eventually vice-president of the Royal Asiatic Society.

7
Imperial Zion: Israel Zangwill and the English Origins of Territorialism

David Glover

The great Anglo-Jewish writer Israel Zangwill (1864–1926) has long represented a difficult case in the history of Zionism, so much so that he might scarcely be said to belong to that history at all, a figure more often omitted than remembered. Certainly in the wake of his notorious 1923 Carnegie Hall address to the American Jewish Congress attacking political Zionism – a speech denounced by Chaim Weizmann as tantamount to 'national treason' – Zangwill seemed to have sealed his reputation as a dangerous apostate.[1] Yet initially, Zangwill's Zionist credentials were impeccable. When Theodor Herzl first came to England in November 1895, he made a point of visiting the celebrated author of *Children of the Ghetto* at his home in Kilburn and, as a direct result of their meeting, Zangwill emerged as one of Zionism's most prominent advocates in a period when many leading figures in the Jewish community were lukewarm or entirely sceptical about Herzl's project.

Despite being an early and enthusiastic supporter of Herzl, Zangwill nevertheless shifted position several times in the course of an eventful career. From being thoroughly immersed in the Zionist movement, a familiar face and voice at its annual congresses, Zangwill embarked on a path that was effectively to lead him into the political wilderness, before wearily returning to the fold towards the end of his life when all other hopes appeared to have been exhausted. Whether Zangwill was ever really readmitted, his detour or deviation forgiven, remains an open question. But it is with that detour – or rather with its peculiarly English character and origins – that this essay is concerned.

In a sense, Zangwill's divergence from Zionism is inseparable from Zionism's own history and can be traced back to Herzl's failure to secure Turkish support for a Jewish settlement in Palestine, a failure that was rooted in the inter-imperial rivalries of the late nineteenth century and that encouraged Herzl to turn to other more or less desperate expedients. For over two decades Zangwill immersed himself in the search for a non-Palestinian homeland, a new colonial space that might for the foreseeable future replace the need for diasporic Jews to fruitlessly pin their hopes to the dream of Eretz-Israel. It was this controversial venture, labelled 'Territorialism' and promoted by his Jewish Territorial Organization (or ITO), that preoccupied Zangwill during his most politically active years and set him at odds with the Zionist Congress after Herzl's untimely death in July 1904. Zangwill was a lively and enormously resourceful rhetorician, but with hindsight the provocative catchphrases that peppered his political speeches too easily resonate as famous last words, stamped with all the finality of an epitaph. 'Zionism without Zion', a slogan tossed off in an address designed to inspire American backing for a Jewish settlement in British East Africa, might well have been inscribed on Zangwill's tombstone.[2] His tireless devotion to the territorialist cause not only broke his health, but also helped to extinguish, or at least overshadow, his once-bright literary reputation.

Even today territorialism remains something of an impediment to those forms of Zionist historiography that view the creation of the modern Israeli state as the capstone and ultimate validation of all Herzl's efforts. For if Herzl's game plan is conceived as the slow, steady, yet always single-minded direction of the Jewish people towards Palestine, irrespective of any tactical adjustments necessitated by the geopolitical exigencies uppermost at any particular moment, then Zangwill's commitment to the exploration of alternative possibilities must *ipso facto* appear not only as a reckless diversion, squandering popular energies on a wholly specious goal, but as an act of betrayal. In fact, far from being unthinkable, territorialist initiatives were an integral part of the Zionist milieu that Herzl created and were partly inspired by the political manoeuvrings that absorbed his later years. Had Herzl not been prepared to consider and actively negotiate for Jewish colonies *outside* Palestine, it is doubtful whether Zangwill would have pursued his cause so fervently and so doggedly.

Signs of the pragmatic nature of Herzl's vision were present almost from the very beginning and undoubtedly prior to the First Zionist Congress of 1897: in his foundational pamphlet *Der Judenstaat* (1896), for example, Herzl envisaged a choice between Palestine and Argentina and, while clearly favouring the former, insisted that '[w]e shall take what is given us, and what is selected by Jewish public opinion'.[3] By the turn of the century, and especially following the Galician pogroms in 1899, the sense of a non-Palestinian option began to take on substance. Indeed, at the Third Zionist Congress of 1899 Herzl was already floating the idea of a Jewish settlement in Cyprus – an idea that had been suggested to him the previous year by fellow Zionist Davis Trietsch – only to find that 'Jewish public opinion' was distinctly unimpressed.[4] But it was Herzl's discussions with Joseph Chamberlain in October 1902 at the Colonial Office in London that precipitated the most sustained consideration of a Jewish statelet by substituting part of East Africa for the Promised Land. Though the prototypical territorialist solution as it tentatively emerged from this ill-starred meeting ultimately proved to be stillborn, Zangwill made it his personal mission to give it life. Why did he do so?

Two very different answers have been proposed by critics and historians, each of them embedded in a specific reading of Herzl's career. According to the first line of argument, Zangwill is the Zionist deserter who abandons the cause for a pale and meretricious imitation and who fails to grasp the short-term tactical improvisations that mask Herzl's grand Palestinian strategy; or, in a more pessimistic version, Zangwill is the political *naïf* who is unable to learn from what Herzl eventually recognized as a disastrous mistake.[5] On this view – which echoes the outrage expressed at the Sixth Zionist Congress in 1903 – Zangwill's most serious shortcoming is his inability to appreciate the strength of commitment, the sheer staying power, displayed by the movement's most visionary figure, not to mention its most dedicated supporters.[6] Put another way, one might say that, unlike Herzl, *Zangwill's* attachment to Zionism was too superficial, too shallow to plumb the true currents of historical change, and so he rashly pursued what was in fact a chimera.

The second explanation offers a curious inversion of this thesis. By this reckoning, Zangwill emerges as Herzl's most sincere disciple, perhaps more candid (or, at worst, more guileless) than his mentor. So Uri Eisenzweig has argued that what Zangwill articulates is the inner logic of Herzl's political thought, insofar as it crystallizes around the dream of an autonomous Jewish territory beyond the murderous reach of antisemitisms old and new.[7] Only a Zionist movement flexible enough to pay the price of forsaking Palestine could guarantee the security and integrity of the Jews in extraordinarily troubled times. However unthinkable such an option might sound, so serious was the plight of the Jews that sooner or later a combination of hard circumstances and practical successes would persuade Zionists everywhere that it was a viable proposition. *This* therefore was the implicit goal of Herzl's Zionism that its leader could never openly acknowledge for fear of exacerbating the tensions and divisions within the movement and losing the bulk of his supporters. But, of course, if Eisenzweig is right, then any distinction between how Herzl understood the Zionist project and what Zangwill called territorialism is entirely illusory, a matter of emphasis at best. The criticism voiced in 1903 by Herzl's main Russian opponent Menahem Ussishkin when he dubbed his Viennese adversary 'a territorialist masquerading as a Zionist' turns out to be correct.[8]

Now there may be something to be said in favour of both these answers. Zangwill's own take on Judaism always emphasized its progressive side, its 'centre of gravity' in the 'here and now', what he came to call its capacity to resonate with 'the very note of "modernity"'.[9] And this perhaps dulled his appreciation of the tenacity displayed by those East European Jews whose unwavering allegiance to Zionist principles derived from the earlier religious, nationalist, *Hibbat Zion* tradition. But one might note that Zangwill's restless pursuit of contemporary relevance was also what made Herzl such an attractive figure to him – and that made Herzl such a problematic figure for others. For, notwithstanding his stature as Zionism's pioneer and champion, it is precisely Herzl's 'modernity' that has so often and so long been at issue, the suspicion that his thinking was not Jewish enough, that at heart he was 'too European.'[10] Among those Zionists like Ahad Ha'am, who believed in the necessity of a Jewish cultural renaissance, Herzl's vision of a future Jewish society was a curiously bloodless exercise in liberal wish-fulfilment in which everything that had made the Jews unique was somehow to be effortlessly sublated through the infinitely expandable horizons of advanced technology and civic tolerance. There is thus some plausibility in Eisenzweig's claim that Herzl and Zangwill were united in a 'double refusal', turning away from the ghetto *and* assimilation in favour of 'a third way' whose 'essential' feature was that it would at last 'leave the Diaspora behind.'[11]

Of course, this brotherhood-in-negation begs all the most important questions, since the indeterminacy or open-endedness of the putative 'third way' effectively gives the idea of a return to Palestine (and *a fortiori* Zionism itself) a curiously neutral status in cultural and religious terms. Nevertheless, it would be a mistake to underestimate the very real affinity between these two men of letters. Despite what Herzl condescendingly called Zangwill's 'long-nosed Negroid' appearance, the East End writer immediately impressed him as 'an honest ambitious man who had made his way after bitter struggles', while for his part Zangwill subsequently described his meeting with the Viennese journalist and playwright as a sort of conversion experience.[12]

What both of these accounts neglect, however, is the decisive role that the British political context played in shaping Zangwill's response to the new agendas brought into being by the rise of Zionism (not to mention Herzl's own love affair with England). Although many of Zangwill's practical commitments – his feminism, his pacifism, and his socialist sympathies – embodied universalistic values and beliefs, it was the pressure of events within the British political arena that nearly always propelled him into word and deed. In spite of his wide interests, generous sympathies, and an understandable desire to ensure that his writing should travel well – reaching out to the largest, most heterogeneous publics – Zangwill was at root a peculiarly British intellectual. From his earliest days as a humorist alongside writers like his friend Jerome K. Jerome to his later insistence that England was uniquely Zionism's 'spiritual home', Zangwill was first and foremost a British voice.[13] And his journey from the Spitalfields of his birth to the country retreat in Sussex where he ended his days was also, in its way, a very British success story. True, Zangwill was never a very easy figure. Temperamentally disputatious, exasperatingly independent-minded, and seldom cowed, he was in many respects a natural malcontent. Yet during the First World War, when the British government wanted to assemble a group of writers to help them find ways of resisting the German propaganda campaign, it was to Zangwill – along with Thomas Hardy, H. G. Wells, John Masefield, Arnold Bennett, and Gilbert Murray – that the government turned.[14] However spiky and unpredictable he might often have been, he did become, if not quite a national treasure, at least something very close to an establishment figure.

Lest this sound too cosy, it should immediately be added that Zangwill's presence raises questions about the cohesiveness and vitality of Britain's intellectual life in the late nineteenth and early twentieth centuries and its purchase upon the public imagination. Like Disraeli before him, Zangwill's elevation to the national-popular stage – 'national in idiom, popular in argument', to use Michael Walzer's suggestive formula – showed that his thinking was inescapably tempered by broader, less parochial loyalties than his origins and obsessions would lead one to expect.[15] At the same time, the fact that his audiences were typically much more diverse, much more complex than those of his non-Jewish forebears and peers, gave Zangwill a singular position amongst the ranks of those 'public moralists' and commentators who endeavoured to act as the consciences of the nation's civic and intellectual life.[16] Not only did Zangwill have to straddle the divide between majority and minority cultures, resorting to an unstable, double-voiced address; but in his speeches and political work he was also constantly forced to confront the internal divisions that defined the contemporary Jewish communities with whose futures he was engaged.

Whether Zangwill possessed the patience and tact that might have secured the kind of mediation between the very various constituencies that his politics required is doubtful in the extreme. He could be blunt and abrasive in his assessments and recommendations, as well as witty and persuasive. Yet in his unsentimental recognition of the intractable tensions that animated Jewish life, in his awareness that the fragmentation of British Jewry was inseparable from its uncomfortable approach towards the national mainstream, Zangwill was far from lacking in 'subtlety' as a social and political observer, as some of his more severe critics have maintained.[17]

His first major foray into Zionist politics came at the end of November 1901, just one month before the Fifth Zionist Congress was due to convene in Basle, when Zangwill organized and headed up a discussion on 'The Commercial Future of Palestine' in the new premises of the Article Club, a body that provided a forum for debates on leading political and economic matters of the day. In opening the proceedings, Zangwill's talk was an attempt to increase general awareness of Palestine's economic opportunities, to suggest some of the ways in which the country needed to be developed, and to explore their implications for Jewish settlement. To further this end he assembled a remarkable collection of sympathetic and interested parties, ranging from colonial administrators with experience in Australia,

Canada, and the Far East to eminent members of the Jewish community such as Dr Moses Gaster and Colonel Goldsmid. Also included were a clutch of well-known and widely-read authors including the novelist Hall Caine (whose romance *The Scapegoat* had led the Chief Rabbi to ask him to travel to Poland and Russia to investigate the plight of the Jews in 1891) and two playwrights: George Bernard Shaw and George Sims, the latter best known for his Adelphi melodramas, as well as his campaigning journalism and popular ballads.

This concoction of imperial knowledge laced with a certain measure of philosemitism was subsequently to prove definitive of Zangwill's vision and tactics: it formed the intuitive baseline from which his thinking evolved. However, at this stage Zangwill's arguments looked over his shoulder at the founding charter of the First Zionist Congress of 1897, echoing the Basle Programme's assertion of the need to create 'a home for the Jewish people in Palestine to be secured by public law'.[18] There is scant reference here to the various backstage negotiations regarding Cyprus or Sinai, for example, endeavours that had formed the unsettling subtext to the previous Congress in August 1899.[19]

On the night, Zangwill's Article Club address rather played down this Zionist pedigree, though it did reappear as the necessary starting-point in the version that he published in *The New Liberal Review* the following month. There Zangwill also struck a characteristically discomforting note, rebuking those 'unbalanced spirits' among his fellow-Zionists who 'mistook the beginning of the movement for its consummation'.[20] In short, correcting this misrecognition and replacing it with a more accurate perspective constituted the principal aim of his survey. Central to Zangwill's argument is the proposition that Palestine is no mere pastoral idyll, but an embryonic industrial nation that will be built on 'the ruins of a great civilized State'.[21] And playing upon the European inter-imperial rivalries that lay at the heart of popular fears about Britain's own international destiny, Zangwill stressed that Germany was currently 'the only country that seriously makes an effort to push her trade in Palestine', was vigorously expanding its industrial and commercial activities, and may by the next generation come to dominate the area (14).

In practice, Zangwill's evidence was slight. As a fairly recent visitor to the country he knew, and frankly admitted, that Palestine lacked the developed infrastructure – 'roads, railways, harbours, and water power' (15) – of which Herzl could only dream in his utopian novel *Altneuland* (1902) and which alone would facilitate the emergence of a truly modern statelet, no matter how abundant the supply of Jewish labour available from Russia and Eastern Europe.[22] The crux of the argument therefore turned on the credibility of Palestine as a possible site for the kind of skilled industrial labour capable of reshaping the social world, a near teleological belief that underpinned a variety of political positions in this period. Thus George Bernard Shaw's rejoinder to Zangwill partly consisted of a sharp reminder – in line with the views he would advance on Ireland's future in *John Bull's Other Island* (1904) – that agricultural workers lacked the 'intellect' to make a real contribution to Palestine's renewal. Similarly, when Shaw insisted that 'the poor and the oppressed and the down-trodden are not the people with whom to build up a great city' (16), his reference to the view that certain types of human material were chronically and permanently unsuitable to the modern division of labour carried clear degenerationist overtones. However, it was George Sims who raised what was to become the main component of Zangwill's political thinking when he emphasized not only the importance of the 'alien immigrant to the maintenance of the commercial supremacy of England by enabling manufacturers to compete in the markets of cheap production', but also the under-appreciation of this fact by the majority of the country's population. Hence the ambivalence of Sims's final remarks: for, while 'there was little probability of *Judenhetze* in England, it would be unwise to ignore signs of the approaching agitation against alien immigration' (17).[23] What Zangwill had done in making the case for the resettlement of Palestine, said Sims, was to show that English Jews were actively seeking their own panacea. If Jewish labour was truly a national asset, then it might equally count as an asset in some other part of the globe, as though the proof of its value lay in its alienability or fungibility, vital but dispensable.

Zangwill took up this question in more detail in his *New Liberal Review* essay. There he argued that antisemitism, previously a form of religious bigotry, was now in its modern incarnation fuelled by 'commercial jealousy' and 'the dislike for all that is unlike' that was endemic to democratic nation-states, 'the crude logic of Demos and demagogues' (an analysis that was close to Herzl's own position on the subject). However many generations of Jews had lived in any given country, they were always in some fundamental respect regarded as permanent aliens. In a direct riposte to George Sims, Zangwill observed how 'vain' was the defence that East End Jews 'have won the mantle trade for England against German importations'. The reaction from their compatriots was nothing less than the formation of the British Brothers' League, mischievous questions in Parliament, and the unwarranted racial slur that English Jews have been unwilling to fight in the Boer War. There was little comfort to be gleaned from conceding that England 'has no Jewish problem in the sense in which other nations have it'.[24] This long hard look at the vicissitudes of English antisemitism went to the core of the anxieties upon which Zangwill's territorialism was founded.

Against such assaults, what resources did modern Jewry possess? What made its plight exceptionally desperate was the fact that the Jewish community faced both 'persecution without and disintegration within'.[25] The latter half of this pungent formula had long been among Zangwill's chief preoccupations. As early as 1889, in a review essay dealing with the question 'What is Judaism?', he had observed that 'all over the world the old Judaism is breaking down,' characterizing *English* Judaism in particular as 'an immense chaos of opinions', racked by internal dissension.[26] At this stage in his thinking, Zangwill regarded the future of Judaism as lying in the direction of what he called 'Natural Judaism' in which the supernatural narrative forms that had been the carriers of the faith were progressively being stripped away to reveal the real moral and intellectual content that gave it meaning. But, of course, this rather neo-Hegelian move was implicitly presented as very much a Western-led phenomenon with England at the epicentre of events. Only one generation away from East European origins, Zangwill seems to have regarded – and perhaps needed to regard –the 'simple heart of the Russian pauper' as a residual matter.[27]

While Zangwill's 'criticism' and attempted 'classification' of the varieties of English Judaism was detailed and complex, it fell short of the full-blown commitment to modernity that began to enliven his work around the time of his first meeting with Herzl. In his article on 'The Position of Judaism' that appeared eight months before Herzl's visit to Kilburn, Zangwill portrayed Judaism as *the* form of consciousness most adequate to contemporary society: as he put it, '[t]here is more in Judaism akin to the modern spirit than there is in any other religion.'[28] The argument is often forced or fanciful – as when Zangwill finds affinities between the remote omnipresence of the God of the Old Testament and the unity underlying the phenomenal world – but the insistence that the crumbling of the ghetto provides the conditions, far too rarely understood at present, for the renewal and possible generalisation of Judaism into a kind of Comtean religion of humanity, binding together sociology, socialism, and natural science, is powerfully articulated.

However, this emergent closeness of fit between Judaism and modernity, requiring – in a typical Zangwillian paradox – that Judaism assimilate or, in his own words, 'absorb the culture of the day so as to bring its own peculiar contribution to the solution of the problems of its time' (438), also extends to some of the more refractory aspects of Western history. The Jews, 'the most remarkable survival of the fittest known to humanity' (433) are, according to Zangwill's vision, among the foremost pioneers and nation-builders. As the metaphor of absorption suggests, there is what amounts to a Jewish genius for the 'unnoticed' work of 'colonization'. Zangwill does not elaborate on this point. Yet by positioning 'the Jew' alongside the British imperialist he makes it plain that the two figures are not the equals they might seem at first glance to be, since the colonial project is truly defensible only when nested within the civilizing process that was the *raison d'être* of 'Israel's mission': to 'enrich humanity by its point of view' (438). In a striking revision of Matthew Arnold's thesis in *Culture and Anarchy* (1869), Judaism is allotted a leading role in the revivification of culture, drawing 'the Hellenic cult of beauty' into the 'white light of the religion of the future' (437) and deepening its sense of ethics and reason. Here 'Hebraism' ceases to be mere racial particularity, a fount of energy in search of transcendence, and becomes instead the cynosure of advancement.

By the time that Zangwill had committed himself to Herzl's cause, all the major elements in his standpoint on the Jewish Question were already in place. What Herzl's influence elicited was a new emphasis upon Jewish statehood, though a nationalist credo was easily adapted to the earlier idea of a civilizing mission. To some extent, this orientation is visible in 'The Future of Palestine' debate, although there Zangwill's primary focus was upon physical rather than moral resources. But certainly in slightly later and more extended discussions of this issue he began to relate Zionism's shifting scenarios to tensions within the British reaction to the deteriorating conditions in Russia and Eastern Europe, conditions that were accelerating international migration by persecuted and impoverished Jews. The years from 1901 to 1904 were especially significant for the resurgence of British antisemitism, for in addition to the formation of the British Brothers' League in February 1901 (to whose existence Zangwill was one of the first commentators to draw attention), a Parliamentary platform against Jewish migrants was secured through the appointment of a Royal Commission on Alien Immigration in February 1902. The Commission brought out its report in August of the following year.

Zangwill immediately grasped the dangers presented by the Commission's Report, setting them out in a speech at a farewell meeting for British delegates to the Sixth Zionist Congress (1903) organized by the English Zionist Federation. After praising the Report for its fairness and objectivity – and making the by now habitual gracious nod towards the gentlemanly conduct of 'anti-alien members' like Major William Evans-Gordon for 'personally travelling to the Jewish lands of oppression to try to trace the evil to its source' – Zangwill briskly dismissed its 'tyrannical and un-English' recommendations as 'petty, vexatious and difficult to carry out'. But, in characterizing the Report as a case of a national body working against the country's own highest traditions by pandering to the 'illogical and semi-civilized' side of 'human nature', Zangwill concluded that there was little point for critics to 'denounce the English outcry' against the Jews as though it 'were entirely unnatural'. Rather, one should appeal to England's best self. Taking up what he saw as England's exceptional generosity in broaching the East African offer, Zangwill's own preferred approach was 'to solve the Jewish problem elsewhere'; in other words, to render a restrictionist Aliens Act unnecessary by making alternative arrangements for Jewish migrants overseas. In the aftermath of the Kishinev massacres – which Zangwill described as 'the turning point in their history' – Jewish refugees needed a place of safety *'and* a place of preparation for Palestine' (my emphasis). The overall perspective remained firmly Zionist, but the order of priorities was beginning to change.[29]

By the time that Zangwill had returned from the Basle Congress a month later, attitudes towards the idea of an East African Zion had hardened appreciably and not merely among Zionists themselves. There had been a flurry of letters to the press that had begun to depict the notion of an East African settlement as though it were an extension of Jewish immigration into London. In response, Zangwill's public utterances on the question, notably in a speech at a second EZF sponsored meeting in early September, became more openly combative. Much of what he had to say followed the broad outline of his previous address. Once again, his main themes were the new urgency of the post-Kishinev situation, the practical solution that East Africa offered to the demand for choking off immigration, and the place that the Jews might occupy within Britain's glorious imperial design. The world as defined by these hazards and prospects was condensed into an imagined series of doors. Russia was 'opening doors of exit', while 'England and New York are closing their doors' and 'the door of Palestine is shut'. Only two choices remained: to seek entry 'by the back door' as Herzl had done in negotiating for territory in the Sinai peninsula or to walk away from the door and to go in search of another opening altogether, as one might do when haggling in a shop in an Arab bazaar – an unguarded reminder of those other Palestinians whose interests were served by Ottoman obduracy.[30] Sooner or later, negotiations would have to resume, albeit from a different place, on a different basis. Such was the rationale behind Zangwill's notion of an East African detour. Whether permanent or temporary, its role was to rekindle the spiritual or political solidarity that the West could never comfortably allow. Behind it lay a nightmare of exits without any corresponding point of entry, or of points of entry that were increasingly liable to summary closure.

Zangwill was not the only writer to voice these worries. In her now long forgotten novel *A Modern Exodus* (1904), Violet Guttenberg conjured up a futuristic spectacle in which Britain was gripped by an anti-alien backlash so extreme that Parliament legislated for the deportation of all Jews. The net result was that the nation found itself facing economic ruin (rapidly becoming a lesser power than Palestine) and was forced to rescind its draconian and unproductive statute.[31] In a similar vein, Zangwill argued that the resettlement of migrant Jews in another part of the world would serve as an object lesson to those who anathematized or oppressed them, releasing an economic dynamo that any host-country could ill-afford to lose. Moreover, one finds an extension of the same logic in Herzl's *Altneuland* when the modernization of Palestine makes some nations reluctant to allow Jews to emigrate, producing 'quite a revolution of public opinion' as civil society takes on a more generous and open-minded cast.[32] The phantasmatic power of this ideal of a full flowering of untrammelled Jewish talent, its benefits overflowing in every direction, was in fact the mirror-image of one of the most pernicious narratives of Jewish degradation. Those hostile to the very idea of Jewish colonization gloomily predicted that the stultification of the ghetto, with all its degeneracy and insularity, would effectively be transferred *tout court* from one place to another since poverty and disadvantage were simply ingrained in the East End soul.

One fantasy could just as easily slide into its opposite – which was why Zangwill could ecstatically discern 'the physical regeneration of our race' in a gymnastic display put on by Zionist students at a special Congress event, describing its 'marvellous' show of 'muscle and skill' as a sign that 'the Jewish life-force *still* runs red in the veins of youth' (485, my emphasis). And why, at the same moment, Zangwill was so concerned to repudiate the views of Anglo-Jewish critics like Lucien Wolf who saw in East Africa merely the prospect of a Whitechapel writ large, bereft of 'the civilising influence' of local Christians or, worse still, the perpetuation of 'a Polish ghetto' (486). It is against this background that Zangwill began to trumpet the grandeur of imperial whiteness, insisting that 'if Britain could attract all the Jews of the world to her colonies, she would double their white population' and strengthen her hand against the indigenous peoples (487). As he told the famous African administrator Sir Harry Johnston in 1906 in even less cautious terms, just one month after the new Aliens Act had come on to the statute-book, an East African settlement would allow the Jews to form a hegemonic colonial bloc, supplying 'the white element' or, more assertively still, 'a better white population' than had hitherto been available, phrases calculated to bring music to a veteran colonialist's ears.[33] Zangwill evidently had no doubts that Uganda was 'eminently a white man's country', describing it in one flight of suburban lyricism as a sub-equatorial equivalent to 'our own Surrey Hills', free from any taint of the East End slums with their sweating and overcrowding (485). And to secure this chain of equivalences, Zangwill was quite willing to float a far more damning association by claiming that the alien Jew decried by Lucien Wolf was objectively the same figure as the caricature that formed the stock-in-trade of the British Brothers' League.

Zangwill's imaginary geography, in which races and territories can be perfectly matched, is as inventive as any of his fictions and shows how potent the fantasy of Empire as a *tabula rasa*, a place of fresh starts and new beginnings, was during the period when the major European powers were scrambling for Africa. And Zangwill was surely no less prone to such fantasies than anyone else. 'Three cheers for England', he is reported to have shouted when the East African offer was announced to the Sixth Congress.[34] Moreover, as the scramble for Africa had demonstrated, imperialism begets imperialism. Zangwill's ambitions stretched beyond the creation of a Jewish imperial enclave or protectorate. The successes of the British Empire provided a model for a progressive Zionist eschatology. The East Africa that Zangwill envisaged would be not merely a colony, but '*the* colony [that] would found the motherland' (486, my emphasis). Patterns of settlement would ensure that, by a process of devolution, Jewish settlers would attain *de facto* self-government and so finally achieve the Zionist dream, offering an example to the world. From Zangwill's perspective, the attraction of East Africa for 'the alien' lay in the fact that it would by-pass the forcing-house of assimilation and would institutionalize specifically 'Jewish rights' (486). In short, it was to be a colony with a difference: an English shell with a Jewish content, an inviolable protected space in which Jewish traditions might flourish and diversify while never ceasing somehow to embody the very best of Britain's imperial legacy, even though one day there would have to be complete independence. This was the fiction that Zangwill ultimately failed to write, an African *Altneuland*.

Notes

My thanks to Eitan Bar-Yosef, Cora Kaplan, and Nadia Valman for helpful comments on an earlier version of this essay.

1. Quoted in Wohlgelernter, *Israel Zangwill*, 43.
2. Israel Zangwill, *The East African Question: Zionism and England's Offer* (New York: Maccabaean Publishing Company [1904]), 34. The full phrase reads: 'No, better Zionism without Zion than Zion without Zionism'.
3. Theodor Herzl, *The Jewish State* (1896), trans. Sylvie D'Avigdor (New York: Dover Publications, 1988), 95.
4. Beller, *Herzl*, 113. Cyprus officially passed into British hands after the Berlin Congress in July 1878.
5. On Herzl's 'blunder' see Avineri, 'Theodor Herzl's Diaries', 34–37.
6. See Friedman, 'Herzl'.
7. Eisenzweig, 'Aux origins'.
8. Quoted by Friedman, 'Herzl', 39.
9. Israel Zangwill, 'The Position of Judaism', *The North American Review*, 160.461 (April 1895), 431. This essay was evidently written just under a year prior to his first meeting with Herzl.
10. Max Nordau (1903), quoted in Stanislawski, *Zionism and the Fin de Siècle*, 17. Nordau was here attempting to summarize the substance of Ahad Ha'am's dismissive review of Herzl's utopian novel *Altneuland* (1902).
11. Eisenzweig, 'Aux origins', 4, 6. My translation.
12. *The Complete Diaries of Theodor Herzl*, ed. Raphael Patai, trans. Harry Zohn, 5 vols. (New York: The Herzl Press, 1960) i, 276. Revealingly, Herzl's reflections differentiate his own political stance from what he calls Zangwill's 'racial' point of view, arguing that the Jews are 'an historical unit, a nation with anthropological diversities' and hence that there can be no 'uniformity of race' in 'the Jewish State'.
13. Zangwill, 'Palestine Regained', *Speeches, Articles and Letters*, ed. Maurice Simon (London: Soncino Press, 1937), 345.
14. Vital, 'Zangwill', 243.
15. Walzer, *The Company of Critics*, 233.
16. To use Stefan Collini's celebrated phrase. See his *Public Moralists*.
17. Cf. David Vital's critique of Zangwill's 'simplicity – both of vision and expression' ('Zangwill', 249).
18. Quoted in full in Vital, *Zionism*, 4.
19. Over the years, and especially between 1902–4, Herzl considered a number of alternatives to Palestine, including (in addition to Cyprus and Sinai) East Africa, Mesopotamia, Mozambique, the Congo, and Libya. See, for example, Stewart, *Theodor Herzl*, 302.

20. Zangwill, 'The Return to Palestine', *New Liberal Review*, 2.11 (December 1901), 615. Another edited version of the same material was published at the same time in the American *Frank Leslie's Popular Monthly*, 8.2 (December 1901): 210–220 under the title 'The Redemption of Palestine by the Jews'.

21. 'The Commercial Future of Palestine. Interesting Speech by Mr. I. Zangwill'. *JC*, 22 November 1901, 14. Subsequent page numbers will be cited parenthetically in the text.

22. Zangwill visited Palestine in April 1897 as part of the first Maccabaean pilgrimage.

23. Sims' ambivalence has an even more unfortunate aspect to it. His highly successful 1889 play *London Day by Day* (jointly written with Henry Pettitt) had been attacked by the *Jewish Chronicle* for its scurrilous portrayal of a Jewish money-lender. See *JC*, 20 September 1889.

24. Zangwill, 'The Return to Palestine', 616–620.

25. Zangwill, 'The Return', 620.

26. Zangwill, 'English Judaism: A Criticism and a Classification', *Jewish Quarterly Review*, 1 (1889), 379, 398.

27. Zangwill, 'English Judaism', 406–407.

28. Zangwill, 'The Position of Judaism', 433. Subsequent page numbers will be cited parenthetically in the text.

29. 'The Jewish Question', *The Times*, 17 August 1903, 10.

30. 'Sixth Zionist Congress. East Africa and Palestine', *The Jewish World*, 11 September 1903, 485–486. Subsequent page numbers will be cited parenthetically in the text.

31. Violet Guttenberg, *A Modern Exodus* (London: Greening & Co., 1904).

32. Theodor Herzl, *Altneuland* (1902), trans. Paula Arnold (Haifa: Haifa Publishing Co. Ltd., 1960), 134.

33. Zangwill to Sir Harry Johnston, 21 February 1906, quoted in Weisbord, 'Israel Zangwill's Jewish Territorial Organization', 105.

34. Wohlgelernter, *Israel Zangwill*, 160.

8

Zionism, Territorialism, Race, and Nation in the Thought and Politics of Israel Zangwill

Meri-Jane Rochelson

Soon after the Balfour Declaration was announced in November 1917, Israel Zangwill wrote to his good friend, the poet and translator Nina Davis Salaman, 'You will see that the ITO & Z have joined – perhaps IZ stands for both.'[1] This rather gleeful announcement of the reunion of Zangwill's Jewish Territorial Organization (the ITO) with the larger Zionist movement reflects a sense of personal optimism that would be short-lived. It also reflects Zangwill's characteristic egoism, his sense of himself so tied up with his work as a Zionist (as with his other endeavours) that he could look at the two movements seeking a homeland for the Jews and come up with his own initials. But while Zangwill's Territorialist activism both promoted and was facilitated by his status as an Anglo-Jewish celebrity, his insistence on looking for a homeland outside Palestine separated him from the mainstream of Zionism and ultimately contributed to the eclipse of his reputation in the Jewish community. His Territorialism needs to be revisited, however, in the context of his experience as a turn-of-the-century English Jew, which shaped his understandings of the world situation and the place of the Jewish people within it. The rhetoric through which he enunciated his versions of Zionism reveals a figure who understood the ambiguous position of the Jews in a world obsessed with race, religion, and nationality, an impassioned defender of Jewish rights who at the same time sought to convince his listeners – in the Jewish as well as the non-Jewish public – of the normalcy of Jewish aspirations, the universality of Jewish ideals, and the inherent continuity between Jewish and Christian religious beliefs.

Zangwill was an early entrant into the Zionist fold, as the Englishman to whom Max Nordau introduced Herzl on 21 November 1895. Zangwill in turn introduced Herzl and Zionism to prominent British Jews, including the circle of professionals and intellectuals who made up the Maccabaeans, and a few wealthy community leaders who could help finance the new movement. As a division developed between the political Zionism of Herzl (the desire to establish the Jews in a sovereign state recognized by the world community) and the cultural Zionism of Ahad Ha'am (which envisioned the settlement in Palestine as a centre for the renewal of Jewish life and not necessarily or immediately a state), Zangwill had clearly allied himself with Herzl in favour of accepting a British offer of land in East Africa.[2] Zangwill formed the Jewish Territorial Organization (known as the ITO) late in 1905, after the Russian Zionists who opposed pursuing Britain's offer gained firm control of the movement's direction at the Seventh Zionist Congress (1905). He then and afterwards – except for a short time right after the 1917 Balfour Declaration – remained committed to obtaining a Jewish homeland with autonomy and a majority presence, in contrast to the Zionist settlements in Palestine that were subject first to Turkish and then to British control, and always in a minority position *vis-à-vis* Palestine's Arab population.

His insistence on creating an autonomous state (which remained remarkably consistent in the pronouncements of a man not notable for consistency) underlay both Zangwill's eventual opposition to Palestine settlement and his at times apparently radical ideas in regard to the Arabs of Palestine. Between 1907 and 1914 the ITO worked with Jacob Schiff's Jewish Immigrant Information Bureau to resettle 10,000 Russian Jews in America via Galveston, an effort which Zangwill argued was a necessary short-term adjunct to the long-term effort of securing a Jewish national home, and was consistent with his overarching goal of rescuing Jews in peril.[3] At the Seventh Zionist Congress and later, Zangwill maintained his insistence that Palestine was not excluded from his hopes for an autonomous homeland. But he increasingly believed that the Jews would never obtain autonomy in Palestine, and so over the years his rhetoric increasingly focused on its disadvantages.[4] Beginning with what David Vital has termed a 'brisk and even cheerful pragmatism'[5] at the founding of the ITO, Zangwill became increasingly embittered as his ideas failed to take hold. By 1920 he was frustrated with the idealism of the Zionists, as well as with the cynicism of the Great Powers who failed to follow their own 'principle of nationalities' in not granting a state to the Jewish people.

Zangwill led the ITO while he continued to work for women's suffrage and peace, and to write, publish, and produce stories, poetry, novels, and plays. The importance he attached to his ITO work appears in his decision in 1920 to publish *The Voice of Jerusalem*, a collection that reprints some of his earlier essays on the Jews with a lengthy new introductory essay explaining Territorialism. *The Voice of Jerusalem* was clearly intended for a non-Jewish as well as a Jewish readership, as were Zangwill's many articles in general interest periodicals making his case for a Jewish homeland. Indeed, after the First Zionist Congress (1897) there was considerable interest in the movement beyond the Jewish community, and articles on the subject appeared in such publications as the *Fortnightly Review,* the *Contemporary Review*, the *Nineteenth Century*, the *Asiatic Quarterly,* the *North American*

Review, and *Cosmopolis,* a favourite of Zangwill's for publishing short fiction and the first venue of 'Dreamers in Congress', which became part of *Dreamers of the Ghetto,* his 1898 collection of stories and fictionalized biographies.[6]

'Dreamers in Congress' shows Zangwill's reluctance, even at the beginning, to embrace Zionism fully, at least in part because of the general scepticism that kept him always a contrarian in the Jewish community. In *Dreamers of the Ghetto,* Zangwill placed the participants of the First Zionist Congress alongside such unhappy idealists as Heine and Spinoza; indeed, his pocket diary for the period indicates that he worked on the Heine essay and 'Dreamers in Congress' more or less simultaneously, and directly after the meetings in Basle.[7] Readers of Michael Stanislawski's *Zionism and the Fin de Siècle* will recognize Heine, Spinoza, and Bar Cochba (whom Zangwill also often evoked in his writings) as representations of Jewish literary, intellectual, and military might brought forward by Max Nordau to take the place of rabbinic figures for a non-religious generation.[8] But Zangwill's elevation of these unorthodox heroes – Heine a convert and Spinoza a heretic in his day – predated Nordau's, and his stories may in fact have influenced his German colleague and contemporary. Like Nordau, Zangwill, too, brought to Zionism the universalist perspective of a *fin-de-siècle* intellectual. In his case, however, having already established his identity as a Jewish writer, Zangwill spent the rest of his career insisting that the Jewish and the universal were one. Indeed, 'Dreamers in Congress' begins with a vision of delegates from all nations, as different in appearance from one another as members of any such large gathering might be. 'Yet some subtle instinct links them each to each', he writes, 'presage, perhaps, of some brotherhood of mankind, of which ingathered Israel – or even ubiquitous Israel – may present the type'.[9] Jewish racial feeling, in Zangwill's terms, here becomes both a call to Jewish unity and an invitation to the rest of the world – as well as to Jews – to transcend racial barriers.

And yet, although in this essay Zangwill praises the idealism and enthusiasm of the Congress, he also places himself above and aloof from its deliberations. The 'open-eyed Jewish idealist has been blest with ignorance of the actual', he writes, alluding to the depressing conditions in Palestine he had seen firsthand earlier that year, and intra-communal rivalries such as those he had detailed in his bestselling novel *Children of the Ghetto* (1892).[10] In 'Dreamers in Congress', he presents the ideas and debates of the First Zionist Congress largely through rhetorical questions, and even ends the essay on an interrogatory note.[11] Reading 'Dreamers in Congress', one has the sense that Zangwill returned from Basle in 1897 energized by the earnestness of visionaries who could imagine a modern Jewish state, yet at the same time sceptical that they could hold on to such visions and provide a refuge for the suffering millions of their own moment in history. Buoyed by the vision of a state independent of religious control, he foresaw, as well, the objections of the devout. 'Dreamers in Congress' in 1898 hinted at the greater distance Zangwill would later create between himself and the Zionist mainstream.

Yet even the mainstream Zionists had difficulty enlisting the support of Jews in such countries as the United States and the United Kingdom. In an article titled 'Zionism', published in the *Contemporary* in 1899, Zangwill wrote that, 'While the Western Christian is generally not unsympathetic towards Zionism, the Western Jew is generally in bitter or contemptuous opposition.'[12] Proponents of Zionism had to counter the arguments of those who believed the future of Judaism lay in assimilation with Western culture, and their fears that the security or hard-won rights of emancipated Jews would be jeopardized by a Jewish state. Like other Zionists, Zangwill in the 'Zionism' essay assured readers that Jews would not be asked 'to migrate *en masse*', and later made clear in the ITO's manifesto that the state proposed was 'for those Jews who cannot or will not remain in the lands in which they at present live'.[13] The 'Zionism' article, like many that would follow, refuted assumptions that a Jewish state was either unnecessary, impractical, or both, asserting, for example, that there was no reason to believe Jews could not be farmers, and affirming that they could revive Palestine from its current neglected state.[14] He was less able, however, to dispose of the problems he foresaw for the Zionists in dealing with the Sultan, and he had no clear answer for what would happen regarding control of Christian and Muslim holy sites; in later articles and speeches he would assert that the Jews – progenitors of each of the other faiths – would guard their shrines more attentively than any other caretakers. But in 1899 Zangwill was also more optimistic about relations with Palestine's Arabs than he would be later; 'if the Turk is a religious cousin, the Arab is a racial cousin', he wrote:[15] '[I]t is the "practical men"... who are really the dreamers'.[16]

Zangwill's biographer Joseph Udelson rightly describes this article as the 'clearest formulation of Zangwill's original attitude toward Zionism'.[17] And yet even in this very idealistic essay there is considerable doubt about Zionism's practicality; the difficulties Zangwill minimizes are never completely explained away, and they will return in his Territorialist writings. Indeed, Zangwill's pessimism opens and closes the essay, although so subtly at first that it might pass unnoticed. He begins, for example, by fondly evoking the name of Mordecai Manuel Noah, the proto-Zionist who dreamed of a Jewish settlement near Buffalo, New York. What he fails to mention is that Noah's scheme never took hold; but readers of his story 'Noah's Ark' – published in *Lippincott's* in the same year the 'Zionism' essay appeared in that magazine – would be more likely to view Noah as the fictionalized con-artist who lures the hapless Peloni to a lifetime of waiting in the barren cold of upper New York state. Similarly, while the conclusion of the 'Zionism' article is overtly upbeat, Zangwill suggests the possibility that in the end a Jewish state may not develop at all, in which case 'the Jew in semi-barbarous countries will, with the gradual advance of civilization, be relieved of his unjust burdens, and...when emancipated politically, he will either disappear or undergo a religious regeneration'.[18] This is an odd conclusion for an essay promoting the Zionist enterprise.

However, the need for *something* as the basis for Jewish persistence, whether it be religion or a state, was an idea that recurred throughout Zangwill's writings. In the 'Zionism' essay, he imagines that national regeneration itself could lead to a religious revival among the world's Jews.[19] In subsequent writings he would emphasize how a Jewish state, governed by the Jewish calendar, would alleviate the problems experienced by observant Jews in the Diaspora, most notably the 'Sabbath problem' that forced Jewish businesses to close two days a week, putting them at an economic disadvantage. Zangwill dramatized this dilemma in 'The Sabbath Question in Sudminster', a story he published in 1907 in his last collection of Jewish fiction, *Ghetto Comedies*. One of the few stories in the book that might in fact be called humorous, its comedy is bittersweet, tainted with a sense of loss as one by one the Jewish merchants in town solve their problem by deciding to open on Saturdays.

Zangwill's concern with 'religious regeneration' as a component of Jewish statehood needs to be looked at, however briefly, since he was not himself observant and in fact spent much time insisting that Christianity was a continuation of Jewish principles, the 'New Testament' a part of Jewish Scripture, and so on.[20] Yet the dichotomy that Udelson ascribes to Zangwill – in which Judaism is preserved in the East while it disappears in the West – is an oversimplification of Zangwill's thought.[21] What Udelson refers to as Zangwill's ' "Hebraic" universalism' is a continued development of the 'mission of Judaism' idea prevalent in liberal Jewish circles of the early twentieth century, that the role of Judaism would be to spread its ethical concepts among humanity, without sectarian trappings. When Zangwill wrote of the 'de-national[ization]' of Judaism,[22] proposing the dissemination of Jewish values beyond communal boundaries, he also managed to present the idea as a reason for Jewish autonomy. In one of Zangwill's most powerful speeches for Territorialism, 'The East Africa Offer' – which he delivered in both Britain and the United States after Herzl's death in 1904 but before the Seventh Zionist Congress – Zangwill urged that a Jewish state would promote the Jewish religious mission because 'being something' is better than talking about it; if a Jewish state exemplified Jewish values, it would be fulfilling the mission of Judaism in the most effective way.[23]

Israel Zangwill's ideas about the Jews as a 'race' may be even more complicated than his views on Judaism, but they, too, were central to his Territorialist vision and rhetoric. Zangwill incorporated the racial terminology applied to Jews in his day, but he also resisted it at every turn. His speech to the Universal Races Congress, held in London in July 1911, emphasized the spiritual and ethical components of Judaism, of which 'the Jewish race is to be the medium and missionary'.[24] Yet his awareness of political and social realities prevented him from joining those who insisted that Judaism was simply a religious belief, which imposed no other connections among its adherents. In his speech to the Congress, titled 'The Jewish Race' – but 'The Problem of the Jewish Race' when reprinted as a pamphlet – Zangwill emphasized not a genetic unity but another close tie, the unity of a people who shared a religious tradition. Like other Zionists, Zangwill was repelled by the assimilationism (which he termed 'Marranoism') of many British and American Jews, regardless of the extent to which he himself had moved away from Jewish observance.[25] In his 1925 introduction to a collection (of works by others) titled *The Real Jew*, Zangwill wrote that it was important for Jews to assert their Jewishness and not allow Judaism to 'lurk too shyly in the background of civilisation'[26] – a principle Zangwill enacted through his own public identification as a Jew. His speech on 'the Jewish race' served his Territorialist purpose, as well, since he allowed the terms 'race', 'nation', and 'religion' considerable slippage into each other. 'The comedy and tragedy of Jewish existence to-day', he wrote, 'derive primarily from this absence of a territory in which the race could live its own life'.[27]

As Zangwill argued for a Jewish homeland in East Africa, however, and, later, in Cyrenaica in North Africa (now Libya), his Territorialist writings were replete with the language of British imperialism. Shortly after the Sixth Zionist Congress, in a speech to an East End audience, he began by presenting the East Africa offer as a source of pride and an occasion for gratitude: 'Whether we establish a colony in British East Africa or not, that is a small issue compared with the unquestionable fact that ours is now a serious political movement, officially recognized by two of the greatest powers of the world, England and Russia, that we have lifted the status of the Jewish people to a height from which it must never go back',[28] that '[e]ven more than a triumph for Zionism is it a moral triumph for England, a victory for humanity',[29] and that 'Really, if the British Empire chooses to be magnanimous to the Jews, it is scarcely the place of the Jew to rebuke her', reminding his listeners that the non-Jewish British colonists in East Africa had already expressed their objections to the government when they heard that large numbers of Jews might be arriving.[30] Zangwill's annoyance at the Zionists' ingratitude would continue in later speeches, as he expressed amazement that with so much Jewish suffering in Russia and elsewhere – including the United States – Jews would reject such a generous offer.[31] Only years later, after he understood the limited way in which the Balfour Declaration would be applied, did Zangwill begin to treat Britain's intentions less respectfully. By 1923, he bluntly told 4,000 listeners gathered by the American Jewish Congress that 'Zionism can ... only rely upon as much of England's Might as suits the policy of England ...'.[32]

In 1903, however, Zangwill expressed not only gratitude, but also his conviction that Jewish settlement in East Africa was in Britain's interest. 'Why, the whole white population of the British Colonies is only some twelve millions,' he declared,

> so that if Britain could attract all the Jews of the world to her colonies, she would just double their white population. ...With all Judea helping us, ... we could create a colony that would be a source of strength, not only to Israel but to the British Empire, a colony second to none in loyalty to the British flag, a colony that would co-operate in extending civilization from Cairo to the Cape, and which, even when Palestine was resettled by our people, would remain one of the brightest gems in the British Imperial Crown.[33]

Of course this rhetoric served Zangwill's immediate Territorialist purpose, but it was based in a general acceptance of and identification with the imperialist worldview that somehow managed to coexist with Zangwill's more progressive orientation. In 1910, for example, in an essay condemning the cruel treatment of rubber field workers in the Belgian Congo, Zangwill wrote, 'Imperialist has been degraded to mean a man who extends the area of the Empire. I should like it to mean a man who extends the honour of the Empire'[34] – the implication being that he, as a British Jew, had the same stake as other Britons in imperial honour. Zangwill's emphasis on Jewish 'whiteness', like his acceptance of imperialism, was thus not simply a rhetorical strategy but a representation of concerns about racial and national identification that he shared with other educated British Jews.[35]

One of Zangwill's most audacious moves in asserting the normalcy of Jews and their aspirations (and, by extension, their 'whiteness'), was to request opinions about an ITO homeland, in 1906, from a cross-section of European literary and political figures, mostly British and Irish, and then publish the letters, with minimal editing and commentary, in the *Fortnightly Review*. His letter of solicitation indicated his desire 'to take advantage of England's offer of a virgin soil under British suzerainty', adding, 'We have elements to offer England in return which are not to be disdained even by so mighty an Empire', since a 'flourishing settlement of one of the most potent white peoples on earth cannot but bring a gain of strength to any Power that accords it a stretch of territory at present waste'.[36] What is most notable about the letters reprinted (and Zangwill seems to have printed all that he received) is that they are by no means all favourable. Arminius Vambéry, Professor of Oriental Languages at the University of Budapest (and a Jew), contributed the longest and most detailed letter of support, while J. M. Barrie, Hall Caine, Arthur Pinero, and Jerome K. Jerome wrote very enthusiastic but brief comments. Thomas Hardy applauded Territorialism as a step toward Palestine (as Zangwill himself did in public pronouncements at that time, while pursuing Territorialist schemes elsewhere); Coulson Kernahan suggested his native Ireland as a welcoming territory; and Mary Ward pledged not only support, but cash, once the plan 'takes practical shape'.[37] Yet Conan Doyle and Quiller-Couch each had difficulty imagining

Jews as farmers, W. S. Gilbert urged against the emigration of British Jews, and W. Pett Ridge expressed a general pessimism that he hoped would be proved wrong. Even worse, Frederic Harrison, John Davidson, Richard Whiteing, and H. Rider Haggard included in their letters – whether ultimately supportive or not – slurs against Jewish religion, Jewish wealth, and Jewish political weakness.[38]

Although Zangwill, in the article, argued with some of his correspondents, he also tried to put the best face on some of the most obviously antisemitic; for example, ignoring Frederic Harrison's expression of disgust at the Jewish religion, Zangwill instead called his 'the most Jewish letter of the series' because it opposed nation-building based on race.[39] To H. G. Wells's at best ambiguous remarks – 'But it's not my doorstep, and I can offer you neither help nor advice. Your people are rich enough, able enough, and potent enough to save themselves' – Zangwill simply says 'Amen!' and ends the article. Ultimately it seems to have mattered less what these notables said than that they associated themselves with Zangwill and his project at all; they were to provide Territorialism's British and European *bona fides*. But a significant difference in perception of the Jews appears as Zangwill points out the magnanimity of his correspondents in ignoring the benefits a Jewish colony would bring to Britain, repeating what he had viewed as a strong selling point. That they might not have seen such a colony as a benefit is left out of consideration.

An incident preceding the 1911 Universal Races Congress illustrates well both the racial otherness of Jews in Europe and the defiant defensiveness of Zangwill's response. A pamphlet had defined the purpose of the Congress as 'to discuss, in the light of modern knowledge and the modern conscience, the general relations subsisting between the peoples of the West and those of the East, between so-called white and so-called coloured peoples, with a view to encouraging between them a fuller understanding, the most friendly feelings, and a heartier co-operation'.[40] Zangwill's correspondence with the secretary of the organizing committee reveals his dissatisfaction with being placed, as he saw it, at the Oriental and 'coloured' end of the continuum. He expressed discomfort at signing the conference 'Appeal' because, as he wrote, 'After speaking of "all the races of the world" it gives a list of races mainly coloured, among which the Jewish race might rather resent being included. In any case this list lends to the Races Congress an air of conde-scension on the part of the dominant white. Surely this is a mistake, and a paper or two should be added on such curious races as say the English and the Germans.'[41] Apparently Zangwill was mollified by secretary G. Spiller's offer to print his name right after that of the conference President, Lord Weardale, 'as the Jewish race has its home now chiefly in Europe'.[42] But Lord Weardale's name in the end appears as a signature set off from the rest, while Zangwill's name, with the parenthetical descriptor "on the Jewish race," is placed at the head of a list of representatives from Asia, Africa, the Caribbean, and 'American Negroes'.[43] The Jewish race was still decidedly 'other', as far as the Congress organizers were concerned.[44]

Zangwill's ambivalence on issues of race is of course relevant to his interest in securing African territory as a homeland for the Jews. As I shall discuss below, Zangwill's desire for a land outside Palestine was due in large part to his recognition that Palestine was already inhabited by 600,000 Arabs, the figure he used repeatedly in his speeches and essays. One wonders, then, why the potential or presumed inhabitants of the Uasin Gishu plateau – the area in East Africa offered to the Jews – did not seem an equivalent obstacle to Jewish settlement. In fact, Zangwill's apparent obliviousness to African inhabitants of the plateau resulted from incomplete information and wishful thinking at least as much as from attitudes toward race that he shared with his contemporaries. His correspondence with Helena (Nellie) Auerbach, who travelled through East Africa at Zangwill's behest and reported back her findings and opinions, illustrates on both sides complex interactions between anti-racist and colonialist worldviews in the search for a Jewish homeland.[45]

Helena Auerbach, who as Treasurer of the National Union of Women's Suffrage Societies also shared Zangwill's active support of the suffrage movement, expressed her allegiance to Territorialism as early as October 1905, when she offered to 'get as near as possible to the "promised" land' at the end of her imminent visit to South Africa.[46] She and her husband, Julius, contributed financially to the ITO and Helena served on its governing council. During extended visits to family in South Africa she advocated for the ITO, speaking at meetings, distributing literature, and helping to develop branches throughout the colony.[47] Zangwill welcomed her offer to take a look at the proposed territory, asking her specifically to assess the danger of fever, and to try to enlist Christians to the cause at a time when many Christian settlers opposed it. '[G]ive people to understand', he wrote, in February 1906, 'that it is not a General Booth scheme for planting pauper aliens upon a country, but a scheme for turning a vast mass or [sic] organized capital and potential labour upon any territory that is lucky enough to get us ...'.[48] Even before she began her tour of the proposed ITOland, however, Auerbach expressed to Zangwill 'one very serious and farreaching objection to the E. African idea':

> It is the presence in that country of a large & I believe, increasing black native population. Now it is no theory but an unfortunate fact that whenever you introduce the white man into countries (such as this for instance) where there exists a ... black population the tendency is for the white man to develop into nothing more than an aristocratic minority. I fear very much that, no matter what efforts were made to the contrary, there would be no openings for our people in E. Africa except in the capacity of capitalist & employer of labour, absurd as this may sound.[49]

Once she travelled to East Africa her objections centred more insistently on the resident Indians who had come to work on the railroad from Mombasa to Lake Victoria that made colonization feasible. Having arrived as unskilled labour, the Indians had become a large presence of merchants, office workers, and artisans who, in the racial economy of the day, would accept lower pay in those areas of employment than any group of white settlers, including Jews. In this case, too, Auerbach combined arguments regarding pragmatic difficulties with a gentle appeal to Zangwill's humanistic instincts: 'I know that any legislation aimed at the exclusion of any one race from ITO-land would be distasteful to you; besides the British Government would be obliged, most probably, to raise objections to it also'.[50] Additionally, she was blunt about local opposition to Jewish settlement and, in particular, Jewish autonomy. In the early months of 1906 she therefore encouraged Zangwill to pursue ITO prospects in northwest Canada.

Zangwill's response underscores his reluctance to abandon a plan unless positively forced to, and an optimism that put off as long as possible the need to recognize inconvenient facts. 'The Black question weighs upon us very much', he wrote, in response to Auerbach's concerns, but 'in Canada you strike a new set of difficulties...There are four million Blacks altogether [in East Africa] so that some part should simply seem teeming with population, but a great deal of the healthy high land seems still available.'[51] Auerbach's subsequent letters neither confirm nor deny the presence of a native population on the plateau, and the question was moot by July 1906 when the Colonial Office withdrew its offer.[52] But as Zangwill pursued prospects in Angola and Cyrenaica, Auerbach, on later visits to the continent, continued to remind him of the difficulties of race and the ethical problems they would pose for a Jewish settlement.[53]

While Zangwill's record on race, as I have discussed, reflects the ambivalence and at times even the racism of the early-twentieth-century liberal white Englishman, the prospect of an African homeland for the Jews never came close enough to fruition to really test his ideals or values. A letter of late July 1906 perhaps best sums up the extent to which he might have been willing to disregard Auerbach's concerns, and the reasons why:

> The real trouble is that some of our most influential friends do not wish to base the Jewish territory on black labour [an issue about which his correspondent, herself, had serious reservations]. ... I have just received a telegram from Russia which I have sent to the papers saying that universal Jewish massacres have been arranged for July 28th. I hope they will be averted.

A few days later he repeated the objection, adding (in a note apparently typed as an afterthought), 'But the Russians [meaning Russian Jews] are not likely to consider that – merely space and possibility.'[54] For Zangwill, the idea of a Jewish land as primarily a place of rescue allowed him to postpone as long as possible any confrontation with difficult racial issues; in the end, when Africa ceased to be an option, he never had to confront them.

Zangwill repeatedly rejected Palestine, however, because he believed that a territory dominated by a non-Jewish population would never allow the formation of an autonomous Jewish national home. He has been called, in fact, the first Zionist to recognize the difficulties that the Palestinian Arab population would pose, and he could see no way around it but to search for a homeland elsewhere. Since this is probably the most misunderstood and misrepresented part of Zangwill's Zionist career, it is worth ending with at least a brief consideration of what he himself had in mind.

In July 1903, Zangwill made a statement that would haunt his reputation ever after: 'Palestine needs a people; Israel needs a country.'[55] Historian Adam Garfinkle has argued that Zangwill was simply repeating a formulation of Lord Shaftesbury's which referred to the idea that Palestinian Arabs did not represent a unified nation, not that Palestine was uninhabited; according to Garfinkle, Shaftesbury (1801–85) had religious as well as political reasons for wanting a restoration of the Jews to Palestine, and used the formulation in 1853 in an attempt to persuade the British government to bring it about.[56] But it is even easier to defend Zangwill by noting that, soon after making the statement in question, he reversed himself completely. In his major speech on 'The East Africa Offer', delivered in 1904 and 1905, Zangwill told his listeners,

> There is...a difficulty from which the Zionist dares not avert his eyes, though he rarely likes to face it. Palestine proper has already its inhabitants. The pashalik of Jerusalem is already twice as thickly populated as the United States, having fifty-two souls to the square mile, and not 25 per cent of them Jews; so we must be prepared either to drive out by the sword the tribes in possession as our forefathers did, or to grapple with the problem of a large alien population, mostly Mohammedan and accustomed for centuries to despise us.[57]

Not surprisingly, this statement and others like it have been quoted by anti-Zionists as an indication of longstanding brutality to the Arabs of Palestine, and by Zionist proponents of forcible ejection as an example of a potentially workable plan.[58] However, when one reads the body of Zangwill's Zionist and Territorialist writings it becomes clear that only at one point – in the two or three years just after the Balfour Declaration – did Zangwill believe that even a peaceful transfer of population might be possible. In this case his idea was grounded in larger hopes for a League of Nations that would create equity among peoples in the postwar division of territories, whereby

> those amicable measures of race redistribution which we have already seen to be an unavoidable part of a final world settlement will be carried out in Palestine as elsewhere. Thus the Arabs would gradually be settled

in the new and vast Arabian Kingdom, to liberate which from the Turk, Jews no less than Arabs have laid down their lives, and with which the Jewish Commonwealth would cultivate the closest friendship and co-operation.[59]

While the phrase 'race redistribution' sounds frighteningly Hitlerian, in February 1919 it was one element of an idealistic plan to create a world of peace and justice, to make Europe – in the terms Zangwill was fond of at the time – more like a 'melting pot' than a 'cockpit'. Not long after making this statement, however, it became clear to Zangwill that the League of Nations would not achieve the ideal world order it promised, that the British mandatory power was not committed to Jewish autonomy, and that its guarantee of rights to all the peoples of Palestine would ensure the persistence of a non-Jewish majority. And although Zangwill would later refer to the period of 1917–19 as a missed opportunity, neither before nor after did he in fact suggest that Arabs be forced out of the land. Instead, the use of force was more often presented–as in the 1904 statement above–as an unthinkable alternative to what Zangwill preferred: the establishment of a Jewish homeland somewhere else.

As Territorialism fell out of favour as an option, and the Zionist movement seemed determined to ignore his warnings about the problems presented by the Arab majority in Palestine, Zangwill became increasingly disgusted with Zionism, leading to the statement, 'Political Zionism is dead', that caused such a furor in his 1923 American address.[60] There was in fact very little in 'Watchman, What of the Night?' that Zangwill had not said or written before, leading one to imagine that the uproar it caused may have resulted, in part, from his uncompromising delivery of a 42-page harangue, or that perhaps his audience had not been keeping up with his political writings but instead had come to hear the masterful interpreter of Jewish life that they knew through his fiction. But the 'Watchman' speech very concisely sums up Zangwill's position on Palestinian Arabs through the years. While asserting that an opportunity for removal with compensation had been missed, Zangwill significantly went on to add that an 'expropriation policy, tolerable in the immense tragedy of the war, would be inadvisable today'. He continued, 'we must forgo our political hopes in Palestine rather than kindle a conflagration that may ravage the whole world.'[61]

Viewing the ITO from the perspective of a later century, it seems unlikely that any territory Zangwill might have obtained would have been free of the problems posed by an already existing population. Zangwill was not prophet enough to see the end of the imperialist worldview on which he based his schemes, nor to envision the relative success of the Jewish state of Israel. But his recognition that the Arabs of Palestine could not be ignored seems more than prescient today, as does his recognition, decades before the Holocaust, of the urgency of finding a place of refuge for East European Jews.

Notes

My work on this chapter was made possible by grants from the College of Arts and Sciences at Florida International University and the Memorial Foundation for Jewish Culture. I am most grateful to Rochelle Rubinstein, Associate Director of the Central Zionist Archives, and Naomi Niv, who served as my very able research assistant in Jerusalem, for making available to me many of the letters and papers in the Zangwill and ITO files that I have drawn upon in preparing this chapter. Without their generous assistance, this chapter would not have been possible, and I am grateful for the Archives' permission to publish extracts from materials in its collections.

1. Cambridge University Library (CUL), Add Ms 8171/61, Letter from Israel Zangwill to Nina Davis Salaman, 23 November 1917.
2. By the time of the Sixth Zionist Congress, in 1903, Ahad Ha'am's views became pre-eminent among Russian Zionists. See Vital, *Zionism*, ch. 9. Vital points out that not long before his death in 1904, Herzl promised his opponents that despite his pragmatic interest in the East Africa offer, 'the solution for us lies only in Palestine' (345).
3. See Udelson, *Dreamer*, 186; Israel Zangwill, 'A Land of Refuge' (Speech delivered at a mass meeting at the Manchester Hippodrome, 8 December 1907), *Speeches, Articles and Letters*, ed. Maurice Simon (London: Soncino Press, 1937), 253–524. The speech was also published as the second ITO pamphlet.
4. Zangwill, 'The East Africa Offer' (Speech delivered at Derby Hall, Manchester, April 1905), *Speeches*, 210. This speech is a republication, with slight changes, of *The East African Question: Zionism and England's Offer* (New York: Maccabaean Publishing Company, [1904]), a reprint of an address given in the United States in December 1904.
5. Vital, *Zionism*, 355.
6. Several of these periodicals are mentioned in Richard Gottheil, 'Zion Night', *The Judaeans: 1897–99* (New York: The Judaeans, 1899), 24.
7. Central Zionist Archives (CZA), A120/73, Israel Zangwill, Pocket Diary for 1897.
8. Stanislawski, *Zionism*, 80–81.
9. Israel Zangwill, *Dreamers of the Ghetto* (1898; Philadelphia: Jewish Publication Society of America, 1938), 433.
10. Zangwill, *Dreamers*, 434. Zangwill's visit to Palestine as part of a delegation of Anglo-Jewish notables is mentioned in Bentwich, 'Anglo-Jewish Travellers', 15–16. Zangwill's handwritten notes recording his impressions (later used in several of his stories and essays) may be found in CZA, A120/73.
11. '[A]nd when the President gravely gives the assurance ... that Judaism has nothing to fear – Judaism, the one cause and consolation of the ages of isolation and martyrdom – does no sense of the irony of history intrude upon his exalted mood?' Zangwill, *Dreamers*, 440.
12. Zangwill, 'Zionism', *Speeches*, 159.
13. Zangwill, 'Zionism', 159, italics in original; Zangwill, 'A Land of Refuge', *Speeches*, 234.
14. Zangwill, 'Zionism', 159, 163.
15. Zangwill, 'Zionism', 164.
16. Zangwill, 'Zionism', 162.
17. Udelson, *Dreamer*, 158.
18. Zangwill, 'Zionism', 166.
19. Zangwill, 'Zionism', 157–158.

20. For a summary of Zangwill's statement of this view near the end of his life, see Israel Zangwill, 'My Religion', *My Religion: Arnold Bennett, Sir Arthur Conan Doyle, Hugh Walpole, E. Phillips Oppenheim, Rebecca West, Compton Mackenzie, J. D. Beresford, H. De Vere Stacpoole, Israel Zangwill, Henry Arthur Jones* (New York: D. Appleton & Co., 1926), 65–74.

21. Udelson, *Dreamer*, 169.

22. Zangwill, 'Zion, Whence Cometh My Help' (July 1903), *Speeches*, 81, and elsewhere in his writings.

23. Zangwill, 'The East Africa Offer', *Speeches*, 204. Udelson is in part correct; Zangwill might have been satisfied with assimilation in the Diaspora, accompanied by a universalist Jewish revival, alongside Jewish nationalism and the renewal of religious observance in a Jewish state. But this is not because he privileged assimilation; indeed, as I will discuss, he knew its limits. Zangwill found it difficult to imagine orthodox Judaism in the West (although in fact he depicted it persuasively in the character Raphael Leon in *Children of the Ghetto*) because in his place and time he saw it most convincingly only in what he termed 'the ghetto', and envisioned Jewish life as being either of a particular kind of orthodoxy or essentially non-observant. He recognized, however, that only in a self-governing homeland could imperilled Jews of all religious orientations be secure. In terms of religion as in other ways, he saw Territorialism as the conception 'in which this abnormal condition [of being everywhere a minority] ... would be replaced by the normal condition of being in the majority' ('Territorialism as Practical Politics', *Speeches*, 310–311).

24. Israel Zangwill, *The Problem of the Jewish Race* (New York: Judaen Publishing Co., n.d), 3.

25. Although he often proposed 'de-nationalization' as a good, he equally decried what he called 'Marranoism', that is, 'adopting a policy of "Lie low and say nothing"', as he put it in 1904, or 'sailing under false racial colours', as he phrased it 11 years later ('The East Africa Offer', *Speeches*, 199; 'Introduction', *The Real Jew: Some Aspects of the Jewish Contribution to Civilization*, ed. H. Newman (London: A. &. C. Black, 1925), xix). In other words, Jews could exert a positive influence on the nations in which they lived without assimilating and submerging their unique identity.

26. Zangwill, 'Introduction', *The Real Jew*, xix.

27. Zangwill, *The Problem*, 8.

28. Zangwill, 'The Sixth Zionist Congress' (speech delivered under the auspices of the English Zionist Federation, at Mile End Road, September 1903), *Speeches*, 181–82. For details of the recognition agreement between Herzl and Plehve, the Russian Minister of the Interior, see Vital, *Zionism*, 148–518; Avineri, 'Theodor Herzl's Diaries', 27–31.

29. Zangwill, 'The Sixth Zionist Congress', *Speeches*, 182.

30. Zangwill, 'The Sixth Zionist Congress', 193.

31. Cf. 'A Land of Refuge', *Speeches*, 259; in the freestanding reprint of the speech, published by the ITO [1907?], 22–23, Zangwill listed 11 different incidents of antisemitism worldwide, all in the previous August. The first was in the United States.

32. Israel Zangwill, *Watchman, What of the Night?* (New York: American Jewish Congress, 1923), 31.

33. Zangwill, 'The Sixth Zionist Congress', 193, 195.

34. Zangwill, 'Mr. Morel and the Congo' (Speech at the City Temple, 20th October, 1910)', *The War for the World* (New York: Macmillan, 1916), 285. Zangwill in this

speech and essay supported E. D. Morel's efforts to relieve the suffering inhabitants of the Belgian Congo, and expressed a hope for their eventual self-determination. But he also lamented the absence of British intervention against cruelties inflicted by the Belgians in the rubber fields, and in that connection made the statement quoted above.

35. For an important discussion of Anglo-Jewish scientists and race, see Endelman, 'Anglo-Jewish Scientists'.

36. Israel Zangwill, 'Letters and the ITO', *Fortnightly Review*, 85, NS 79 (1906), 633.

37. Zangwill, 'Letters', 647.

38. Some notable quotations from Zangwill, 'Letters': 'Why, some States would begin to live by going for the Jews' (Richard Whiteing, 647); 'the crucifixion [of Jesus] ... makes a second exodus to Palestine impossible in the meantime – perhaps for ever' (John Davidson, 636); 'Why cannot some of the richer members of your community buy the place? They would hardly miss the money' (H. Rider Haggard, 638); 'Strict Judaism – in so far as it means the perpetuation of the observances, laws, ideals, and beliefs of Moses, is to me even more barbarous and retrograde than strict Christianity, or strict Buddhism, or Islamism. ... I see that some sort of ground – I do not say excuse – for the Russian fanaticism is to be found in the tendency of some East European Jews to avoid sharing in the nationality of the country in which they were born and bred' (Frederic Harrison, 640).

39. Zangwill, 'Letters', 640. In fact, of course, Zangwill recognized antisemitism when it appeared. In response to Helena Auerbach's characterization of Harrison's and Davidson's comments as 'idiotic & entirely untrue', and her question as to whether he had noticed Harrison's self-contradictions regarding Jews and Englishmen (CZA, 36/23, 22 April 1906), Zangwill replied, 'I quite agree with you about Frederic Harrison. His unconscious bias is most comic in a man who prides himself upon his internationality' (CZA, A36/23, 16 May 1906).

40. CZA, A120/484, *First Universal Races Congress* (London, 1911), 8.

41. CZA, A120/484, Letter from Israel Zangwill to G. Spiller, 23 January 1911 (carbon copy).

42. CZA, A120/484, Letter from G. Spiller to Israel Zangwill, 24 January 1911.

43. CZA, A120/484, *First Universal Races Congress* (London: 1911, n.p.).

44. Probably the clearest explication of what was in fact Zangwill's own ambivalence toward the 'coloured races' appears in the 'Afterword' to the 1914 edition of *The Melting Pot*. The Afterword seems intended generally to soften the assimilationist message of the play, with Zangwill pointing out that 'The process of American amalgamation is not assimilation or simple surrender to the dominant type, ... but an all-round give-and-take by which the final type may be enriched or impoverished' (Israel Zangwill, 'Afterword', *The Melting Pot: A Drama in Four Acts* (new and rev. ed., 1914; rpt. New York: Macmillan, 1932; North Stratford, NH: Ayer, 1999), 203). In the play Zangwill welcomes all races to the American crucible, and in the 'Afterword' notes approvingly that American 'negrophobia' is in decline. Yet he also stops short of endorsing intermarriage between blacks and whites, citing pragmatic drawbacks: '[I]n view of all the unpleasantness, both immediate and contingent, that attends the blending of colours, only heroic souls on either side should dare the adventure of intermarriage' (207). Thus, although in most other writings of the period Zangwill denounced the prohibition on marriage between Jews and non-Jews, here he drew upon what he saw as a nearly insurmountable racial difference to reassure Jewish readers who opposed the play's assimilationist theme. If blacks and whites could be reshaped

as Americans in 'the melting pot' without marrying each other, then it was clear that desirable cultural intermingling among all groups might still occur 'without any gamic interaction' (207).

45. I am grateful to conference participant Mark Levene for urging me to explore further the issue of Africans in East Africa, and to Eitan Bar-Yosef for directing me to the Auerbach correspondence.
46. CZA, A36/23, Letter from Helena Auerbach to Israel Zangwill, 5 October 1905.
47. See Abrams, 'Jewish Women', 58.
48. CZA, A120/237, Letter from Israel Zangwill to Helena Auerbach, 15 February 1906.
49. CZA, A36/23, Letter from Helena Auerbach to Israel Zangwill, 18 March 1906.
50. CZA, A36/23, Letter from Helena Auerbach to Israel Zangwill, 18 May 1906. On the Indians of East Africa, see also Weisbord, *African Zion*, 19–22 and elsewhere.
51. CZA, A120/237, Letter from Israel Zangwill to Helena Auerbach, 10 April 1906.
52. Vital, *Zionism*, 441.
53. A very long letter from Auerbach to Zangwill (CZA, A36/23, 8 July 1907) treats the issue of 'the Native' in detail and makes clear both the ambivalence towards the subject of even broadminded individuals and the limited nature of perceived options. The letter appears both in typescript and handwritten, both sent from Port Elizabeth, South Africa, although on different stationery. In it Auerbach describes the social stratifications based on race that inevitably occur when white colonists arrive. Regarding education, Auerbach writes,

> Is the white man to consider it his duty to raise up the African Native & drag him along paths which, of his own initiation, he never would have discovered or may he with a clear conscience bring him only under such civilizing influence as suits his own convenience and no more? – In the one alternative he is faced with the ignominious prospect of seeing the Native absorb all his own ideals & aspirations & thereafter marching with him side by side & pari passu to the same goal. In the other alternative he subjects himself to the demoralising effects of constant contact with a human species that must permanently emain on a lower plane of civilization than his own...

She also reminds Zangwill that education renders any individual, black or white, more sensitive to social and political inequality, and thus it is not 'remarkable that anti-white sentiment should invariably increase with every increase in Native Education'. For these and other reasons, Auerbach concludes, 'I would much prefer our Itoland where the Native problem can never arise – so that I, the negrophile & others of the Council who are negrophobe, come to the same conclusion – as often happens – from opposite premises' (quoted from handwritten copy).
54. CZA, A36/23, Letters from Israel Zangwill to Helena Auerbach, 23 and 25 July 1906.
55. Zangwill, 'Zion, Whence Cometh My Help', *Speeches*, 80.
56. Garfinkle, 'On the Origin'.
57. Zangwill, 'East Africa Offer', *Speeches*, 210.
58. See, for example, Rabbi Dr Chaim Simons, *A Historical Survey of Proposals to Transfer Arabs from Palestine*, 1998, http://www.geocities.com/CapitolHill/Senate/7854/; and *Israel Zangwill Quotes*, PalestineRemembered.com, 23 October, 2001, http://www.palestineremembered.com/Acre/Famous-Zionist-Quotes/Story646.html.
59. Zangwill, 'Before the Peace Conference', *Speeches*, 341. It is worth noting, however, that Redcliffe Salaman warned Zangwill 'that your utterances are being

used by the Arabs primarily[?] as weapons against us' (CZA, A120/199, Letter from Redcliffe Nathan Salaman to Israel Zangwilll, 1 April 1920). Two years earlier he had repeated to Salaman a few lines of verse which, he reported, got a gleeful reception in speeches at the time: 'that going was the Arab's metier: "Fold their tents like the Arabs/ And as silently steal away"' (CUL, Add. Ms. 8171/61, Box 24, Letter from Zangwill to Salaman, 31 May 1918; the quotation is a metaphor from a poem by Longfellow). Although Zangwill would not have forced the Arabs to 'trek', the prospect of voluntary resettlement seemed possible to him for a short period of time.

60. Zangwill, *Watchman*, 36.
61. Zangwill, *Watchman*, 34–35.

9

'By Whom Shall She Arise? For She Is Small': The Wales-Israel Tradition in the Edwardian Period

Jasmine Donahaye

Welsh culture has been strongly marked by a long tradition of identification and sympathy with Jews, an identification that arose in part out of the emphatically Old Testament focus of the several Nonconformist denominations that made up the bulk of Welsh religious affiliation into the twentieth century, and in part out of a belief in liberty of conscience, which was an important component of dissenting denominational belief. From the seventeenth century until the twentieth, this identification with Jews was often expressed in terms of an identification of the Welsh *as* the Biblical Jews, and it included an identity of the geography of Wales with that of Palestine and subsequently Israel, the construction of Welsh linguistic descent from Hebrew, and the construction of ethnic descent from the Biblical Gomer.[1] In the Edwardian period, this identification with notional, Biblical Jews shifted to a political identification with historical Jews, as the rise of Zionism coincided with the rise of Welsh cultural nationalism and the Welsh cultural renaissance. As a religious motif, however, it also continued to inform the literature into the late twentieth century. In *Sacred Place, Chosen People*, Dorian Llywelyn names this folkloric substratum 'the Wales-Israel tradition' and claims that it is 'the most resonant bourdon in Welsh history'.[2]

This essentially folkloric tradition, so pervasive in the literature, also constituted a fundamental part of traditional Welsh historiography which, up until 1911, relied on a mixture of a recent heroic past and mythological and Biblical origins and descent, and was promulgated most overtly in the form of the widely-read *Drych Y Prif Oesoedd* by Theophilus Evans. This pseudo-history had originally been published in 1716, and was later translated into English as *The Mirror of the First Ages*. It enjoyed an enormous number of editions and reprints, and was, according to Prys Morgan, 'the most widely read history book in Welsh in the eighteenth and nineteenth centuries'.[3] In 1911 the traditional historiography that drew from such sources was displaced by the publication of J. E. Lloyd's new *A History of Wales*, which was to provide a more useable Welsh past.[4]

Despite the ubiquity in literature of the Wales-Israel tradition, Welsh literature in both languages also reveals the range of both positive and negative Jewish stereotypes that constitute more typical semitic discourse. However, a folkloristic approach to understanding the tradition of identification with Jews reveals aspects and attitudes that an analysis of semitic discourse does not – namely, that with this identification, the Welsh expanded the Welsh folkgroup or identity group to include Jews in a binary opposition to England and to Englishness.

Unfortunately, despite the widespread expression of this tradition, which is very much in evidence in writing, in place names, and in the consciousness of those who were raised in Welsh-language chapel culture, Welsh attitudes to Jews in the Edwardian period have been analysed in Anglo-Jewish historiography almost exclusively in relation to the Tredegar riots of 1911. These events have received substantial and, arguably, disproportionate attention; in the absence of analysis of other aspects of Jewish history in Wales, they have come to erroneously represent Welsh Jewish experience and Welsh attitudes to Jews, not only in the Edwardian period but also more generally.[5] Where Wales, rarely, does garner a mention in histories of British Jews, such reference occurs almost always in relation to the riots. In *The Jews of Britain: 1656–2000*, Todd Endelman follows this scholarly pattern. In his brief discussion of these events, he repeats the received wisdom first promulgated by Geoffrey Alderman in 1972 and subsequently minimally modified by historians Anthony Glaser, Colin Holmes, and Neil Evans, and he summarizes the causes of the riots as comprising 'xenophobia, Nonconformist antisemitism, Jewish rack-renting and labour unrest'.[6] By citing 'Nonconformist antisemitism' he implicitly rejects W. D. Rubinstein admittedly problematic reassessment of the riots.[7]

Rubinstein's examination of the evidence used by Alderman shows it to be tenuous in the extreme, and hence the conclusions drawn from it by Alderman and subsequently by other historians are unreliable. However, Rubinstein's own argument about the philosemitism of Welsh culture, the evidence he uses to support such an argument, and his reductive definition of philosemitism all prove to be equally tenuous. Nevertheless, historians have on the whole ignored his challenge to the original evidence used to argue the case of widespread Welsh antisemitism and, unlike him, have continued to overlook Welsh-language sources.[8]

In his account of British Jewry, Endelman emphatically subsumes Welsh Jewish history under Anglo-Jewish history, arguing that 'since the number of Jews who lived in Wales and Scotland was never large, folding them into "Anglo"-Jewry does not distort the overall picture'.[9] Perhaps this does not distort the overall *Anglo*-Jewish picture, but Endelman's synecdoche – the substitution of 'Anglo-Jewry' for 'British Jewry' – is another kind of distortion. To fold the Jews of Wales into Anglo-Jewry erases the particularity of Welsh Jewish experience, and this essay seeks, in part, to correct such a distortion by examining aspects of the Jewish-Welsh encounter in the Edwardian period.

The influence of the tradition of Welsh identification with the Jews, and the evidence of its transitional state from religious to political identification in the Edwardian period, is marked in the work of two writers in particular: that of D. Wynne Evans, who published several articles in 1901 and 1902, and that of the Welsh Jewish writer Lily Tobias, whose earliest, undated stories were written before 1914, and whose later fiction, though published between the wars, was fundamentally informed by her experiences as a young adult in the Swansea Valley before her marriage in 1911. In addition to exploring this tradition of identification, therefore, this essay also examines the work of these two writers and what it reveals about Welsh attitudes to both historical and notional Jews, and Jewish responses to these attitudes in the Edwardian period.

Definitions

Given the failure to recognize the several distinct national cultural contexts of the United Kingdom in much of the scholarship about nominally British – but more accurately about *English* – Jews, it is necessary to state pedantically that in this essay, the terms 'Anglo-Jewish', 'Anglo-Jewry', 'Britishness', and 'Englishness' have specific rather than general meanings. While Endelman may be correct in stating that with devolution 'the meanings of Britishness and Englishness are again much disputed',[10] in this essay the terms 'Anglo-Jewish', 'Anglo-Jewry' and 'Englishness' refer specifically to England and to Jews in England, and do not imply or incorporate Jews elsewhere in the United Kingdom; 'Britain' and 'British' refer to the United Kingdom as a whole.

Contrary to suggestions that have been made about the provincial typicality of the Jewish communities in Wales – a provincial typicality extrapolated from the *Anglo*-Jewish provinces[11] – in bilingual and predominantly Nonconformist Wales the reception of the languages, culture, and religion of Jewish immigrants was distinct from their reception in predominantly Anglican, monolingual England (notwithstanding the varieties of dialect and class and hence of attitudes that exist within the English language). In Wales, the relationship between Jews and non-Jews was, and still is, informed by the language, religion, class tensions, politics, and economics particular to the Welsh cultural context.

Whether in the anglicised towns of the north and south coasts or in the Welsh-speaking western valleys and rural areas, Jews and other minorities had to struggle with a dual and sometimes a triple pressure to assimilate and become anglicised: they had to negotiate a relationship both with Welsh and with English society and, within Welsh society, had to negotiate a relationship both with its Welsh-speaking and its anglicised cultures. This process of assimilation was further complicated for the Jewish community, as distinct from that of some Welsh minority groups, by an orientation towards the institutions of the Anglo-Jewish centre.

The use of terms such as anglicisation and assimilation must evidently differ in Wales from their use in England. In Wales, anglicisation denotes not only a primary orientation towards England and the acquisition of the English language and of English social attitudes and behaviours, but also the acquisition of English attitudes to the Welsh, to Welsh culture, and to the Welsh language. For Welsh Jews to assimilate to English society means not only partially or wholly to abandon Jewish practice, language, and accent, but also to abandon Welsh ones. In the Victorian and Edwardian periods, anglicisation – which was mediated by the class issues associated with the two languages – was a process of social change that not only pertained to immigrants, but also to the Welsh-speaking community and to second generation Jews who grew up in Welsh-speaking areas. Jewish adaptation to this social environment is complex, particular, and difficult to generalize, but is surely no more complex or particular than in comparable situations, and such a difficulty therefore does not justify its neglect in scholarship, nor its dismissal as merely 'piquant and arresting in human terms'.[12]

Like the particular meaning of anglicisation in the context of Wales, this essay also deploys a specific meaning for the term 'folkgroup'. My understanding of folkgroup in this context relies more on an adaptation of a definition in American folkloristics than on traditional notions of a *volk*: Alan Dundes, for example, defines a folkgroup at its most elemental as constituting any group of people who share one or more linking factors, and who produce and share a body of folk*lore*.[13] The repeating motifs of the Wales-Israel tradition constitutes a form of *blason populaire*, the genre of folklore that identifies common characteristics shared by members of a group, and which defines membership in (and exclusion from) a folkgroup.[14] These shared factors render folkgroups very flexible, with membership categories able to expand or contract according to political expedience.

The Welsh tradition of identification with the Jews was distinguished from a not uncommon Protestant and often millenarian identification, by the motif of Welsh self-identification in binary opposition to *Englishness*; this identification effectively incorporated the Jews – originally in terms of borrowed Biblical election but later in terms of parallel national sentiment and national aspirations – into an expanded Welsh folkgroup. It is this construction of a species of 'Welsh-Israelite' identity group that suggests the tradition – which, unlike Hobsbawm's definition of tradition as a set of practices, is, in this case, a set of motif references – might be usefully understood in folkloric terms, particularly *blason populaire*, and in terms of the construction of folkgroup.[15]

The Welsh as Jews: pre-Edwardian religious identification

In his reassessment of the Tredegar riots, W. D. Rubinstein argues that Welsh culture is fundamentally philosemitic, and the work of D. Wynne Evans is one of several examples, including David Lloyd George and the Reverend John Mills, that he cites. However, Evans, like Rubinstein's other examples, proves problematic: his work is overtly millenarian, and his attitudes, as discussed later, cannot be adequately accommodated by W. D. Rubinstein and Hilary Rubinstein's binary definition of philosemitism as 'support and/ or admiration for the Jewish people by non-Jews', which they regard 'as the other side of the coin of antisemitism (hostility to, or dislike of, Jews)'.[16] This definition cannot take account of the nuances and contradictions in Welsh semitic discourse, nor can it account for the construction of a Welsh-Israelite folkgroup that is characteristic of the tradition of identification with the Jews. Indeed, Rubinstein reduces a range of Nonconformist denominations to a single cultural monolith, and in the process projects onto Welsh culture a construct of Protestant philosemitism as reductive as Endelman's passing reference to 'Nonconformist antisemitism' or indeed Rubinstein's parallel construct of Catholic antisemitism.[17]

What Rubinstein perceives at work in Welsh culture – as expressed by D. Wynne Evans, Lloyd George and many others – is the interaction of the Welsh tradition of religious liberalism (which recognizes the rights of other dissenting faiths, such as Judaism) with the complex and multifaceted folk-loric tradition of identification with the Jews. Continually reinvented according to the needs of a contemporary agenda, elements of the folkloric tradition can be traced back to Gildas in the sixth century, and its primary, repeating motifs may be seen at work in Charles Edwards, Henry Rowlands, and Theophilus Evans in the seventeenth and eighteenth centuries.[18] In the nineteenth and early twentieth centuries the tradition of identification still formed an integral part of traditional Welsh historiography, which continued to incorporate foundation myths until the end of the Edwardian period.

Principled support for other dissenting religious views was fundamental to Welsh Nonconformist belief: for example, in 1838, Hugh Pugh, a prominent Independent minister maintained, according to E. T. Davies, 'that it was the glory of nonconformity that it could not deprive others of this liberty without denying their own faith'.[19] Nevertheless, Welsh Nonconformists were equally committed to the practice of evangelism, and the tension between these two positions is one of the many contradictions in Nonconformist attitudes to Jews that cannot be accommodated by a binary definition of philosemitism and antisemitism.

Religious liberalism on the part of Nonconformists was tied to the political movement in Wales for the disestablishment of the Church of England and the removal of its privileges, for only a small minority of the Welsh population was Anglican. This support therefore extended, at times reluctantly, to Catholics as much as to Jews: indeed the proportionately greater hostility to Catholics than Jews in Wales, especially during the time of mass immigration to industrial Wales, is of particular importance when considering the Tredegar riots in context.[20]

Notwithstanding revisionist history that has queried the extent of religious observance in Wales in the nineteenth century, the predominance of Nonconformity and of Calvinistic Methodism in particular marked Wales culturally, linguistically, and politically well into the twentieth century. The inheritance and reinvention in the nineteenth and twentieth centuries of traditional Welsh historiography and, with it, the tradition of identification with Jews, has had often surprising consequences, among them, for example, a strongly defended notion – if not necessarily a fact – of the inherent tolerance of Welsh culture.[21] This is a notion to which many Jews have responded positively – indeed, in Welsh Jewish literature, Wales is consistently constructed as a haven from antisemitism.[22] Another surprising consequence, arising from the traditional association between Welsh and Hebrew, has been the identification with the aspirations of the Hebrew language revival among those seeking models for Welsh language survival: the intensive study of the Welsh language is still called an Ulpan (spelled in Welsh as 'wlpan').[23]

Although it was distinct in many ways, the Welsh tradition of identification with Jews shared some superficial similarities with what developed, in England, into the Anglo-Israel and British Israel theories. The Anglo-Israel theory, which through complex eschatological arguments posits that the English are descended from the lost tribes of Israel and that the English language is descended from Hebrew, enjoyed wide debate in England both within and outside the Church of England in the late nineteenth and early twentieth century. The theory has roots in Puritan eschatology, the Fifth Monarchy Men movement, and Cromwellian millenarianism; it has influenced white suprematist groups in the United States and it still enjoys support in the form of the Anglo-Israel Federation, which disseminates the version of the belief articulated by John Wilson in 1840.[24]

In the 1870s and 1880s a certain F. W. Phillips, who wrote under the pen name 'Philo-Israel', produced a large number of publications on the Anglo-Israel theory and edited *The Banner of Israel*, the journal of the movement.[25] While Phillips argues that English is descended from Hebrew, he clearly had to account for other languages in Britain in order to co-opt all into what became the British Israel theory, and in order to evangelize the Welsh. Whereas in 1879 he commented on the relation of Welsh to Hebrew (citing, among others, Henry Rowlands[26]), in 1880 he produced a more substantial appeal to the Welsh entitled *Proofs for the Welsh that the British Are the Lost Tribes of Israel* and *Y Genedl Gymreig yn Deillio oddiwrth Ddeg Llwyth Colledig Tŷ Israel: Sef, Epistol at y Cymry* [*The Origins of the Welsh Nation in the Ten Lost Tribes of the House of Israel: Namely, an Epistle to the Welsh*].[27] It is perhaps this latter manifestation of the theory that influenced D. Wynne Evans, whom I discuss later.

The Welsh tradition of identification with the Jews was distinct from this 'theory' in many ways, one of which was the identification with Jews in opposition to England and Englishness. Before the Edwardian period, and going back to the sixth century, this oppositional identification is with notional, Biblical Jews: it may be seen in *De Excidio Britanniae*, in which Gildas constructs the Proto-Welsh (that is, the Britons) as the true chosen people in opposition to the pagan Anglo-Saxons (the proto-English).[28] In a similar fashion, in the seventeenth century Charles Edwards equates the English attack on the Welsh chosen people with the Assyrian attack on the Biblical chosen people.[29]

Another distinguishing feature is that of the nature of election. In his lecture *'Canys Bechan Yw': Y Genedl Etholedig yn Ein Llenyddiaeth* [*'For She Is Small': The Chosen People in Our Literature*], Derec Llwyd Morgan observes that national self-construction as the new chosen people, which is common to many Protestant cultures, has traditionally taken two forms:

> Beth sy'n dod yn amlwg i'r neb a astudia phenomen y genedl etholedig Brotestannaidd o'r cyfnod modern cynnar hyd y dydd heddiw yw hyn – sef bod dau ddosbarth o genhedloedd etholedig, dau deip, dau fath. Y rhai llwyddiannus, a dybiant mai llwyddiant yw eu rhan yn wastadol; a'r rhai methiannus y mae eu llwyddiant eto i ddod.[30]
>
> [What becomes obvious to anyone who studies the phenomenon of the elect Protestant nation from the early modern period to the present day is this – that there are two classes of elected nations, two types, two kinds. The successful ones, who imagine that success is their perpetual fate, and the failed ones, whose success is yet to come.]

England is one of those 'successful' elect nations, the English believing (in the nineteenth century) that their success as an imperial power was a signal of divine favour. 'Nid bechan yw', Llwyd Morgan concludes – 'she is *not* small'.[31] But the image of the Welsh as the latter kind of elect nation, a chosen people whose 'success' is yet to come, is, according to Llwyd Morgan, pervasive in Welsh literature. He sees the myth of the small and powerless nation and the question 'how will she [Wales-as-Israel] rise, for she is small?' being asked in Welsh literature from the sixteenth century to the twentieth.

The qualities that define the Welsh as a 'small' chosen people remain stable across time. Dorian Llywelyn sees the work of the twentieth-century writer Saunders Lewis as 'the latest layer of a palimpsest: the struggle of

Naboth against Jezebel, of the Britons against the Saxons, of culture against ignorance, salvation against damnation, Welsh pacifism against English imperialism, are all part of the same pattern, in which the whole is visible through the various strata.'[32] Llwyd Morgan observes:

> The totalizing Biblical influence has been very great in our literature. In the modern period, it is religious literature from root to branch, and it is not surprising that its main readers should see themselves as a spiritual Israel living in Bethlehem and Carmel, whether in Carmarthenshire or in Caernarfonshire...[33]

However, although this Biblical identification is pervasive in the literature (but not in the visual culture), the attitudes towards Jews in Gildas, Charles Edwards, Theophilus Evans, and others, and in the discussions of these texts by subsequent commentators, do not constitute *philosemitism*, as Rubinstein defines it.[34] Even less do they suggest antisemitism or allosemitism, for the Jews are neither demonised nor are they placed outside the boundaries of known experience: they are more often than not simply replaced by the Welsh. The Welsh *become* the Biblical Jews, and the Jews as a historical rather than a metaphorical people are themselves absented from the discourse. Llywelyn analyses this in terms of a theological equation:

> The metaphor, where x *is* y, identifies or joins the two realities.... Gildas' description is more than a literary device: in a typological sense the Christian Britons *are* the inheritors of the Old Testament promise.[35]

Consequently, these are not 'semitic' discourses, as such, at all – perhaps instead they could be termed *a-semitic* or *de-semiticized* discourses, and they exist alongside more typical Welsh semitic discourse, whose negative stereotypes do not appear to be greatly modified or informed by this prominent tradition of close identification.

Much of the literary discourse that does pertain to historical rather than to notional or Biblical Jews is concerned with their conversion. In a long poem published in 1826 entitled *Golwg ar Gyflwr yr Iuweddon* [*A Look at the State of the Jews*], the poet Daniel Evans, for example, upbraids the Jews for their stubbornness and intransigence, while other conversionist texts construct Jews in terms of positive stereotypes.[36] Besides this conversionist discourse, the full range of negative stereotypical attributes may occasionally be seen in the work of writers such as O. M. Edwards in the 1880s or in Crwys (the bardic name for the poet William Williams) in 1918.[37] What is curious about these instances of negative stereotyping is their co-existence with such a strong identification with the Jews.[38] Perhaps more remarkable is the belief, by some commentators, that they are exceptional and hence not representative of what is constructed as the essential tolerance of Welsh culture.[39]

The shift to political identification

In the Edwardian period, a new expression of political identification with contemporary Jewish oppression and national aspirations began to emerge alongside the older Biblical motifs. While this new political identification was certainly informed by the growth of Zionism – which coincided with and, in Wales, was in part nurtured by the rise of Welsh cultural nationalism – Welsh responses to Zionism were also informed by residual and sometimes overtly millenarian sentiment. The intimate interrelation of religion and nationalism in Wales, which proved so strongly resonant with Zionism, is eloquently expressed in 1905 by Alderman Edward Thomas, who writes under his bardic name 'Cochfarf'. Like Derec Llwyd Morgan many years later, he frames the argument of his essay, which was published in the *South Wales Jewish Review*, in terms of the influence of Hebrew and the Bible on Welsh literature:

> Hebrew ideals, and the writings of the Hebrew prophets have impregnated the minds of the writers of Wales to such an extent that for the best part of a century, scriptural idioms have become as prevalent among the Welsh as the idioms of their own language.[40]

He suggests that this Biblical influence has affected Welsh political life:

> Wales is intensely national in matters of government, and its inhabitants are as patriotic as they are religious, and it is a fair subject for enquiry as to what extent its nationalism has been fostered by the example of the Jewish people, and which is, as it were, breathed by the writings of their prophets. (29)

Most significant of its publication in the *South Wales Jewish Review* is not Cochfarf's observation that 'it is no discredit to the Cambrian to have chosen his patriotic ideal in a God-chosen people', but his suggestion about the role that the Welsh can play in Jewish life:

> Wales has long ago learned the lesson of religious equality, and its sons are ever the standard-bearer of liberty of conscience. This with their exceptional knowledge of Hebrew aspirations as enunciated in the Hebrew Scriptures may fit the Cymry to be interpreters of Jewry, as disinterested third parties, to rulers and potentates who will not give ear to the decendants [*sic*] of Abraham, gifted as their sons are with all the talents that the human race can command. (29)

As already mentioned, this 'liberty of conscience' and the belief in religious equality are themes that disposed Welsh Nonconformists to support Jewish emancipation. Cochfarf concludes his article by quoting a prophesy that he attributes to the sixth-century poet Taliesin, which predicts that the Welsh will hold onto their language, will glorify their God, and will lose their land except for 'Wild Wales', and he asks:

> Who can realise the pathos of these well-known lines more readily than the Jewish people? And if so, should not the sentiment it proclaims prove a channel of sympathy between the two people? (29)

D. Wynne Evans

Three years earlier, in several eschatological essays that were published in a prominent journal of cultural nationalism entitled *Young Wales*, D. Wynne Evans similarly drew parallels between the Welsh and the Jews.[41] His essays are concerned with millenarianism, but by his incorporation of the Jews into an argument about the crucial contribution of Welsh culture to the British Empire, he illustrates the transition of the tradition of identification with Jews to a political plane in this period. His essays offer a concise summary of the motifs of this tradition and, by their use of a wide range of source material, effectively demonstrate its wide distribution.

Evans suggests that 'it was from the boundless wilderness of the east the Cymro [Welshman] came', adding that 'when it is remembered how adapted to the Cymro's mind is the Old Testament, it is not difficult to believe that the Welshman and the Hebrew are brothers from the wilderness'.[42] Among those whose work he cites is the author Ernest Rhys, editor of *Everyman*, who wrote, also in 1901, in a review of the *Jewish Encyclopoedia* in his 'Welsh Literary Notes' column in the *Manchester Guardian*:

> It is not a mere ingenious idea that the Welsh people have felt at times in their history that it had a very strange parallel in the history of the Jews. There is even a spiritual affinity between the two races that lies deeper than we know; and when a Welshman thinks of the Holy Land he is very apt to think of it as another Wales in the East. So today there is no section of readers more eager than ours for anything that helps to lighten and explain the inner and outer world of Jewish life and all that belongs to it.[43]

According to Evans, in this review Rhys 'touched on this Hebrew-Celtic chord, which must have vibrated sympathetically in many hearts belonging to the two nations'.[44] Evans reports that in the *Western Mail* he himself repudiated a claim made by a correspondent that the Welsh were antisemitic, and that in his repudiation he had argued 'that the Welsh had always been exceptionally partial to the Jews; that Welsh bishops fought valiantly in the House of Lords for their emancipation' and that 'the checkered [*sic*] career of Israel finds a sympathetic echo in the warm Cymric heart'.[45] To bolster his argument, he used extracts from a lecture by Dean Howell, who had observed:

> There is a striking similarity in the geographical features of Wales and of Palestine...There is also the same sentiment of intense and undying patriotism, which is characteristic of the two nationalities. There is again much in common between the Welsh and Hebrew languages, and I have it on good authority that our Welsh translation of the Old Testament Scriptures comes nearer to the Hebrew original than almost any other.[46]

Proud of what he effectively argues is his country's philosemitic tradition, Evans reports that he sent the two newspaper letters to Chief Rabbi Adler, who responded: 'I fully agree with you as to the kindly sentiments which the Welsh nation has at all times entertained for my fellow-religionists. I believe that the Welsh and the Irish are the sole nationalities that have not practised any active persecution against the Jews.'[47] Consistent with the older uses of the folkloric tradition, such as that of Charles Edwards or Gildas, Evans attempts to secure for Wales the moral high ground over England, for Adler's response is quoted, he explains, 'to show that the Celtic race, in its Welsh and Irish branches, is the one solitary exception among the nations of the earth that has never suffered from that periodical epidemic of suicidal madness, called antisemitism'.[48]

The clearest indication of Evans' agenda is apparent in his discussion of an article by J. H. Edwards, the editor of *Young Wales*. According to Evans, Edwards argued that 'every country had some special purpose to accomplish – some special destiny to fulfil', and that allotted to Wales 'was that the Celt was destined to carry on the work of the Hebrew as bearers of a message to the hearts of the people'.[49] According to Evans, Edwards

> looked to the Celts to rescue England from the danger of becoming grossly materialistic, and to the conquered, in this case, establishing a moral and beneficent superiority over their conquerors, so that all-powerful England might turn to Wales, not only for its coal and water supply, but also for purer national aspirations and nobler national ideals.[50]

One may perceive in the constructions of Welsh culture by Evans those same layers of the palimpsest identified by Llywelyn in the later work of Saunders Lewis. Throughout his essays Evans invokes all the motifs of the tradition of identification – that of linguistic relationships, geographic similarity, and moral purity, constructing a noble lineage for Wales that partakes of the traditional historiography definitively displaced, in 1911, by the publication of J. E. Lloyd's *A History of Wales*. But perhaps the most telling motif in the work of Evans is the definition of the Welsh and the Jews as 'brothers in the wilderness': the Welsh no longer supplant the Jews in divine election but struggle in parallel against oppression.

The essays by Evans and Cochfarf indicate how the identification with Jews as a folkloric substratum was challenged, in the Edwardian period, by the splintering of political nationalism after the demise of the Cymru Fydd movement, and by the cultural renaissance that had begun to discover an indigenous Celtic and increasingly historical Welsh past. Their essays show how the tradition of identification combined old religious and new political expressions, but also how the tradition had not yet moved in the early Edwardian period to a clear, contemporary political comparison, which it would do in the post-war period, particularly in association with the Balfour Declaration. In contrast, Lily Tobias, in her earliest stories, which are discussed below, decisively translated this identification into one of solidarity with national aspirations, thus re-Judaizing a tradition that had primarily concerned notional Jews.

During the Edwardian period, the religious context that had given rise to the tradition still limited it. Evans' essays, for example, are framed by the conversionist poetry of the seventeenth-century Puritan mystic, Morgan Llwyd, and indeed the overall message of his work is eschatological and millenarian. Thus, although his work indicates an overt sympathy with Jews and with Jewish national aspirations, due to this equally overt millenarianism (though only covert conversionism) it cannot be construed as being philosemitic.

This millenarianism was certainly widespread in Wales up to and beyond the beginning of the twentieth century, but arguably it was qualitatively distinct from English millenarianism, informed as it was by the self-image of the Welsh as a 'small' elect nation. One may deduce that its subtextual conversionism may also have been somewhat moderated – though it was certainly not erased – by the Nonconformist respect for dissenting belief. In the nineteenth century the strange case of the abduction of Esther Lyons indicates that such conversionism was at times and in certain circumstances explicit and malign, and that millenarianism might therefore have been viewed with suspicion.[51] John Mills, however, who was sent to London by the Calvinistic Methodists to convert the Jews in the 1840s, was himself accused of courting conversion, because of his sympathy.[52] Nevertheless, by the Edwardian period, it would appear that on the whole such millenarianism (and more specifically its conversionist subtext) was seen by Jews in Wales as considerably more benign than the English variety, at least in terms of its attitudes to Jews.

Lily Tobias

The clearest evidence for this Jewish attitude to Welsh millenarianism appears in a short story by Lily Tobias (discussed below), in which an encounter with millenarian sentiment, presented as positive in its attitude to Jews, precipitates in the assimilationist Jewish protagonist an interest in Zionism, which (in Tobias' understanding of the value of Zionism), offers a solution to the protagonist's difficult situation as a Jew. However, in 1938, in her last novel (which is set in the 1930s), the millenarianism of a Welsh missionary is constructed as ignorant and hostile – a change that suggests Tobias later came to view millenarian support for Zionist endeavour with considerable suspicion.[53]

While Lily Tobias' work explores the subtleties of social relationships between Welsh Jews and the non-Jewish Welsh, such complexities are largely absent from the work of Jewish writers who grew up in the heavily anglicised capital Cardiff. These writers, including Bernice Rubens, Maurice Edelman and Tobias' nephew Dannie Abse, reveal an internalisation of attitudes of anglicised south Wales.[54] However, the complexity of these social relations is very much in evidence in the work of those writers who engage with Welsh-speaking Wales, such as Tobias or, in the 1970s, the Israeli writer Judith Maro.[55]

Tobias was born in Ystalyfera in the Swansea Valley in 1887, and her work is informed by her background in this Welsh-speaking environment, and by her upbringing in an immigrant, Yiddish-speaking family. Several of her stories and her first novel trace the experiences of Jewish protagonists in Swansea and the Swansea Valley from the late nineteenth century up until the First World War, and her work is complemented by that of sociologist Leonard Mars, in particular his essay on the troubled tenure of Simon Fyne as Minister at the Swansea Hebrew Congregation between 1899 and 1906.[56] This focus on the Jewish community of Swansea is not only the result of an accident of history, which largely preserved the records of the synagogue when those of Cardiff were lost, but is also a reflection of the rich culture of Swansea and its industrial valley, which has been neglected as much in Welsh as in Jewish historiography in favour of the dominant histories of Cardiff, Merthyr Tydfil, and the Rhondda. Swansea has the oldest Jewish community in Wales, with roots that go back to the 1730s, and the city and valley have produced prominent Jewish political and cultural figures.[57]

While Ursula Henriques claims that the difference between the establishment and immigrant communities in the Jewish community of Swansea 'was more one of generation than of class', the sociological history by Mars and fiction by Tobias indicate that, on the contrary, these differences were indeed class-based.[58] But although Mars acknowledges the failure of Simon Fyne to recognize the particularity of Wales, he analyses the tensions between the immigrant and establishment Jewish communities (tensions that led to the formation of a new immigrants' synagogue) solely in terms of Anglo-Jewish concerns with class and immigration status.[59] In contrast, Tobias's work suggests that the tensions within the Swansea Valley Jewish community were class-based within the very particular Welsh context of rural versus urban, and Welsh-speaking versus anglicised differences.

In Tobias's stories and in her first novel, immigrant Jews are seen as a threat by the middle-class and largely assimilated Jewish establishment in Swansea.[60] This establishment is acculturated to the class, linguistic, and political attitudes of the anglicised urban Welsh, and it is among this anglicised Welsh middle class, who in turn have exaggerated *English* aspirations, that expressions of antisemitism are to be found. Immigrant and second-generation Jews, such as Tobias herself, who are both Welsh- and Yiddish-speaking, rural, poor, and predominantly Zionist, are too Welsh and too 'foreign' (which is to say too Orthodox and continental) for the establishment Jews to accept.

In the story 'Glasshouses', set in the early Edwardian period and written before 1914, this Jewish establishment is represented by a 'Mrs Knacker' who, like the Anglo-Jewish establishment she imitates, stands for 'the right attitude in Jewish-Gentile relationships', which entailed emulating 'the life and behaviour of the Goyim as much as possible, while retaining some ineradicable old Hebrew customs that, under judicious treatment, should not show too marked a line of cleavage'.[61]

However, the questioning protagonist of the story, Sheba, rejects Mrs Knacker's attitudes, along with the assertion by Mrs Knacker's son that 'as we live with the Goyim, we must act similar to make 'em like and respect us'. 'Oh, respect,' Sheba exclaims, 'I don't believe that's the way to do it...If there was a Jewish country, one wouldn't have to worry' (48–49). Sheba's fledgling Zionism develops in response to what she describes as her 'betwixt and between' status as the daughter of an immigrant couple; in response to her exposure to antisemitism, expressed by the anglophilic shop-girl Miss Howells, whose casual contempt for 'greasy old Jews' is equal to her casual contempt for all things Welsh; and, most interestingly, in response to the millenarian expostulations of a Welshman named Christmas Jones.[62]

This story sketches what becomes, in Tobias' first novel, *My Mother's House*, an extended examination of the abject status of the would-be assimilated Jew. The novel's Jewish protagonist, Simon, is born in about 1895 and grows up in a thinly fictionalised Ystalyfera, and he first encounters antisemitism when he enters the County School. Here he is 'made aware, beyond all previous experience, of the acuteness of "Christian" hostility'.[63] The children of the village where he had grown up

> had, on the whole, accepted him as one of themselves; the constant sense of familiarity prevailing over the occasional sense of difference. But the County scholars came to judgement from strange and less charitable courts. Mostly the offspring of prosperous shopkeepers, they thought it an offence to their gentility to have a 'dirty Jew' among them. The phrase was oftenest on the lips of...the anglicised son of a country vicar. (55)

The novel subtly explores issues of class and language: the rural working-class Jewish protagonist Simon, for example, experiences mortification at the hands of his urban cousin, who mocks him for coming to town in hobnail boots, and 'a funny suit – like the colliers buy in the shops' (48). Tobias indicates that anglicised, socially aspiring Welsh Jews like Simon's cousin had to contend with the dual social disability of Welshness and Jewishness, for this cousin reveals her middle-class English aspirations when she complains about the social habits of immigrant Jews:

> 'But there, indeed!' she said in a loud whisper to her sister, forgetting to avoid being 'Welshy' in her indignation. 'What can you expect of *foreigners*? No idea how to behave...' (49)

The quest by Simon for complete English assimilation, the doomed nature of which is the didactic message of the novel, is stimulated when he is ten years old by hearing, for the first time, 'English perfectly spoken by an Englishwoman' (7). His anglophilia is fuelled by a growing hatred of all things Welsh and Jewish and he expresses a particular horror of Welsh, Anglo-Welsh, and Yiddish. The central concern with language as a carrier of culture appears in the novel's opening scene, which suggests how sensitive Tobias was to the complexities of the linguistic situation around her.[64]

When Simon does eventually escape Wales, his almost ecstatic emergence from the Severn Tunnel into England is a moment of high tragicomedy: it is clear that in England he will have a rude awakening to the legacy of his Welsh and Jewish birth and upbringing. Simon 'had come to regard himself the victim of a twofold difference – that which he felt as a barrier between himself and his parents, and that which others felt as a barrier between himself and them', and unlike other assimilated Jews who, despite their efforts and their own self-image, are unable to cross the 'dividing line' because of their inability to 'obliterate the featured stamp of their race', he feels 'himself free of all "foreign" flaws – born incontestably a native heir to English life' (64–65). In England, however, he finds that his Jewishness, his Welshness, and the working-class Welshness of his Patagonian-Welsh wife are severe social disabilities that he tries, and fails, to eradicate. The conflicts that Simon experiences are only finally resolved when he re-engages with his Jewish identity and embraces Zionism: the novel closes with his death in Palestine as a Jewish Battalion soldier in the First World War.

The influence on Tobias of her Zionist father was no doubt also felt by her brother, Joseph Shepherd, who articulates belief in two kinds of Jews – 'the non-Jewish Jew and the Zionist Jew'.[65] This bipartite view of Jews is also to be found in Tobias' work and is a parallel to her bipartite construction of the non-Welsh Welsh and the nationalist Welsh. In the two pre-war stories, 'Glasshouses' and 'The Nationalists', the Zionism of the Jewish protagonists is directly informed by the Welsh nationalism of their surroundings.[66]

Indeed, 'The Nationalists', whose narrative, set in Ystalyfera, unfolds between the turn of the century and the riots in 1911, details the parallels and sympathies between Welsh and Jewish political aspirations, and constitutes an overt response to the tradition of Welsh identification with the Jews, a consciousness of which suffuses all Tobias' work.[67]

Tobias came to political awareness in the late 1890s at the height of the Cymru Fydd movement for national autonomy, and her young adulthood in the Swansea Valley exposed her to the vibrant cultural nationalism of Edwardian Wales. Ystalyfera was home to *Llais Llafur* [*Labour Voice*], an influential socialist paper that was a focus for the active political and cultural life of the valley. After the war, Tobias lived in Rhiwbina in Cardiff, which was an enclave of Welsh intellectual activity in the interwar years.[68] As with her arguably autobiographical protagonists, it is clear that the political environment in and around Ystalyfera informed her Zionism, which throughout her fiction she situates in a comparative Welsh national context. The cover of her collection of short stories, many of which were first published in *The Zionist Review*, depicts a Welsh dragon entwined with a Star of David, and in reviewing the book in 1922, Paul Goodman observed:

> Mrs Tobias has introduced us to a new *milieu*, for Welsh Nationalism, unknown to most of us, has had its effect on her, blending harmoniously with the Jewish Nationalism with which Mrs Tobias is so deeply imbued. Those of us who only England know are struck by the self-assertion of Welsh Nationalism in its own home.[69]

Tobias constructs as antisemitic those anglicised Welsh who reject their culture and language in favour of Englishness. In contrast, her working-class and often culturally or politically nationalist Welsh-speakers warmly welcome Jews as 'the people of the Book', and Tobias thus suggests that antisemitism in Wales is a product of anglicisation.[70]

In 'Glasshouses', the sympathy with Jews that Tobias attributes to the nationalist Welsh is millenarian in tone. Christmas Jones, a character whose name is probably a reference to the famous Welsh preacher Christmas Evans, greets the Jewish girl Sheba:

> Merch annwyl [dear girl], and proud I am to meet you, for sure. Why, I do love the Jews, indeed I do. You are the people of the book and the lord will show His wonders through you yet. You have got a big job in front of you my gell... the return to Zion. (46)

Jones reveals his millenarian beliefs in response to a story that he is told about the experiences of a Romanian pogrom refugee: 'I would be telling him it is the Lord's will, and the sign that the prophecies are coming true,' he exclaims. 'For, indeed, if the afflictions have come true, it is certain that the joy and happiness will come after' (47). Despite the fact that Tobias is highly sensitive to conversion and conversionism, she does not make anything of the conversionism that is always an implicit (and often explicit) subtext of millenarianism; this suggests that, in practical terms, in this context such conversionism is seen as benign.

However, the millenarian Jewish sympathy of Christmas Jones is only one of a range of positive attitudes to Jews that Tobias attributes to the Welsh. In *My Mother's House* she ascribes such sympathy to the religious liberalism of a village school teacher: he is described as 'a conscientious nonconformist, whose principles approved the freedom of another faith' (31). The attitudes of this village teacher contrast with those encountered by Simon in the County School, where it is not just the anglicised students who are hostile to a Jew, but also the teacher and the anglicised school inspector. The latter, on noting Simon's academic gifts, asks:

'What's his father – a miner?'
'No,' said the schoolmaster – 'a Jew.'
...'Well, well,' he said pettishly. 'Fancy that – didn't know you had 'em here. Amazing how the breed gets about…Shouldn't encourage 'em too much, anyhow. They'll swamp us.' (23)

The teacher agrees with the sentiment 'not only in words but in his heart', but he is well disposed towards Simon, for, as Tobias suggests, 'the soundest of generalities can be discounted by individual experience' (24). Tobias' brother Joseph Shepherd recalls that at the religious service on his first day at the County School in 1909, 'the Nonconformist headmaster' announced:

This is an unusual day…today I understand we are being honoured by the presence for the first time of a Jewish boy. He cannot be expected to take part in a service of this kind which is predominantly Christian. So in welcoming him – and I trust you will all welcome him – I want him to stand up and walk outside…because he's not expected to participate in this service which would be contrary to his religion.[71]

Although this can be read as an exclusionary and perhaps hostile way of highlighting difference, the manner in which Shepherd reports this incident indicates the deep respect he had for the religious liberalism of the headmaster, and he recalls humorously how he was expected, as a Jew, to excel in any matter relating to the Hebrew Bible.[72]

Perhaps most importantly, Shepherd comments on the absence of antisemitism in his childhood and upbringing, an observation made later by Dannie Abse, his brother Leo, and many other Welsh Jews and Jewish immigrants to Wales, who, as already mentioned, construct Wales as a refuge from affliction. This is also echoed by Maurice Silverglit, a Jewish miner born in Aberfan, who was interviewed when an old man in 1978:

> I consider myself more Welsh than these other buggers...There's no antisemitism here – it's wonderful. The Welsh were very religious – you'd go to certain places – you'd see an Old Testament, not the New Testament – the Old Testament, and the father would say certain portions of the Bible to his children. In English it was, see – in Welsh too. I used to like to go to their chapels: I was very friendly with some of the boys. Sincere Protestants, you know – not the Catholics, the Irish – [though] I went to their churches as well.[73]

Another of Tobias' liberal humanists, a north Walian Welsh-speaking nationalist who learned Hebrew and who believes that 'the Jews are the best people in the world', is, like Christmas Jones, constructed as being representative of Welsh-speaking Wales and, consequently, as expressing an increasingly marginalized position.[74] In attributing to the Welsh-speaking and nationalist Welsh such positive attitudes to Jews – including identification with Jewish political aspirations, millenarian sympathy with and support for Zionism, and religious liberalism – and by situating the Jewish struggle with assimilation and culture loss within a comparative Welsh context of culture loss, Tobias effectively re-Judaizes the Welsh tradition of identification with Jews. She also effectively incorporates the Welsh-speaking Welsh into an expanded *Jewish* folkgroup of political sympathies, in counterpoint to the tradition of Welsh identification with Jews, which incorporates the Jews into an expanded *Welsh* folkgroup.

Conclusion

It may be the very *notionality* of Biblical Jews, with whom the Welsh closely identified themselves for so long, that, in the pre-Edwardian period, enabled such a folkloric tradition of identification with Jews to co-exist with widespread conversionist discourse and with the antisemitic stereotypes that sometimes appear in Welsh literature and elsewhere.[75] While invocation of the tradition of identification and expressions of positive stereotypes may have obscured such negative stereotyping, the occurrence of negative stereotype in Welsh literature in both languages is nevertheless occasional rather than frequent. However, this by no means justifies the claim, made by Rubinstein, that 'Philosemitism...permeated every aspect of Welsh culture until very recent times'.[76] The difference in the degree of negative Jewish stereotyping in Welsh and in English literature may be due to the fact that in Wales the Jews have not occupied the place of prime 'other' in the way that they often have in England and on the continent. On the contrary, one might argue that this place has been occupied, in Wales, by the English. It is for this reason that understanding the elements of the tradition of identification as examples of *blason populaire*, deployed in the construction of an 'us/other' folkgroup or identity group, is perhaps more helpful than analysing it solely in terms of semitic discourse. It is certainly more helpful and revealing than understanding the tradition in binary terms of antisemitism and philosemitism.

Before the Edwardian period, the notional Jews were effectively replaced by the Welsh, as occurs in the question by Charles Edwards: 'By whom shall Wales arise, for she is small?' In the Edwardian period itself, however, when the shift from religious to political identification occurs, and for a long time afterwards, the Jews were situated within the margin of a larger folkgroup of Welsh identification (as distinct from Welsh *nationality*): the Jews are another small nation like this small nation, and in this period the question posed was: 'How will she, Wales, arise? For she, like Israel, is small.' In these still religiously-inflected but by now politically-focused constructions, the Jews and the Welsh are fellow brothers in the wilderness of statelessness, sharing a 'small' sense of nation, language, and distinctive history, which they retain in binary opposition to the politically, linguistically and culturally dominant 'other', the English.

Notes

1. See for example Glanmor Williams, 'Fire on Cambria's Altar', *The Welsh and Their Religion*.
2. Llywelyn, *Sacred Place*, 77.
3. Prys Morgan, 'The Clouds of Witnesses', quoted in James, ' "The New Birth of a People" ', 23. According to Glanmor Williams (*The Welsh and Their Religion*, 23), Evans' *Drych Y Prif Oesoedd* was 'the most influential book on the subject of the history of religion in Wales'.
4. J. E. Lloyd, *A History of Wales: From the Earliest Times to the Edwardian Conquest* (London: Longmans, Green & Co., 1911).
5. This has been reinforced in the Oscar-nominated (and hence widely-seen) S4C-sponsored film *Solomon and Gaenor*, written and directed by Paul Morrison (1999).
6. Endelman, *The Jews of Britain*, 162. See Alderman, 'The Anti-Jewish Riots'; Alderman, 'The Jew as Scapegoat?'; Glaser, 'The Tredegar Riots'; Holmes, 'The Tredegar Riots'; Neil Evans, 'Immigrants and Minorities'.
7. Rubinstein, 'The Anti-Jewish Riots'.
8. For analysis of the interpretation of the riots, see Donahaye, 'Jewish Writing in Wales', ch. 1.
9. Endelman, *The Jews of Britain*, 12.
10. Endelman, *The Jews of Britain*, 162.
11. Henriques, 'The Conduct of a Synagogue', 107.
12. Endelman, *The Jews of Britain*, 130.
13. Dundes, *International Folkloristics*, vii.
14. See for example Oring, *Folk Groups*.
15. Hobsbawm, 'Introduction'.

16. Rubinstein and Rubinstein, 'Philosemitism', 5.
17. See also Rubinstein, Review of *The Chosen People* by Grahame Davies.
18. Charles Edwards, *Y Ffydd Ddi-ffuant* [*The Unfeigned Faith*] (1667); Theophilus Evans, *Drych Y Prif Oesoedd* [*Mirror of the First Ages*], (1716; 1740); Henry Rowlands, *Mona Antiqua Restaurata – an Archaeological Discourse on the Antiquities, Natural and Historical, of the Isle of Anglesey, the Antient Seat of the British Druids in Two ESSAYS* (1723).
19. Davies, *Religion and Society*, 18.
20. See for example O'Leary, *Immigration and Integration*. See also John Mills, *The British Jews: Their Religion, Ceremonies, Social Conditions etc...* (London: 1853; 1862), in which, by castigating 'Popery', he reassures his Calvinistic Methodist readers of his credentials, which might be queried given the highly sympathetic account he gives of Jewish life and religion.
21. See for example Neil Evans, 'Immigrants and Minorities', 5; Rubinstein, 'The Anti-Jewish Riots'.
22. See Donahaye, '"Gartref – bron"'.
23. See for example Crowe, *Yr Wlpan yn Israel*; Crowe and Solomonik, *Adfywiad yr Hebraeg*. Gensler's revisit of the linguistic 'CHS problem' ('A Typological Evaluation') suggests there is some linguistic basis for this association.
24. The latter-day racist aspect of the British Israel theory is detailed in Katz and Popkin, *Messianic Revolution*.
25. Katz and Popkin (*Messianic Revolution*, 274 n. 24) identify Philo-Israel as Edward Wheeler Bird, the founder of the Anglo-Israel Association, but the publications by Philo-Israel identify him as F. W. Phillips.
26. F. W. Phillips, *The Historical, Ethnic and Philological Arguments in Proof of British Identity with the Lost Ten Tribes of Israel...* (London: 1879).
27. Both pieces were published in Bangor (*The North Wales Chronicle*, 1880).
28. See *Gildas: The Ruin of Britain and Other Works*, ed. and trans. Michael Winterbottom (London: Phillimore & Co., 1978). For discussion of Gildas in this context, see Llywelyn, *Sacred Place*.
29. Edwards, *Y Ffydd Ddi-ffuant*. For discussion see Llywelyn, *Sacred Place*.
30. Morgan, *'Canys Bechan Yw'*, 7. The title of the lecture refers to the question in the Book of Amos 'by whom shall Jacob arise? For he is small', which Charles Edwards (*Y Ffydd Ddi-ffuant*, 1) transforms into the feminine 'pwy a gyfyd Gymru, canys bechan yw?' [by whom shall Wales arise, for she is small?]. The translations in the text are my own, except where indicated otherwise.
31. Morgan, *'Canys Bechan Yw'*, 8. The emphasis (indicated by word order), is in the original. Evidently, the Anglo-Israel theory, which had almost no following in Wales, expresses this latter form of identification as the chosen people.
32. Llywelyn, *Sacred Place*, 110.
33. Morgan, 'Y Beibl a Llenyddiaeth Gymraeg' [The Bible and Welsh Literature], 84, quoted in translation in Llywelyn, *Sacred Place*, 112.
34. Although John Harvey argues in *Image of the Invisible* that this tradition of identification exists in the visual culture, he presents no compelling visual evidence except for a turn-of-the-century map. Indeed, the art is notable for the *absence* of the evidence. See Lord, *The Visual Culture of Wales* series and Lord, *Words With Pictures*.
35. Llywelyn, *Sacred Place*, 89.
36. Daniel Evans, *Golwg ar Gyflwr yr Iuddewon* (Aberystwyth: 1826).

37. Crwys, 'Yr Iddew' [The Jew], *Y Geninen*, 36 (1 January 1918). Excerpted in translation in Grahame Davies, *The Chosen People*, 65–70.
38. The range of material anthologized in Davies' *The Chosen People* reveals a spectrum of stereotypical semitic discourse as defined by Cesarani, 'Reporting Antisemitism', 5.
39. Notions of Welsh tolerance have recently been challenged by the publication of work such as Charlotte Williams *et al*, *A Tolerant Nation?*.
40. Cochfarf, 'The Influence of Hebrew Literature upon Wales and Welshmen', *The South Wales Jewish Review* (February 1905), 28. Subsequent page numbers will be cited parenthetically in the text.
41. D. Wynne Evans, 'Studies in...', *Young Wales*, 7.75 (March 1901), 55–57; *Young Wales*, 7.78 (June 1901), 121–125; *Young Wales*, 7.80 (August 1901), 172–177; *Young Wales*, 8.88 (April 1902), 87–91, and *Young Wales*, 8.90 (June 1902), 121–127.
42. D. Wynne Evans, 'Studies in Iberic-Hebraic Eschatology', *Young Wales*, 7.78 (June 1901), 121.
43. From the *Manchester Guardian*, 13 April 1901, quoted in Evans, 'Studies' (June 1901), 121.
44. Evans, 'Studies' (June 1901), 122.
45. Evans, 'Studies' (June 1901), 123.
46. Evans, 'Studies' (June 1901), 123.
47. Evans, 'Studies' (June 1901), 123.
48. Evans, 'Studies' (June 1901), 123. This is published before the Limerick boycott in 1904 and the Irish-Jewish scuffles at Dowlais in Wales in 1903.
49. Evans, 'Studies in Britannic-Hebraic Eschatology', *Young Wales*, 8.88 (April 1902), 89.
50. Evans, 'Studies' (April 1902), 90.
51. Henriques, 'Lyons versus Thomas'. Esther Lyons' family saw their daughter's conversion as the product of abduction and coercion.
52. For discussion of Mills, see Donahaye, 'How Are The Mighty Fallen'. In 1852 he published the highly sympathetic and progressive work of Jewish ethnography entitled *Iddewon Prydain* (Llanidloes: 1852), an earlier version of his *The British Jews*.
53. Lily Tobias, *The Samaritan: An Anglo-Palestinian Novel* (London: Robert Hale, 1939), 182–185. For discussion of this novel and other work by Tobias see Donahaye, '"A Dislocation"'; and Donahaye, '"The Link of Common Aspirations"'.
54. See Donahaye, '"Gartref – bron"'.
55. See for example Judith Maro, *Hen Wlad Newydd: Gwersi i Gymru* [Old-New Land: Lessons for Wales] (Talybont: Y Lolfa, 1974).
56. Mars, 'The Ministry'. See also Mars, 'Immigration and Anglicisation'.
57. These include the Monds, the Nefts, Lily Tobias, and Mervyn Levy. Dannie and Leo Abse also have family roots in the Swansea Valley, through their mother, the sister of Lily Tobias.
58. Henriques, 'Conduct of a Synagogue', 108.
59. Fyne subsumes Wales under a generalisation of England in a public lecture. Mars, 'The Ministry', 124.
60. Lily Tobias, *The Nationalists and Other Goluth Stories* (London: C. W. Daniel, 1921) and Tobias, *My Mother's House* (London: George Allen & Unwin, 1931).
61. Tobias, 'Glasshouses', *The Nationalists*, 45. Subsequent page numbers will be cited parenthetically in the text.

62. The subtleties in this social portrait are reinforced by the names of her protagonists – Sheba's name evoking a Biblical legitimacy and that of Mrs Knacker evoking both the slaughterhouse and (for those familiar with Yiddish) a cheap worthlessness. I am grateful to Bryan Cheyette for his observation about the latter meaning.

63. Tobias, *My Mother's House*, 55. Subsequent page numbers will be cited parenthetically in the text.

64. Her sensitivity to both Hebrew and Yiddish is informed by the Welsh-speaking environment in which she grew up, in which it would appear that Yiddish did not suffer the negative status it suffered in England. See Donahaye, 'Hurrah for the Freedom'.

65. Oral History Archive, Museum of Welsh Life at Sain Ffagan, 6010–6011, Interview with Joseph Shepherd (recorded by David Jacobs), 8 November 1976.

66. Both stories were written before 1914, and published in Tobias' collection *The Nationalists*.

67. This is discussed in Donahaye, ' "A Dislocation" '.

68. See for example Peate, *Rhwng Dau Fyd* [*Between Two Worlds*].

69. Paul Goodman, 'Jewish and Welsh Nationalism', *Zionist Review*, 5.10 (February 1922), 161.

70. Leo Abse similarly attributes a Welsh welcome of the Jews as 'the People of the Book' to those whom he, like Tobias, terms the 'real' Welsh, and antisemitism to alien influence. But whereas Abse constructs these 'real Welsh' as Nonconformist socialists of the Welsh Labour party, and the political nationalism of Plaid Cymru as the alien incursion, Tobias constructs her anglicised antisemitic Welsh as cultural traitors and her 'real' Welsh as nationalists faithful to their culture and language. See Abse, 'A Tale of Collaboration'.

71. Interview with Joseph Shepherd.

72. This must be compared, however, with the experience of the Belgian Jewish painter Karel Lek, who emigrated to north Wales in 1940, where he was humiliated by a similar exclusion imposed by an abusive and violent teacher nicknamed Mochyn [Pig]. Interview with the artist, 16 November 2003.

73. Oral History Archive, Museum of Welsh Life at Sain Ffagan, 6017, Interview with Morris Silverglit (recorded by David Jacobs), 22 May 1978.

74. Tobias, *My Mother's House*, 35.

75. See for example, the reference to the Conservatives' 'cywaid cyfalafwyr Iuddewig' [gang of Jewish capitalists] in *Llais Llafur* on 9 December 1905. Quoted in Robert Smith, *'In the Direct'*, 8–9. The translation is Smith's.

76. Rubinstein, 'The Anti-Jewish Riots', 670.

10
Spying Out the Land:
The Zionist Expedition
to East Africa, 1905

Eitan Bar-Yosef

In a leader entitled 'Jews as Colonists', published in February 1896, the *Jewish Chronicle* proudly declared that 'Jews possess at least three of the most important qualifications which go to make successful Colonists – climactic adaptability, linguistic talents, and trading instincts.' This colonizing impetus, noted the *Chronicle*, could be traced all the way back to the ancient Israelites' mythical ties with both England and Africa:

> Both the clear language of Scripture and the vaguer hints of a less reliable popular tradition have associated the ancient Hebrews with England and with some of its present colonies. MR. RIDER HAGGARD startled a prosaic generation with an old-world romance of South Africa, in which gruesome horrors and fascinating dreams of wealth untold clustered round the name of 'King Solomon's Mines.' ... It is certain that in the gold districts of South and Eastern Africa, traces are still discoverable of very old workings which may have attracted Jewish operators long before the days of Syndicates and Mining Banks. Whether this be true or not, Judea, itself a 'Colony' formed by immigrant Jews, sent out shoots long before the Diaspora.[1]

By 1900, the smug satisfaction with which the *Chronicle* discussed the Jewish contribution to the imperial cause in Africa was replaced by a more anxious tone; after all, it was precisely the success of those Jewish syndicates and mining banks that allowed so many Britons to insist that the South-African War was in fact a Jewish War, serving the interests of a clique of rich Jews.[2] Indeed, by the summer of 1903, the *Jewish Chronicle* no longer seemed to cherish the prospect of a Jewish colonial adventure in Africa. Responding to the British Government's offer to establish in East Africa an autonomous Jewish province – the 'Uganda plan', as it came to be known – the weekly sympathized with those who were horrified to discover that the dream of returning to Palestine must be given up 'for the sake of a settlement among half savage tribes, remote from the haunts of civilisation. ...Is Zion to be exchanged for Kikuyu and the cedars of the Lebanon for the Taru jungle?' And while the *Chronicle* was forced to admit that British East Africa 'was not a swamp, as our hazy ideas... might at first suggest', it concluded by insisting that the 'future of Jewry does not lie in the tropics'.[3] One could only wonder what had happened to the Jew's climactic adaptability, linguistic talents, or trading instincts.

The playful energy which characterized the *Chronicle*'s response suggests that although the Uganda plan was swiftly aborted, Africa did play – and continues to play, even today – a significant role in Zionism's self-fashioning. It is a space in which personal and national fantasies can be acted out and made explicit: from a blunt analogy like the former Israeli Prime Minister Ehud Barak's recent claim that 'Israel is a villa in the jungle' to more disturbing instances, like the novels of Amos Oz, in which, Jacqueline Rose has noted, South Africa occasionally flickers 'as the unlived life of Israel: mundanely, almost contingently, as the place where the Israeli might have chosen to go; more troublingly, as the sign wherever it appears – hysteria, fanaticism, apocalypse – of the barely imaginable, barely acknowledgeable, political unconscious of the nation'.[4]

It is perhaps not surprising that an African daydream is already present in the first pages of the diary Theodor Herzl began writing in June 1895, as he became increasingly preoccupied with his vision of a Jewish state. 'For some time past I have been occupied with a work of infinite grandeur. At the moment I do not know whether I shall carry it through. It looks like a mighty dream,' he writes, and then goes on to offer a striking analogy: 'Stanley interested the world with his little travel book *How I Found Livingstone*. And when he made his way across the Dark Continent, the world was enthralled – the entire civilized world. Yet how petty are such exploits when compared to mine.' A few months later he imagined how, for the sake of 'the future legend', the first Jewish colonists would land in Palestine wearing 'a distinctive cap designed, *à la* Stanley'.[5]

Struggling to define his Zionist mission, then, Herzl's imagination turned, of all places, to Stanley's adventure. Was it because Stanley, like Herzl, was a journalist? Or was it Herzl's conviction that, just like the enigma of Livingstone's disappearance in the jungle, the Jewish 'problem' could only be solved by a bold, imaginative stroke? Perhaps; but the allusion to Africa also hints at the Zionist fantasy of transforming the dark effeminate Jews into vigorous white men. No wonder Herzl associated his project with a thrilling African escapade, a manly mission to explore that 'Dark Continent' in which white bodies always appear whiter.[6] The Uganda proposal offered a unique chance to realize this racial fantasy: defined against the local savages, the Jews' paleness would shine afar. Even the British settlers in East Africa, who fiercely resisted Chamberlain's vision of an African Zion, had to admit that the Jews were 'possibly the lowest class of white men'.[7] Barely, but still white.

Defending the Uganda Plan, Herzl explained that the Jewish colony would function as 'a miniature England in reverse'.[8] He meant that whereas the British metropolitan centre established colonies overseas, the Jewish colonies overseas would eventually establish a metropolitan centre in Palestine itself.[9] Nevertheless, just like witnesses to the Royal Commission on Alien Immigration, who were complaining that Jews were both the epitome of difference *and* so alarmingly alike, Herzl's phrase – 'a miniature England in reverse' – preserves the imperfect colonial mimicry that stands at the heart of the Zionist project.[10]

The following discussion explores the role of Africa in the Zionist imagination by looking closely at the work of the special commission sent out by the Zionist Congress to inspect the East African territory, its general physical condition, natural resources, commercial possibilities, and political situation. Drawing on the different narratives generated by and about the expedition – official reports, journalistic accounts, speeches, diaries, and letters – this chapter will ask: how do these narratives relate to other colonial texts, like Haggard's imperial romances or Stanley's travel accounts? What does the African fantasy tell us about Zionism's most coveted yearnings, chief among them, as we have seen, the yearning to be white? To what extent does this African fantasy represent what Jacqueline Rose has called 'the unlived life of Israel' – or, indeed, the life that Israel *has* lived? What, in other words, is at stake in imagining, or refusing to imagine, Zion in Africa? Africa in Zion?

To explore these questions, I will concentrate primarily on the work of Nahum Wilbusch, one of the first Zionist industrialists in Palestine and the only Jewish member in the delegation sent to East Africa. In 1963, 60 years after Herzl first introduced the Uganda plan, Wilbusch published *The Journey to Uganda*, a more verbose, even literary adaptation of his original report to the Zionist Congress. Juxtaposing the two narratives allows us to recognize the changes in Wilbusch's understanding of the commission's work. As we shall see, reproducing, on a miniature scale, the Biblical story of the spies who set out to explore Canaan, Wilbusch's accounts testify to the complicated ties between these two territories, East Africa and the Land of Israel. Indeed, if the East African adventure began with the attempt to project the sacred image of 'The Promised Land' onto East Africa, ultimately it was the symbolic aura of 'Africa' – the African fantasy with its significant colonialist, racist, and cultural implications – that shed light on the Zionist project in the Promised Land and helped define its nature and goals.

Africa as the Promised Land

The Sixth Zionist Congress, which convened in Basle in August 1903, opened with Herzl's presidential address. The situation seemed bleak: his negotiations with the Ottoman Sultan about the possibility of a Jewish colonization of Palestine were unsuccessful; attempts to obtain from Britain a land concession in the Sinai Peninsula were equally thwarted. But Herzl then astonished the crowd by declaring that the British government had proposed to establish a Jewish colony in East Africa. Stunned, then thrilled, the delegates soon became anxious and indignant: how could Zion be forsaken? In a last-minute attempt to pacify his opponents, Herzl proposed to send an expedition which would assess the designated African territory. A resolution, passed by a vote of 295 to 178, declared that only a congress specially convened for that purpose would be allowed to reach a final decision on the East Africa settlement, based on the commission's report.[11]

Delayed by Herzl's untimely death in July 1904 and by a range of financial difficulties, the expedition was eventually organized by the Anglo-Zionist activist and journalist Leopold Greenberg, in cooperation with Professor Otto Warburg, a Jewish botanist from Berlin University who advised the German colonial service.[12] Leaving Berlin by the Express train to Basle, where the contract was signed on Christmas Day 1904, the commissioners travelled to Trieste and embarked on board the appropriately-named *S.S. Africa*, arriving at Mombasa on 12 January 1905. After hiring porters and organizing the caravan, they took the newly-built Uganda railway to Nairobi, then to Nakuru; from there it was a four-day march to the Uasin Gishu (in some accounts, Guas Ngishu) plateau, the territory offered for the Jewish colony (then in the East Africa Protectorate, now part of Kenya). They reached the area on 29 January and spent about five weeks there; by 7 March the commission was once again in Mombasa, ready to sail back to Europe. Its report, presented in May 1905, was published as a Zionist Blue Book in both English and German. By that stage, even a glowingly positive report (and this was certainly not the case) would have done little to change the Zionist suspicion; following a vote in the Seventh Zionist Congress, the British proposal was declined.[13]

The expedition included three men. Appointed in command was an Englishman, Major A. St Hill Gibbons, a Boer War veteran and well-known African traveller who, following Livingstone's work in the Zambezi, had published two travel accounts. The second member was Professor Alfred Kaiser, a Swiss advisor to the Northwest Cameroons Company who had been active in scientific surveys in both Africa and Sinai. The third commissioner was a young Jewish Russian engineer, Nahum Wilbusch, who was added after Greenberg acknowledged that it was absurd to send a commission 'and not have one of our own people part of it'.[14]

Born in 1879 near Grodno in Russia, son of a wealthy mill-owner, Wilbusch belonged to an ardent Zionist family: his older brother, Itzhak, emigrated to Palestine as part of the *Bilu* society, the first Zionist group committed to the colonization of Palestine; his sister, Manya Shohat, became a legend among Zionist circles after helping in 1909 to establish *HaShomer*, a secret militia guarding Jewish settlements;[15] one brother-in-law was Dr Yosef Hazanovitz, who established the Jewish National Library in Jerusalem; another was Avshalom Feinberg, a central figure in the Nili spying movement which contributed to the British conquest of Palestine in 1917.[16] Other brothers were inventors and entrepreneurs; with their support, Wilbusch became one of the first Jewish industrialists in Palestine, associated mainly with *Shemen*, a leading oil factory which exists to this day. In 1903, after attending the Sixth Zionist Congress in Basle, Wilbusch journeyed to Palestine, where he embarked on an extensive survey to determine the land's economic potential. Determined to establish a factory for the extraction of oil press residue, he travelled to Berlin for more technical and financial advice. There he met Warburg, who convinced him to join the expedition. From Mombasa he returned, in March 1905, to Palestine; having acquired one hundred dunams near the Arab village of Hadita, not far from Lydda, he renamed the place *Hadid* (after Ezra 2:33) and set to work to establish his factory, which he called *Atid* (future).[17]

Whether Greenberg intended it or not, the commission resembled one of Haggard's imperial romances: a reserved, stiff-upper-lipped English soldier; a good-natured Swiss scientist, short and plump; and an inexperienced, yet overconfident, Jewish youth. Moreover, since Kaiser had converted to Islam a few years earlier (in the hope of facilitating his research in Arabia[18]), the three commissioners even represented the three monotheistic religions. But whereas Haggard's child-like protagonists usually work well together, the Zionist commission was fraught with personal tensions. These are certainly reflected in the official report, which was made up of four different narratives: the three individual accounts, as well as a supplemental report written by Gibbons, in which he rejected many of the assumptions made by his two colleagues, especially Wilbusch, whose study

> leaves on the mind an impression of supreme disappointment. A young man serving his first apprenticeship in Africa returns after a short six weeks' experience and dogmatises with supercilious self-confidence. I can best describe this report as the result of the crude conjectures of a very limited and unmethodised experience, and cannot recommend that it be taken into serious consideration.[19]

On one level, Gibbons' disappointment stems from Wilbusch's negative report.[20] Whereas Gibbons was more optimistic as to the colonial prospects of the territory, and Kaiser (true to his Swiss nationality) remained quite neutral, Wilbusch's account was unapologetically damming. All he could see was dry desolate land, with no prospects whatsoever. His report ended with the harsh verdict, 'Where nothing exists, nothing can be done' (90). To be sure, even Gibbons' report did not constitute an unqualified recommendation of the site, but he did conclude by advocating a pilot experimental scheme that would give a better idea of the territory's possibilities. It was one thing, moreover, to disagree about the land's general prospects; but the commissioners could not even agree about its appearance – even when they were travelling in one caravan. So, whereas Wilbusch describes the scenery in the first two days spent together in the tendered territory as 'dry and desert plains. ... No timber, no pasturage, no game' (59), Gibbons saw 'one of the finest pieces of country within my experience – rolling grass downs with a thick growth of "sour veldt" pasture ... anything but a desert' (19). In addition, there was a curious disparity between Gibbons' more cautious account in the official Report and the claim he made in a Reuters interview immediately after returning to Britain: 'There is no healthier country in Africa than the spot offered by the Government for the Zionists. It seems almost impossible to be ill there. It is an ideal region for white settlement.'[21]

To this we can add the observations made by others, like Sir Harry Johnston, the celebrated African explorer, who asserted that the territory 'is covered with rich alluvial soil; it is admirably well-watered. In many districts one would think one was in a wild part of England. The climate is as near perfection as that of any part of the world I have ever visited. It is like perpetual mild summer, with April showers.'[22] None of the commissioners went that far in their praises. Nevertheless, Mr Sulski, one of the few Jewish farmers who actually settled in the area, wrote an angry letter to the *Jewish Chronicle* in March 1905, in which he described the land's assets, 'splendid forests of timber, abundance of water, good soil, a very healthy climate to live in, and also cheap labour ... I have traveled through the Nandi, the nearest district to the Gwas Ngishu Plateau. I could not pass through a village without being offered honey and milk and some sheep.'[23]

Even without this explicit allusion to milk and honey, one can easily perceive that the question at the heart of the debate surrounding the Uganda proposal was not only ideological, or practical, but representational as well: to what extent was it possible to imagine East Africa as an alternative Promised Land? Davis Trietsch, a Dresden-born Zionist activist who advocated Jewish settlement in Cyprus and Sinai as part of a 'greater Palestine' scheme, exhibited in the Sixth Zionist Congress a map which demonstrated that although the East African territory was situated at a distance of almost 3,000 miles from Palestine, its western border, the Elgeyo valley, was a natural continuation of the Syrian-African rift, that is, the Jordan valley.[24] Rather than being the opposite of Palestine, as the *Jewish Chronicle* suggested in its juxtaposition of Zion and Kikuyu, Trietsch seemed to believe that East Africa (just like Cyprus or Sinai) could be imagined as an *extension* of the actual Promised Land.

Indeed, even on the official level, attempts were made to project Zion's symbolic power onto the African settlement. According to the draft of the Charter (prepared by the solicitor David Lloyd George MP), the prospective settlement was to be called 'New Palestine' or such other name as might from time to time be approved of.[25] Israel Zangwill, an ardent supporter of the plan, came up with some other options, typical of 'new world' naming: New Sinai, British Judea, British Palestine, or New Judea.[26] Zangwill, in particular, revelled in the symbolic parallels between Africa and Palestine. 'There are lions in East Africa, but what would Judah be without the lion of Judah? Our ancestors grappled with lions, and why should not we?' And elsewhere: 'There are wild beasts in East Africa, but in Jerusalem there are wilder creatures. There are religious fanatics, both Mohammedan and Christian, and wherever we go we shall find no absolutely safe proposition.'[27]

The Zionist commission reinforced this analogy because it repeated, in a condensed form – one could say, following Herzl, in a reversed miniature form – the Biblical story of the spies sent out by Moses to view the Holy Land:

> And Moses sent them to spy out the land of Canaan, and said unto them, Get you up this way southward, and go up into the mountain: And see the land, what it is, and the people that dwelleth therein, whether they be strong or weak, few or many; And what the land is that they dwell in, whether it be good or bad; and what cities they be that they dwell in, whether in tents, or in strong holds; And what the land is, whether it be fat or lean, whether there be wood therein, or not. (Numbers 13:17–20)

Like the spies, who come back and report that the land is both exceedingly good *and* exceedingly bad, a land of milk and honey but also a land that devours its inhabitants, the Zionist report – with its many inconsistencies and self-contradictions – also presents an image of the land that is unstable, fluid, ambiguous, almost dreamlike. Some of the images even recall the scriptural emphasis on nature beyond measure: Gibbons, for example, describes a 'great entanglement of rope-like vines, creepers, giant thistles and other underscrub', and 'huge trees, some of them many feet in diameter, [that] rise to a height of eighty feet and upwards' (6). Various pests, like caterpillars or locusts which can 'clear a whole harvest in a single day' (13), appear in a vast, almost legendary mass.

The analogy with the Biblical story was not lost on Wilbusch. In the German version of his report (but not in the English one), he referred to the Plateau, in English, as 'The Promised Land'.[28] Wilbusch, it seems, was being sarcastic: for him, an ardent East European Zionist, there was only one possible Zion. This explains his tone throughout the report: whereas the Biblical spies react with awe and confusion to the sights of the land, Wilbusch responds with a wry sense of patience, irritated at times, but never really disappointed at what he sees. This tone is reinforced in his 1963 account, *The Journey to Uganda* (published in Hebrew by the Zionist Library):[29] 'Our entrance into the Designated Land was not pleasing. The plains and the hills were covered with dry grass; there were no flocks or wild herds, only a few crooked trees and bushes.' And the following day: 'a plain covered with dry grass, little thickets of miserable-looking and crooked trees, fit only for heating...Where the soil is bad, only inferior and sour grass can grow, and bushes instead of trees.'[30]

I told you so, Wilbusch's tone appears to suggest: *This is no Promised Land.* And yet, Wilbusch seems unaware of the textual trap that the Biblical narrative is setting up for him. Paradoxically, the more he rejects the notion that this is a land of milk and honey, the more he reinforces the original Biblical story, casting himself in the role of the spy who 'spread among the Israelites a bad report about the land they had explored' (Numbers 13:32), and thus constructing Africa as the Promised Land after all. Wilbusch's reluctance to admit the analogy between the two territories merely reinforces the analogy.

Africa as the Dark Continent

All this points to Wilbusch's ability – or need, or refusal – to read Africa as if it were Canaan; and I will return to this analogy shortly. In the meanwhile, we should ask, what about Wilbusch's ability – or need, or refusal – to read Africa as if it were *Africa*?

This brings us back to the Gibbons' claim that Wilbusch was 'a novice to African travel who showed himself absolutely incapable of taking care of himself when left for a few days to his own resources!' (20). There is a correct way of experiencing Africa, Gibbons seems to be saying, but Wilbusch is not familiar with it. And what is this 'correct' way? Even though the report is essentially a scientific text, Gibbons writes with the gusto of a veteran explorer, emphasizing the linear progress and the different hazards facing the expedition, hazards that merely delight the skilled traveller. He mentions, for example, a certain valley which he names the 'Valley of the Lions'; for 'I never heard so many of these animals in any one place as I did during the two nights I was encamped here' (8). Gibbons constantly goes up to view the panoramic scenery and writes enthusiastically of the view, lying 'like a map 3,000 feet below' (7), in what Mary Louise Pratt has famously called the monarch-of-all-I-survey scene.[31] He also makes numerous observations about the East African natives in general, and more specifically about the expedition's porters, who are depicted as perverse but also helpless, continuously turning to the fearless white man for guidance and assistance.

In this respect, his account in the Zionist report is clearly a textual continuation of his previous travel accounts. *Exploration and Hunting in Central Africa, 1895–96* (1898) contains a wealth of material on African game and even includes, on its cover, a dramatic illustration of a lion about to leap;[32] *Africa from South to North through Marotseland* (1904), a work in two volumes dedicated to the memory of Cecil Rhodes, begins with a long description of the members of the expedition, all of them gallant, unselfish, practical Englishmen, whose work satisfied Gibbons in a way that Wilbusch's would never do. Frequent references are made to the natives' perverseness: it is enough to note that the index entry for 'boys' includes categories like 'suspicious', 'restless', 'desertion of, expected', 'greed of, requited', 'desert', 'less fastidious' and 'one boy left to die by comrades'.[33]

Gibbons' energetic representation of the African adventure as a colourful and exotic quest received a more heightened retelling in the stories that circulated in East Africa about the hardships allegedly experienced by the Zionist expedition. According to Elspeth Huxley, the biographer of Lord Delamere, early in 1904 a delegation of settlers met with Sir Charles Eliot, His Majesty's Commissioner for the East Africa Protectorate, to reiterate their protests. Eliot replied cryptically that he was sure the settlers would be able to show members of the commission 'many things that they would not otherwise see'. In Huxley's account, based on settlers' testimonies, the three commissioners were escorted to the Uasin Gishu by an officer sent out by the Foreign Office and a group of settlers. Since they were not used to walking, they soon 'learnt that blisters could be a painful affliction'. At night a huge herd of noisy elephants passed very close to their tents. The following day they supposedly encountered a column of Masai, dressed in full war kit. The painted warriors surrounded them, brandishing their spears and 'shouting hideous war-cries'. Following the settlers' intervention, the Masai eventually retreated, but not before they performed a terrible war-dance, with the commissioners gazing with distaste and disgust. Once again, there was little sleep in the camp than night: no natives attacked, but lions were growling outside the tents. 'The commission only stayed about three days on the plateau', concludes Huxley: 'They returned to England and reported the district to be, on the whole, unsuitable for the settlement of fugitives from Russia.'[34]

This account is gripping, but inaccurate. As Weisbord notes, the Zionist Report does not mention any escort by settlers; nor is there any evidence to suggest that the meeting with the Masai or the trouble with elephants and lions in fact happened; and certainly the commission spent more than three days in the area. Some of the commission's porters were attacked by a group of Nandi natives, but this occurred on the way back and did not resemble the alarming encounter described by Huxley.[35] Indeed, more than anything else, Huxley's narrative is a white settlers' fantasy, which says very little about the actual Zionist expedition, but reveals a great deal about the settlers' notions of what a Jewish commissioner would be like (cannot walk, timid) and what a real African journey should include (elephants, lions, bloodthirsty savages). As I have suggested, although Gibbons' tale does not mention the incident with the Masai, it does bear a certain resemblance, in tenor and scope, to Huxley's narrative: not only because he mentions the elephants and lions (described in his account as exciting rather than threatening), but also because his account shares the fantasy of the Jew as unfit for African excursions.

Wilbusch's report, in comparison, is highly laconic. He, too, occasionally encounters wild animals – though the only lion he saw was a solitary beast about 1,000 paces from camp (64) – but his narrative lacks the sense of excitement that permeates Gibbons' account. Indeed, nothing much seems to happen: 'owing to its uniformly waste and desert character there was unfortunately little to be found or to investigate', he writes (68). While Gibbons is progressing linearly, Wilbusch seems to be moving in circles or short, one-day excursions from the camp. This, to be sure, has to do with the nature of the specific assignments, but his dry style could also be read as an attempt to write against the conventions of African travel-writing – maybe because the Jew insists on approaching the Uganda proposal as a 'serious' matter that should not be confused with juvenile escapades; or maybe because his fervent dismissal of the plan does not allow Wilbusch to acknowledge a colonial desire to play the African adventure out.

What Wilbusch is essentially ridiculing is the notion of a 'white man's country', a notion which appears again and again in the British descriptions of the land. Gibbons claims that Wilbusch is a novice in African travel? Wilbusch will react by mocking the English obsession with hunting: 'If a country is uninhabited there are probably natural reasons which make it unsuitable for human habitation, for humanity is actuated by reasons entirely different to those of the English Colonial enthusiasts. It does not pine after beautiful climate and happy hunting grounds as the latter seek, but its aspirations are founded on the possibility of eking out an existence' (72). And in his later account, commenting on Harry Johnston's observation, he declares, 'only a hunting-loving Englishman can recommend a place like this' (84).

Whereas Wilbusch ridicules Gibbons' 'white' sensibilities, Gibbons, in turn, suggests that in Wilbusch's case, 'All things seem to have been looked on with the eyes of the son of a Russian landowner.' Exploring these small African rivers, 'The writer seems to have expected a Volga or a Danube' (20). There is an intriguing slippage here: on the one hand, the Jew cannot appreciate the African journey because he is not white enough – not courageous enough, not able physically; but, on the other hand, his distorted views of Africa emerge because he is *too* European, too genteel, almost – one could say – too white. This is where Gibbons' construction of the Jew as overly refined, the complete antithesis to the brave Anglo-Saxon members of Gibbons' former African expedition, seems to acquire a gendered perspective which carries us back to Herzl's anxieties about the effeminate Jewish body: the only thing whiter than white masculinity is white femininity.

The difficulty of defining the Jew's colour raises the inevitable question: if this is indeed a white man's country, is the Jew white enough for it? Zangwill, in particular, was obsessed with this racial aspect of the proposal. Writing to Johnston in 1905 in an attempt to revive the plan as part of his territorialist project (ITO), Zangwill remarked, 'The British Empire, indeed, is largely a black Empire, and over its thirteen million or so square miles, it has less than one white man per square mile. Under these circumstances I imagine that the accession of a potent white population would be a boon even for our great Empire.'[36] In other words, 'As it is impossible for England to get more than a tiny white population of Britons [into East Africa] I cannot see how or whence she could get a better white population than ourselves.'[37] This insistence on the whiteness of the Jew is particularly ironic, considering Zangwill's own physical appearance. Following their first meeting in Kilburn in November 1895, Herzl described Zangwill as 'the long-nosed Negro type, with woolly deep-black hair, parted in the center…. He maintains, however, the racial point of view – something I can't accept, for I merely have to look at him and at myself.'[38]

Africa and the Jewish settler

Considering the cultural and ideological disparity between Wilbusch and Gibbons that surfaces in their 1905 Report, it is telling that Wilbusch's 1963 narrative is very different from his original diary of 1905. Not only in its style – no longer committed to scientific precision, this book reads like a conventional travel account – but also in its outlook. Wilbusch's paternalistic attitude towards the black servants, his description of the panoramic views, and, in general, his more energetic narration – all these create a text that is now much closer to Gibbons' 1905 report, even including a dramatic encounter with a lion:

> Near the bush was a gray hind, slain, its back and neck covered with blood. 'The hind has just been hunted down by a lion. It's satiated', said Kaiser, 'and close by. After a rest, it will start its dinner'. Kaiser had hardly finished his sentence, when a lion leapt from a nearby bush, about ten yards from us, and ran off. The servant, horrified, fell down with the rifle. I was stunned at first. I did not know what to do, but a minute later the lion was far away. The event left quite an impression on me and remained engraved in my memory. (91–92)

Engraved as it may have been in Wilbusch's memory, this terrifying incident did not appear in his 1905 report, although another lion, 1,000 paces away, was mentioned.

The heightened sense of adventure which dominates the revised account is also reflected in Wilbusch's readiness to expose moments of crisis which were naturally obliterated from the official account. These calamities emerged particularly after 30 January 1905, when, following Gibbons' suggestion, each of the commissioners set out independently to explore a separate portion of the plateau; it was decided that Kaiser, heading north, would set out the main camp, where the others would convene a week later. In a chapter entitled 'I Walk Alone' – alone, that is, with seven porters, a cook, an armed Masai and his 'own servant boy' (68) – Wilbusch describes his many hardships. The food runs out, the porters despair, and still he is unable to locate the main camp:

> I was so tired, I fell to the ground, stretched out and motionless. Suddenly a large bird, like a vulture, circled the air above my head. It must have thought me a corpse, circling down towards me. I rose, jumped on my feet, and welcomed the vulture with fire from my pistol. (78)

A few pages earlier, Wilbusch narrates a disturbing encounter which seems to have anticipated these calamities:

> We were walking in the empty plain, with no trees or animals about, only dry straw below and a scorching sun above, when suddenly we saw in the distance a tree, the size of an acacia. Its fruit was round, large and magnificent, shining in the brightness. I walked towards it and was amazed. It was a leafless acacia, and on its branches were human skulls, dozens of skulls, which sparkled in the strong sunlight. The spectacle was horrible. I do not believe in superstitions or bad omens, but I must confess that from that moment onwards my luck in the journey changed for the worse. (73)

On the one hand, this remarkable scene once again calls to mind the analogy between Africa and the Promised Land: the fear of cannibalism, which the tree seems to evoke, echoes the Biblical image of the land as a devouring mother who swallows up her children.[39] On the other hand, the scene reads like something out of Haggard – maybe even Conrad – as if Wilbusch, 50 years after his original narrative, is finally prepared to disclose his moments of calamity and thus narrate a real, spine-tingling African adventure. In other words, while the 1905 report calls into question the link between the two territories (only, as we have seen, to reinforce it), the later book offers a belated acceptance of the conventions of African travel-writing, as if the fulfillment of the Zionist project in Palestine somehow allows Wilbusch to embrace, at last, the African adventure. Why? Maybe because it is no longer threatening to the Zionist cause to admit that Africa's white man's country was in fact exceedingly good (good, at least, for white men who are ready to face hair-raising adventures). Or maybe because it is by experiencing the Zionist adventure in Palestine that one can finally look back and acknowledge the nature of its discarded African counterpart.

The affinity between the two adventures is reflected, in the 1963 account, in the story of the commissioners' meeting with another Jewish settler in the area, Mr London, 'about thirty years old, tall and healthy, a pioneer in appearance and dress'. Having emigrated from Kovna to America, he had spent some years in South Africa. 'Growing weary of the devious trade and the hustle and bustle of the city, he escaped to this remote place, where he wishes to create new life on virgin soil...When he first came here he lived in a tent, and then built himself a hut...and made all the furniture, the bed and the chair and the carpet, from the skins of hinds' (54). Wilbusch was thrilled: 'The meeting with London, healthy in both body and spirit, setting out courageously to change the laws of creation in this wild place, just like Robinson Crusoe, left a huge impression on us' (55). And elsewhere he adds:

> I was enthralled by the presence of Jewish settlers in this place, in evergreen forests, among wild Negroes and predatory animals, Jews who live in primitive conditions in clay huts and intend to settle here and create new life and change the face of creation. I was envious of them, and I thought these pioneers should settle in Palestine and strengthen the *Bilu* ranks which have thinned out, and cheer up the younger generation in the colonies who had grown weak and had become materialistic and adopted territorial ideals. (56)

In this reversal of the Biblical text, the young Zionist pioneers in Palestine become the 'Desert Generation', too weak to take on the responsibility of nation-building. Indeed, when Wilbusch says he is 'envious' of these Jewish settlers in Africa he suggests not only that their commitment to the cause is greater, but also that their colonial project is somehow more demanding, more genuine, the 'real thing' (and note his phrase, 'change the face of creation'). It is only the pioneer from Africa, this modern-day Robinson Crusoe, who can show the way for those involved in the Zionist project in Palestine.

The story of Mr London, the pioneer, points to the ease with which the two territories, Africa and Palestine, could be interchanged; the ease with which colonial energy could be directed from one territory to the other. It is telling that Wilbusch also performs this movement, at least symbolically, as if the African adventure is a crucial stage, a dress rehearsal, for the Zionist project in Palestine. Wilbusch writes in 1963:

> My tent was made of green fabric, square and pretty, and it included folding furniture, a bed and table and chair...all of them made of green fabric. This pleased me a great deal, and when I returned to Palestine I took everything with me and set the tent in the grounds of Bet-Arif for the summer of 1905, when I built the first factory for extracting oil from olive residue, and where I enjoyed the tent and the furniture for many months. (52)

Settling in Arab land which he purchased with the backing of the Anglo-Palestine colonial bank, and having performed the crucial act of naming the place – after the Biblical Hadid, which is actually a few miles away[40] – Wilbusch's new project is a smooth continuation of his African adventure. Refusing to accept the idea that Africa could function as Zion, he approaches Zion as if it were Africa.

Africa as a land without a people

Africa, in other words, offers equipment with which one can now colonize Palestine: a perfect green tent, but also racial perceptions; capacity for colonial appropriation; and, most significantly, a better idea of the kind of land that is required. It is here that Wilbusch's account offers a final reversal of the scriptural story. In the Bible, the land is not good because it is occupied, inhabited: 'The Amalekites dwell in the land of the south: and the Hittites, and the Jebusites, and the Amorites, dwell in the mountains: and the Canaanites dwell by the sea, and by the coast of Jordan' (Numbers 13:29). Now, on the other hand, the Promised Land – that is, Africa – is not good because it is empty, uninhabited. This is Wilbusch in his 1905 report:

> The chief and most characteristic feature of the territory in question is the total absence of any population.... if the territory offered is really one of the beautiful countries of the world, as Sir H. Johnston for one has asserted, then following the law of the survival of the fittest, it ought to belong to any strongest tribe that might have adapted itself to the country. This latter tribe [the nomad tribes of the Eldoma Ravine], according to the Lord's promise to mankind, would have multiplied and populated the land. (71–72)

In Africa, the Zionist pioneer suddenly admits that the vision of a land without a people for a people without a land is pure fantasy:[41] it is precisely an inhabited land that Wilbusch wants for his colonial project. This, in turn, raises a problem:

> The Native Question appears to be one of the most difficult and most burning questions with all Colonial politicians. We, however, are absolutely free, there is no population whatever, and the native question is solved, and there now arises the labour question. To work without negro labour is out of the question, for first of all a European labourer, even if he *is* a Jew, could never perform the work done by negroes under the burning equatorial sun, and secondly, he can never compete with negroes. (81; italics in the original)

Even the Jew, white but not quite, cannot compete with the local natives. Wilbusch does not explain how this assumption might affect the Zionist project in Palestine, under the scorching Mediterranean sun; but his conclusion is clear: 'Natives must and shall be imported' (81). With no native problem, Wilbusch seems intent on importing one.[42]

Zangwill was quick to note and mock this disturbing ambiguity. In a witty address in July 1905, he made fun not only of the contradictions that fill Wilbusch's report, but also of the demographical question which lies at its heart. Zangwill begins by quoting Wilbusch's diary entry for 11 February 1905:

> Territory first four or five miles moderately good pasture grass, last nine miles rather bad, the grass being short and dry, not a sign of water or wood. Numerous antelopes everywhere. Camp on a river ending in a swamp, on the banks of which there are isolated bushes. At the last mile, abandoned stone Kraals; no people. (Laughter.)
>
> What can be more dismal! No wood, no water, no people, no anything. (Laughter.) But let us examine this entry. There is no water, yet Mr. Wilbusch camps on a river. (Laughter.) There is no wood, yet there are bushes with which he doubtless hit his camp fire. (Laughter.) There is no raw material of any kind, yet there are uncountable antelopes, and the hoofs and horns and skins of antelopes have always been widely used for manufacture, not to mention their flesh. There are no people—but this is exactly what we want. (Loud laughter and applause.) The stone kraals show that men could and did live there once. But Mr. Wilbusch writes gloomily again and again: —'We did not see a single man.' (Laughter.) I suppose if he travelled through Palestine, he would report joyously: 'Saw half a million Arabs.' (Laughter.) For such, alas! is the number of our rivals already in possession of Palestine. The East African territory being empty is just its attraction; it is free for development without opposition and under our own laws. That has always been the greatest attraction of the scheme. ...
>
> There are only two possibilities. Either you must have a developed land or an undeveloped land. Now, developed lands are inhabited—and you must fight the inhabitants and turn them out. But ... if you cannot fight man, you must fight nature.[43]

Despite Zangwill's enthusiasm, the land, of course, was not empty. Not only because Wilbusch, as Zangwill himself had noted, continuously encountered signs of human habitation – a deserted camp, a fire – but, more generally, because other peoples had greater claim to the land. Kaiser noted in his report that while the Wakuefi tribe, which lived on the outskirts of the area, is 'a very unimportant tribe', 'If Europeans settled in the Guas Ngishu Plateau they would very likely assert their claims to the land, and would ... regard the best agricultural land in the territory as their property' (32). But Zangwill, of all people, should have known, because he, too, sent an envoy to spy the Promised Land in Africa: Helena Auerbach, a South-African Jewish friend and a devout territorialist.[44] Where the men saw uninhabited land, she saw trouble. Having surveyed the desired territory in East Africa, she reported to Zangwill that the possibility of acquiring the land for the Jews seemed to her increasingly remote: the '"Black" question', she confessed candidly, was in fact much blacker than she had anticipated.[45]

Auerbach's formulation is hardly politically correct, but at least she was aware of the real situation in Kenya, as the Mau Mau movement would make clear less than 40 years later. This tells us something about Zangwill's own colonial vision. At the end of the day – the long Zionist day that might begin in another territory around the world but must end in Jerusalem – there was no real difference between his own vision and Wilbusch's. In the same lecture, quoted above, Zangwill shrewdly noted how ITO's territorial vision was already encapsulated, in a nutshell, in Wilbusch's journey: '"Left Berlin by Basle Express. Arrived Basle. Started for East Africa. Left East Africa. Arrived in Palestine." That was Wilbusch's journey,'[46] Zangwill concluded as the audience cheered, but this was to be Zangwill's journey as well, as he moved closer to Canaan, no longer an anxious spy, but a starry-eyed Joshua, ready at last to inherit the land.

Notes

1. *JC*, 21 February 1896, 13.
2. Holmes, *Anti-Semitism*, 66–70, 81–3.
3. *JC*, 28 August 1903, 15.
4. Rose, *States of Fantasy*, 45.
5. *The Diaries of Theodor Herzl*, ed. Raphael Patai, trans. Harry Zohn, 5 vols. (New York: Herzl Press, 1956), 1:3, 4, 91. See also Bar-Yosef, 'A Villa in the Jungle'.
6. Boyarin, *Unheroic Conduct*, 271–312.
7. Weisbord, *African Zion*, 84.
8. Quoted in Elon, *Herzl*, 375.
9. He did not state how, exactly, this would come about. When the Zionists were still hoping to colonize Sinai, Chamberlain jokingly asked Herzl to promise that he wasn't 'planning a Jameson Raid from El Arish into Palestine'. See *The Diaries of Theodor Herzl*, 4:1369.
10. On 'Jewish mimicry' see Geller, 'Of Mice and Mensa'. Also see Cohen, 'Who Was Who?'.
11. Weisbord, *African Zion*, 78–80.
12. On Warburg's contribution to both German colonialism and Zionism see Penslar, 'Zionism, Colonialism, and Technocracy'.
13. On the commission see Weisbord, *African Zion*, 198–223.
14. Central Zionist Archives (CZA), W78, Letter from Leopold Greenberg to David Wolffsohn, 21 November 1904.
15. See Raider and Raider-Roth, *The Plough Woman*, esp. 3–4, 274.
16. Mrs Wilbusch's first cousin, Dora Bloch (née Feinberg), was among the Israeli citizens kidnapped in June 1976 at Entebbe, Uganda, where she was murdered by Idi Amin's men.

17. On Wilbusch see Avitzur, *The Industry of Action*. Unless otherwise stated, all translations from Hebrew in this chapter are mine.

18. Nahum Wilbusch, *The Journey to Uganda* (Jerusalem: The Zionist Library – Zionist Congress, 1963) [Hebrew], 43–44.

19. Major A. St Hill Gibbons, Alfred Kaiser, and Nahum Wilbusch, *Report on the Work of the Commission Sent Out by the Zionist Organization to Examine the Territory Offered by H.M. Government to the Organization for the Purposes of a Jewish Settlement in British East Africa* (London: Werthimer, Lea & Co., 1905), 19. Subsequent page numbers will be cited parenthetically in the text. Unless otherwise stated, all references are to the English section of the Report.

20. Wilbusch (*The Journey*, 92) believed that Gibbons was paid a considerable sum to present a positive report. According to the contract prepared by Greenberg (CZA, A355/147), Gibbons was paid £750 sterling, in addition to about £300 to cover costs; Kaiser received 6,000 marks (about £300 sterling); Wilbusch, who was not paid, received thanks for 'presenting his report without any fee, and solely with the desire of serving the Zionist Organization, of which he is an earnest and loyal supporter'. See Gibbons et al, *Report*, 4.

21. *JC*, 7 April 1905, 17.

22. Quoted in *Jewish Missionary Intelligence*, February 1905, 24.

23. *JC*, 10 March 1905, 22.

24. Wilbusch, *The Journey*, 42.

25. Weisbord, *African Zion*, 74.

26. CZA, A36/91, Letter from Israel Zangwill to Alfred Lyttleton, 30 November 1905.

27. Israel Zangwill, *The East African Question: Zionism and England's Offer* (New York: The Maccabaean Publishing Company, [1904]), 49, 51.

28. Gibbons et al, *Report*, German version, 63, 64.

29. Wilbusch completed the manuscript in the early 1950s in the hope, it seems, of publishing the book in commemoration of the commission's fiftieth anniversary. Due to bureaucratic difficulties, the book was only issued in 1963. See correspondence in CZA, A355/10.

30. Wilbusch, *The Journey*, 66. Subsequent page numbers will be cited parenthetically in the text.

31. Pratt, *Imperial Eyes*, 201–208.

32. A. St Hill Gibbons, *Exploration and Hunting in Central Africa, 1895–96* (London: Methuen, 1898).

33. A. St Hill Gibbons, *Africa from South to North through Marotseland* , 2 vols. (London: John Lane & the Bodley Head, 1904), 2:274.

34. Huxley, *White Man's Country*, 1:124–125. Weisbord notes (*African Zion*, 211–212) that the story is repeated in Hill, *Permanent Way*, 275–279.

35. Weisbord, *African Zion*, 212–213.

36. CZA, A36/125, Letter from Israel Zangwill to Harry Johnston, 15 February 1906.

37. CZA, A36/125, Letter from Israel Zangwill to Harry Johnston, 21 February 1906.

38. *The Diaries of Theodor Herzl*, 1:276.

39. Pardes, *The Biography of Ancient Israel*, 112; Greenblatt, *Marvellous Possessions*, 136.

40. Avitzur, *Industry of Action*, 32.

41. On the phrase 'a people without people for a people without land', usually attributed to Zangwill, see Garfinkle, 'On the Origin'. See also Chapter 8 in this volume.

42. In due course, the Zionist establishment did 'import' Oriental Jewish 'natives' from North Africa and other Arab countries.

43. *JC*, 14 July 1905, 14.

44. For more details see Chapter 8 in this volume.

45. Weisbord, *African Zion*, 241–242. See also CZA, A36/23, Letter from Helena Auerbach to Israel Zangwill, 29 May 1906.

46. *JC*, 14 July 1905, 15.

11

Herzl, the Scramble, and a Meeting that Never Happened: Revisiting the Notion of an African Zion

Mark Levene

> ... Mr Wilcox said that one sound man of business did more good to the world than a dozen of your social reformers.[1]
>
> E. M. Forster, Howards End (1910)

> The world will be liberated by our freedom, enriched by our wealth, magnified by our greatness.[2]
>
> Theodor Herzl, The Jewish State (1896)

E. M. Forster's quintessential Edwardian novel, *Howards End*, may seem a slightly odd place to begin a consideration of the classic Herzlian text, *Der Judenstaat*. Yet to me its relevance is so palpable that the temptation cannot be resisted. Jews, of course – unless they are extraordinarily well camouflaged – do not figure in the Forster story. The narrative follows the fortunes of the temperamentally bohemian, certainly cosmopolitan (indeed half-German) but nevertheless very comfortable Schlegel sisters and their relationship with the much more wealthy, practical, horribly confident but decidedly roast-beef English Wilcoxes. There is in these pages a hardly hidden treatise on the conflict between a money-driven materialism and a free-thinking, literary idealism. Caught in the middle and destroyed by both is the figure of Leonard Bast, a near impoverished clerk.

However, there is another set of more subterranean themes in the story, part of whose purpose is to hint at the less than salubrious way that Henry Wilcox may have arrived at his wealth and status. The novel is situated primarily in a rapidly changing London and its environs, with the relentless, destabilizing energy of the metropolis notably conveyed by railway and new motor car motifs. But the capital that drives it all is metaphorically situated behind the closed doors of Henry's business, 'The Imperial and West Africa

Rubber Company'. We learn very little of how the business actually operates. There are the normal ledgers and counters and some maps of Africa on the office walls, and there is a son out in Nigeria who flits in and out of the story. Although she encounters the office, Margaret Schlegel, Henry's fiancée, never penetrates the inner sanctum and remains unable to fathom how Africa is the source of so much wealth, or indeed to bring into focus what is otherwise 'the formlessness and vagueness that one associated with Africa'.[3]

If Africa and Empire, at the *fin de siècle*, are distant and not quite explicable to Forster's cosmopolitan Margaret, how much further and irrelevant must they have seemed to Jews. What, after all, has black Africa to do with the fortunes of a European Jewry of the Edwardian period – or, indeed, a more contemporary Western or Western-centric Jewry? True, there are some colourful figures in the so-called Scramble for Africa who turn out to be Jewish, not least Emin Pasha, (a.k.a. Dr Eduard Schnitzner, formerly of Oppeln, Prussian Silesia), the famously beleaguered governor of Anglo-Egyptian Equatoria, who in 1888 was 'rescued' – though quite unrequested – by Henry Stanley from the supposed clutches of the *mahdiyya*.[4] Then, of course, there is Herzl himself, honoured in 1903 by the British Colonial Secretary Joseph Chamberlain with the offer of a slice of British East Africa: part of Kenya, suitably mislabelled as Uganda, and regarded as a 'virgin' territory for Jewish settlement. In mainstream Zionist annals, however, one senses here not so much a sense of oddity as sheer embarrassment that anybody might think that Zionists, let alone Herzl, might have seriously considered the creation of an autonomous Jewish entity anywhere other than in Palestine. Better that the apparent mistake is airbrushed out of the saga altogether, rather than that the whole rumpus (in which a substantial minority of the sixth Zionist Congress – effectively Herzl's own great creation – voted against him on the matter) is regurgitated again.[5] One consequence is the dearth of scholarly research on the 'Uganda plan'.[6]

British South Africa alone, perhaps, has a place within Jewish consciousness, but only because large-scale white settlement and immigration there, mostly preceding a major Jewish influx from the 1880s onwards, made the latter's presence part of a 'normative' process, a process that bears obvious comparisons with the development of the United States. Unlike the American case, however, where the majority of the Indian natives *were* exterminated or driven onto reservations, the black populations of southern Africa were able, at least in demographic terms, to remain the majority. Even so, the region's subsequent political and economic trajectory continued to be fixed in the European imagination within a mainstream narrative of Western 'progress'.[7]

Actually, there is an unfortunate blemish in this assumption, occasioned by the existence before 1902 of the independent Boer republics of Transvaal and Orange Free State, where – in the former case – large numbers of Jewish would-be entrepreneurs had ventured as a result of the discovery of Rand gold two decades earlier.[8] Their wholly disproportionate role in the origins of the Anglo-Boer War of 1899–1902 is undoubtedly an issue of some historical import. Viewed from the perspective of the wider modern Jewish experience, however, the role of Jewish entrepreneurs in South Africa is of primary interest for the way in which some of the leading protagonists like Beit, Barnato, Lippert, and Albu were cast in stereotypical guise as conspiring 'imperial-Jew' villains. This seemed to demonstrate the escape of Europe's antisemitic virus to Africa.[9]

Resisting the connections between black Africa and the Jewish experience thus involves utopian elements (Herzl's flights of fancy), as well as more obviously dystopian ones. The latter would certainly reach their nadir in the altogether nightmare vision of Madagascar as a dumping ground-cum-sealed reservation for European Jewry as dreamt up by various European politicians and bureaucrats, before finally coming to a head, then fizzling out, with the infamous Nazi scheme for the island.[10] If anything, however, these fleeting incidents only tend to confirm the ongoing Jewish disinterest in black Africa: the destinies of Jews and Africans are seen to be entirely unrelated; if they do at any point intersect, it is clearly some sort of solecism, as summed up in the title of the recent film, *Nowhere in Africa*, based on the quasi-biographical story of German-Jewish refugees in Kenya in the years of the Holocaust.[11]

Against such an unpromising background, this essay seeks to argue that Herzl's big idea as put forward in his 1896 tract – perhaps prospectus – for a Jewish state, may not mention Africa by name but is, nevertheless, profoundly influenced by the then ongoing European colonial impact on the continent. This argument, then, places Herzl's *Judenstaat* all the more firmly within the mainstream thrust of the *Zeitgeist*. And, like all agendas and actions which emanated from that *Zeitgeist,* it carried its own potentiality for a 'heart of darkness'. This is not to propose that the Zionist colonizing project could have been translated into an African setting. The one speculation in these pages – on what might have happened had the Viennese journalist met his English hero, Cecil Rhodes – is, thus, not to develop a counterfactual history.[12] Rather, I consider the unfulfilled meeting between these two only ephemerally, in order to bring into closer focus the guiding ideas and principles driving Herzl's neo-Africanist, neo-imperialist, agenda.

This proposition certainly carries with it a challenge. The colonialist features of Zionism have become quite a *cause célèbre* in recent years, as historians and others have attempted to chart the origins of an increasingly dark and relentless turn in the Israel-Palestine conflict. But their examination, necessarily, has been largely conducted within that Palestinocentric context.[13] The question of how the broader imperial mindset impinged on Herzl has been passingly alluded to in some analysis of early Zionism, most memorably in a few tantalizing paragraphs in J. L. Talmon's *Israel among the Nations*.[14] More recently, Steven Beller has referred to a 'colonial air' about the Herzlian project.[15] More recently still, Daniel Boyarin has brilliantly penetrated into the Viennese journalist's complex psyche to persuasively argue that, through a mimicry of 'white man' colonization, what Herzl was actually attempting was a European escape from 'the stigma of Jewish difference'.[16] However, a fuller consideration of the relationship between Herzl's vision and *Africa* itself has yet to be firmly charted. This chapter is intended as no more than a proposal for such further exploration. At the outset, however, one thing needs clarifying: the raw – not to say catastrophic – African context in the final years of the Scramble.

Africa: rivers of blood, rivers of gold[17]

The years from 1895 to 1904 – in other words, the years in which Herzl took his quest for an international solution to the Jewish question into the public domain – also happened to mark the climacteric in the partition of sub-Saharan Africa. On two accounts: firstly, these years marked the final surge of Great Power efforts to wrest an absolute control over the continent; secondly, and clearly in dialectical relationship to this trajectory, these years were also ones of heightened, even millenarian, African resistance and consequent suffering.

The ensuing catastrophe was played out most fully at Africa's very heart, in the Congo. Here the economic asset-stripping of the country's raw ivory and rubber wealth – at the behest of King Leopold of the Belgians' internationally recognized Free State (*sic*) regime – produced such an extraordinary cycle of hyper-exploitation, resistance, and retaliation, that the ultimate result was a population collapse from an estimated 20 million to possibly only half that number.[18] The atrocities meted out both by Leopold's Force Publique and by the franchised rubber companies themselves – as tribal Congolese increasingly refused the forced labour tapping of the wild rubber vines – began to seriously escalate in the mid-1890s.[19] By the turn of the century, Western public awareness of the scope, scale, and sheer viciousness of the regime was beginning to make itself felt. Joseph Conrad's famous indictment in the form of *Heart of Darkness* appeared in 1899.[20] By the following year what was now being dubbed 'the Congo Question' was, thanks in part to humanitarian campaigners such as E. D. Morel and the British government investigation compiled by Roger Casement, firmly on the *political* agenda.[21]

Of course, one might argue that suffering, immiseration, and disaster were nothing new to black Africans – cycles of famine, drought, and epidemic being common to their experience with or without the presence of Europeans. Nor was outside interference and ensuing violence only the latter's preserve: massive destabilisation and brutality at the hands of Arab slavers had been a legitimate matter of international concern in the 1870s and 1880s, and, paradoxically, had been fundamental to the formation of an International African Association headed by Leopold.

However, the widespread breakdown or even collapse of sub-Saharan societies in the 1890s was not only arguably in a class of its own, but profoundly exacerbated by a chain reaction of climatic, ecological, and epidemiological crises, either operating closely in tandem with or directly precipitated by Western imperialist intervention. The estimated half a million Congolese deaths from sleeping sickness in 1901 alone, for instance, would not have arisen without the mass dislocation and exhaustion of the population as a result of Leopold's depredations.[22] Meanwhile, the expansion of sleeping sickness in other corners of the continent was in large part due to a livestock wipe-out as a result of a Biblical epidemic of rinderpest, apparently caused by the arrival of infected Russian cattle, destined as meat ration for the Italian invasion of Eritrea.[23] As sleeping sickness is normally held in check by the cattle upon which the tsetse fly carriers of the disease feed, the interaction between these bovine disasters should be discernible. Worse, however, the livestock collapse happened to coincide with a major series of droughts and consequent famine associated with the periodic shift in tropical weather systems known as El Niño. With further epidemics ensuing, plus the arrival of jiggers (another devastating but transoceanic imported disease), the link between the high phase of the imperial land grab and the exposure of the tipping point in Africa's fragile ecology becomes all too evident.[24]

The impact of these disasters may also have had some causative relationship to the degree of violent, desperate, resistance to the invaders and hence to the consequent, exterminatory *modus operandi* of imperial military forces. 1896, for instance, was significant not only in that it produced a defeat for the invaders (in this case, the Italians) at the hands of an authentic and itself utterly ruthless African empire, the Amharic-led Ethiopians, at the battle of Adowa.[25] Closer to our interest, it was also the year of the last ditch uprisings of the Umkuvela and even more tenacious Chimurenga in the recently British-subjugated southern African territories henceforth known as Rhodesia. The extremely bloody extirpation of these revolts involved scorched earth tactics and, in the case of the Chimurenga, a general lack of distinction between combatants and non-combatants, whether men, women, or children.[26] These strategies became almost standard procedure in subsequent punitive expeditions by all the major imperial contenders on the continent. In addition to the well-known British destruction of the independent Islamic theocracy in the Sudan in 1898, there was a whole sequence of less publicized French and Portuguese campaigns involving extensive atrocities.[27] Even closer to the site of our putative African Zion, in the Kenya highlands, Sir Arthur Hardinge, the British East Africa Protectorate's first commissioner, was busy expostulating in the early 1900s that 'these people must learn submission by bullets – it's the only school, after that you can begin more modern and humane methods of education'.[28] Indeed, here, according to one historian, the British were 'employing violence on a locally unprecedented scale'.[29] To cap it all, in 1904, the year of Herzl's death, the most public and overtly genocidal of imperial retributions took place, in the form of the attempted liquidation of the 80,000-strong Herero people in German South West Africa.[30] Even then, in terms of fatalities, the Herero catastrophe was actually surpassed the following year when, in response to the pan-tribal Maji-Maji revolt in their East African Tanganyika colony, the German military contrived a man-made famine. The tactics are believed to have led to a quarter of a million deaths.[31]

Legitimately, one might ask, what has any of this to do with Herzl? Neither he, nor Zionism, can be held responsible in any shape or form for any of the Great Powers' crimes against African humanity. What, however, can be held against the Viennese journalist is an agenda which closely followed and sought to emulate the essential contours of European empire-building in Africa.

Let us remind ourselves of what exactly Herzl had in mind in his seminal tract. *The Jewish State* is premised on the notion that 'a portion of the globe',[32] adequate to the needs of the Jews, will be made available as a sovereign entity through the imprimatur of the Great Powers, that is to say through the provision of some form of international treaty or, as Herzl later described it, 'charter'. On the Jewish side, the initial organizing kernel that would prescribe the necessary political and scientific tasks for the foundation of the State would be 'the Society of Jews' – an elite body of notables drawn from industrialists, financiers, politicians, as well as the rabbinate.[33] Actual implementation of this blueprint would in turn be the responsibility of a 'Jewish Company'. This, on the one hand, would be 'the liquidating agent for the business interests of departing Jews',[34] and, on the other, the motor for the economic and political development of the new polity. Herzl emphasized here that 'it is the financial soundness of the enterprise which will chiefly be called into question'.[35] In other words, the Company would run the State.

Now, we could treat this simply as a case of fantasy wish-fulfilment, albeit not the first of its kind in modern times: Moses Hess, Leo Pinsker, and Nathan Birnbaum all expounded on the theme previously. What, however, was different about Herzl was his almost terrifying insistence on the practicability of his formula. In one regard this is certainly strange, as he was also notably vague about where his State was going to be situated. Argentina or Ottoman Palestine were both proffered as possibilities without much explication.[36] Perhaps it is just as well. The Argentine republic, over the course of the previous generation, had been involved in some extraordinarily bloody conflicts, both internal and inter-state, over the very issue of territorial control and border consolidation – as indeed had all of its immediate southern cone neighbours.[37] The idea, thus, that Argentina would somehow relinquish part of its territory in favour of another putative polity was entirely in the realm of cloud-cuckoo land. True, the Ottomans, faced with both internal and external efforts to prise territory away from their imperium, had had to concede Great Power adjudication and consequent losses following Balkan uprisings and the Russo-Turkish War of the late 1870s. But the result was that Abdul Hamid's regime, at the time of Herzl, was busily fighting tooth and nail to deny Armenians, Greeks, or anybody else, any more slices of Ottomania.[38]

A lot of energy has been expended determining how Herzl came by his particular answer to European antisemitism and the plight of the Jews. Yet, if neither Argentina, nor Palestine, could actually be imagined as the end-goal of the desire for sovereign sanctuary, from where did Herzl – that is, in his practical as against utopian mode – draw his otherwise bizarre notion that a portion of the globe could be made available for it?

Role-model I: King Leopold of the Belgians

Because Herzl never stated the answer, ours, necessarily, must be speculative. Indeed, to what extent was Africa, and the imperialist partition of it, really on his brain in 1895 and 1896? There are only occasional relevant references in his diaries. Interestingly, though, at the very outset he proffers an almost snide comparison between the way Stanley was able to exploit his finding of the lost explorer Livingstone through his published travelogue of 'the Dark Continent', and thereby to enthral 'the entire civilized world' – and his own yet to be accomplished dreams, which, Herzl implies, will make Stanley's seem 'petty'.[39] The empirical problem, nevertheless, remains that there is no direct evidence linking Africa with 'the Jewish State'. The German colonial exhibition in Berlin, with its specially created camp of black human exotica, may have been all the rage when set up in 1896.[40] But there is no evidence that Herzl visited or reported upon it. Perhaps it is just as well that there is no direct reference either to the Congo Free State – the one most obvious source for Herzl's proposition – as this really might have saddled his dream with long-term obloquy.[41]

In early 1904, a few months before Herzl's death, the British journalist, E. D. Morel – who had spent the previous decade attempting to expose the horror of Leopold's regime to the world – formed the Congo Reform Association.[42] The movement has interesting parallels with Herzl's World Zionist Organization. Like the latter, the CRA – though effectively run by a single, dynamic, figure – sought to create a grass-roots and thereby incipiently democratic base in order to foster and bring to resolution a single issue of humanitarian concern. Its intended reach, too, was international, by which was primarily meant an educated, thinking, and concerned Western public. What the WZO was to antisemitism, the CRA was to racism. Yet if

208 'The Jew' in Late-Victorian and Edwardian Culture

Herzl's proposed route to Jewish salvation was through the creation of something along the lines of Congo Free State, then something was very amiss.

As Jean Stengers, one leading expert on the central African polity, posits: 'The Congo is the archetype of the political entity brought into being on African soil by the will of a European.'[43] The complex story of how this arose is not for detailed examination here. Nor does it necessarily fit a standard prescript. Derek Penslar notes that 'settlement colonialism was usually sanctioned by a sovereign state, often via the licensing of one of more private companies to bear the risk of the colonizing venture'.[44] The notion of a colonial entity being underpinned by venture capitalism is of particular significance to this discussion. But it is not how Leopold's entirely more personal domain actually emerged. Far from the Belgian state conjuring up the Congo into a colonial existence on its own behalf, it was the Great Powers at an international conference in Berlin in 1884–85, who conferred the territory on the king. The whole process indeed sounds peculiarly Herzlian, and, as Talmon astutely notes, 'must have been known and remembered by Herzl'.[45] A 'neutral' sovereignty over the Congo basin, guaranteed by the Great Powers, was placed into the hands of the International African Association, no more, no less than Leopold's own front organization. The administration's purposes, moreover, were on paper entirely guided by humanitarian principles: to provide for the wellbeing of the region's natives and for the prevention of slave-trading, alongside clauses on internationally free trade and movement which were assumed to be the motor force to the basin's development.[46]

Not only did this in effect mean that Leopold was being given leave to run the territory as his very own fief (only later, in 1908 – just before his death – did the issue of sovereignty come within the Belgian state's purview), but with a financial return from its resource potential as its main driving force. Nor was this some small affair, the powers having granted the territory to the Belgian king in an absence of mind. The Congo Free State really was 'a portion of the globe' and successfully extended by Leopold himself – by crafty realpolitik against the contending interests of the other 'scramblers' – to embrace some 900,000 square miles of central Africa, or, put another way, a territory 80 times the size of Belgium.[47]

Certainly, there was no primary issue of white settlement in this mostly tropical region. And one might argue, too, equally contra Herzl's vision, that what Leopold developed hardly represents an object lesson in sound or even 'kosher' finances. It was his very vaunting ambition to make huge profits at minimum outlay that led him to ditch the free trade regime – always rather a case of sophistry anyway – in favour of an effective rubber and ivory state monopoly (through a variety of closely controlled and interrelated company concessions). At the same time, he increasingly turned to forced labour, thereby unravelling the regime's almost unrivalled descent into exterminatory violence.[48]

As a result, the Congo certainly lagged far behind equivalent British colonies in pure developmental terms, heavily distorted as it was by the get-rich-quick imperatives galvanized by the rubber boom.[49] But as long as it lasted, nobody could deny it was a roaring success.[50] Leopold had proved that a great deal of money could be made from a colonial 'virgin' (*sic*) territory,[51] thus overturning the initial warnings from his Jewish financier friends, Gerson Bleichroder and Charles de Rothschild, that his agenda was not a good banking proposition.[52] Such a precedent could not but be significant to Herzl, the whole thrust of whose proposal was predicated on enticing the great Jewish financiers to his cause. Without their cash, the specifically Herzlian 'Jewish state' truly remained a mirage. But if only he could convince them that there was a financial return, then perhaps he, too, could play the Leopold.

This personal element cannot be ignored. Recent studies of Herzl, notably Jacques Kornberg's iconoclastic but otherwise thoroughly revealing portrait, confirm just how much in Herzl's case the personal was political, and the degree to which the man craved celebrity status and a world stage upon which to play it out.[53] At first sight, Leopold may seem an odd comparison, not least that, already having a crown on his head, he had ostensibly all the status he could possibly desire. The likeness, however, is rather telling. As an individual, Leopold was by turns obnoxious and charming, restless and visionary, a megalomaniac, a man who believed himself to have been repeatedly cheated of his due recognition – in short, a classic case of a self-proclaimed hero of our time wrestling with a serious inferiority complex, with a strong dose of misogyny thrown in for good measure.[54] How to resolve it all? Do something extraordinary.

Of course, we are in murky waters here. How much were Leopold's very public commitments to save black Africans from Arab slavers just a convenient prop to hide a project of naked profiteering? Or is this to miss the actual point that Leopold's greed was not financial *per se* but rather a means of building monuments, literally, to his own glory?[55] The same may well also be true of Herzl. All his efforts to open the coffers of bankers were clearly not for their own sake; the resolutely literary and elitist Herzl hated such a reminder of Jewish *parvenu* wealth and all the philistinism associated with it.[56] Nevertheless, he could hardly do without this filthy lucre in order to arrive at *his* eternal monument: 'the Jewish state'. And, additionally, his own *chutzpah* perhaps suggested that if a rather minor European prince could claim to deliver on behalf of the negroes in the heart of Africa, why could not Herzl accomplish the same, not only for the persecuted Jews but also, thereby, 'for many other downtrodden and oppressed beings' too?[57] The big difference, of course, is that Herzl never achieved the financial backing for his project, even though he continued to work unceasingly, tirelessly, single-mindedly for it. Indeed, the effort probably ensured his early death at the age of 44.

None of this proves Herzl's inspiration for the Jewish state by way of Leopold. In 1903, at the time he was negotiating with the British Colonial Office for Uganda, we know that Herzl – through the Jewish Colonization Association (ICA) office in Brussels – did attempt to sound out the king as to the possibility of a Jewish settlement in the Congo.[58] Nothing, however, seems to have come of it. But if all this does is to confirm that the case for our first role model remains tendentious, there is, in fact, a much more obviously verifiable one.

Role model II: Cecil Rhodes

Strangely, though we know Cecil Rhodes was someone whom our Viennese journalist tenaciously pursued, few of the Herzl biographers or commentators on early Zionism have given the issue more than passing attention. Strangely, because the two who have – Desmond Stewart and Geoffrey Wheatcroft[59] – have also noted some striking similarities and affinities between these two men. We could make it a threesome: many of the qualities and weaknesses we have already noted with regard to Leopold were also pertinent to Rhodes. And some more besides: Rhodes has been described as overweening, manipulative, petulant, thoroughly misogynist, as well as inspiring. A 'neurotic…bundle of energy',[60] he was nothing if not obsessive. He was also certainly something of a loner – again, shades of the Herzlian great man above it all – which only, of course, intensifies the sense of enigma surrounding him.[61] Perhaps the crucial clue is his awareness of his own mortality, hence his Herculean efforts to accomplish his dreams before it was too late. Rhodes had a hole in the heart, knew it, and had many scares on this account before finally predeceasing Herzl by two years, utterly exhausted at the age of 48.

Again, we can be unnecessarily reductive here. Herzl may have been very curious to meet a man as driven as himself. But there were obvious practical reasons why he might have urgently wanted to make the connection. Throughout almost the entire period of Herzl's Zionist career, Rhodes remained the star in the imperial firmament. Randlord *par excellence*, mover and shaper of an emerging British South Africa, key (and subsequently judicially censured) player in the abortive 1896 attempt to overthrow the Boers in favour of the gold mining and hence British commercial interest in the Rand, Rhodes was above all the mastermind behind the British advance north to the Zambesi. And that was only the beginning. Beyond the Cape, Rhodes envisaged a railway running all the way to Cairo, confirming the entire African continent in effect for the British; and, beyond that, with a little help from a United States reincorporated within the Empire – and some German support too – the authentic creation of a British super-power.[62]

In the context of the Scramble, what may strike one today as plain daft, narcissistic, delusions of grandeur – were they were not both pernicious and dangerous – were often treated by metropolitan publics as grounds for adulation. Stanley or Carl Peters (the leading advocate for a German empire in Africa) were merely two among the many other celebrated monomaniacs who had already trampled over as much of the continent as they could manage, spreading mayhem and misery in the process.[63] What made Rhodes a cut above the rest was that he had made the forward advance through his own marriage of initiative and financial acumen. The result, in 1888, had been the creation of the British South Africa Company, a new crown chartered enterprise. Closely following historic precedents (such as the British East India Company), the BSAC sought – with royal approval – to develop lands beyond the Limpopo 'by any concession, agreement, grants, or treaty sale of any rights, interests, authorities, jurisdictions, and powers of any kind, whatever, including powers necessary for the purposes of government and the preservation of public order'.[64]

No northern limit was put on the BSAC's territorial remit by Her Majesty's Government. The result was the conquest of a great swathe of southern-central Africa, henceforth known as Rhodesia, the agenda being that it would be both the basis for major gold or other mining development *and* white settlement. No wonder Herzl thought that he could not do without Rhodes for his own Zionist project. 'It is an effort which carries the colonial effort in it,' he wrote to the latter, adding: 'what I want from you is not that you should contribute a few guineas to our fund or that you should lend them to me but that you should place the stamp of your authority on the Zionist scheme'.[65]

Nor was the notion of Rhodes' assistance implausible. For all the obvious racism in his grander design, the one thing Rhodes could not be accused of was antisemitism. De Beers Consolidated Mines, the original basis of his wealth from Kimberley diamonds, had actually been arrived at by striking a series of deals with mostly Jewish competitors, some, like Beit, with whom he remained very closely associated. Moreover, famously, Rhodes had said of his BSAC territory, 'my country is all right if the Jews come'.[66]

Gaining Rhodes' support also carried with it a series of potentially critical openings. One was to the leading banking house of the era. One may remember that the draft of *The Jewish State* began as an 'Address to the Rothschilds'.[67] Of course, there had already been before that an unsuccessful approach to Baron de Hirsch, the German-Jewish financier and railway magnate who had set up shop in Brussels where he had been duly ennobled by Leopold, had gone on to found ICA (aimed at micro-managing Jewish settlement in Argentina), and, it also so happened, maintained a Piccadilly address, mostly so that he could go to the races with his friend the Prince of Wales, later Edward VII.[68]

To what extent Herzl had done his homework on these connections we do not know. But they were certainly the sort of thing at the forefront of his game-plan. After the initial false start with de Hirsch, not to say with leading members of both the Austrian and French branches of the Rothschild clan, there still remained the British wing, above all, their head, Lord Nathaniel ('Natty') Rothschild. Through this potential opening lay 'the biggest concentration of financial capital in the world' of the time.[69] Moreover, Lord Rothschild, as well as being a leading shareholder in De Beers, was also heavily involved in BSAC, effectively 'its unpaid financial adviser'.[70] Gaining the ear of Rothschild potentially opened up access to the entire Rhodes operation – just as, conversely, gaining the attention of Rhodes paved the way to Rothschild. And so, too, to some of the most senior British politicians of the day, including former Prime Minister, Lord Rosebery, none other than Rothschild's son-in-law.[71]

Perhaps this largely explains why Herzl was in earnest about coming to make his case in Britain even before *The Jewish State* had been properly written. The early meetings, in late 1895 and 1896, with Anglo-Jewish literati and journalists like himself, (not to say the first public outing of his thesis in the *Jewish Chronicle*), were surely intended to clear the path to more lofty and esteemed men of influence, both Jewish and Gentile. Indeed, by the middle of 1896 he had, according to Stuart Cohen, 'already begun to envision a possible community of interest between World Jewry and Great Britain'.[72]

Certainly, everything we know suggests that Herzl was unashamedly enthusiastic about Britain, but most especially about its industry, commerce, and imperial world power. As a result he was insistent that the epicentre of the Zionist operation should be in London, close to the Rothschild millions, and that both Society and Company should be registered there.[73] In 1900 he spelt out this positive appraisal in a Vienna speech in which he described Zionism as a colonial policy in the English style.[74] Even when proposing to the Kaiser a location for the colony in Palestine, Herzl would still insist that it should be along the lines of the 'British chartered company for South Africa'.[75] Nor was there anything in the British or indeed Rhodesian record from which he wished to demur. On the contrary, in the key conflict of the period, it was the Boer state which was 'religiously fanatic and xenophobic',[76] while the British themselves represented 'the civilising mission'.[77]

Herzl's big obstacle in all this, however, was access to, and hence the support of, those two critical players, Rothschild and Rhodes. When the Jewish Colonial Trust was set up in 1898, it was intended to have a share capital of £2,000,000 – double that with which the BSAC had begun – but, interestingly, equivalent to the original capital of de Hirsch's ICA fund. Herzl had done well to raise £250,000 by the time of the third Congress in 1899.[78] But without the big guns, the notion of Great Britain 'as the Archimedian point where the lever is applied',[79] as Herzl proudly asserted to the opening English Zionist conference in Clerkenwell in 1898, was beginning to look decidedly thin.

Ironically, despite his primary efforts to make the acquaintance of Rhodes, it was Rothschild whom Herzl finally got to meet, inadvertently, at the 1902 hearings of the Royal Commission on Alien Immigration. Rothschild, however, was not playing ball.[80] By then Rhodes was more than two months dead. But he had previously been in brief contact with Herzl, sending him a message in which he tersely proposed that Herzl put 'money in his purse'.[81]

The profit and loss of empire

Here, then, was the nub of Herzl's conundrum. His intuition told him that the idea of 'the Jewish state' – that is, in the context of empire – was quite conceivable. The problem was that as its unknown advocate, without serious knowledge of things practical, financial, or organizational, let alone of the workings of the stock exchange,[82] his personal ability to translate idea into practice lacked credibility. Yet equally we might speculate that a successful Rhodes-Herzl meeting which in turn had cajoled serious Rothschild cash into play might have genuinely enabled Herzl to resume his original colonial march, even regardless of what the Palestinocentric Zionists might have had to say.

After all, looked at logically, the imperial way at the *fin de siècle* was the only show in town. Herzl may have been a German-speaking continental living in an empire without extra-European territories, but he could hardly have been unaware of the increasing direction of Austrian alongside German, Belgian, and French capital flows by this juncture. Before 1895, issues of undercapitalization had placed a major question mark over the direction, and indeed practicability, of future Great Power colonization in Africa. The needs of European emigration – hardly an exclusively Jewish problem – were certainly part of this issue. But without sufficient capital to support organized mass 'white' settlement, such settlement looked increasingly uncertain, or utopian. It is surely no coincidence, then, that Herzl begins *The Jewish State* with a hardly veiled lampooning of the popular 1890 Austrian novel, *Freiland*, by Theodor Hertzka – a man with a strangely parallel existence to that of himself – which imagines just such a communitarian paradise in Central Africa.[83]

Herzl, by contrast, sought to hitch up capital behind his emigrationist project, not only because this was the single way to provide it with firm foundations, but because European state planners themselves, by the mid-1890s, were firmly of a view that any colonial enterprise was also required to make a profit.[84] The only discrepancy, from a Herzlian standpoint, lay in the fact that a serious and rapid return was much more likely to be made by a mineral prospecting concession, usually allied to a railway opening up a great tract of country, rather than that same tract being handed over to large numbers of European smallholders. Herzl thus was not wrong to seek out a major venture capitalist and railway financier like de Hirsch to back his idea, or to assume that an African portion of the globe could be made available and developed through significant capital investment. The turn of the century concession of a mere 57 million acre job lot in Portuguese Angola – to a syndicate formed by Rhodes, Wernher, Beit and co. and the German-Jewish entrepreneur Viscount Adolphe Wertheimer, in return for the initial capitalization on a railway-line into the territory – rather underscores this potentiality.[85] Indeed, the fact that the capital funding for this, and other concessions of this period, crossed national lines was equally propitious in that it suggested that imperial rivalry might be giving ground to a new international cooperation. Wilcox in *Howards End* might justify the British being in Africa to keep the Germans out,[86] but the evidence from a few years earlier, when Herzl was writing, suggests not only that the development of a territory like German South-West Africa was dependent on British and South African shareholders, but that one likely conclusion to these corporate interrelationships was a German-British political marriage, which Chamberlain, indeed, at the turn of the century, was within a whisker of bringing to fruition.[87]

With the financial shakers and movers to help him get there, Herzl's plugging into this particular political-economic nexus, in the Jewish 'national' interest, was more than plausible. Without them he was back at square one. No wonder, then, that the primary source material contains so much of Herzl's exasperation with them. 'There is always plenty of Jewish money for Chinese loans, for Negro railroad enterprises in Africa, for the most extravagantly adventurous ideas', yet apparently not for 'the most immediate and tormenting needs of the Jews themselves', he expostulated to de Hirsch in June 1895.[88] Yet Herzl, in this early period, would have handed more than a virtual Jewish state to the Rothschilds *et al.* on a plate, if only they had accommodated themselves to his vision.[89] The degree to which they were those who especially mattered in this reckoning is palpably evident in the tract itself. The prescribed role of the actual emigrants, plebeians and 'intellectual mediocrities' – in other words, the Jewish equivalents of the Leonard Basts of the world – was simply to provide the hard labouring graft;[90] to be, in other words, no more than Jewish 'Hottentots'.[91] The profits and glory would go to the financial entrepreneurs. Even after they had so obviously shown him the door, and Herzl had had to devise his alternative plan, based on popular mobilization, he could never quite let go of the original intention, privately admitting, in 1901, that he had run himself 'ragged' to obtain 'a hearing from the wretched crew'.[92]

So when Chamberlain made his belated offer of the Uasin Gishu plateau almost eight years after the Viennese journalist had put forward his original blueprint, is it all that surprising that Herzl was prepared to put on hold all the considerably unsatisfactory dealings with Abdul Hamid, the Kaiser, or Chamberlain himself, over Palestine or its environs? Not to say be prepared to incur the wrath of the Tschlenows, Ussishkins and Weizmanns who would have – and did – stand in his way? On the contrary, East Africa represented a return to the original pristine idea: a colony which would be developed as a 'joint stock Moses', driven by the quest for diamonds, gold, or whatever minerals could be found, and so firmly hitching the Rothschilds and the other banking houses to its venture capital opportunities. It would, of course, in the Herzlian mind's eye, also be a beacon of European civilization through and through. But at its aristocratic helm would be 'enlightened administrators and talented entrepreneurs' whose governance would be 'based on shrewd capital investments'.[93]

The fact, however, that none of this came to pass does not mean that there is not a reckoning, or legacies, to be considered. The linkage to Britain and its Empire, through the Balfour Declaration and the subsequent British mandate in Palestine, is an obvious one – one which would have been even more firmly entrenched had the trajectory remained African or globally imperial, as Israel Zangwill and the most devoted followers of the Herzlian brand of Zionism envisaged.[94] When Zangwill created the Jewish Territorial Organization (ITO), in 1905, it was with the firm intention of following through Herzl's remit and negotiating with the British to create a large but autonomous Jewish colony in East Africa, or, if that failed, in some other territory such as Cyrenaica, Angola, or Mozambique which Herzl had already considered.[95] The preference of both men, of course, was that the colony should be under the aegis of the premier imperial power on the world stage. But even without Britain, the chartered company concept remained key. Under a *dirigiste* mainstream Zionism, something of this concept also held. As Penslar notes, 'The World Zionist Organization tried to assume the role of a colonizing state. It overtly emulated European practices by establishing a colonial bank, funding agricultural research and development and supporting capitalist joint-stock companies that were hoped to yield, eventually, a profit to their shareholders.'[96]

All this might be read as a tribute to Herzl's acumen and foresight. But to do so, while ignoring the darker and more problematic aspects of his agenda, would be to grossly mislead. Let us remember that at the time Herzl was negotiating for the Uasin Gishu plateau, its inhabitants, primarily the Nandi people, were having their lands expropriated, their livelihoods denied, their lives expunged by the British. This was not some small or passing matter. Even that hard-headed imperialist and soon-to-be Colonial Secretary, Winston Churchill, would describe the Kenya Highlands situation as 'butchery', as it built up to a crescendo.[97]

Of course, again, it was not Herzl or the Zionists doing the slaughtering. But they were effectively colluding in it. How? Primarily by doing to the black inhabitants of Africa what all good imperialists do: making them invisible. Herzl, in his great tract, never for once posed the possibility that there might be indigenous human beings in the territory to be apportioned to the Jews. The implication rather is that it would be truly virginal,[98] a *tabula rasa*, or, to use the correct legal sophistry, a *territorium nullius*.[99] The definition, of course, does not quite mean that the territory would be entirely uninhabited. Rather the assumed aboriginals, in failing to be productive with the land, would have no proprietorial connection or obligation to it and might as well just be passing through. Just recently, for instance, in 1889, the British had used this legal ruling to declare the whole continent of Australia to have been an unoccupied 'waste' prior to its eighteenth-century 'discovery' by themselves.[100]

Armed with this sophistry, there were really only two options available for the colonizer with regard to the colonized. The first was to convince oneself that the indigenes one came across, in accordance with the standard nineteenth-century racial hierarchical ordering of the species, were so low down its scale that they really might as well be non-existent. Here, for instance, is a public statement from Chaim Weizmann at the fourteenth Zionist Congress, in Vienna, in 1925: 'Palestine is not Rhodesia. There are 600,000 Arabs living there who in the world's eyes have as much right to live in Palestine as the Jews have to a national home.'[101]

Weizmann's sin here is not with regard to the Palestinians but rather the native peoples of Rhodesia. Significantly, their prior fate, in the 1890s, provides us with our second option: that of military subjugation. And Herzl fully knew and approved of it: the notion of a Jewish army conquering the would-be Jewish territory was firmly presented by him in his meeting and early correspondence with de Hirsch.[102]

There is, then, a final, terrible irony. At the very time when Jews throughout the world were reeling from what had been done to their kith and kin in Kishinev, when the whole thrust of the East European Jewish experience – overwhelmed, that is, by the impact of tsarist persecution, prejudice, and violence – was driving vast multitudes of *yidn* into the ranks of left-wing, anti-imperial movements, a Viennese Jewish journalist was busy promoting a quintessential imperial project. And in terms which, borrowing directly from Rhodes, or Leopold, would have required the most raw and unadulterated methods for dealing with the 'natives', or making them bend to one's will. If that had actually transpired, the lives of Jews and black Africans would have undoubtedly met in the most grotesque and violent of fashions. Yet, to arrive at that point, it required that Jewish questions and Congo questions travel in entirely separate compartments, not only as if there were no congruence between them but no basis – even for the vast majority of East European Zionists – for that precious item we call empathy.

Of course, if one accepted the prevalent social Darwinian view of the world at the *fin de siècle* there would be no grounds for such empathy anyway; only for finding a way to become and remain strong within that world. In these terms Herzl's genius as the critical interlocutor within a protean Zionist movement was to put substance on the idea that the route out of the dilemmas of powerlessness and vulnerability to violence was through the assertion of a collective, *Jewish*, destiny. In East Africa, British settler opponents to Zionism strove to wreck this insolent effrontery by proclaiming that, as the preserve of superior white men, there was no place for such 'undesirable aliens'.[103] Yet the whole thrust of Herzl's agenda had been to counter this claim in advance through what amounted to a scheme of political transcendence. The Jew belonged to the imperialist camp: he, too, was unequivocally a superior white man.[104]

That meant taking it as a given that the black – or Arab – man's land was either, or both, vacant or legitimate for exploitation; which meant, in turn, treating the other as 'other', as any white man would. The quest for Zion in Africa may have become an Edwardian colonial cul-de-sac before it had even begun, but it surely carries a warning from history, the resonances of which are to be found not just in the tortuous history of Israel-Palestine, but in the ongoing struggles of the third world against the rapacity and violence of corporate capitalism. It is time to finish as we began with the writer of *Howards End*: 'But the imperialist is not what he thinks or seems. He is a destroyer. He prepares the way for cosmopolitanism, and though his ambitions may be fulfilled, the earth that he inherits will be grey.'[105]

Notes

1. E. M. Forster, *Howards End* (London: Edward Arnold, 1910), 21–22. Film version: *Howards End*, dir. James Ivory, Merchant Ivory productions (1992).
2. Theodor Herzl, *The Jewish State* (1896), in Arthur Hertzberg (ed.), *The Zionist Idea: A Historical Analysis and Reader* (New York: Atheneum, 1973), 226.
3. Forster, *Howards End*, 193.
4. Iain R. Smith, *The Emin Pasha Relief Expedition*, 12.
5. See, for instance, Friedman, 'Herzl', 39–40. Friedman circumvents the problem by vehemently repudiating the notion that Uganda was anything other than a 'ploy' with which to arrive at the prize of Palestine.
6. The one, not particularly penetrating monograph is Weisbord, *African Zion*. Weisbord, too, follows the standard line that Herzl never once deviated from the ultimate goal of Palestine (252).
7. Crosby, *Ecological Imperialism*.
8. Wheatcroft, *The Randlords*.
9. Wheatcroft, *The Randlords*, 196–206; Holmes, *Anti-Semitism*, 66–70.
10. For the most up-to-date overview of the Nazi Madagascar Plan see Browning, *The Origins of the Final Solution*, 82–89.
11. *Nowhere in Africa* (*Nirgendwo in Afrika*), dir. Caroline Link, Zeitgeist Films (2002).
12. At its conference outing, an eminent colleague objected to the thrust of this piece on grounds of its counterfactuality, a ruse operated by some historians to criticize a 'what might have happened' argument. However, in his defence of counterfactuality, Niall Ferguson ('Virtual History', 86) posits that 'we should consider as plausible or probable only those alternatives which we can show on the basis of contemporary evidence that contemporaries actually considered'. The brief counterfactual argument herein follows exactly this procedure.
13. See notably Penslar, 'Zionism, Colonialism, and Postcolonialism'; Bareli, 'Forgetting Europe'.
14. Talmon, *Israel among the Nations*, 120–121.

15. Beller, *Herzl*, 135.
16. Boyarin, *Unheroic Conduct*, 303.
17. The November 1904 turn-of-phrase used by the General von Trotha, the German commanding officer describing his promised annihilation of revolting Herero and other tribes in German South-West Africa; subsequently commandeered by Mark Cocker as the title of his comparative study, *Rivers of Blood, Rivers of Gold: Europe's Conflict with Tribal Peoples* (1998).
18. Hochschild, *King Leopold's Ghost*, 233.
19. Marchal, *L'Etat Libre du Congo*, esp. vol. I, Part 3, 'La Regne de la Terreur'.
20. Joseph Conrad, *Heart of Darkness* (serialized 1899; published as a book 1902; Harmondsworth: Penguin, 1973).
21. Hochschild, *King Leopold's Ghost*, 194–208.
22. Hochschild, *King Leopold's Ghost*, 231.
23. Lonsdale, 'The Conquest State', 101.
24. Lonsdale, 'The Conquest State', 101; Pankhurst and Johnson, 'The Great Drought', 48–52. See also Davis, *Late Victorian Holocausts*, for a searing overview and analysis.
25. Vandervort, *Wars of Imperial Conquest*, 156–164. For the implications and consequences of the African victory see Rainero, 'The Battle of Adowa'.
26. Major studies include Ranger, *Revolt in Southern Rhodesia*; Kepple-Jones, *Rhodes and Rhodesia*. For the impact on Africans themselves see Vambe, *An Ill-Fated People*, chs. 6–11.
27. See Lindqvist, *'Exterminate all the Brutes'*, for a highly polemical but thought-provoking account of some of these events, most notably the 1898 French campaign to conquer the Western Sudan (163–171). See also Vandervort, *Wars of Imperial Conquest*, 146–156, for the 1895–96 Portuguese campaign in Gazaland, Mozambique.
28. Lonsdale, 'The Conquest State', 95.
29. Lonsdale, 'The Conquest State', 87.
30. Drechsler, *Let Us Die Fighting*, 212–214, for the casualty breakdown. See also Zimmerer, *Deutsche Herrschaft über Afrikaner*.
31. Iliffe, *Tanganyika under German Rule*, ch. 6, 'The Maji-Maji Rebellion, 1905–7'.
32. Herzl, *The Jewish State*, 219.
33. Berkowitz, *Zionist Culture*, 10–11.
34. Herzl, *The Jewish State*, 220–221.
35. Herzl, *The Jewish State*, 215.
36. Herzl, *The Jewish State*, 222.
37. Geyer and Bright, 'Global Violence', esp. 639–645.
38. See Bloxham, *The Great Game of Genocide*, ch. 1.
39. *The Diaries of Theodor Herzl*, trans. and ed. Marvin Lowenthal (London: Victor Gollancz, 1958), 4.
40. Zimmerman, *Anthropology and Antihumanism*, ch. 1.
41. The work of a Belgian historical commission, at the instigation of the state-funded Royal Museum for Central Africa, is currently investigating the claim – implicit, or explicit, in Hochschild and Marchal's work – that Leopold's rule in the Congo led to genocide. See Andrew Osborn, 'Belgium Exhumes Its Colonial Demons', *The Guardian*, 13 July 2002.
42. See Hochschild, *King Leopold's Ghost,* esp. 209–217, for the CRA's origins and initial development.
43. Stengers, 'The Congo Free State', 261.
44. Penslar, 'Zionism, Colonialism, and Postcolonialism', 85.

45. Talmon, *Israel among the Nations*, 120.
46. Lucas, *The Partition and Colonization of Africa*, 82–83. See, by comparison, Herzl's emphasis on a neutral state, but also one linked to and guaranteed by Europe (*The Jewish State*, 222).
47. Gann and Duigan, *The Rulers of Belgian Africa*, 41.
48. Gann and Duigan, *The Rulers of Belgian Africa*, 125–126.
49. Alas, in other regions of the globe, where red (wild) rubber could be tapped by enforced labour, there were similar results. See Hochschild, *King Leopold's Ghost*, 280–81, on the neighbouring French Congo; Hardenburg, *The Putumayo*, on a smaller scale but nevertheless devastating human catastrophe in Peru.
50. Gann and Duigan, *The Rulers of Belgian Africa*, 141–142.
51. Gann and Duigan, *The Rulers of Belgian Africa*; Hochschild, *King Leopold's Ghost*, 168.
52. Pakenham, *The Scramble for Africa*, 397–398.
53. Kornberg, *Theodor Herzl*.
54. See Hochschild, *King Leopold's Ghost*, for elements of this portraiture, as well as Kornberg, *Theodor Herzl*.
55. Hochschild, *King Leopold's Ghost*, 168–169, 293–294.
56. Kornberg, *Theodor Herzl*, 71–76.
57. Herzl, *The Jewish State*, 208.
58. Weisbord, *African Zion*, 64.
59. Stewart, *Theodor Herzl*, 188–191; Wheatcroft, *The Controversy of Zion*, 73.
60. See Wheatcroft, *The Randlords*, 7.
61. Wheatcroft, *The Randlords*, 138–143, for a not entirely flattering portrait.
62. Wheatcroft, *The Randlords*, 141–142.
63. On Stanley see Hochschild, *King Leopold's Ghost*, 67–69; On Peters see Gay, *The Cultivation of Hatred*, 85–86.
64. Quoted in Bodley, *Victims of Progress*, 65.
65. Quoted in Wheatcroft, *The Randlords*, 264. See also Stewart (*Theodor Herzl*, 190): 'Herzl's stencil for obtaining a territory and then claiming it for settlement was cut after the Rhodesia model.'
66. Quoted in Kepple-Jones, *Rhodes and Rhodesia*, 355–356.
67. Hertzberg, *The Zionist Idea*, 202.
68. Stewart, *Theodor Herzl*, 174.
69. Ferguson, *Empire*, 223.
70. Ferguson, *Empire*, 224. Interestingly, the official catalogue at the New Court Rothschild archives confirms that the De Beers interest remained an important part of the banking house portfolio, but is much more coy about its role in BSAC, arguing that the Rothschilds declined to give backing for the 'northward march of imperialism'. While Ferguson is the most forthright in contesting this notion, other commentators (Pakenham, *The Scramble for Africa*, 341; Kepple-Jones, *Rhodes and Rhodesia*, 304–305) agree that New Court was prepared to back the BSAC, notwithstanding Rothschild's own concern that there should not be any financial irregularities in the form of De Beers money finding its way into BSAC accounts.
71. On the Rosebery-Rothschild connection see Bermant, *The Cousinhood*, 153–164.
72. Stuart A. Cohen, *English Zionists*, 26; also 52–53.
73. Beller, 'Herzl's Anglophilia', 55.
74. Beller, 'Herzl's Anglophilia', 56.
75. Stewart, *Theodor Herzl*, 188.

76. Kornberg, *Theodor Herzl*, 168.
77. Beller, 'Herzl's Anglophilia', 56.
78. Stewart, *Theodor Herzl*, 174, 189, 285.
79. Cohen, *English Zionists*, 80.
80. *The Diaries of Theodor Herzl*, 360–371, for Herzl's illuminating commentary on these meetings.
81. Wheatcroft, *The Randlords*, 81.
82. Berkowitz, 'Herzl'.
83. Herzl, *The Jewish State*, 205; Weisbord , *African Zion*, 23–24. Hertzka, like Herzl, was also Hungarian born, and a leading journalist on the *Neue Frei Presse*.
84. Voeltz, *German Colonialism*, 55–56.
85. Voeltz, *German Colonialism*, 66–67.
86. Forster, *Howards End*, 127.
87. Voeltz, *German Colonialism*, 17, 55; Judd, *Radical Joe*, 204.
88. *The Diaries of Theodor Herzl*, 24.
89. *The Diaries of Theodor Herzl*, 47: 'To the (Rothschild) Family Council (June 1895): Your older men will stand by with advice as to finances, banking, railroads and politics, and will enter our diplomatic service. Yours sons...will play their part in the army, diplomatic corps, etc....and govern provinces'.
90. Herzl, *The Jewish State*, 221.
91. Boyarin, *Unheroic Conduct*, 303, for an acute commentary on this theme.
92. Letter to Dr Mandelstamm, 1901, quoted in Bein, *Theodore Herzl*, 369.
93. Edward Timms, 'Ambassador Herzl', 23.
94. On Zangwill as the authentic mouthpiece of Herzlian Zionism after the leader's death see Eisenzweig, 'Aux Origines'.
95. Weisbord, *African Zion*, 63, 274. On ITO see Cohen, *English Zionists*, 85–105.
96. Penslar, 'Zionism, Colonialism, and Postcolonialism', 86.
97. Mungeam, *British Rule in Kenya*, 171–180, for the concern of Churchill and others within the Colonial service on what was taking place in the highlands.
98. Eisenzweig, 'Aux Origines', 12.
99. Bodley, *Victims of Progress*, 63–64.
100. Reece, *Aborigines and Colonists*, 168–169.
101. Quoted in Lavsky, *Before Catastrophe*, 168.
102. *The Diaries of Theodor Herzl*, 17, 23. See also Stewart, *Theodor Herzl,* 182, 187. Ironically, Herzl was in good company. In 1888, Lord Rothschild financed the £1.9 million merger which created the Nordenfelt Gun and Ammunition Company, providing for industrial production of the Maxim automatic machine gun – the same gun which ensured Rhodes' conquest of Matabeleland five years later. See Ferguson, *Empire*, 221.
103. Bodley, *Victims of Progress*, 95, quoting High Commissioner, Sir Charles Eliot. Also Weisbord, *African Zion*, 82–84.
104. Boyarin, *Unheroic Conduct*, esp. 293–308.
105. Forster, *Howards End*, 323.

Bibliography

Abrams, Ruth. 'Jewish Women in the International Woman Suffrage Alliance, 1899–1926'. PhD diss., Brandeis University, 1997.

Abse, Leo. 'A Tale of Collaboration not Conflict with the "People of the Book"'. Review of *The Jews of South Wales*, ed. Ursula Henriques. *New Welsh Review*, 6.2 (1993): 16–21.

Ackroyd, Peter. *London: The Biography*. London: Chatto & Windus, 2001.

Alderman, Geoffrey. 'The Anti-Jewish Riots of August 1911 in South Wales'. *Welsh History Review*, 6.2 (1972): 190–200.

———. 'The Jew as Scapegoat? The Settlement and Reception of Jews in South Wales before 1914'. *Jewish Historical Society of England: Transactions*, 26 (1974–78): 62–70.

———. *Modern British Jewry*. Oxford: Oxford University Press, 1992.

Alleyne, Brian. 'An Idea of Community and Its Discontents: Towards a More Reflexive Sense of Belonging in Multicultural Britain'. *Ethnic and Racial Studies*, 25.4 (2002): 607–627.

Arata, Stephen D. 'The Occidental Tourist: Dracula and the Anxiety of Reverse Colonization'. *Victorian Studies*, 33.4 (1990): 62–45.

Avineri, Shlomo. 'Theodor Herzl's Diaries as a Bildungsroman'. *Jewish Social Studies*, 5.3 (1999): 1–46.

Avitzur, Shmuel. *The Industry of Action: A Collection on the History of Israeli Industry, in Commemoration of Nahum Wilbusch, Pioneer of the New Hebrew Industry in Israel*. Tel-Aviv: Milo, 1974. [Hebrew].

Back, Les. *New Ethnicities and Urban Culture: Racisms and Multiculture in Young Lives*. London: Routledge, 1996.

Bakhtin, Mikhail. *Rabelais and His World*. Trans. Helene Iswolsky. Cambridge, MA: MIT Press, 1968.

Bar-Avi, Israel. *Dr Moses Gaster*. Jerusalem: Cénacle Littéraire 'Menorah', 1973.

Bareli, Avi. 'Forgetting Europe: Perspectives on the Debate about Zionism and Colonialism'. In Penslar and Shapira (eds), *Israeli Historical Revisionism*. 99–120.

Bar-Yosef, Eitan. 'A Villa in the Jungle: Herzl, Zionist Culture, and the Great African Adventure'. In Mark Gelber and Vivian Liske (eds), *Theodor Herzl between Europe and Zion*. Tübingen: Niemeyer, 2007. 85–102.

———. *The Holy Land in English Culture, 1799–1917: Palestine and the Question of Orientalism*. Oxford: Clarendon, 2005.

———. 'I'm Just a Pen: Travel, Performance, and Orientalism in David Hare's *Via Dolorosa* and *Acting Up*'. *Theatre Journal*, 59.2 (2007): 259–277.

Bauman, Zygmunt. 'Allosemitism: Premodern, Modern, Postmodern'. In Cheyette and Marcus (eds), *Modernity, Culture and 'the Jew'*. 143–156.

———. 'Exit Visas and Entry Tickets: Paradoxes of Jewish Assimilation'. *Telos*, 77 (1988): 45–77.

———. *Modernity and Ambivalence*. Cambridge: Polity, 1991.

———. *Modernity and the Holocaust*. Cambridge: Polity, 1989.

Bayme, Steven. 'Jewish Leadership and Anti-Semitism in Britain, 1898–1918'. PhD diss., Columbia University, 1977.

Beer, Gillian. *George Eliot*. Brighton: Harvester Press, 1986.

Bein, Alex. *Theodore Herzl: A Biography*. Philadelphia: Jewish Publication Society of America, 1940.

Beller, Steven. *Herzl*. London: Halban, 1991.

———. 'Herzl's Anglophilia'. In Robertson and Timms (eds), *Theodor Herzl*. 54–61.

Benjamin, Walter. *The Arcades Project*. Trans. Howard Eiland and Kevin McLaughlin. Cambridge: Belknap Press, 1999.

Bentwich, Norman. 'Anglo-Jewish Travellers to Palestine in the Nineteenth Century'. *Miscellanies, Part IV: The Jewish Historical Society of England* (1942): 9–19.

Bentwich, Norman and John M. Shaftesbury. 'Forerunners of Zionism in the Victorian Era'. In John M. Shaftesbury (ed.), *Remember the Days: Essays on Anglo-Jewish History Presented to Cecil Roth*. London: Jewish Historical Society of England, 1966. 207–239.

Berkowitz, Michael. 'Herzl and the Stock Exchange'. In Gideon Shimoni and Robert P. Wistrich (eds), *Theodor Herzl, Visionary of the Jewish State*. Jerusalem: Magnes, 1999. 99–111.

———. *Zionist Culture and West European Jewry before the First World War*. Cambridge: Cambridge University Press, 1993.

Bermant, Chaim. *The Cousinhood: The Anglo-Jewish Gentry*. London: Eyre and Spottiswoode, 1971.

Bhabha, Homi K. *The Location of Culture*. London: Routledge, 1994.

Black, Eugene C. 'A Typological Study of English Zionists'. *Jewish Social Studies*, 9.3 (2003): 20–55.

———. *The Social Politics of Anglo-Jewry, 1880–1920*. Oxford: Blackwell, 1988.

Bloch, Howard. *Earlham Grove Shul: One Hundred Years of West Ham Synagogue and Community*. London: West Ham and Upton Park Synagogue, 1997.

Bloxham, Donald. *The Great Game of Genocide: Imperialism, Nationalism, and the Destruction of the Ottoman Armenians*. Oxford: Oxford University Press, 2005.

Bodley, John H. *Victims of Progress*. 2nd ed. Palo Alto, CA: Mayfield, 1982.

Boyarin, Daniel. *Unheroic Conduct: The Rise of Heterosexuality and the Invention of the Jewish Man*. Berkeley: University of California Press, 1997.

Brantlinger, Patrick. *Rule of Darkness: British Literature and Imperialism, 1830–1914*. Ithaca, NY: Cornell University Press, 1988.

Browning, Christopher R. *The Origins of the Final Solution: The Evolution of Nazi Jewish Policy, September 1939–March 1942*. London: Heinemann, 2004.

Cesarani, David. *The Jewish Chronicle and Anglo-Jewry, 1841–1991*. Cambridge: Cambridge University Press, 1994.

———. (ed.). *The Making of Modern Anglo-Jewry*. Oxford: Blackwell, 1990.

———. 'Reporting Antisemitism: The *Jewish Chronicle* 1879–1979'. In Siân James, Tony Kushner, and Sarah Pierce (eds), *Cultures of Ambivalence: Studies in Jewish – Non-Jewish Relations*. London: Vallentine and Mitchell, 1998. 247–282.

Cheyette, Bryan. *Constructions of 'the Jew' in English Literature and Society: Racial Representations, 1875–1845*. Cambridge: Cambridge University Press, 1993.

———. 'From Apology to Revolt: Benjamin Farjeon, Amy Levy and the Post-Emancipation Anglo-Jewish Novel, 1880–1900'. *Transactions of the Jewish Historical Society of England*, 29 (1982–86): 253–265.

———. ' "Ineffable and usable": Towards a Diasporic British-Jewish Writing'. *Textual Practice*, 10.2 (1996): 295–313.

———. 'Introduction: Unanswered Questions'. In Bryan Cheyette (ed.), *Between Race and Culture: Representations of 'the Jew' in English and American Literature*. Stanford: Stanford University Press, 1996. 1–15.

———. 'The Other Self: Anglo-Jewish Fiction and the Representation of Jews in England, 1875–1903'. In David Cesarani (ed.), *The Making of Modern Anglo-Jewry.* 97–111.

Cheyette, Bryan and Laura Marcus (eds). *Modernity, Culture and 'the Jew'.* Cambridge: Polity, 1998.

Cocker, Mark. *Rivers of Blood, Rivers of Gold: Europe's Conflict with Tribal Peoples.* London: Jonathan Cape, 1998.

Cohen, Deborah. 'Who Was Who? Race and Jews in Turn-of-the-Century Britain'. *Journal of British Studies*, 41.4 (2002): 460–483.

Cohen, Stuart A. *English Zionists and British Jews: The Communal Politics of Anglo-Jewry, 1895–1920.* Princeton: Princeton University Press, 1982.

Coleman, Terry. *Passage to America: A History of Emigrants from Great Britain and Ireland to America in the Mid-Nineteenth Century.* London: Hutchinson, 1972.

Colley, Linda. *Britons: Forging the Nation, 1707–1837.* New Haven: Yale University Press, 1992.

Collini, Stefan. *Public Moralists: Political Thought and Intellectual Life in Britain, 1850–1930.* Oxford: Oxford University Press, 1991.

Collins, Kenneth E. 'Scottish Transmigration and Settlement: Records of the Glasgow Experience'. In Newman and Massil (eds), *Patterns of Migration.* 49–58.

———. *Be Well! Jewish Immigrant Health and Welfare in Glasgow, 1860–1914.* East Linton: Tuckwell Press, 2001.

———. *Second City Jewry: Jews of Glasgow in the Age of Expansion, 1790–1919.* Glasgow: Scottish Jewish Archives, 1990.

Comaroff, John and Jean Comaroff. *Of Revelation and Revolution: Christianity, Colonialism, and Consciousness in South Africa.* Vol. 1. Chicago: Chicago University Press, 1991.

Cowen, Anne and Roger Cowen (eds). *Victorian Jews through British Eyes.* Oxford: Oxford University Press for the Littman Library, 1986.

Crosby, Alfred W. *Ecological Imperialism: The Biological Expansion of Europe 900–1900.* Cambridge: Cambridge University Press, 1986.

Crowe, Richard M. *Yr Wlpan yn Israel.* Aberystwyth: Canolfan Ymchwil Cymraeg i Oedolion, 1988.

Crowe, Richard M. and Avraham Solomonik. *Adfywiad yr Hebraeg.* Aberystwyth: Canolfan Ymchwil Cymraeg i Oedolion, 1988.

Davies, E. T. *Religion and Society in the Nineteenth Century.* Llandybïe: Christopher Davies, 1981.

Davies, Grahame. *The Chosen People: Wales and the Jews.* Bridgend: Seren, 2002.

Davis, Mike. *Late Victorian Holocausts: El Niño Famines and the Making of the Third World.* London: Verso, 2001.

Davison, Carol Margaret. *Anti-Semitism and British Gothic Literature.* New York: Palgrave, 2004.

Docker, John and Gerhard Fischer (eds). *Race, Colour, and Identity in Australia and New Zealand.* Sydney: New South Wales University Press, 2000.

Donahaye, Jasmine. ' "A Dislocation Called a Blessing": Three Welsh-Jewish Perspectives'. *Welsh Writing in English: A Yearbook of Critical Essays*, 7 (2001–2): 154–173.

———. ' "Gartref – bron": Adversity and Refuge in the Jewish Literature of Wales'. In Daniel Williams and Alyce von Rothkirch (eds), *Beyond the Difference: Welsh Literature in Comparative Contexts.* Cardiff: University of Wales Press, 2004. 38–53.

———. 'How Are The Mighty Fallen: Welsh Attitudes to Israel and Palestine'. *Planet*, 183 (2007): 41–49.

———. 'Hurrah for the Freedom of the Nations!' *Planet*, 147 (2001): 28–36.

————. 'Jewish Writing in Wales'. PhD diss., University of Wales, Swansea, 2004.

————. ' "The Link of Common Aspirations": Wales in the Work of Lily Tobias'. In Claire Tylee (ed.), *In the Open: Jewish Women Writers and British Culture*. Newark: University of Delaware Press, 2006. 147–163.

Dorson, Richard M. *The British Folklorists: A History*. London: Routledge and Kegan Paul, 1968.

————. 'Folklore Studies in England'. *The Journal of American Folklore*, 74.294 (1961): 302–312.

————. 'The Great Team of English Folklorists'. *The Journal of American Folklore*, 64.251 (1951): 1–10.

Drechsler, Horst. *Let Us Die Fighting: The Struggle of the Herero and Nama against German Imperialism, 1884–1915*. London: Zed Press, 1980.

Dundes, Alan (ed.). *International Folkloristics*. Lanham, Maryland: Rowman and Littlefield, 1999.

Efron, John M. *Defenders of the Race: Jewish Doctors & Race Science in Fin-de-Siècle Europe*. New Haven: Yale University Press, 1994.

Eisenzweig, Uri. 'Aux Origines du Sionisme Politique: Theodore Herzl, Israel Zangwill et la Negation de Sion'. *Esprit*, 4 (1983): 3–15.

Elon, Amos. *Herzl*. New-York: Holt, Rinehart, and Winston, 1975.

Endelman, Todd M. 'Anglo-Jewish Scientists and the Science of Race'. *Jewish Social Studies*, 11.1 (2004): 52–92.

————. 'Communal Solidarity and Family Loyalty among the Jewish Elite of Victorian London'. *Victorian Studies*, 28.3 (1985): 491–526.

————. 'English Jewish History'. *Modern Judaism*, 11.1 (1991): 91–109.

————. 'The Englishness of Jewish Modernity in England'. In Jacob Katz (ed.), *Toward Modernity: The European Jewish Model*. New Brunswick, NJ: Transaction Books, 1987. 225–246.

————. 'The Frankaus of London: A Study in Radical Assimilation, 1837–1967'. *Jewish History*, 8.1+2 (1994): 117–154.

————. *The Jews of Britain 1656–2000*. Berkeley: University of California Press, 2002.

————. *The Jews of Georgian England, 1714–1830: Tradition and Change in a Liberal Society*. Ann Arbor: University of Michigan Press, 1999.

Endelman, Todd M. and Tony Kushner (eds). *Disraeli's Jewishness*. London: Vallentine Mitchell, 2002.

Englander, David. 'Booth's Jews: The Presentation of Jews and Judaism in *Life and Labour of the People in London*'. *Victorian Studies*, 32.4 (1989): 551–571.

————. (ed.). *A Documentary History of Jewish Immigrants in Britain 1840–1920*. Leicester: Leicester University Press, 1994.

Eskenazy, Victor. 'Gaster and His Memoirs – The Path to Zionism'. *Shvut: Jewish Problems in Eastern Europe*, 16 (1993): 161–183.

————. (ed.). *Memorii (fragmente) Correspondată/Moses Gaster*. Bucharest: Editura Hasefer, 1998.

Evans, Neil. 'Immigrants and Minorities in Wales, 1840–1990: A Comparative Perspective'. *Llafur*, 5.4 (1991): 5–21.

Evans, Nicholas J. 'Aliens *en Route*: European Transmigration via Britain, 1836–1914'. PhD diss., University of Hull, 2006.

————. 'Indirect Passage from Europe: Transmigration via the UK, 1836–1914'. *Journal for Maritime Research* (June 2001). http://www.jmr.nmm.ac.uk/server/show/conJmrArticle.28

Evans, Richard J. *Death in Hamburg: Society and Politics in the Cholera Years, 1830–1910*. Oxford: Clarendon, 1987.

Feldman, David. *Englishmen and Jews: Social Relations and Political Culture, 1840–1914*. New Haven: Yale University Press, 1994.

———. 'Jews and the British Empire c.1900'. *History Workshop Journal*, 63.1 (2007): 70–89.

———. 'Was Modernity Good for the Jews?' In Cheyette and Marcus (eds), *Modernity, Culture and 'the Jew'*. 171–187.

Felman, Shoshana. 'Education and Crisis, or the Vicissitudes of Teaching'. In Shoshana Felman and Dori Laub, *Testimony: Crises of Witnessing in Literature, Psychoanalysis, and History*. New York: Routledge, 1992. 1–56.

Felsenstein, Frank. *Anti-Semitic Stereotypes: A Paradigm of Otherness in English Popular Culture, 1660–1830*. Baltimore: Johns Hopkins University Press, 1999.

Ferguson, Niall. *Empire: How Britain Made the Modern World*. London: Penguin, 2004.

———. 'Introduction. Virtual History: Towards a "Chaotic" Theory of the Past'. In Niall Ferguson (ed.), *Virtual History: Alternatives and Counterfactuals*. London: Picador, 1997. 1–90.

Field, Geoffrey G. 'Anti-Semitism with the Boots off: Recent Research on England'. *The Weiner Library Bulletin*, Special Fiftieth Anniversary Issue (1983): 25–46.

Finestein, Israel. *Jewish Society in Victorian England*. London: Vallentine Mitchell, 1993.

Fishman, Williams J. *East End 1888: A Year in a London Borough among the Labouring Poor*. London: Duckworth, 1988.

———. *East End Jewish Radicals*. London: Duckworth, 1975.

Frankel, Jonathan. *The Damascus Affair: 'Ritual Murder', Politics and the Jews in 1840*. Cambridge: Cambridge University Press, 1997.

Freedman, Jonathan. *The Temple of Culture: Assimilation and Anti-Semitism in Literary Anglo-America*. Oxford: Oxford University Press, 2000.

Friedman, Isaiah. 'Herzl and the Uganda Controversy'. In Robertson and Timms (eds), *Theodor Herzl*. 39–53.

———. *The Question of Palestine; British-Jewish-Arab Relations 1914–1918*. 2nd ed. New Brunswick: Transaction, 1992.

Fromkin, David. *A Peace to End All Peace: Creating the Modern Middle East, 1914–1922*. London: André Deutsch, 1989.

Galchinsky, Michael. ' "Permanently Blacked": Julia Frankau's Jewish Race'. *Victorian Literature and Culture*, 27.1 (1999): 171–183.

Gann, L. H. and Peter Duignan. *The Rulers of Belgian Africa, 1884–1914*. Princeton: Princeton University Press, 1979.

Garfinkle, Adam M. 'On the Origin, Meaning, Use and Abuse of a Phrase'. *Middle Eastern Studies*, 27.4 (1991): 539–552.

Garrard, John. *The English and Immigration, 1880–1910*. London: Oxford University Press, 1971.

Gay, Peter. *The Cultivation of Hatred*, Vol. 3 of *The Bourgeois Experience: Victoria to Freud*. London: Harper Collins, 1994.

Geller, Jay. 'Of Mice and Mensa: Antisemitism and the Jewish Genius'. *Centennial Review*, 38 (1994): 361–385.

Gensler, Orin. 'A Typological Evaluation of the Celtic/Hamo-Semitic Syntactic Parallels'. PhD diss., University of California, Berkeley, 1993.

Geyer, Michael and Charles Bright. 'Global Violence and Nationalizing Wars in Eurasia and America: The Geopolitics of War in the Mid-Nineteenth Century'. *Comparative Studies in Society and History*, 38.4 (1996): 619–657.

Gidley, Ben. 'Citizenship and Belonging: East London Jewish Radicals, 1903–1918'. PhD diss., University of London, 2003.

Gilman, Sander L. *Jewish Self-Hatred: Anti-Semitism and the Hidden Language of the Jews*. Baltimore: Johns Hopkins University Press, 1986.

———. *The Jew's Body*. London: Routledge, 1991.

Gilroy, Paul. *Between Camps: Race, Identity and Nationalism at the End of the Colour Line*. London: Allen Lane, 2000.

Glaser, Anthony. 'The Tredegar Riots of August 1911'. In Henriques (ed.), *The Jews of South Wales*. 151–175.

Green, Abigail. 'The British Empire and the Jews: An Imperialism of Human Rights?'. *Past and Present*, 199 (2008): 175–205.

Greenblatt, Stephen. *Marvellous Possession: The Wonder of the New World*. Oxford: Clarendon, 1991.

Halberstam, Judith M. 'Technologies of Monstrosity: Bram Stoker's *Dracula*'. *Victorian Studies*, 36.3 (1993): 333–352.

Hall, Catherine. *Civilising Subjects: Metropole and Colony in the English Imagination 1830–1867*. Cambridge: Polity, 2002.

Hardenburg, W. E. *The Putumayo: The Devil's Paradise*. London: T. Fisher Unwin, 1912.

Harper, Marjory. 'Settling in Saskatchewan: English Pioneers on the Prairies, 1878–1914'. *British Journal of Canadian Studies*, 16.1 (2003): 88–101.

Harris, Clive. 'Beyond Multiculturalism? Difference, Recognition, and Social Justice'. *Patterns of Prejudice*, 35.1 (2001): 13–34.

Hart, Mitchell B. 'Jews, Race and Capitalism in the German-Jewish Context'. *Jewish History*, 19.1 (2005): 49–63.

———. 'Picturing Jews: Iconography and Racial Science'. *Studies in Contemporary Jewry*, 11 (1995): 159–175.

———. *Social Science and the Politics of Modern Jewish Identity*. Stanford: Stanford University Press, 2000.

Harvey, John. *Image of the Invisible: The Visualization of Religion in Welsh Nonconformist Tradition*. Cardiff: University of Wales Press, 1999.

Henriques, Ursula. 'The Conduct of a Synagogue: Swansea Hebrew Congregation, 1895–1914'. In Henriques (ed.), *The Jews of South Wales*. 85–110.

———. (ed.). *The Jews of South Wales: Historical Studies*. Cardiff: University of Wales Press, 1993.

———. 'Lyons versus Thomas: The Jewess Abduction Case 1867–68'. In Henriques (ed.), *The Jews of South Wales*. 131–149.

Hill, M.F. *Permanent Way: The Story of the Kenya and Uganda Railway*. Nairobi: East African Railways and Harbours, 1950.

Hirshfield, Claire. 'The Anglo-Boer War and the Issue of Jewish Culpability'. *Journal of Contemporary History*, 15.4 (1980): 619–631.

———. 'The British Left and the "Jewish Conspiracy": A Case Study of Modern Antisemitism'. *Jewish Social Studies*, 63.2 (1981): 95–112.

Hobsbawm, Eric. 'Introduction: Inventing Traditions'. In Eric Hobsbawm and Terence Ranger (eds), *The Invention of Tradition*. Cambridge: Cambridge University Press, 1984. 1–14.

Hochschild, Adam. *King Leopold's Ghost: A Story of Greed, Terror, and Heroism in Colonial Africa*. Boston: Houghton Mifflin, 1998.

Holmes, Colin. *Anti-Semitism in British Society, 1876–1939*. London: Edward Arnold, 1979.

————. 'J. A. Hobson and the Jews'. In Colin Holmes (ed.), *Immigrants and Minorities in British Society*. London: George Allen & Unwin, 1978. 125–157.

————. 'The Tredegar Riots of 1911: Anti-Jewish Disturbances in South Wales'. *Welsh History Review*, 2.2 (1982): 214–225.

Huxley, Elspeth. *White Man's Country: Lord Delamere and the Making of Kenya*. 2 vols. London: Macmillan, 1935.

Hyde, Francis E. *Cunard and the North Atlantic, 1840–1973*. London: Macmillan, 1975.

Hyman, Jonathan. *Jews in Britain during the Great War*. Manchester: University of Manchester Working Papers in Economic and Social History 51, 2001.

Iliffe, John. *Tanganyika under German Rule, 1905–1912*. Cambridge: Cambridge University Press, 1969.

Jaffe, Benjamin. 'The British Press and Zionism in Herzl's Time (1895–1904)'. *Jewish Historical Society of England: Miscellanies* 24 (1974): 89–100.

James, E. Wyn. ' "The New Birth of a People": Welsh Language and Identity and the Welsh Methodists c.1740–1820'. In Robert Pope (ed.), *Religion and National Identity: Wales and Scotland c.1700–2000*. Cardiff: University of Wales Press, 2001. 14–42.

Judd, Dennis. *Radical Joe: A Life of Joseph Chamberlain*. Cardiff: University of Wales Press, 1993.

Kadish, Sharman. *Bolsheviks and British Jews: The Anglo-Jewish Community, Britain and the Russian Revolution*. London: Frank Cass, 1992.

Kalmar, Ivan Davison and Derek J. Penslar (eds). *Orientalism and the Jews*. Waltham: Brandeis University Press, 2005.

Kanfer, Stefan. *The Last Empire: De Beers, Diamonds, and the World*. London: Hodder & Stoughton: 1993.

Kaplan, Mendel and Marian Robertson (eds). *Founders and Followers: Johannesburg Jewry, 1887–1915*. Cape Town: Vlaeberg, 1991.

Katz, David S. and Richard H. Popkin. *Messianic Revolution: Radical Religious Politics to the End of the Second Millennium*. London: Allen Lane, 1999.

Kaufman, Heidi. 'King Solomon's Mines?': African Jewry, British Imperialism, and H. Rider Haggard's Diamonds'. *Victorian Literature and Culture*, 33.2 (2005): 517–539.

Kelly, Ninette and Michael Trebilcock (eds). *The Making of the Mosaic: A History of Canadian Immigration Policy*. Toronto: University of Toronto Press, 1998.

Kenefick, William. 'Jewish and Catholic Irish Relations: The Glasgow Waterfront c.1880–1914'. In David Cesarani and Gemma Romain (eds), *Jews and Port Cities 1590–1990: Commerce, Community, and Cosmopolitanism*. London: Vallentine Mitchell, 2006. 215–234.

Kepple-Jones, Arthur. *Rhodes and Rhodesia: The White Conquest of Zimbabwe, 1884–1902*. Kingston and Montreal: McGill-Queen's University Press, 1983.

Kimmerling, Baruch. *Zionism and Territory: The Socio-Territorial Dimensions of Zionist Politics*. Berkeley: University of California Press, 1983.

Knowles, Valerie. *Strangers at Our Gates: Canadian Immigration and Immigration Policy, 1540–1997*. Toronto: Dundurn Press, 1997.

Kornberg, Jacques. *Theodor Herzl: From Assimilation to Zionism*. Bloomington: Indiana University Press, 1993.

Krebs, Paula M. *Gender, Race and the Writing of Empire: Public Discourse on the Boer War*. Cambridge: Cambridge University Press, 1999.

Kristeva, Julia. *Powers of Horror: An Essay on Abjection*. Trans. Leon S. Roudiez. New York: Columbia University Press, 1982.

Kushner, Tony. 'Jew and Non-Jew in the East End of London: Towards an Anthropology of "Everyday" Relations'. In Geoffrey Alderman and Colin Holmes (eds), *Outsiders and Outcasts*. London: Duckworth, 1993. 32–52.

——. *The Persistence of Prejudice: Anti-Semitism in British Society during the Second World War*. Manchester: Manchester University Press, 1989.

Lavsky, Hagit. *Before Catastrophe: The Distinctive Path of German Zionism*. Detroit: Wayne State University Press, 1996.

Leasor, James. *Rhodes and Barnato: The Premier and the Prancer*. London: Leo Cooper, 1997.

Lee, Charles E. *The Blue Riband: The Romance of the Atlantic Ferry*. London: Sampson Low, 1930.

Leftwich, Joseph. *Israel Zangwill*. London: James Clarke, 1957.

Levene, Mark. *War, Jews, and the New Europe: The Diplomacy of Lucien Wolf, 1914–1919*. Oxford: Oxford University Press, 1992.

Lindeborg, Ruth H. 'The "Asiatic" and the Boundaries of Victorian Englishness'. *Victorian Studies*, 37.3 (1994): 381–404.

Lindqvist, Sven. *'Exterminate All the Brutes': One Man's Odyssey into the Heart of Darkness and the Origins of European Genocide*. Trans. Joan Tate. London: Granta Books, 1998.

Lipman, Vivian D. *A Century of Social Service, 1859–1959: The History of the Jewish Board of Guardians*. London: Routledge & Kegan Paul, 1959.

——. *A Social History of the Jews in England*. London: Watts, 1954.

Llywelyn, Dorian. *Sacred Place: Chosen People*. Cardiff: University of Wales Press, 1999.

Lonsdale, John. 'The Conquest State of Kenya'. In Moor and Wesseling (eds), *Imperialism and War*. 87–120.

Looker, Ben. 'Exhibiting Imperial London: Empire and City in Late-Victorian and Edwardian Guidebooks'. MA diss., Goldsmiths College, University of London, 2001.

Lord, Peter. *The Visual Culture of Wales: Imaging the Nation*. Cardiff: University of Wales Press, 2000.

——. *The Visual Culture of Wales: Industrial Society*. Cardiff: University of Wales Press, 1998.

——. *The Visual Culture of Wales: Medieval Vision*. Cardiff: University of Wales Press, 2003.

——. *Words with Pictures: Images of Wales and Welsh Images in the Popular Press, 1640–1860*. Aberystwyth: Planet, 1995.

Lucas, Charles. *The Partition and Colonization of Africa*. 1922; New York: H. Fertig, 1972.

Lyotard, Jean-François. *Heidegger and 'the Jews'*. Trans. A. Michel and M. S. Roberts. Minneapolis: University of Minnesota Press, 1990.

Maidment, Brian. 'Joseph Jacobs and English Folklore in the 1890s'. In Dov Noy and Issachar Ben-Ami (eds), *Folklore Research Center Studies*, Vol. 5, *Studies in the Cultural Life of the Jews in England*. Jerusalem: Magnes, 1975. 185–196.

——. 'The Literary Career of Joseph Jacobs, 1876–1900'. *The Jewish Historical Society of England: Transactions*, 24 (1974): 101–113.

Malchow, H. L. *Gothic Images of Race in Nineteenth-Century England*. Stanford: Stanford University Press, 1996.

Marchal, Jules. *L'Etat Libre du Congo, Paradis Perdu, L'Histoire du Congo, 1876–1900*. 2 vols. Borgloon: Editions Paula Bellings, 1996.

Maro, Judith. *Hen Wlad Newydd: Gwersi i Gymru*. Talybont: Y Lolfa, 1974.

Marriott, John. 'In Darkest England: The Poor, the Crowd, and Race in the Nineteenth-Century Metropolis'. In Phil Cohen (ed.), *New Ethnicities, Old Racisms*. London: Zed Books, 1999. 82–100.

Mars, Leonard. 'Immigration and Anglicisation: Religious Education as an Issue in the Swansea Hebrew Congregation, 1894–1910'. *Jewish Journal of Sociology*, 39.1+2 (1997): 76–86.

———. 'The Ministry of the Reverend Simon Fyne in Swansea, 1899–1906'. In Henriques (ed.), *The Jews of South Wales*. 111–130.

Marx, Karl. 'The Fetishism of the Commodity and Its Secret'. *Capital: A Critique of Political Economy*. Vol. 1. Trans. Ben Fowkes. London: Penguin, 1976.

McClintock, Anne. *Imperial Leather: Race, Gender, and Sexuality in the Colonial Conquest*. New York: Routledge, 1995.

Mendelsohn, Richard. 'The Jewish Soldier: Anglo-Jewry at War, 1899–1902'. *Jewish Affairs*, 54.3 (1999): 11–19.

Mintz, Alan L. and David G. Roskies (eds). *Kishinev in the Twentieth Century*. Spec. issue of *Prooftexts*, 25.1+2 (2005): 1–234.

Mitchell, Harvey. 'Hobson Revisited'. *Journal of the History of Ideas*, 26.3 (1965): 397–416.

Moor, J. A. de and H. L. Wesseling (eds). *Imperialism and War: Essays on Colonial Wars in Asia and Africa*. Leiden: Brill and University of Leiden Press, 1989.

Morgan, Derec Llwyd. *'Canys Bechan Yw': Y Genedl Etholedig yn ein Llenyddiaeth*. Aberystwyth: University of Wales, 1994.

———. 'Y Beibl a Llenyddiaeth Gymraeg'. In R. Geraint Gruffudd (ed.), *Y Gair ar Waith: Ysgrifau ar yr Etifeddiaeth Feiblaidd yng Nghymru*. Cardiff: University of Wales Press, 1988. 87–112.

Morgan, Prys. 'The Clouds of Witnesses: The Welsh Historical Tradition'. In R. Brinley Jones (ed.), *Anatomy of Wales*. Peterston-super-Ely: Gwerin Publications, 1972. 17–42.

Mufti, Aamir R. *Enlightenment in the Colony: The Jewish Question and the Crisis of Postcolonial Culture*. Princeton: Princeton University Press, 2007.

Mungeam, G. H. *British Rule in Kenya, 1895–1912*. Oxford: Clarendon, 1966.

Narayan, Uma. *Dislocating Cultures: Identities, Traditions, and Third World Feminisms*. New York: Routledge, 1997.

Newman, Aubrey. *Migration and Settlement*. London: Jewish Historical Society of England, 1971

———. 'The Poor Jews' Temporary Shelter: Directed Migration'. In Newman and Massil (eds), *Patterns of Migration*. 175–186.

Newman, Aubrey, and Stephen Massil (eds). *Patterns of Migration, 1850–1914: Proceedings of the International Academic Conference of the Jewish Historical Society of England and the Institute of Jewish Studies, University College London*. London: Jewish Historical Society of England, 1996.

O'Day, Rosemary. 'Before the Webbs: Beatrice Potter's Investigations for Charles Booth's Inquiry'. *History*, 78 (1993): 218–242.

O'Leary, Paul. *Immigration and Integration: The Irish in Wales, 1798–1922*. 2000; Cardiff: University of Wales Press, 2002.

Omer-Sherman, Ranen (ed.). *The Cultural and Historical Stabilities and Instabilities of Jewish Orientalism*. Spec. issue of *Shofar: An Interdisciplinary Journal of Jewish Studies*, 24.2 (2006): 1–233.

Oring, Elliott (ed.). *Folk Groups and Folklore Genres*. Logan: Utah State University Press, 1986.

Pakenham, Thomas. *The Scramble for Africa: White Man's Conquest of the Dark Continent from 1876 to 1912*. New York: Random House, 1991.

Pankhurst, Richard and Douglas H. Johnson, 'The Great Drought and Famine of 1888–92 in Northeast Africa'. In Douglas H. Johnson and David Anderson (eds), *The Ecology of Survival: Case Studies from Northeast African History*. London: Lester Crook Academic Publishing, 1988. 47–72.

Pappé, Ilan. 'Zionism as Colonialism: A Comparative View of Diluted Colonialism in Asia and Africa'. In Yehiam Weitz (ed.), *In Between Vision and Revision: One Hundred Years of Zionist Historiography*. Jerusalem: Zalman Shazar Center, 1997. 345–365. [Hebrew].

Pardes, Ilana. *The Biography of Ancient Israel: National Narratives in the Bible*. Berkley: University of California Press, 2000.

Patai, Raphael and Jennifer Patai. *The Myth of the Jewish Race*. Rev. ed. Detroit, MI: Wayne State University Press, 1989.

Peate, Iorwerth. *Rhwng Dau Fyd*. Dinbych: Gwasg Gee, 1976.

Pellew, Jill. 'The Home Office and the Aliens Act, 1905'. *The Historical Journal*, 32.2 (1989): 369–85.

Penkower, Monty Noam. 'The Kishinev Pogrom of 1903: A Turning Point in Jewish History'. *Modern Judaism*, 2.3 (2004): 187–225

Penslar, Derek J. 'Zionism, Colonialism, and Postcolonialism'. In Penslar and Shapira (eds), *Israeli Historical Revisionism*. 84–98.

———. 'Zionism, Colonialism, and Technocracy: Otto Warburg and the Commission for the Exploration of Palestine, 1903–1907'. *Journal of Contemporary History*, 25.1 (1990): 143–160.

Penslar, Derek J. and Anita Shapira (eds). *Israeli Historical Revisionism from Left to Right*. London: Frank Cass, 2003.

Persell, Michelle. 'Capitalism, Charity, and Judaism: The Triumvirate of Benjamin Farjeon'. *Victorian Literature and Culture*, 27.1 (1999): 203–218.

———. 'Dickensian Disciple: Anglo-Jewish Identity in the Christmas Tales of Benjamin Farjeon'. *Philological Quarterly*, 73.4 (1994): 451–468.

Pick, Daniel. *Faces of Degeneration: A European Disorder, c.1848–c.1918*. Cambridge: Cambridge University Press, 1989.

———. *Svengali's Web: The Alien Enchanter in Modern Culture*. New Haven: Yale University Press, 2000.

Pragai, Michael J. *Faith and Fulfilment: Christians and the Return to the Promised Land*. London: Valentine Mitchell, 1985.

Pratt, Mary Louise. *Imperial Eyes: Travel Writing and Transculturation*. London: Routledge, 1992.

Ragussis, Michael. *Figures of Conversion: 'The Jewish Question' and English National Identity*. Durham, NC: Duke University Press, 1995.

Raider, Mark A. and Miriam B. Raider-Roth (eds). *The Plough Woman: Records of the Pioneer Women of Palestine*. Hanover: Brandeis University Press, 2002.

Rainero, Romain H. 'The Battle of Adowa on 1st March 1896: A Reappraisal'. In Moor and Wesseling (eds), *Imperialism and War*. 189–200.

Ranger, Terence O. *Revolt in Southern Rhodesia, 1896–97: A Study in African Resistance*. London: Heinemann, 1967.

Reece, R. H. W. *Aborigines and Colonists: Aborigines and Colonial Society in New South Wales in the 1830s and 1840s*. Sydney: Sydney University Press, 1974.

Robertson, Ritchie and Edward Timms (eds). *Theodor Herzl and the Origins of Zionism*. Edinburgh: Edinburgh University Press, 1997.

Rochelson, Meri-Jane. ' *"They That Walk in Darkness"*: *Ghetto Tragedies*: The Uses of Christianity in Israel Zangwill's Fiction'. *Victorian Literature and Culture*, 27.1 (1999): 219–233.

Rose, Jacqueline. *States of Fantasy*. Oxford: Oxford University Press, 1996.

Roskies, David G. *Against the Apocalypse: Responses to Catastrophe in Modern Jewish Culture*. Cambridge, MA: Harvard University Press, 1984.

———. *The Literature of Destruction: Jewish Responses to Catastrophes*. Philadelphia: Jewish Publication Society, 1988.

Roth, Cecil. *A History of the Jews in England*. Oxford: Oxford University Press, 1941.

Rubinstein, W. D. 'The Anti-Jewish Riots of 1911 in South Wales: A Re-examination'. *Welsh History Review*, 18.4 (1997): 667–699.

———. *A History of the Jews in the English-speaking World: Great Britain*. London: Macmillan, 1996.

———. Review of *The Chosen People: Wales and the Jews*, by Grahame Davies. *New Welsh Review*, 57 (2002): 110–111.

Rubinstein, W.D. and Hilary Rubinstein. 'Philosemitism in Britain and in the English Speaking World, 1840–1939: Patterns and Typology'. *Jewish Journal of Sociology*, 40.1+2 (1998): 5–47.

Said, Edward W. *Orientalism: Western Conceptions of the Orient*. 1978; Harmondsworth: Penguin, 1995.

Salbstein, M. C. N. *The Emancipation of the Jews in Britain: The Question of the Admission of the Jews to Parliament, 1828–1860*. Rutherford: Fairleigh Dickinson University Press, 1982.

Schindler, Bruno (ed.). *Gaster Centenary Publication*. London: Percy Lund, Humphries and Co., 1958.

Schreuder, D. M. *The Scramble for Southern Africa, 1877–1895*. Cambridge: Cambridge University Press, 1980.

Shapiro, James. *Shakespeare and the Jews*. New York: Columbia University Press, 1996.

Shafir, Gershon. *Land, Labour and the Origins of the Israeli-Palestinian Conflict, 1882–1914*. Cambridge: Cambridge University Press, 1989.

Shimoni, Gideon. 'Postcolonial Theory and the History of Zionism'. *Israel Affairs*, 13.4 (2007): 859–871.

———. *The Zionist Ideology*. Hanover, NH: Brandeis University Press, 1995.

Singer, Alan H. 'Great Britain or Judea Nova? National Identity, Property, and the Jewish Naturalization Controversy of 1753'. In Sheila A. Spector (ed.), *British Romanticism and the Jews: History, Culture, Literature*. London: Palgrave, 2002. 19–36.

Smith, Iain R. *The Emin Pasha Relief Expedition, 1886–1890*. Oxford: Clarendon, 1972.

Smith, Robert. *'In the Direct and Homely Speech of the Workers': Llais Llafur 1898–1915*. Aberystwyth: University of Wales Centre for Advanced Welsh and Celtic Studies, 2000.

Sokolow, Nahum. *History of Zionism 1600–1918*. 2 vols. London: Longman, 1919.

Sollors, Werner. *Beyond Ethnicity: Consent and Descent in American Culture*. New York: Oxford University Press, 1986.

Stanciu, Măriuca. 'A Promoter of the Haskala in Romania – Moses Gaster'. *Studia Hebraica*, 1 (2003). http://www.unibuc.ro/eBooks/filologie/hebra/2-4.htm.

Stanislawski, Michael. *Zionism and the Fin de Siècle: Cosmopolitanism and Nationalism from Nordau to Jabotinsky*. Berkeley: University of California Press, 2001.

Stengers, Jean. 'The Congo Free State and the Belgian Congo before 1914'. In L. H. Gann and Peter Duigan (eds), *Colonialism in Africa 1870–1960*. Vol 1. Cambridge: Cambridge University Press, 1969. 261–292.

Stewart, Desmond. *Theodor Herzl: Artist and Politician*. London: Quartet, 1981.

Steyn, Juliet. *The Jew: Assumptions of Identity*. London: Cassell, 1999.

Stocking, George W. *Victorian Anthropology*. New York: Free Press, 1987.

Stratton, Jon. 'The Color of Jews: Jews, Race, and the White Australia Policy'. In Sander L. Gilman and Milton Shain (eds.), *Jewries at the Frontier: Accomodation, Identity, Conflict*. Urbana: University of Illinois Press, 1999. 309–334.

Talmon, J. L. *Israel among the Nations*. London: Weidenfeld & Nicolson, 1970.

Timms, Edward. 'Ambassador Herzl and the Blueprint for a Modern State'. In Robertson and Timms (eds), *Theodor Herzl*. 12–26.

Traverso, Enzo. *The Marxists and the Jewish Question*. Atlantic Highlands, NJ: Humanities Press, 1994.

Udelson, Joseph. *Dreamer of the Ghetto: The Life and Works of Israel Zangwill*. Tuscaloosa: University of Alabama Press, 1990.

Valman, Nadia. *The Jewess in Nineteenth-Century British Literary Culture*. Cambridge: Cambridge University Press, 2006.

———. 'Semitism and Criticism: Victorian Anglo-Jewish Literary History', *Victorian Literature and Culture*, 27.1 (1999): 235–248.

Vambe, Lawrence. *An Ill-Fated People: Zimbabwe before and after Rhodes*. London: Heinemann, 1972.

Vandervort, Bruce. *Wars of Imperial Conquest, 1830–1914*. London: University College London Press, 1998.

van Wyk Smith, M. 'The Boers and the Anglo-Boer War (1899–1902) in the Twentieth-Century Moral Imaginary'. *Victorian Literature and Culture*, 31.2 (2003): 429–446.

Vital, David. *The Origins of Zionism*. Oxford: Clarendon Press, 1975.

———. 'Zangwill and Modern Jewish Nationalism'. *Modern Judaism*, 4.3 (1984): 243–253.

———. *Zionism: The Formative Years*. Oxford: Clarendon Press, 1982

Voeltz, Richard A. *German Colonialism and the South West Africa Company, 1894–1914*. Ohio: Ohio University Press, 1988.

Walkowitz, Judith R. *City of Dreadful Delight: Narratives of Sexual Danger in Late-Victorian London*. London: Virago, 1992.

———. 'The Indian Woman, the Flower-Girl, and the Jew: Photojournalism in Edwardian London'. *Victorian Studies*, 42.1 (1998/9): 3–46.

Walzer, Michael. *The Company of Critics: Social Criticism and Political Commitment in the Twentieth Century*. New York: Basic Books, 1988.

Weber, Max. *The Protestant Ethic and the Spirit of Capitalism*. Trans. Talcott Parsons. New York: Scribner, 1958.

Weisbord, Robert G. 'Israel Zangwill's Jewish Territorial Organization and the East African Zion'. *Jewish Social Studies*, 30.2 (1968): 89–108.

———. *African Zion: The Attempt to Establish a Jewish Colony in the East Africa Protectorate 1903–1905*. Philadelphia: The Jewish Publication Society of America, 1968.

Werses, Shmuel. 'The Jewish Reception of *Daniel Deronda*'. In Alice Shalvi (ed.), *Daniel Deronda: A Centenary Symposium*. Jerusalem: Jerusalem Academic Press, 1976. 9–43.

Wheatcroft, Geoffrey. *The Controversy of Zion or How Zionism Tried to Resolve the Jewish Question*. London: Sinclair-Stevenson, 1996.

———. *The Randlords*. London: Weidenfeld & Nicolson, 1985.

White, Jerry. *Rothschild Buildings: Life in an East End Tenement Block, 1887–1920*. London: Routledge, 1980.

Williams, Bill. *The Making of Manchester Jewry, 1740–1815*. Manchester: Manchester University Press, 1976.

Williams, Charlotte, Neil Evans, and Paul O'Leary (eds). *A Tolerant Nation? Exploring Ethnic Diversity in Wales*. Cardiff: University of Wales Press, 2003.

Williams, Glanmor. *The Welsh and Their Religion: Historical Essays*. Cardiff: University of Wales Press, 1991.

Wistrich, Robert S. *Revolutionary Jews: From Marx to Trotsky*. London: Harrap, 1976.

Wohlgelernter, Maurice. *Israel Zangwill: A Study*. New York: Columbia University Press, 1964.

Young, Robert, J. C. *Colonial Desire: Hybridity in Theory, Culture, and Race*. London: Routledge, 1995.

Zimmerer, Jürgen. *Deutsche Herrschaft über Afrikaner: Staatlicher Machtanspruch und Wirklichkeit im kolonialen Namibia*. 2nd ed. Munster, Hamburg, and London: Lit Verlag, 2002.

Zimmerman, Andrew. *Anthropology and Antihumanism in Wilhelmine Germany*. Chicago: Chicago University Press, 2002.

Index